JOURNAL FOR THE STUDY OF THE OLD TESTAMENT
SUPPLEMENT SERIES
238

Sheffield Academic Press

The Chronicler as Historian

**M. Patrick Graham, Kenneth G. Hoglund
and Steven L. McKenzie**

Journal for the Study of the Old Testament
Supplement Series 238

Copyright © 1997 Sheffield Academic Press

Published by Sheffield Academic Press Ltd
Mansion House
19 Kingfield Road
Sheffield S11 9AS
England

Printed on acid-free paper in Great Britain
by Bookcraft Ltd
Midsomer Norton, Bath

British Library Cataloguing in Publication Data

A catalogue record for this book is available
from the British Library

ISBN 1-85075-651-1

CONTENTS

PART I
FRAMING AN APPROACH

PART II
ELEMENTS OF THE NARRATIVE

PART III
SPECIALIZED STUDIES

ABBREVIATIONS

AASOR	Annual of the American Schools of Oriental Research
AB	Anchor Bible
ABD	*Anchor Bible Dictionary*
ABRL	Anchor Bible Reference Library
AJA	*American Journal of Archaeology*
AJP	*American Journal of Philology*
AnBib	Analecta biblica
ANET	J.B. Pritchard (ed.), *Ancient Near Eastern Texts Relating to the Old Testament* (Princeton: Princeton University Press, 3rd edn, 1969)
AOAT	Alter Orient und Altes Testament
AS	Assyriological Studies
ASOR	American Schools of Oriental Research
ATANT	Abhandlungen zur Theologie des Alten und Neuen Testaments
ATD	Das Alte Testament Deutsch
BARev	*Biblical Archaeology Review*
BASOR	*Bulletin of the American Schools of Oriental Research*
BBET	Beiträge zur biblische Exegese und Theologie
BDB	F. Brown, S.R. Driver, and C.A. Briggs, *A Hebrew and English Lexicon of the Old Testament*
BEATAJ	Beiträge zur Erforschung des Alten Testaments und des antiken Judentums
BethM	*Beth Mikra*
BETL	Bibliotheca ephemeridum theologicarum lovaniensium
BEvT	Beiträge zur evangelischen Theologie
BH	Biblical Hebrew
BHS	*Biblia hebraica stuttgartensia*
Bib	*Biblica*
BJS	Brown Judaic Studies
BKAT	Biblischer Kommentar, Altes Testament
BR	*Biblical Research*
BSac	*Bibliotheca Sacra*
BTB	*Biblical Theology Bulletin*
BUS	Brown University Studies
BWANT	Beiträge zur Wissenschaft vom Alten und Neuen Testament
BZAW	Beihefte zur *Zeitschrift für die alttestamentliche Wissenschaft*

CBC	Cambridge Bible Commentary
CBQ	*Catholic Biblical Quarterly*
Chr	The Chronicler
ConBOT	Coniectanea biblica, Old Testament
CTM	*Concordia Theological Monthly*
DBHE	L. Alonso Schökel, *Diccionario bíblico hebreoespañol* (Madrid: Trotta, 1994)
DtrH	The Deuteronomistic History/Historian
Ebib	Etudes bibliques
ErIsr	*Eretz Israel*
ExpTim	*Expository Times*
FOTL	Forms of Old Testament Literature
FRLANT	Forschungen zur Religion und Literatur des Alten und Neuen Testaments
FTS	Freiburger theologische Studien
GTS	Gettysburg Theological Studies
HAR	*Hebrew Annual Review*
HAT	Handbuch zum Alten Testament
HKAT	Handkommentar zum Alten Testament
HSM	Harvard Semitic Monographs
HTR	*Harvard Theological Review*
HUCA	*Hebrew Union College Annual*
ICC	International Critical Commentary
IDB	*Interpreter's Dictionary of the Bible*
IDBSup	*IDB, Supplementary Volume*
IEJ	*Israel Exploration Journal*
Int	*Interpretation*
JANESCU	*Journal of the Ancient Near Eastern Society of Columbia University*
JARCE	*Journal of the American Research Center in Egypt*
JBL	*Journal of Biblical Literature*
JCS	*Journal of Cuneiform Studies*
JETS	*Journal of the Evangelical Theological Society*
JJS	*Journal for Jewish Studies*
JNES	*Journal of Near Eastern Studies*
JPSV	Jewish Publication Society Version (*Tanakh, A New Translation of the Holy Scriptures*)
JQR	*Jewish Quarterly Review*
JSOT	*Journal for the Study of the Old Testament*
JSOTSup	*Journal for the Study of the Old Testament*, Supplement Series
JSP	*Journal for the Study of Pseudepigrapha*
JSPSup	*Journal for the Study of the Pseudepigrapha*, Supplement Series
JSS	*Journal of Semitic Studies*

JTS	*Journal of Theological Studies*
KAI	H. Donner and W. Röllig, *Kanaanäische und aramäische Inschriften*
KAT	Kommentar zum Alten Testament
KB	L. Koehler and W. Baumgartner (eds.), *Lexicon in Veteris Testamenti libros*
KHCAT	Kurzer Hand-Commentar zum Alten Testament
LCL	Loeb Classical Library
LS	*Louvain Studies*
LTQ	*Lexington Theological Quarterly*
LUÅ	Lunds universitets årsskrift
NCB	New Century Bible
NEAEHL	E. Stern (ed.), *The New Encyclopedia of Archaeological Excavations in the Holy Land* (Jerusalem: Israel Exploration Society & Carta; New York: Simon & Schuster, 1993)
NEB	New English Bible
NEB	Neue Echter Bibel
NICOT	New International Commentary on the Old Testament
NorTT	*Norsk Teologisk Tidsskrift*
NRSV	New Revised Standard Version
NTS	*New Testament Studies*
ÖBS	Österreichische biblische Studien
OIP	Oriental Institute Publications
OTL	Old Testament Library
OTS	*Oudtestamentische Studiën*
PAAJR	*Proceedings of the American Academy of Jewish Research*
PEGLMBS	*Proceedings, Eastern Great Lakes and Midwest Biblical Societies*
PEQ	*Palestine Exploration Quarterly*
RB	*Revue biblique*
REB	Revised English Bible
ResQ	*Restoration Quarterly*
RSV	Revised Standard Version
SBB	Simor Bible Bibliographies
SBL	Society of Biblical Literature
SBLDS	Society of Biblical Literature Dissertation Series
SBLMS	Society of Biblical Literature Monograph Series
SBLSPS	Society of Biblical Literature Seminar Papers Series
SBT	Studies in Biblical Theology
SJOT	*Scandinavian Journal of the Old Testament*
TBC	Torch Bible Commentary
TECC	Textos y Estudios 'Cardinal Cisneros'
ThW	Theologische Wissenschaft
TPQ	*Theologisch-Praktische Quartalschrift*
TynBul	*Tyndale Bulletin*

VT	*Vetus Testamentum*
VTSup	*Vetus Testamentum*, Supplements
WBC	Word Biblical Commentary
WMANT	Wissenschaftliche Monographien zum Alten und Neuen Testament
WO	*Die Welt des Orients*
WTJ	*Westminster Theological Journal*
ZA	*Zeitschrift für Assyriologie*
ZAW	*Zeitschrift für die alttestamentliche Wissenschaft*
ZDPV	*Zeitschrift des deutschen Palästina-Vereins*

LIST OF CONTRIBUTORS

Samuel E. Balentine, Baptist Theological Seminary at Richmond,
    Richmond, VA
William H. Barnes, Southeastern College of the Assemblies of God,
    Lakeland, FL
Christopher T. Begg, Catholic University of America, Washington, DC
Ehud Ben Zvi, University of Alberta, Alberta, Canada
Roddy L. Braun, Our Savior Lutheran Church, Arlington, VA
M. Patrick Graham, Emory University, Atlanta, GA
Alan Groves, Westminster Theological Seminary, Philadelphia, PA
Kenneth G. Hoglund, Wake Forest University, Winston-Salem, NC
Isaac Kalimi, Brookline, MA
Ralph W. Klein, Lutheran School of Theology at Chicago, Chicago, IL
Gary N. Knoppers, Pennsylvania State University, University Park, PA
Tremper Longman III, Westminster Theological Seminary,
    Philadelphia, PA
Steven L. McKenzie, Rhodes College, Memphis, TN
Anson F. Rainey, Tel Aviv University, Tel Aviv, Israel
William M. Schniedewind, University of California Los Angeles, Los
    Angeles, CA
Mark A. Throntveit, Luther Seminary, St Paul, MN
John Van Seters, University of North Carolina at Chapel Hill, Chapel
    Hill, NC
John W. Wright, Point Loma Nazarene College, San Diego, CA

INTRODUCTION

This collection of fourteen essays has its roots in the work of the Chronicles–Ezra–Nehemiah Section of the Society of Biblical Literature. The section was founded and ably led for many years by Ralph W. Klein. He has continued to serve on the program committee for the section as it is currently constituted, along with the three editors of the present volume, Christopher T. Begg, Tamara C. Eskenazi, Gary N. Knoppers, Mark A. Throntveit, and John W. Wright. It was this committee that chose the topic, 'Was the Chronicler a Historian?', for the section's theme session at the 1994 annual meeting of the SBL.

The first three papers of this book were presented on 19 November at that conference and address the issue from what can be generally designated comparativist (Hoglund), historical and geographical (Rainey), and literary (Kalimi) approaches. The diversity of their perspectives and answers to the question posed illustrates the rich ferment that characterizes the contemporary study of Chronicles. The second part of the book consists of articles that investigate a particular theme or genre of material in Chronicles and attempt to assess its value for historical reconstruction. Once more, the reader will notice a variety of opinions among the contributors. While some have considerable confidence in the reliability of Chronicles for the reconstruction of the pre-exilic history of Israel, others find little in Chronicles that is useful to the historian working on the period. The three final articles are explorations of specific historical issues related to texts from Chronicles. By the publication of these studies, it is our hope that further research on Chronicles will be stimulated.

The editors would like to express appreciation to three groups for their contributions to the present volume. First, thanks are due to the SBL and especially to its executive office for assistance with the annual meeting. It has been an honor to work with such dedicated and capable colleagues. Second, we are indebted to Philip R. Davies and David J.A. Clines of Sheffield Academic Press for accepting this collection of essays into the JSOT Supplements Series. Their energetic and talented efforts with Sheffield Academic Press have indeed served to promote biblical scholarship and have placed many in their debt. Finally, we want to express appreciation to Douglas W. Stott, a superb translator of German theological and philosophical works. He has reviewed the translations of German texts that appear in this volume and has made numerous helpful suggestions. For any mistakes that remain, however, the editors accept responsibility.

Finally, we turn to the one to whom this book is dedicated. From the birth of the Chronicles–Ezra–Nehemiah Section of the Society of Biblical Literature until his death, Raymond B. Dillard served on its program committee, offering advice on program topics and speakers and assistance with other business of the section. The respect and admiration of committee members for Ray grew as the years passed and Ray made his contributions to Chronicles research. He was known to all as a kind man of sincere Christian faith, a congenial and generous colleague, and a diligent and insightful scholar. It was with shock and deep sorrow that we learned of Ray's death. His presence has indeed been missed, and this will doubtless continue to be the case. As a tribute to Ray's memory, these essays are offered by his friends and colleagues with gratitude and affection.

M. Patrick Graham
Kenneth G. Hoglund
Steven L. McKenzie

Raymond B. Dillard

1944–1993

In Memoriam

Those of us who knew Ray Dillard will know that he was a passionate man. He loved his God and his family. He cared deeply for his friends and his seminary. He relished hunting and carpentry. And he was devoted to the Bible, the object of his personal and professional study. For almost two decades he made Chronicles the focus of his scholarly attention, writing numerous articles and an important commentary on 2 Chronicles.

It is therefore fitting that this volume on Chronicles be dedicated to his memory. It is particularly appropriate that the volume concentrate on the role of history in Chronicles, because this was an especially intriguing and difficult issue for Ray. As an evangelical Protestant scholar, he held a high view of the Bible's authority and a firm confidence in its trustworthiness. At the same time, he refused to approach the Bible in general, and Chronicles in particular, with any preconceived notion of the book's intention and style. Ray often found himself in turmoil as he wrestled with the issue of the Chronicler's picture of Israel's history.

In a word, Ray would have loved to participate in this project. He would be highly honored to think that the editors and contributors of the volume thought to dedicate this book to his memory. It is certainly an honor for us, Ray's former colleagues, to write the following reminder of the life and career of our friend and mentor.

Raymond Bryan Dillard was Professor of Old Testament Language at Westminster Theological Seminary from 1969 until his death at the age of 49 in 1993. He graduated from Westminster Seminary in 1969 and completed his PhD at Dropsie College of Hebrew and Cognate Learning in 1975. He did other postgraduate work at Temple

University, the University of Pennsylvania, and Tel Aviv University.

Ray was the author of numerous articles and monographs. His earliest scholarly work was as a major translator of the New International Version of the Bible. Besides the commentary on 2 Chronicles in the Word Biblical Commentary series, he published a commentary on the book of Joel (Baker, 1992) and was co-author of *An Introduction to the Old Testament* (Zondervan), published posthumously at the end of 1994.

Though a productive research scholar and writer, Ray was perhaps best known for his mastery of classroom drama. He captivated minds and hearts, imparting his passion for the Bible to students who went on to the Christian ministry, as well as to a surprisingly large number of men and women who presently teach Hebrew Bible not only in America, but also Asia, Europe, Australia, Africa, and South America.

Ray died of a heart attack while in the woods that he loved near his home. He is survived by his wife, Ann, and his three sons, Joel, Jonathan, and Joshua.

Tremper Longman III and Alan Groves

PART I
FRAMING AN APPROACH

THE CHRONICLER AS HISTORIAN:
A COMPARATIVIST PERSPECTIVE

Kenneth G. Hoglund

At first glance, 'The Chronicler as Historian' would seem to be a straightforward topic—1 and 2 Chronicles presents us with a narrative more or less chronologically arranged and more or less focused on the political events affecting Jerusalem and the southern kingdom of Judah. It would seem that 'history' would be an appropriate label for such a narrative, and that as the author of a 'history', the Chronicler (Chr)[1] should be judged on the basis of how well this narrative reflects the reality of what happened in Israel's past.

It is precisely at the point of assessing this narrative that one encounters those well-known tendencies of the work that have given scholars difficulty in applying the designation 'history' to this complex of narrative, hymns, speeches, genealogies, and assorted lists. While not intending to be exhaustive, one could cite the selective adaptation of materials in 2 Samuel–2 Kings, the apparent free-handed revision of some of these materials, and the insertion of narrative details into some borrowed accounts without attribution of sources. Worse still, we find the appeal to otherwise unknown sources for authentication and the recurring notices of otherwise unknown prophetic figures within the warp and woof of Chr's narrative fabric.

It is no wonder then that scholars of earlier generations sought to qualify their use of the term 'history' to designate this work. Some sought to mitigate their use of the term by explaining that Chr sought only to present an 'idealized' portrayal of Israel's past in which the

---

1. 'Chr' will be used in this study to designate the author of the books of Chronicles, a work that is independent of Ezra–Nehemiah. My views on the relationship of these two works are discussed more fully in my *Achaemenid Imperial Administration in Syria-Palestine and the Missions of Ezra and Nehemiah* (SBLDS, 125; Atlanta: Scholars Press, 1992), pp. 36-40.

author self-consciously recast the 'facts' of the past to fit a polemical scheme.[2] Others, less charitable, talked of Chr's 'fictionalized' history and chastised the author for disregarding the canons of accuracy and fidelity to sources.[3]

It is into this environment of predominantly negative assessments of Chr's work that several contemporary authors have stepped with the intention of redefining the genre of the work. If the work fails to meet *our* criteria for a 'history', then perhaps it is something else entirely, they apparently argue. Taking their cue from how Chr has revamped his work's presumed source in the Deuteronomistic History (DtrH), terms such as 'exposition' or 'midrash' have been used to characterize the books of Chronicles.[4] More enigmatic yet are terms such as 'midrashic-like', which seem only to obscure the genre.[5]

Given this confusion over genre and uneasiness with the application of the term 'history' to Chronicles, it seems that additional attention should be given to methodological questions: On what grounds do we assign this narrative to the genre 'history'? And if it is to be assigned to this genre, how do we assess the narrative's value for modern reconstructions of Israel's past?

The subject of our discussion is primarily the matter of how we regard *historiography*, the process of creating a narrative that possesses cohesion, while treating a variety of different events and chronological periods. Now, our primary evidence for assessing Chr's work is the evidence of Chr's narrative itself, taken as a whole. If we are to understand that narrative, we must position ourselves with Chr's framework, that is to say, how did Chr perceive his task of creating a narrative and how did he go about his work. Only then are we able to judge how successfully Chr completed his task and the manner in which Chr's narrative may be used by modern historians.

2.   C.C. Torrey, *The Composition and Historical Value of Ezra–Nehemiah* (BZAW, 2; Giessen: Ricker, 1896), p. 52.

3.   E.g., E.L. Curtis and A.A. Madsen, *A Critical and Exegetical Commentary on the Books of Chronicles* (ICC; Edinburgh: T. & T. Clark, 1910), p. 14; R.H. Pfeiffer, *Introduction to the Old Testament* (New York: Harper, 1948), p. 806.

4.   H.G.M. Williamson, *1 and 2 Chronicles* (NCB; Grand Rapids, MI: Eerdmans, 1982), p. 21; W.E. Barnes, 'Chronicles a Targum', *ExpTim* 8 (1896), pp. 316-17.

5.   R.L. Braun, *1 Chronicles* (WBC, 14; Waco, TX: Word Books, 1986), p. xxiv.

It should be self-evident that it is both methodologically flawed and the height of modern *hubris* to assess Chr's work using the criteria and standards of modern, positivistic historiography. It is equally unacceptable to select only portions of Chr's narrative (e.g., the synoptic passages—those places where Chr is largely relying on the pre-existent DtrH) to characterize Chr's work. These passages represent only a portion of the narrative's body and can only provide partial insight into Chr's conception of the historiographic task.

Since the narrative, as we have it, treats events and the reigns of kings in a sequence, and since the narrative possesses cohesion both in writing style and in recurring thematic elements, we may begin by calling it a 'history'. How then, does Chr conceptualize the writing of this narrative? There are two possible sources for a paradigm or model. First, since Chr has clearly made use of DtrH, it may be that he is simply working with the same understanding of the historiographic task as employed by DtrH. However, as I hope to demonstrate in this paper, several compositional elements that are present in Chr's narrative are absent from DtrH's compositional technique, and thus we must look outside the biblical corpus for the models—and thus, the criteria—that Chr has employed.

This is the second possibility, that Chr was seeking to compose an ἱστορία on the basis of models and methods derived from the Hellenic world. The process by which Chr has gone about assembling the narrative, the narrative formulas employed to carry the flow towards the issues that Chr wished to highlight, and the means employed in the narrative to authenticate the work for the reader—all are modeled on customary and accepted practices within Hellenic historiography. Thus we are led to a comparativist approach, bringing our knowledge of the world of Greek historiography to bear on Chr's narrative. By so doing, we clarify not only the way that Chr conceptualized the historiographic task, but we also find some guidance for assessing the value of Chr's narrative for modern reconstructions of Israel's past. An examination of several specific elements in Chr's narrative will illustrate these points.

Genealogy

It is the bane of most commentators that 1 Chronicles 1–9 consists largely of genealogical materials with pitifully little in the way of narrative interspersed among lists of 'begats'. Rudolf termed these chapters 'the genealogical vestibule' ('die genealogische Vorhalle') of Chr's *real* history,[6] and in general, commentators have regarded the genealogical materials as a late redactional addition to the narrative.[7] Even when taken as a component of the entire work, composed largely by Chr and not attached by a later redactor, commentators often express confusion over the role of such genealogical materials in the history as a whole.

It needs to be noted that there is nothing like this sustained genealogy in the DtrH. Consequently, working on this difference from DtrH and drawing comparisons to the ethnic concerns of Ezra–Nehemia, some have tried to see in 1 Chronicles 1–9 an attempt to define the community. Thus, the genealogical chapters of the narrative serve only to define the racial boundaries of the nation, reflecting a purely 'Yehudian' concern to be on guard against intermarriage.[8]

It is only when we turn to Hellenic historiography that such a particularistic understanding of these materials is called into severe question. Throughout the historical compilations of the Greek world, genealogies play a central role as carriers of the organization of society. Thus, Acusilaus of Argo (early fifth century BCE) writes of primeval times and includes extensive accounts of the heroes' lineages with the gods. Pherecydes of Athens (mid-fifth century BCE) wrote ten books of history, largely filled with genealogies drawn from all across Greece. Such is the case as well with the histories of Hecataeus, Hellanicus of Mytilene, and Damastes of Sigeum. As M.L. West has observed, 'The total mass of Greek genealogical literature was very considerable.'[9] Why did Greek historiography indulge such interests? These genealogical materials gave a sense of place and succession, a rooting of a person (and thus the family) in a specific place. Genealogies also established relationships between persons, families, and political entities. No one

---

6.   W. Rudolph, *Chronikbücher* (HAT, 21; Tübingen: Mohr, 1955), pp. 6-7. T. Willi (*Die Chronik als Auslegung: Untersuchungen zur literarischen Gestaltung der historischen Überlieferung Israels* [FRLANT, 106; Göttingen: Vandenhoeck & Ruprecht, 1972], p. 14) traces the use of the expression 'genealogischen Vorhalle' for 1 Chronicles 1–9 back to J. Wellhausen. The most recent extensive treatment of Chr's genealogies is that of M. Oeming, *Das wahre Israel: Die 'genealogische Vorhalle' 1 Chronik 1–9* (BWANT, 128; Stuttgart: Kohlhammer, 1990).

7.   E.g., M. Noth, *The Chronicler's History* (JSOTSup, 50; Sheffield: JSOT Press, 1987), pp. 36-42; see also the summary in Braun, *1 Chronicles*, p. 11.

8.   E.g., Curtis and Madsen, *Chronicles*, pp. 16-17.

9.   M.L. West, *The Hesiodic Catalogue of Women: Its Nature, Structure, and Origins* (New York: Oxford University Press, 1985), p. 7.

has argued that all this genealogical information in the Greek world is the result of a late redactor of the narrative materials that accompanied the descent lists.

Returning to the narrative of Chr, we can see that the genealogical prologue provides a sense of order, from Creation to the ordering of the ritualistic family offices of ch. 9. Taken as a whole, it provides the reader with an impressive sense of continuity and position. De Vries has noted, 'The tribal groups are placed in relationship to one another, their responsibility (cultic or military) is assigned, and tribes, clans, or individuals are identified for each slot'.[10]

In sum, we may conclude three points about the genealogical prologue of Chronicles. First, since it is not a feature of DtrH, its presence suggests that Chr is working from a different conceptualization of his task—thus a comparison with Hellenic historiography is warranted. Second, the commonness of genealogical materials in fifth–fourth century Greek historiography indicates that the historical prologue, 1 Chronicles 1–9, is an intentional part of Chr's historiography and thus plays a role in understanding the narrative as a whole. Finally, the purpose of these materials is not to establish ethnic boundaries for Yehud but rather, along the lines of the role of genealogical materials in Greek historiography, to show how all of Israel has been organized and interrelated.

Role of Prophets

Prophetic figures abound in Chronicles, and in many ways this is one of the most interesting features of the narrative.[11] In Chronicles the appearance of such figures and their message takes on a literary formula that varies little from place to place in the narrative.[12]

For example, 2 Chron. 25.5-24 is a stirring narrative about Amaziah's rule over Judah.[13] It opens with the mustering of troops (for no apparent

---

10. S.J. De Vries, *1 and 2 Chronicles* (FOTL, 11; Grand Rapids, MI: Eerdmans, 1989), p. 27.

11. The most recent extensive treatment of prophecy in Chronicles is W.M. Schniedewind's *The Word of God in Transition: From Prophet to Exegete in the Second Temple Period* (JSOTSup, 197; Sheffield: JSOT Press, 1995).

12. De Vries, *1 and 2 Chronicles*, pp. 287-88.

13. For a recent treatment of this text, see M.P. Graham, 'Aspects of the Structure and Rhetoric of 2 Chronicles 25', in M.P. Graham *et al.* (eds.), *History*

reason), and 300,000 are found among Judah (v. 5). Amaziah hires an additional 100,000 Ephraimites to join his army. But, in vv. 7-8 a 'man of God' comes abruptly on the scene and commands the king to leave the Ephraimites behind. If the king will do this, God will go with him. The king agrees and the Ephraimites are left behind. Amaziah invades the Valley of Salt, strikes down 10,000 men of Seir, and captures another 10,000, who are then executed. Amaziah returns from a triumphant 'slaughter of the Edomites' but unaccountably worships the gods of Edom. So God sends another unnamed prophet to warn the king against his idolatry—but Amaziah interrupts him and snaps, 'Have we made you a royal advisor? Stop! Why should you be put to death?' So the prophet mutters, 'I know that God has determined to destroy you' (v. 16). Because he would not listen, Amaziah now abruptly calls for an encounter with King Joash of Israel. Joash's insulting reply contains a moral observation: 'You say, "See I have defeated Edom," and your heart has lifted you up in boastfulness' (v. 19a). As the story unfolds, Joash and Amaziah meet in battle; Amaziah is defeated; and Joash proceeds to attack Jerusalem and despoil the temple.

This narrative is a major expansion of the treatment of Amaziah in 2 Kgs 14.7-14, where Amaziah kills 10,000 Edomites in the Valley of Salt (v. 7) and then requests a meeting with Joash of Israel (vv. 8-10). There is no 'man of God' to guarantee the victory if the Ephraimites are sent home, and no prophet to warn the king about worshiping the gods of Edom. Indeed, despite the DtrH's considerable interest in the peril of idolatry, there is no mention of Amaziah's defection to the gods of Edom. What then is the role of the 'man of God' or the prophet in this pericope, or generally, in Chr's narrative?

If we turn to Greek historiography we find an apt parallel in the 'wise counsellor' type-scenes from Herodotus. Immerwahr pointed out decades ago that Herodotus uses a type-scene of a wise counsellor coming before a ruler to offer specific advice. When the advice is accepted, the ruler goes on to victory. When the advice is rejected, disaster follows.[14] A classic example is an account in Book 5 of Herodotus's *History* in which the king of Miletus debates whether to revolt against Persia. All urge the king to revolt—with the exception of

and Interpretation: Essays in Honour of John H. Hayes (JSOTSup, 173; Sheffield: JSOT Press, 1993), pp. 78-89.

14. H.R. Immerwahr, *Form and Thought in Herodotus* (Philological Monographs, 23; Cleveland: American Philological Association, 1966), pp. 72-75.

Hecataeus, who foresees great community harm in such an action (36). Hecataeus's advice is ignored; the king goes off on his own; and the city revolts. The end is a disaster in which Miletus pays dearly. The point of the wise counsellor scene in Herodotus is to point out the pride or *hubris* of the ruler when such advice is ignored. It also serves to delineate power relationships that the counsellors understand but that kings and rulers do not always choose to recognize.

Returning to our scene with Amaziah, we note that in one instance advice finds a positive reception, but in the second instance it meets with a negative one. In the first, the 'man of God' reflects on the need to discharge the Ephraimite mercenaries—'for the Lord is not with Israel'. Rather, God will be with Amaziah (and Judah) if the king is obedient. The 'man of God' reflects an understanding of power relationships by which Amaziah must abide, or face disaster. In the second encounter, Amaziah has displayed haughtiness before God by turning to the gods of Edom. The prophet comes to warn but is immediately prevented from bringing the message by Amaziah's satire—'Have we made you a royal counsellor?' So judgment is proclaimed, and even the words of his enemy highlight Amaziah's failure. The parallel here with the wise counsellor type-scenes of Herodotus is quite strong.

Throughout Chr's narrative, the scenes in which a prophet, named or unnamed, confronts a king serve to direct the flow of the narrative toward the issues that Chr feels compelled to raise—the power relationships between God and the community, and the moral responsibility of the reigning king. The king, confronted with such a structure of reality, has but two choices—accept God's decision and prosper, or reject the determination of God and suffer certain disaster. The conclusions of the scenes in which reward and disaster, respectively, are recounted serve to validate the issues that Chr wishes to highlight.

Another classic case of the prophetic message is found at 2 Chron. 15.1-7 during the reign of Asa of Judah.[15] Here Azariah, son of Oded, comes and states:

> The Lord is with you while you are with him. If you seek him, he will be found by you; but if you abandon him, he will abandon you...[historical

---

15. Cf. Ray Dillard's examination of Asa's reign for the light that it sheds on the Chr's theological method and as an *entrée* into several historical and interpretative issues: 'The Reign of Asa (2 Chronicles 14-16): An Example of the Chronicler's Theological Method', *JETS* 23 (1980), pp. 207-18.

retrospective]. But you, take courage! Do not let your hands be weak for
your work shall be rewarded! (vv. 2b, 7)

This is a generic message, as applicable to Chr's post-exilic setting as
to its narrative setting in Asa's reign.[16] Asa takes the prophet's advice
seriously and puts away idolatrous worship, repairs the altar and temple
complex, and leads the nation to commit to seeking God 'with all their
heart and all their soul'. God responds by giving the nation rest. Asa
later ignores the advice of a prophet, however, and dies of severe foot
disease.

What we see is a historiographic device, the employment of a type-
scene to bring out central concerns of the historian. There is little probability that a prophet confronted Amaziah or that a prophet named
Azariah gave such encouraging words to Asa, king of Judah. Rather,
Chr has generated such figures to confront the rulers (and readers!) of
his narrative with the central concerns of his own day, that is, understanding how God and people interact.

Authentication

Under this rubric we can place a number of narrative elements, but for
the purposes of this study I wish to examine only two: numbers and
sources. Part of the way that Chr weaves history is to note in passing
various quantities, particularly those related to military affairs.[17] In
the pericope mentioned earlier we saw 300,000 Judeans and 100,000
Ephraimite mercenaries. Other numbers abound. For example, prior to
Azariah's speech, Asa musters an army of 300,000 from Judah and
another 280,000 from Benjamin (2 Chron. 14.8). They confront an
Egyptian army of a million and defeat them. No matter what system of

---

16. S. Japhet, for example, remarks on the thoughtfully crafted statement in
v. 2b, 'Through this fine structure the Chronicler gives fullest expression to a major
tenet of his philosophy of history...': *I & II Chronicles: A Commentary* (OTL;
Louisville, KY: Westminster/John Knox, 1993), p. 718.

17. Cf. also in this connection P. Welten's *Geschichte und Geschichtsdarstellung in den Chronikbüchern* (WMANT, 42; Neukirchen–Vluyn:
Neukirchener Verlag, 1973), pp. 5-6, 201-206. Welten uses the literary-critical term
'topos' to designate literary elements (e.g., references to building activities, composition of the military, and battle reports) that Chr introduced in his efforts to
advance his theological or historiographic agenda. Typically, this material does not
derive from any particular source but is the creation of Chr.

demography is used, such numbers are patently too large for the population of Judah prior to the exile. But through the use of such numbers in
the context of a battle report, the reader is brought into the narrative in
the belief that the writer is thoroughly competent for his task—after all,
surely the historian knows how many troops were there.

Again, if we turn to Hellenic historiography, we find this to be a common practice. If one consults many of the battle scenes of the Persian
period in Diodorus of Sicily (who may be relying on a fourth-century
source, Ephorus), one finds the use of stock numbers for the purposes of
authentication. In every battle narrative involving the Persian military
after the battle of Marathon, the Persians always have 300,000 troops
and 300 Phoenician vessels. This is true for every military expedition,
no matter how serious the strategic mission. Other Greek historians play
with equally fantastic numbers. Finley cites the example of a second-
century CE compiler, who claimed that Aristotle reported there were
470,000 slaves on the island of Aegina, an impossible number for an
island of only 80 sq. km.[18] The point here is that in Hellenic historiography it was permissible to supplement gaps in knowledge with numbers. But why not simply say it was a 'great number' or 'a multitude of
slaves'? By citing exact quantities, the historian appears to be in command of his report, even down to the fine details of quantities. The use
of such details in the narrative serves to authenticate it and indicate that
the historian had access to privileged knowledge.

Returning to Chronicles, the numbers presented in the narrative seem
frequently to reflect this same historiographic technique. The numbers
offered, usually in the context of military discussions, serve to lend
credence to the larger framework of the historian's narrative of specific
military engagements, so much so that modern scholars have speculated
about the precise military sources to which Chr had access.[19] In reality,
the numbers are probably Chr's invention. But Chr is not guilty of dis-
tortion or fictionalization—only of abiding by the accepted historiographic conventions of the day.

A second way authentication is established in Chr's narrative is by
the citation of sources.[20] The narrative makes abundant reference to

18. M.I. Finley, *Ancient History: Evidence and Models* (New York: Viking,
1986), p. 43.

19. For example, Japhet (*I & II Chronicles*, pp. 708-709), who generally finds
considerable evidence of Chr's use of non-biblical sources (pp. 14-23).

20. Cf. Schniedewind, *Word of God*, pp. 209-28; and n. 17, above.

unique sources, but the question that has plagued scholarship is, 'Are these real sources?' For example, in 2 Chron 20.34 we read of the 'Annals of Jehu son of Hannani' in connection with the narrative of King Jehoshaphat's reign. Such citation formulas provide the semblance of inner knowledge on the part of the writer and so lend credibility to the flow of the narrative.

In classical historiography similar source puzzles present themselves. Finley uses the example of the detailed narratives of early republican Rome authored by Livy and Dionysius of Halicarnassus. Admittedly, they did have sources that took them back to approximately 300 BCE, but they write and cite sources for accounts of much earlier periods. Finley commented, 'The ability of ancients to invent and their capacity to believe are persistently underestimated. How else could they have filled their blatant gaps of knowledge?'[21] For example, Herodotus speaks of going to Egypt and attests that many otherwise impossible things are true on the basis that he had seen it 'with my own eyes'. Even as mild a critic as A.H. Sayce noted in the late nineteenth century that these appeals to personal observation are inserted in precisely those narratives most suspect,[22] and more recent critics have been able to demonstrate that these narrative materials reflect Greek misperceptions of Egypt during the time of Herodotus.[23]

Returning to Chr's narrative, there is no compelling reason to suspect that these citations of sources represent anything more than an authentication device. The fact that such devices are used by Hellenic historiographers serves to enhance the probability that Chr would have been concerned to incorporate references to sources in his own narrative in order to suspend the reader's suspicions.

The consideration of the possible use of sources by Chr directly relates to a pervasive problem in Chronicles research, namely the relationship between these books and the pre-existing DtrH. Is the extensive use of the latter by Chr a sign that the DtrH has achieved a 'canonical' status in the community? Or, conversely, is the free handling of the DtrH by Chr a sign that this source was not 'canonical' at the time the

---

21. Finley, *Ancient History*, p. 9.

22. A.H. Sayce, *The Ancient Empires of the East: Herodotos I-III* (London: Macmillan, 1883), pp. xxv-xxvii.

23. O.K. Armayor, 'Did Herodotus Ever Go to Egypt?', *JARCE* 15 (1978), pp. 59-73.

narrative was being written, or at the least was not so authoritative that it was viewed as the last word on the matter?

Again, a comparativist perspective offers some suggestions on how to approach this issue. In the classical world, borrowing without attribution from earlier narratives was an accepted convention. Livy borrows extensively from Polybius without attribution and frequently with editorial selection and expansions. Diodorus Siculus relied on Ephorus, often rewriting his source considerably where the moral focus did not suit his purpose.[24]

The stance of Chr toward the materials that he borrowed from the DtrH is that of a writer tapping a source of earlier narratives. In this, there is no need to raise the question of canonical status or variant text families to account for the changes and alterations that appear in Chr's version. Adapting a source in ancient historiography did not carry with it any premise of slavishly copying the source or even sticking to the basic story line. Rather, like other historiographers, Chr makes use of whatever suits his larger historiographic purpose.

Conclusions

Looking at Chronicles through the lens of the historiographic practices of the Hellenic world both rehabilitates Chr and raises new questions about the value of his narrative for contemporary historical understandings of Israel. It seems apparent that Chr is no evil fictionalizer trying to mislead his audience. Chr is, rather, an accomplished historiographer, writing in accord with the accepted practices of his time. At the same time, such practices are not those that we would countenance in our own day, and just as we have grave difficulties in knowing what to do with Thucydides' narratives of the early years of the Delian League, so we have serious problems determining historical reality in Chr's narratives. Without external confirmation, such narratives are perhaps best left as part of an enticing storyline woven by Chr.

24. R. Drews, 'Diodorus and his Sources', *AJP* 83 (1962), pp. 383-92.

THE CHRONICLER AND HIS SOURCES—
HISTORICAL AND GEOGRAPHICAL

Anson F. Rainey

Introduction

The subject of this paper is a controversial issue among biblical scholars. It is not my purpose to survey the wide spectrum of opinions concerning the composition and sources of Chr[1] However, it may prove worthwhile to cite the opinion of M. Noth, whose analysis of the ancient biblical historical traditions has had such a profound influence on subsequent scholarship:

> It seems, therefore, that Chr had available to him an ancient source in which he found various items concerning the defensive building work undertaken by the kings of Judah. On the basis of this, he seems to have developed his own presentation of the royal armaments which he applied primarily to his favorite characters in the history of the kings of Judah.[2]

After reviewing several war stories recounted by Chr but missing in Kings, Noth also admits:

> It thus seems as though Chr was able to draw some material on the theme of the wars of the Judaean kings from an alternative tradition to which he had access but which has since been lost to us.[3]

---

1. W. Rudolph, *Chronikbücher* (HAT, 21; Tübingen: Mohr, 1955); R.H. Pfeiffer, 'Chronicles, I and II', *IDB* (1962), I, pp. 572-80; O. Eissfeldt, *The Old Testament: An Introduction* (Oxford: Basil Blackwell, 1965); P.R. Ackroyd, 'Chronicles, I and II', *IDBSup* (1976), pp. 156-58; H.G.M. Williamson, *1 and 2 Chronicles* (NCB; Grand Rapids, MI: Eerdmans, 1982); S. Japhet, *I & II Chronicles: A Commentary* (OTL; Louisville, KY: Westminster/John Knox, 1993).

2. M. Noth, *The Chronicler's History* (JSOTSup, 50; Sheffield: JSOT Press, 1987) (=*Überlieferungsgeschichtliche Studien. Die sammelnden und bearbeiten Geschichtswerke im Alten Testament* [Tübingen: M. Niemeyer, 2nd edn, 1957]), p. 59.

3. Noth, *Chronicler's History*, p. 60.

So Noth, followed by some of the commentators mentioned above, admits that some of the materials in Chronicles pertaining to building projects and military actions must derive from sources not available to us now. It is the purpose of the following discussion to attempt a definition of that source.

Sources Cited for 2 Samuel and the Book of Kings

First we must look at the DtrH pertaining to the kings from David to the end of the monarchy. The latest recorded date in that history is the release of Jehoiachin from prison in Babylonia:

ויהי בשלשים ושבע שנה לגלות יהויכין מלך־יהודה בשנים
עשר חדש בעשרים ושבעה לחדש נשא אויל מרדך מלך
בבל בשנת מלכו את־ראש יהויכין מלך־יהודה מבית כלא:

> And it happened in the thirty-seventh year of the exile of Jehoiachin, king of Judah, in the twelfth month on the twenty-seventh day of the month, that Evil-merodach, king of Babylon, in his accession year, granted an amnesty to Jehoiachin, king of Judah from the house of detention (2 Kgs 25.27 = Jer. 52.31-34).

This twenty-seventh day of the twelfth month of the thirty-seventh year of Jehoiachin's captivity (by Tishre reckoning)[4] gives an absolute date of 2 April, 561 BCE.[5] The final Deuteronomistic editor, perhaps one of Jehoiachin's close associates,[6] was evidently present at that event. From certain points discussed below, he will be seen to have had a special interest in preserving the honor and integrity of Jehoiachin and his grandfather, Josiah.

The following compositions are cited in the book of Kings as sources for the information treated in various parts of the book. Concerning the reign of Solomon, the author/editor credits a work called ספר דברי שלמה 'Chronicles of Solomon' (1 Kgs 11.41). As a source for subsequent reigns of kings of Judah, reference is made to ספר דברי הימים

---

4. E.R. Thiele, *The Mysterious Numbers of the Hebrew Kings* (Grand Rapids, MI: Zondervan, 3rd edn, 1983), p. 140, n. 14.

5. R.A. Parker and W.H. Dubberstein, *Babylonian Chronology 626 B.C.—A.D. 75* (BUS, 19; Providence, RI: Brown University Press, 1956), p. 28.

6. E.F. Weidner, 'Jojachin, König von Juda, in babylonischen Keilschrifttexten', in *Mélanges syriens offerts à Monsieur René Dussaud* (Bibliotheque archéologique et historique, 30; Paris: P. Geuthner, 1939), II, pp. 923-35; see Text B, Vs. II, 40.

למלכי יהודה 'Chronicles of the Kings of Judah' (15×): 1 Kgs 14.29; 15.7, 23; 22.45; 2 Kgs 8.23; 12.20; 14.18; 15.36; 16.19; 20.20; 21.17, 25; 23.28; 24.5. Likewise, for the Kings of Israel the source credited is ספר דברי הימים למלכי ישראל 'Chronicles of the Kings of Israel' (14×): 1 Kgs 14.19; 15.31; 16.27; 22.39; 2 Kgs 1.18; 10.34; 13.8, 12; 14.28; 15.11, 15, 26, 31. Frequently, the statement is made to the effect that more details on the reign in question may be found in one or the other of these sources. The author/editor seems to be assuming that the source books, the Chronicles of the Kings of Judah and of Israel, were available and could be consulted.

In parallel passages, the book of Chronicles describes the sources for information on the kings of Judah (it doesn't treat the kings of Israel in detail) in a more explicit manner. Many commentators have denied the authenticity of Chr's citations.[7] Various criticisms and negative theories will be dealt with in the subsequent discussion, but first the relevant evidence must be presented in an organized fashion. In the final analysis, it is the nature of the internal evidence from the citations that must determine their plausibility. The parallel texts from Samuel and Kings on the one hand and from Chronicles on the other are juxtaposed below to facilitate comparison.

Samuel

0. David – blank

Chronicles

0. 1 Chron. 29.29 – David

ודברי דויד המלך הראשנים
והאחרנים הנם כתובים על־דברי
שמואל הראה ועל־דברי
נתן הנביא ועל־דברי גד החזה:

And the acts of King David, from first to last, are written in the Chronicles of Samuel the seer, and in the Chronicles of Nathan the prophet, and in the Chronicles of Gad the seer.

1. 1 Kgs 11.41 – Solomon

ויתר דברי שלמה וכל־אשר
עשה וחכמתו הלוא־הם כתבים
על־ספר דברי שלמה:

1. 2 Chron. 9.29 – Solomon

ושאר דברי שלמה הראשנים
והאחרונים הלא־הם כתובים
על־דברי נתן הנביא ועל־נבואת
אחיה השילוני ובחזות יעדי [יעדו]
החזה על־יר בעם בן־נבט:

---

7.   Cf. Eissfeldt's remarks in *Old Testament*, p. 532.

Samuel

And the rest of the acts of Solomon, and all that he did, and his wisdom, are they not written in the book of the acts of Solomon?

Chronicles

And the rest of the acts of Solomon, from first to last, are they not written in the Chronicles of Nathan the prophet, and in the prophecy Ahijah the Shilonite, and in the visions of Je'do the seer concerning Jeroboam the son of Nebat?

2. 1 Kgs 14.29 – Rehoboam

ויתר דברי רחבעם וכל־אשר
עשה הלא־המה כתובים על־ספר
דברי הימים למלכי יהודה:

And the rest of the acts of Rehoboam, and all that he did, are they not written in the book of the Chronicles of the Kings of Judah?

2. 2 Chron. 12.15a – Rehoboam

ודברי רחבעם הראשנים
והאחרונים הלא־הם כתובים
בדברי שמעיה הנביא ועדו החזה

And the acts of Rehoboam, from first to last, are they not written in the Chronicles of Shemaiah the prophet and Iddo the seer?

3. 1 Kgs 15.7a – Abijam (Abijah)

ויתר דברי אבים וכל־אשר עשה
הלא־הם כתובים על־ספר דברי
הימים למלכי יהודה

The rest of the acts of Abijam, and all that he did, are they not written in the Book of the Chronicles of the Kings of Judah?

3. 2 Chron. 13.22 – Abijam (Abijah)

ויתר דברי אביה ודרכיו ודבריו
כתובים במדרש הנביא עדו:

And the rest of the acts of Abijah, his ways and his words, are written in the history of the prophet Iddo.

4. 1 Kgs 15.23a – Asa

ויתר כל־דברי־אסא וכל־גבורתו
וכל־אשר עשה והערים אשר בנה
הלא־המה כתובים על־ספר דברי
הימים למלכי יהודה

And the rest of the acts of Asa and all his might, and all that he did, and the cities which he built, are they not written in the Book of the Chronicles of the Kings of Judah?

4. 2 Chron. 16.11 – Asa

והנה דברי אסא הראשנים
והאחרונים הנם כתובים על־ספר
המלכים ליהודה וישראל:

And behold the acts of Asa, from first to last, are written in the Book of the Kings of Judah and Israel.

5. 1 Kgs 22.46 (EVV, v. 45) – Jehoshaphat

ויתר דברי יהושפט וגבורתו
אשר־עשה ואשר נלחם הלא־הם
כתובים על־ספר דברי הימים
למלכי יהודה:

5. 2 Chron. 20.34 – Jehoshaphat

ויתר דברי יהושפט הראשנים
והאחרנים הנם כתובים בדברי יהוא
בן־חנני אשר העלה על־ספר מלכי
ישראל:

Samuel

And the rest of the acts of Jehoshaphat and his might that he exhibited and how he warred, are they not written in the Book of the Chronicles of the Kings of Judah?

6. 2 Kgs 8.23 – Joram
ויתר דברי יורם וכל־
אשר עשה הלא־הם כתובים
על־ספר דברי הימים למלכי יהודה:

And the rest of the acts of Joram and all that he did, are they not written in the Book of the Chronicles of the Kings of Judah?

7. 2 Kgs 12.20 (EVV, v. 19) – Joash
ויתר דברי יואש וכל־אשר עשה
הלא־הם כתובים על־ספר דברי
הימים למלכי יהודה:

And the rest of the acts of Joash, and all that he did, are they not written in the Book of the Chronicles of the Kings of Judah?

8. 2 Kgs 14.18 – Amaziah
ויתר דברי אמציהו הלא־הם
כתובים על־ספר דברי הימים
למלכי יהודה:

Now the rest of the acts of Amaziah, are they not written in the Book of the Chronicles of the Kings of Judah?

9. 2 Kgs 15.6 – Azariah (Uzziah)
ויתר דברי עזריהו וכל־אשר עשה
הלא־הם כתובים על־ספר דברי
הימים למלכי יהודה:

Chronicles

And the rest of the acts of Jehoshaphat, the first and the last, are written in the Chronicles of Jehu the son of Hanani, which are recorded in the Book of the Kings of Israel.

6. Joram – blank

7. 2 Chron. 24.27a – Joash
ובניו ורב המשא עליו
ויסוד בית האלהים הנם כתובים
על־מדרש ספר המלכים

And his sons and the many oracles concerning him and the strengthening of the House of God, behold they are written in the history of the Book of the Kings.

8. 2 Chron. 25.26 – Amaziah
ויתר דברי אמציהו הראשנים
והאחרונים הלא הנם כתובים
על־ספר מלכי־יהודה וישראל:

And the rest of the acts of Amaziah, the first and the last, are they not written in the Book of the Kings of Judah and Israel?

9. 2 Chron. 26.22 – Uzziah
ויתר דברי עזיהו הראשנים
והאחרונים כתב ישעיהו בן־אמוץ
הנביא:

Samuel

And the rest of the acts of Azariah, and all that he did, are they not written in the Book of the Chronicles of the Kings of Judah?

Chronicles

And the rest of the acts of Uzziah, the first and the last, Isaiah the prophet the son of Amos wrote.

10.　　2 Kgs 15.36 – Jotham

ויתר דברי יותם אשר עשה הלא־
הם כתובים על־ספר דברי הימים
למלכי יהודה:

And the rest of the acts of Jotham, and all that he did, are they not written in the Book of the Chronicles of the Kings of Judah?

10.　　2 Chron. 27.7 – Jotham

ויתר דברי יותם וכל־מלחמתיו
ודרכיו הנם כתובים
על־ספר מלכי־ישראל ויהודה:

And the rest of the acts of Jotham, and all his wars, and his ways, behold they are written in the Book of the Kings of Israel and Judah.

11.　　2 Kgs 16.19 – Ahaz

ויתר דברי אחז אשר עשה הלא־
הם כתובים על־ספר דברי הימים
למלכי יהודה:

And the rest of the acts of Ahaz which he did, are they not written in the Book of the Chronicles of the Kings of Judah?

11.　　2 Chron. 28.26 – Ahaz

ויתר דבריו וכל־דרכיו הראשנים
והאחרונים הנם כתובים
על־ספר מלכי־יהודה וישראל:

And the rest of his acts and all his ways, the first and the last, behold, they are written in the Book of the Kings of Judah and Israel.

12.　　2 Kgs 20.20 – Hezekiah

ויתר דברי חזקיהו וכל־גבורתו
ואשר עשה את־הברכה ואת־התעלה
ויבא את־המים העירה הלא־חם
כתובים על־ספר דברי הימים
למלכי יהודה:

And the rest of the acts of Hezekiah, and all his might, and how he made the pool and the conduit and brought water into the city, are they not written in the Book of the Chronicles of the Kings of Judah?

12.　　2 Chron. 32.32 – Hezekiah

ויתר דברי יחזקיהו וחסדיו
הנם כתובים בחזון ישעיהו בן־אמוץ
הנביא על־ספר מלכי־יהודה
וישראל:

And the rest of the acts of Hezekiah and his good deeds, behold, they are written in the vision of Isaiah the prophet the son of Amoz, in the Book of the Kings of Judah and Israel.

Samuel	*Chronicles*

13.   2 Kgs 21.17 – Manasseh

ויתר דברי מנשה וכל־אשר עשה
וחטאתו אשר חטא הלא־הם כתובים
על־ספר דברי הימים למלכי יהודה:

And the rest of the acts of
Manasseh, and all that he did, and
the sin that he committed, are they
not written in the Book of the
Chronicles of the Kings of Judah?

13.   2 Chron. 21.17 – Manasseh

ויתר דברי מנשה ותפלתו אל־
אלהיו ודברי החזים המדברים אליו
בשם יהוה אלהי ישראל הנם על־
דברי מלכי ישראל: ותפלתו
והעתר־לו וכל־חטאתו ומעלו
והמקמות אשר בנה בהם במות
והעמיד האשרים והפסלים לפני
הכנעו הנם כתובים על דברי חוזי[ו]:

And the rest of the acts of Manasseh,
and his prayer to his God, and the
words of the seers who spoke to him
in the name of the God of Israel, and
his prayer, and how God received his
entreaty, and all his sin and his faith-
lessness, and the sites on which he
built high places and set up the
Asherim and the images, before he
humbled himself, behold, they are
written in the Chronicles of his seers
(LXX).

14.   2 Kgs 21.25 – Amon

ויתר דברי אמון אשר עשה
הלא־הם כתובים על־ספר
דברי הימים למלכי יהודה:

And the rest of the acts of Amon
which he did, are they not written
in the Book of the Chronicles of the
Kings of Judah?

14.   Amon – blank

15.   2 Kgs 23.28 – Josiah

ויתר דברי יאשיהו וכל־אשר
עשה הלא־הם כתובים על־ספר
דברי הימים למלכי יהודה:

And the rest of the acts of Josiah,
and all that he did, are they not
written in the Book of the
Chronicles of the Kings of Judah?

15.   2 Chron. 35.26-27 – Josiah

ויתר דברי יאשיהו וחסדיו
ככתוב בתורת יהוה: ודרכיו
הראשנים והאחרנים הנם כתובים
על־ספר מלכי־ישראל ויהודה:

And the rest of the acts of Josiah, and
his good deeds according to what is
written in the Law of the Lord, and
his acts, the first and the last, behold
they are written in the Book of the
Kings of Israel and Judah.

16.   2 Kgs 24.5 – Jehoiakim

ויתר דברי יהויקים וכל־אשר עשה
הלא־הם כתובים על־ספר דברי
הימים למלכי יהודה:

And the rest of the acts of
Jehoiakim, and all that he did, are
they not written in the Book of the
Chronicles of the Kings of Judah?

16.   2 Chron. 36.8 – Jehoiakim

ויתר דברי יהויקים ותעבתיו אשר־
עשה והנמצא עליו הנם כתובים
על־ספר מלכי ישראל ויהודה:

And the rest of the acts of Jehoiakim,
and the abominations that he did,
and what was found against him,
behold, they are written in the Book
of the Kings of Israel and Judah.

It is obvious from the examples cited above that Chr meant that the
same material derived by the Deuteronomist(s) from the 'Book of the
Chronicles of the Kings of Judah' was derived by him from works
ascribed to various prophets. This naturally explains the Jewish tradition
that the books of Samuel and Kings were written by prophets.[8] The
most logical conclusion, if we take Chr's statements at face value, is
that the 'Book of the Chronicles of the Kings of Judah' was composed
of a series of works written from reign to reign by prophets contemporary with the respective kings.[9] This is the clear intention of entries
such as 2 Chron. 20.34,

> And the rest of the acts of Jehoshaphat, the first and the last, are written
> in the Chronicles of Jehu the son of Hanani, which are recorded in the
> Book of the Kings of Israel,

and 2 Chron. 32.32,

> And the rest of the acts of Hezekiah, and his good deeds, behold, they
> are written in the vision of Isaiah the prophet the son of Amoz, in the
> Book of the Kings of Judah and Israel.

Chr's כתובים על־ספר מלכי ישראל ויהודה 'written in (literally 'on') the
Book of the Kings of Israel and Judah (or: 'Judah and Israel')' (2 Chron.
16.11; 25.26; 27.7; 28.26; 35.27; 36.8) is obviously the equivalent of
the Deuteronomist's כתובים על־ספר דברי הימים למלכי יהודה 'written
on the Book of the Chronicles of the Kings of Judah' (*passim*). Only
once does Chr use the expression דברי הימים when he speaks about the
census total not being recorded in דברי הימים למלך דויד 'the Chronicles
of King David' (1 Chron. 27.24). On the other hand, he once uses
מדרש ספר המלכים 'the midrash of the Book of the Kings' (2 Chron.

---

8.   Eissfeldt, *Old Testament*, pp. 565-66; cf. Noth, *Chronicler's History*,
pp. 56 and 160, n. 37.
9.   Thiele, *Mysterious Numbers*, pp. 194-97.

24.27), which has caused infinite confusion in the minds of those who associate the term 'midrash' with its meaning in later Jewish literature.[10] It is quite likely that this term represents one of the titles by which Chr's particular source (apart from the DtrH) was known in his day. The question is: What does it signify? The term 'midrash' occurs only twice in the Hebrew Bible, both times in Chr's source citations: 'the midrash of the prophet Iddo' (2 Chron. 13.22) and 'the midrash of the Book of the Kings' (2 Chron. 27.24) discussed above. The verbal root דרש√ signifies 'to seek (after)', but also 'to investigate', as seen, for example, in Deut. 13.15 (EVV, v. 14), ודרשת וחקרת ושאלת 'and you shall search out and investigate and inquire' (cf. also Deut. 17.4; 19.18). The parallel in that passage with the root חקר√ permits us to render the cognate term 'midrash' as 'investigation'.[11] The semantic usage I am proposing for 'midrash' is like that for the Greek ἱστορία 'inquiry', but also the 'written account of one's inquiries'. Therefore, I have rendered מדרש by the term 'history'. It also follows then that Chr's מדרש ספר המלכים 'the midrash of the Book of the Kings' and also his ספר המלכים 'Book of the Kings' are the equivalent of the Deuteronomist's ספר דברי הימים למלכי יהודה 'Book of the Chronicles of the Kings of Judah'.

Therefore, it would seem obvious that the witness of the citation formulas used by Chr confirms that the 'Book of the Chronicles of the Kings of Judah' was composed of prophetic historical essays written from reign to reign. Another conclusion is that the corresponding 'Book of the Chronicles of the Kings of Israel', cited by the Deuteronomist as the source for the data on the kings of Israel, must also have been a similar composition, built up from historical essays by prophets in the northern kingdom. Unfortunately, no one has preserved the names of those northern prophets in the same way that Chr has done for those in Judea.

10. For example, 'a reconstructed history of Israel embellished with marvellous tales of divine interposition and prophetic activity': E.L. Curtis and A.A. Madsen, *A Critical and Exegetical Commentary on the Books of Chronicles* (ICC; Edinburgh: T. & T. Clark, 1910), p. 23.

11. Eissfeldt, *Old Testament*, p. 534; W.M. Schniedewind, 'History or Homily: Toward Understanding the Chronicler's Purpose', in *Proceedings of the Eleventh World Congress of Jewish Studies, Division A* (Jerusalem: World Union of Jewish Studies, 1994), pp. 92-93.

Some scholars[12] have assumed that the Chronicles of the Kings of Judah and Israel were official records of the respective governments. However, this can hardly be the case. It is appropriate in this regard to repeat a point made by Thiele, 'that royal scribes had little if anything to do with most of this material as it has come down to us'.[13] There is too much criticism of the monarchy for these works to have been the official records of the kingdom. Noth had also recognized that the Chronicles of the Kings of Judah and of Israel could not be the official monarchical records, although their respective authors had had access to official materials.[14] Official records would hardly deal with the king's 'sin that he sinned' (2 Kgs 21.17). On the other hand, it is likely that some of the prophets who contributed to the 'Chronicles', especially in Judah, would have had access to official records. At least one of those cited by Chr is known to have served the reigning king in an official capacity.[15] This is Gad, who is known as גד הנביא חזה דוד 'Gad the prophet, David's seer' (2 Sam. 24.11) or simply גד חזה דויד 'Gad, David's seer' (1 Chron. 21.9; also 2 Chron. 29.25); the head of one of the musical guilds in the temple was also הימן חזה המלך 'Heman, the king's seer' (1 Chron. 25.5). Isaiah's well-known sessions with Hezekiah also suggest that the prophet may have been acting in a similar function as advisor to the king.

A common assertion, following Noth,[16] is that Chr simply adopted a literary convention of citing prophets known from Kings and crediting them with writing the history of their respective contemporary monarchs. This theory was taken up with a vengeance by Micheel.[17] Noth has a problem, however, with יעדי = [יעדו] החזה 'Ye'dî/Ye'dô, the seer' of 2 Chron. 9.29 and עדו החזה 'Iddô, the seer' in 2 Chron. 12.15.[18] At least he agrees that they are most likely the same person, but his argument that Chr has simply made him up and given him a

---

12. J.A. Montgomery, *A Critical and Exegetical Commentary on the Books of Kings* (ICC; Edinburgh: T. & T. Clark, 1951), pp. 30-32.

13. Thiele, *Mysterious Numbers*, p. 194.

14. *Chronicler's History*, pp. 57-58, 60.

15. W.M. Schniedewind, *The Word of God in Transition: From Prophet to Exegete in the Second Temple Period* (JSOTSup, 197; Sheffield: JSOT Press, 1995), pp. 31-54.

16. *Chronicler's History*, pp. 53-54.

17. R. Micheel, *Die Seher- und Propheten-Überlieferungen in der Chronik* (BEATAJ, 18; Frankfurt am Main: Peter Lang, 1983).

18. *Chronicler's History*, pp. 156-57, n. 11

name from the root עד׳׳ד√ is simply snatching at straws. For the reign of Solomon, Chr already has two star prophets, Nathan and Ahijah; there is no need for inventing another seer! Furthermore, the source citations are hardly uniform; there are many instances where Chr simply refers to 'the Book of the Kings of Judah and Israel' (2 Chron. 16.11) or a similar locution. Why did he not invent prophets for all the kings? If no name of a contemporary prophet was available from the DtrH for some kings, he could have invented someone just as he is supposed to have invented 'Iddo'. The most obvious solution to the problem is that Chr did have the names of many of the prophetic authors in his own copy of the Chronicles of the Kings of Judah/Israel, but that some chapters were either anonymous or had lost the superscription naming the particular author. Certain chapters may have been the work of several writers combined, who decided not to sign their names to the work. Whatever the case, the variations in the citation formulas of Chr's work are in themselves a strong argument for their authenticity. The Book of the Chronicles of the Kings of Judah must have been composed of chapters written by prophets of the Jerusalem 'circle' during the course of the Judean monarchy.

Noth assumed that Chr borrowed Jehu the son of Hanani from Kings, where he is presumed to have been a northern prophet because of his message to Baasha (1 Kgs 16.1-7).[19] However, his father, חנני הראה 'Hanani the seer', is credited by Chr with an oracle to Asa (2 Chron. 16.7), so there is no need to assume that the two were northern prophets. But even if they were, the reign of Jehoshaphat was marked by close political ties with the northern kingdom under Ahab, and it is just at this time that the Judeans adopted the non-accession system of chronology in vogue in the north (cf. discussion below). There must have been close ties between the two prophetic circles, the northern and the southern, during this very period.

The chronological fabric of our book of Kings actually provides some important insights concerning the two circles of prophets, which preserved the respective chronicles in the north and in the south from reign to reign. Thiele has shown that the historians keeping the northern records used the non-accession year system, while those in the south used the accession year system.[20] In the mid-ninth century BCE, when a covenant was made between the two states, the southern writers adopted

---

19. *Chronicler's History*, pp. 156-57, n. 11.
20. *Mysterious Numbers*, pp. 79-101.

the non-accession system in vogue in the north. Later, during the beginning of the eighth century when a new treaty was made, both schools returned to the accession year system. The precision demonstrated by Thiele for the various synchronisms in the DtrH cannot be dismissed as J.M. Miller[21] would have us believe. Miller seems impervious to the weight of Thiele's evidence. Thiele is not merely adopting 'unreported variables such as co-regencies, calendar changes, variant reckoning procedures, and the like'.[22] Each of the phenomena posited by Thiele not only is proven by the mathematics involved, it is also supported by various hints and allusions in the text and, especially in the case of co-regencies, by impeccable historical logic. Note that 2 Kgs 8.16 MT plainly describes a co-regency. This is in contrast to opposing systems such as that followed by Miller himself,[23] which depends, for example, on the LXX Lucianic chronology, which Thiele has thoroughly explained as a late attempt to make sense out of data that the Lucianic editor could not comprehend.[24] Miller's own reconstructions rely on supposedly sophisticated literary theories and on unsupportable assumptions, for example, that Ahab could not have died a violent death or that he did not engage in any wars.[25] Competing systems of chronology must adopt 'the conjecture that in a significant number of places there have been scribal errors in transmission',[26] believing that '...it is incredible that all these numbers can have been handed down through so many editors and copyists without often becoming

21. 'Israelite History', in D.A. Knight and G.M. Tucker (eds.), *The Hebrew Bible and its Modern Interpreters* (The Bible and its Modern Interpreters, 1; Chico, CA: Scholars Press, 1985), pp. 15-17.

22. 'Israelite History', p. 15.

23. 'Israelite History', pp. 16-17.

24. *The Mysterious Numbers of the Hebrew Kings: A Reconstruction of the Chronology of the Kingdoms of Israel and Judah* (Chicago: University of Chicago Press, 1951), pp. 167-203; *idem*, 'Coregencies and Overlapping Reigns among the Hebrew Kings', *JBL* (1974), pp. 174-200.

25. Cf. A.F. Rainey, 'The Moabite Invasion of Judah (2 Chron. 20.1-30)' (paper delivered at the SBL Annual Meeting, Washington, DC, November 22-24, 1993).

26. H. Tadmor, 'The Chronology of the First Temple Period: A Presentation and Evaluation of the Sources. Appendix 2', in J.A. Soggin, *An Introduction to the History of Israel and Judah* (Valley Forge, PA: Trinity Press International, 2nd edn, 1993), p. 395.

corrupt'.[27] With Thiele all numbers in MT are intact. Some recent attempts to juggle the data in Kings, including chronology, have led to outlandish chaos and can be safely ignored.[28]

The northern chronicles were evidently brought to Judah with the fall of Samaria, where they became available to the circle of prophets there and could be used by the (first) Deuteronomist in the compilation of a combined history of the Israelite/Judean monarchy. Jepsen had postulated a synchronistic chronicle comprised of the main regnal formulas and selected additional materials that he gleaned from Kings.[29] His work is ingenious but is negated by a major flaw: Jepsen himself recognized that the chronological data were not internally consistent, which seemed strange in what was supposed to be a homogeneous text.[30] In fact, Thiele has demonstrated the different systems at work in the citations from Kings, and that clearly indicates that the northern rulers were treated in a document separate from that of the southern kings. When information from the two documents was combined, the redactor/editor did not dare alter the numbers in his two original sources. Jepsen recognized the existence of 'annals' for the kings of Israel and Judah, but he thought that it was one document; for Jepsen, the distinction between the 'Chronicles of the Kings of Israel' and the 'Chronicles of the Kings of Judah' was of no consequence.[31] That two separate documents were involved is further demonstrated by the introductory and concluding formulas that form the basic framework of our book of Kings; the phraseology pertaining to kings of Israel has its own distinct patterns that differ from those for the kings of Judah.[32]

Finally, the existence of two circles or schools of prophets in Israel and Judah respectively, as demonstrated by Thiele's research, finds a remarkable parallel in the similar conclusions concerning the authors of

27. W.F. Albright, 'The Chronology of the Divided Monarchy of Israel', *BASOR* 100 (1945), p. 17.

28. J. Strange, 'Joram, King of Israel and Judah', *VT* 25 (1975), 191-201; J.H. Hayes and P.K. Hooker, *A New Chronology for the Kings of Israel and Judah and its Implications for Biblical History and Literature* (Atlanta: John Knox, 1988).

29. A. Jepsen, *Die Quellen des Königsbuches* (Halle [Saale]: M. Niemeyer, 2nd edn, 1956), pp. 30-40.

30. Jepsen, *Die Quellen*, pp. 41-54.

31. Jepsen, *Die Quellen*, pp. 54-60.

32. For details cf. S. Bin-Nun, 'Formulas from the Royal Records of Israel and Judah', *VT* 18 (1968), pp. 414-32.

the E document (in the north) and the J document (in Jerusalem).[33] Is it not highly likely that the Books of the Chronicles of the Kings of Israel and of Judah were compiled by the same two prophetic circles that produced the E and the J versions of Israel's traditions of origin? Is it not likely that the same refugees from Israel who found asylum in Jerusalem after the fall of Samaria brought with them the E document and the Chronicles of the Kings of Israel (plus other works)? Their reception in Jerusalem would have paved the way for the eventual combining of northern and southern literary works and, of course, the continuance of these productions during the seventh century.

Some Chronicles Passages Not in Kings

Now it remains to examine some of the material in Chr's narrative that is lacking in the biblical Kings. It each case it will be argued that while Chr may have had a tendentious reason for including the various passages, the Deuteronomist may also have had a tendentious reason for omitting them. In other words, I am suggesting that these texts were part of the original prophetic compilation known as the Chronicles of the Kings of Judah but that one author chose not to use them, while another (Chr) decided to include them. It is not denied that Chr usually incorporates these entries in a framework designed to stress his theological point of view.[34]

At this point it is worth noting the Deuteronomist's own testimony concerning some of the specific materials that might be found in the 'Chronicles of the Kings of Judah' and also in the 'Chronicles of the Kings of Israel'. From the former document we are informed that it recorded for Asa כל־גבורתו וכל־אשר עשה והערים אשר בנה 'all his military prowess and all that he did and the cities which he built' (1 Kgs 15.23); for Jehoshaphat גבורתו אשר־עשה ואשר נלחם 'his military prowess, what he did and how he warred' (1 Kgs 22.46 [EVV, v. 45]); for Hezekiah כל־גבורתו ואשר עשה את־הברכה ואת־התעלה ויבא את־המים העירה 'all his military prowess and what he did, and the pool and the channel and how he brought the water into the city' (2 Kgs 20.20); and

33. For example, R.E. Friedman, *Who Wrote the Bible?* (New York: Summit Books), pp. 70-88.

34. This has been discussed for the relevant passages most recently by Japhet (*I & II Chronicles*), to whom I have made constant reference in the ensuing discussion.

for Manasseh כל־אשר עשה וחטאתו אשר חטא 'all that he did and his sin which he sinned' (2 Kgs 21.17). So it should be expected that if Chr really had a copy of the 'Chronicles of the Kings of Judah', he would have found information about military events and building projects, as well as some degree of moral critique. As for the 'Chronicles of the Kings of Israel', we are told that it contained similar data: for Jeroboam I אשר נלחם ואשר מלך 'how he warred and how he reigned' (1 Kgs 14.19); for Ahab כל־אשר עשה ובית השן אשר בנה וכל־הערים אשר בנה 'all that he did and the ivory house that he built and all the cities that he built' (1 Kgs 22.39); for Joash כל־אשר עשה וגבורתו אשר נלחם עם אמציה מלך־יהודה 'all that he did and his military prowess, how he warred with Amaziah king of Judah' (2 Kgs 13.12); for Jeroboam II כל־אשר עשה וגבורתו אשר־נלחם ואשר השיב את־דמשק ואת־חמת ליהודה בישראל 'all that he did and his military prowess, how he warred and how he won back Damascus and Hamath (the ancient ally) of Judah for Israel' (2 Kgs 14.28); and for Shallum וקשרו אשר קשר 'and his plot which he fomented' (2 Kgs 15.15). So if the northern document were available, further information about military and political activities and building projects would be found recorded there. There is no cause to doubt that the Deuteronomist is telling the truth, since there is no reason for him to invent these almost casual statements in his own credit lines. The following passages are grouped according to categories reflected in the passages just cited: political activity, building projects, and military preparations and exploits.

Concerning Relations with the Northern Kingdom

The Deuteronomist (probably the first)[35] wanted to aggrandize the final covenant ceremony in the reign of Josiah with the passover that he celebrated and his campaign to win the allegiance of faithful Israelites in the north (cf. the passage below). Therefore, it appears that he deliberately suppressed similar actions on the part of two previous kings.

Asa. The first of these events took place during the reign of Asa. After Asa's victory over the Cushite invaders,[36] he returned to Jerusalem and

---

35. F.M. Cross, *Canaanite Myth and Hebrew Epic: Essays in the History of the Religion of Israel* (Cambridge, MA: Harvard University Press, 1973), pp. 284-85.

36. From the northern Hejaz, Rainey *apud* Y. Aharoni and M. Avi-Yonah (*The Macmillan Bible Atlas* [rev. A. F. Rainey and Z. Safrai; New York: Macmillan, 3rd

was encouraged by prophetic oracle to instigate a cultic reform:

2 Chron. 15.8-9

וכשמע אסא הדברים האלה והנבואה [אשר נבא עזריהו בן־]
עדד חנביא התחזק ויעבר השקוצים מכל־ארץ יהודה ובנימן
ומן־הערים אשר לכד מהר אפרים ויחדש את־מזבח יהוה אשר
לפני אולם יהוה ויקבץ את־כל־יהודה ובנימן והגרים עמהם
מאפרים ומנשה ומשמעון כי־נפלו עליו מישראל לרב בראתם
כי־יהוה אלהיו עמו:

And when Asa heard these words of the prophecy [which Azariah the
son of] Oded [prophesied, Vulgate], he took courage and put away the
abominations from all the land of Judah and Benjamin and from the
towns that he had taken from Mt Ephraim, and he renewed the altar of
the Lord that was in front of the vestibule of the Lord. And he assembled
all of Judah and Benjamin and all those sojourning with them from
Ephraim and from Manasseh and from Simeon, because many had
defected to him from Israel when they saw that the Lord his God was
with him.[37]

Shortly afterwards comes the passage about Baasha's military action
against Asa (2 Chron. 15.19–16.1//1 Kgs 15.17):

ומלחמה לא היתה עד שנת־שלשים וחמש למלכות אסא:
בשנת שלשים ושש למלכות אסא עלה בעשא מלך־ישראל
על־יהודה ויבן את־הרמה לבלתי תת יוצא ובא לאסא מלך יהודה:

And there was not war until the thirty-fifth year of the reign of Asa. In
the thirty-sixth year of the kingdom of Asa, Baasha, king of Israel, came
against Judah and built Ramah to prevent anyone from going or coming
to Asa, king of Judah.

As it stands in 1 Kgs 16.17, the passage appears like a bolt from the
blue with no obvious rationale, but against the background of 2 Chron.
15.8-9 it makes sense. The usurpation of the throne in Israel by Baasha
(909/908 BCE) and the systematic extermination by him of the remaining members of the family of Jeroboam I (1 Kgs 15.29) must have
created considerable unrest in the northern kingdom. Furthermore, the
military conflict with the Philistines, which was centered at Gibbethon
when Baasha came to power (1 Kgs 15.27), was apparently still

edn, 1993], p. 93). Map 122 is corrected accordingly in the Hebrew edition (Aharoni
and Rainey, *Carta's Atlas of the Bible* [Jerusalem: Carta, 3rd edn, 1995], p. 82).

37. Japhet, *I & II Chronicles*, p. 723; *et al., contra* Williamson, *1 and 2
Chronicles*, p. 269.

unsettled and may have remained so until the end of Baasha's reign in 885 BCE (1 Kgs 16.15). Therefore, it is not surprising that many people of the north would be attracted to Asa because of his successes, both in the direct border conflicts with Israel and in his victory over Zerah.

Incidentally, the problem of the allusions to the thirty-fifth and thirty-sixth years of Asa in the verses cited above is best explained by Thiele's proposal that these are years of the Judean kingdom from the split in 930 BCE and that they equal the actual fifteenth and sixteenth years of Asa respectively.[38] Chr may have somehow connected the thirty-fifth and thirty-sixth years to Asa because of the later (and appropriate) reference to Asa's illness in his thirty-ninth year (2 Chron. 16.12).

The allusion to Simeon (2 Chron. 15.9) refers not to the tribe that settled in southern Judah, but to the town by that name on the northwestern side of the Jezreel Valley.[39] Its appearance in this passage concerning the reign of Asa (2 Chron. 15.9) might be considered anachronistic. But it is more likely that in Asa's day Megiddo was still not rehabilitated after its conquest by Shishak. In Josiah's day, Simeon appears again in a similar context (2 Chron. 34.6), when Megiddo was an Assyrian administrative center.

Hezekiah. Likewise, in the reign of Hezekiah, that king is credited with making an appeal to residents of the north. This took place in his first year of reign, 715 BCE.[40] It could hardly have taken place while there was a king in Samaria, and in fact, Chr's account confirms the 715 date for Hezekiah's succession to the throne.[41] That only a limited number of northerners heeded the invitation of Hezekiah is another confirmatory feature: had Chr wanted to fabricate an event rivaling that of Josiah, he would surely have contrived to make the response more positive.[42] Instead, there is a certain disappointment in the report (2 Chron. 30.10-11):

---

38. Thiele, *Mysterious Numbers*, p. 84; Williamson, *1 and 2 Chronicles*, p. 256; S.J. De Vries, 'Chronology of the OT', *IDB* (1962), I, p. 587, 590-91.

39. A.F. Rainey, 'Toponymic Problems (cont.), The Way of the Sea, Shim'on— Shimron Once Again', *Tel Aviv* 8 (1981), pp. 149-50; cf. Rainey, 'Toponymic Studies (cont.), Shim'on—Shimron', *Tel Aviv* 3 (1976), pp. 57-69, pl. 1.

40. Thiele, *Mysterious Numbers*, pp. 174-76.

41. Thiele, *Mysterious Numbers*, pp. 174-76.

42. J. Rosenbaum, 'Hezekiah's Reform and the Deuteronomistic Tradition', *HTR* 72 (1979), pp. 35-36, 41-42.

ויהיו הרצים עברים מעיר | לעיר בארץ־אפרים ומנשה ועד־
זבלון ויהיו משחיקים עליהם ומלעגים בם: אך־אנשים מאשר
ומנשה ומזבלון נכנעו ויבאו לירושלם

And the messengers were passing from town to town in the land of
Ephraim and Manasseh and as far as Zebulun, and they were laughing
at them and mocking them; however, (some) men from Asher and
Manasseh and from Zebulun humbled themselves and came to Jerusalem.

A later verse (2 Chron. 30.18, מאפרים ומנשה יששכר וזבלון) substitutes
Issachar for Asher, and this in fact is more reasonable, since the territory of Asher had long been under direct Phoenician control, while
Issachar would have become part of an Assyrian province after Tiglath-
pileser III's campaign in 733-732. There is no reason to assume that
residents of Assyrian provinces would have been prevented by Assyrian
governors from making the pilgrimage to Jerusalem. Hezekiah was
making a religious, not a political, appeal. Although the narrative of
2 Chronicles 30 bears all the marks of Chr's own composition, there are
various details (especially the geographical references) that point to a
genuine historical source for the factual background.[43]

Josiah. Finally, there is the description of Josiah's appeal to the
northern Israelites still in the land. Here the geographical description in
Chronicles is more specific, and once again 'Simeon' refers not to the
tribe[44] but to the town located at Tell es-Seim-nîyeh (today Tel
Shimron) on the northwest side of the Jezreel Valley. Its appearance in
a Josianic context is explicable in as much as Megiddo had long since
become an Assyrian base and could not represent the residents in the
Jezreel Valley. The passage in question is 2 Chron. 34.5b-6a.

ויטהר את־יהודה ואת־ירושלם ובערי מנשה ואפרים ושמעון
ועד־נפתלי...

And he purified Judah and Jerusalem and in the towns of Manasseh and
Ephraim and Simeon, and as far as Naphtali ....

43. Japhet, *I & II Chronicles*, pp. 934-36; Williamson, *1 and 2 Chronicles*,
pp. 361-64.
44. Rainey, 'Toponymic Studies' (1976, 1981), *contra* Curtis and Madsen,
Books of Chronicles, p. 504.

Building Programs and Economic Projects

Another category of entries that are hardly the invention of Chr consists of statements about royal building projects. These have a ring of authenticity and there is no reason to assume that Chr invented them as indications of prosperity for the kings whom he favored.

Rehoboam. The list of towns reputedly fortified by Rehoboam has long been a controversial text. As it stands, it can hardly be a complete description of the defensive network of Judah, but the groups of towns represented in the list (not very systematically) do make some kind of geographical sense (2 Chron. 11.5-12).[45]

וישב רחבעם בירושלם ויבן ערים למצור ביהודה:

> So Rehoboam dwelt in Jerusalem and he built towns for time of seige in Judah. (v. 5)

Some of the towns in the list (Azekah and Beth-zur), whose sites have been identified, have been investigated archaeologically, and remains that could be assigned to Rehoboam's construction were not in evidence. Therefore, some scholars have dated the list to the reign of Josiah[46] or to that of Hezekiah.[47] The excavator of Lachish does not seem to have a clear opinion about what might be assigned to Rehoboam's reign.[48] As for the latter site, one might suggest that Lachish Stratum IV actually originated in Rehoboam's reign and that it continued in use for a very long time. The triple gate there was of the type known from tenth century Hazor and could very well have been constructed in the last quarter of the tenth-century at Lachish.

---

45. Rainey *apud* Aharoni and Avi-Yonah, *Macmillan Bible Atlas*, p. 90, map 118. Cf. also J.M. Miller, 'Rehoboam's Cities of Defence and the Levitical City List', in L.G. Perdue, L.E. Toombs, and G.L. Johnson (eds.), *Archaeology and Biblical Interpretation: Essays in Memory of D. Glenn Rose* (Atlanta: John Knox, 1987), pp. 273-86, who dates the list in Rehoboam's reign and views it as the king's attempt to strengthen his hold on a potentially rebellious populace.

46. A. Alt, 'Festungen und Levitenorte im Lande Juda', in *Kleine Schriften zur Geschichte des Volkes Israel* (Munich: Beck, 1953-59), II, pp. 306-15; V. Fritz, 'The "List of Rehoboam's Fortresses" in 2 Chr. 11:5-12 — A Document from the Time of Josiah', in B. Mazar (ed.), *Y. Aharoni Memorial Volume* (ErIsr, 15; Jerusalem: Israel Exploration Society, 1981), pp.46*-53*.

47. N. Na'aman, 'Hezekiah's Fortified Cities and the LMLK Stamps', *BASOR* 261 (1986), pp. 5-21.

48. D. Ussishkin, 'Lachish', *NEAEHL* (1992), III, p. 858b. (Hebrew)

Unless Chr has inserted a later list in this place, it may be that Rehoboam began his constructions but did not complete them. Whatever he did do, however, is clearly placed before the campaign by Shishak, and in fact the towns of Rehoboam's list (except Aijalon) do not appear in Shishak's roster of conquered towns.

Asa. During the first decade of his reign, Asa enjoyed a period of stability (ca. 909–899 BCE), since his father had successfully pushed the border of Judah northward into Jeroboam's territory (2 Chron. 13.2-20).[49] The time was invested in strengthening the kingdom's fortifications (2 Chron. 14.5-7 [EVV, vv. 6-8]).

ויבן ערי מצורה ביהודה כי־שקטה הארץ ואין־עמו מלחמה
בשנים האלה כי־הניח יהוה לו ויאמר ליהודה נבנה את־
הערים האלה ונסב חמה ומגדלים דלתים ובריחים עודנו הארץ
לפנינו כי דרשנו את־יהוה אלהינו דרשנו וינח לנו מסביב ויבנו
ויצליחו: ויהי לאסא חיל נשא צנה ורמח מיהודה שלש מאות
אלף ומבנימן נשאי מגן ודרכי קשת מאתים ושמונים אלף כל־
אלה גבורי חיל:

He built siege towns in Judah because the land was quiet, and there was no war against him during these years because the Lord gave him a respite. And he said to Judah, 'Let us build these towns and let us surround them with walls and towers, gates and bars; the land is still before us, because we have sought the Lord our God; we have sought him and He has given us respite round about.' So they built and prospered. And Asa had an army of three hundred thousand men armed with bucklers and spears from Judah, and two hundred and eighty thousand men from Benjamin, who carried shields and drew bows; all these were mighty men of valor.

Jehoshaphat. The building projects of Jehoshaphat are closely associated with the appointment of his sons as local commanders in towns throughout the kingdom. This later detail is especially relevant for the subsequent history, since Jehoram, the successor, executed all his brothers who had been posted in those fortified centers. Therefore, one has no reason to doubt that Chr is furnishing information from an authentic source, and that source would most logically be 'the Chronicles of Jehu son of Hanani, which are recorded in the Book of the Kings of Israel' (2 Chron. 20.34). The three key passages are noted below.

49. Rainey *apud* Aharoni and Avi-Yonah, *Macmillan Bible Atlas*, pp. 92-93, map 121.

2 Chron. 17.2

ויתן־חיל בכל־ערי יהודה הבצרות ויתן נציבים בארץ יהודה
ובערי אפרים אשר לכד אסא אביו:

He posted forces in all the fortified towns of Judah, and he appointed
commissioners in the land of Judah and in the towns of Ephraim that his
father Asa had occupied.

2 Chron. 17.12-13

ויהי יהושפט הלך וגדל עד־למעלה ויבן ביהודה בירניות
וערי מסכנות: ומלאכה רבה היה לו בערי יהודה ואנשי
מלחמה גבורי היל בירושלם:

And Jehoshaphat grew steadily greater and he built in Judah fortresses
and store cities, and he had great stores in the towns of Judah, and he
had soldiers, men of valor, in Jerusalem.

The term בירניות, a loanword from Akkadian, is unique to Chr (here
and 2 Chron. 27.4). It was hardly an original term in the 'Chronicles of
the Kings of Judah'. Still, there is no reason to doubt that this context
reflects a historical reality,[50] even if its present form shows clear indications of Chr's style.

The continuation of the narrative has as an essential link the placing
of Jehoshaphat's sons in towns throughout the kingdom (2 Chron. 21.2-
3a).

ולד־אחים בני יהושפט עזריה ויחיאל וזכריהו ועזריהו ומיכאל
ושפטיהו כל־אלה בני יהושפט מלך־ישראל: ויתן להם אביהם
מתנות רבות לכסף ולזהב ולמגדנות עם־ערי מצרות ביהודה

He (Jehoram) had brothers, the sons of Jehoshaphat: Azariah, and Jehiel,
and Zechariah, and Azarjahu, and Michael, and Shephatiah, all these
were sons of Jehoshaphat king of Judah. Their father gave them great
gifts, of silver and of gold and of valuable possessions, together with
fortified towns in Judah.

Azariah/Uzziah. The building projects and royal industries of
Azariah/Uzziah (2 Chron. 26.9-10) were the topic of a previous
discussion.[51] The passage has to be properly divided in accordance with
the respective territories to be understood:

50. Japhet, *I & II Chronicles*, pp. 707-709.
51. A.F. Rainey, 'Wine from the Royal Vineyards', *BASOR* 245 (1982), pp. 57-
62.

ויבן עזיהו מגדלים בירושלם על־שער הפנה ועל־שער הגיא
ועל־המקצוע ויחזקם:

And Uzziah built towers in Jerusalem at the corner gate and at the valley
gate and at the Angle, and he strengthened them.

ויבן מגדלים במדבר ויחצב ברות רבים כי מקנה־רב היה לו

And he built towers in the wilderness (of Judah) and he hewed out many
cisterns because he had much cattle,

ובשפלה ובמישור אכרים וכרמים בהרים ובכרמל

and cultivators in the Shephelah and on the Coastal Plain, and
husbandmen in the mountains and in Carmel (S. Judah).

This description according to region is similar to—but independent
of—the usual Deuteronomistic cross section of Judah (e.g., Josh. 12.8).
The details are quite specific with the respective branches of agriculture
matched to their correct regions. Chr would hardly have invented this
text, and there is no reason to doubt that these activities would be
included among 'the rest of the acts of Azariah and all that he did'
(2 Kgs 15.6), which were written in the 'Book of the Chronicles of the
Kings of Judah' in the chapter that Isaiah son of Amoz contributed
(2 Chron. 26.22). Incidentally, these royal enterprises are not associated
with the Negeb.

Jotham. Even the Deuteronomist credits Jotham with building the
upper gate of the temple complex (2 Kgs 15.35), but in keeping with
his usual practice, he does not elaborate on building projects. Chr is
obviously adding material from the original context where the upper
gate is mentioned. The details that he adds seem authentic enough,
except for his use of בירניות (2 Chron. 27.3-4).

הוא בנה את־שער בית־יהוה העליון ובחומת האפל בנה לרב:
וערים בנה בהר־יהודה ובחרשים בנה בירניות ומגדלים:

It was he who built the upper gate of the House of the Lord, and as for
the wall of the Ophel, he built it extensively, and as for towns, he built
forts and towers in the hill country of Judah and in the forests.

Hezekiah. It is here in the reign of Hezekiah that Chr has been credited
with the use of authentic sources for describing the defensive building
operations conducted in preparation for the war against Assyria,

especially the work on the Siloam tunnel.[52] In spite of the negative arguments of North,[53] there is no reason to assume that Chr was basing his entire description on what he already had in 2 Kings.[54] A key passage is 2 Chron. 32.2-6a.

וירא יחזקיהו כי־בא סנחריב ופניו למלחמה על־ירושלם:
ויועץ עם־שריו וגבריו לסתום את־מימי העינות אשר מחוץ
לעיר ויעזרוהו: ויקבצו עם־רב ויסתמו את־כל־המעינות ואת־
הנחל השוטף בתוך־הארץ לאמר למה יבואו מלכי אשור ומצאו
מים רבים: ויתחזק ויבן את־כל־החומה הפרוצה ויעל על־
המגדלות ולחוצה החומה אחרת ויחזק את־המלוא עיר דויד
ויעש שלח לרב מגנים: ויתן שרי מלחמות על־העם

And Hezekiah saw that Sennacherib was coming for the purpose of making war on Jerusalem; so he took counsel with his officers and his warriors to stop the water of the springs that were outside the city, and they helped him. So a great many people were assembled and they stopped all the springs and the brook that flowed through the land, saying, 'Why should the kings of Assyria come and find plenty of water?' And he gained strength and built all the broken down segments of the wall, and he heightened the towers; and he strengthened the Millo, the city of David. And he produced swords and shields in abundance. And he appointed commanders over the people.

Additional information is found in 2 Chron. 32.30a.

והוא יחזקיהו סתם את־מוצא מימי גיחון העליון ויישרם
למטה־מערבה לעיר דויד

And he, Hezekiah, closed the upper outlet of the waters of the Gihon and directed them down westward to the city of David.

There is no reason to doubt that these details were taken by Chr from his source,[55] in this case, the chapter written by Isaiah, son of Amoz. As

---

52. E.g., W.F. Albright, 'The Judicial Reform of Jehoshaphat', in *Alexander Marx Jubilee Volume* (New York: Jewish Theological Seminary of America, 1950), p. 67.

53. R. North, 'Does Archaeology Prove Chronicles' Sources?', in H.N. Bream, R.D. Heim, and C.A. Moore (eds.), *A Light Unto My Path: Old Testament Studies in Honor of Jacob M. Myers* (GTS, 4; Philadelphia: Temple University Press, 1974), pp. 375-79.

54. B.S. Childs, *Isaiah and the Assyrian Crisis* (SBT, 2nd series, 3; London: SCM, 1967), pp. 104-11.

55. Williamson, *1 and 2 Chronicles*, pp. 379-80; Japhet, *I & II Chronicles*, p. 976.

for the following summary passage (2 Chron. 32.27-29), it could also
be from the same source but is hardly suitable as a description of
Hezekiah's position after Sennacherib's campaign.

ויהי ליחזקיהו עשר וכבוד הרבה מאד ואצרות עשה־לו
לכסף ולזהב ולאבן יקרה ולבשמים ולמגנים ולכל כלי חמדה:
ומסכנות לתבואת דגן ותירוש ויצהר וארות לכל־בהמה
ובהמה ועדרים לאורות: וערים עשה לו ומקנה־צאן ובקר
לרב כי נתן־לו אלהים רכוש רב מאד:

And Hezekiah had very great riches and honor; and he made for himself
treasuries for silver, for gold, for precious stones, for spices, for shields,
and for all kinds of precious vessels; and storehouses for the produce of
grain, wine, and oil; and stables for all kinds of cattle, and sheepfolds;
and he furnished cities for himself and flocks and herds in abundance,
because God gave him very great possessions.

One must assume that if this passage were really based on Chr's source,
then it applied to Hezekiah's position prior to the war with Assyria,
when he was truly the political leader of the revolt during the years
following the death of Sargon II. Thus 2 Chron. 32.22b-23 would apply
to that same phase:

וינהלם מסביב: ורבים מביאים מנחה ליהוה לירושלם
ומגדנות ליחזקיהו מלך יהודה וינשא לעיני כל־הגוים מאחרי־כן:

And he led them and many were bringing tribute to the Lord, to
Jerusalem, and precious things to Hezekiah king of Judah, and he became
exalted in the eyes of all the nations after that.

It was also during that time, when Hezekiah had achieved a position of
prominence among his allies and had amassed considerable wealth and
military supplies, that the delegation arrived from Babylon and was
shown all of Hezekiah's riches (2 Kgs 20.12-13):

בעת ההיא שלח מרדך (Isa. 39.1!) בלאבן בן־בלאדן מלך־
בבל ספרים ומנחה אל־חזקיהו כי שמע כי חלה חזקיהו:
וישמח (Isa. 39.2!) עליהם חזקיהו ויראם את־כל־בית נכתה
את־הכסף ואת־הזהב ואת־הבשמים ואת שמן הטוב ואת בית
כליו ואת כל־אשר נמצא באוצרתיו לא־היה דבר אשר לא־
הראם חזקיהו בביתו ובכל־ממשלתו:

And at that time, Merodach-baladan, son of Baladan, king of Babylon,
sent letters and a gift to Hezekiah because he had heard that Hezekiah
had been sick. And Hezekiah rejoiced over them and he showed them all
of his treasure house, the silver and the gold and the spices and the fine

oil and his armory and all that was in his treasuries; there was nothing in
his house or in all his realm that he did not show them.

This visit took place after Hezekiah's illness, which must have been in
701 BCE,[56] on the eve of the war with Sennacherib.

Manasseh. Elsewhere,[57] it has been argued that Manasseh's building
projects were inaugurated after 648 BCE, when he was allowed to return
from Babylon with the support of Asshurbanipal (2 Chron. 33.14-16):

ואחרי־כן בנה חומה חיצונה לעיר־דויד מערבה לגיחון
בנחל ולבוא בשער הדגים וסבב לעפל ויגביהה מאד וישם
שרי־חיל בכל־הערים הבצרות ביהודה:
ויסר את־אלהי הנכר ואת־הסמל מבית יהוה וכל־המזבחות
אשר בנה בהר בית־יהוה ובירושלם וישלך חוצה לעיר:
ויכן [ויבן] את־מזבח יהוה ויזבח עליו זבחי שלמים ותודה
ויאמר ליהודה לעבוד את־יהוה אלהי ישראל:

Afterwards, he built an outer wall for the city of David west of Gihon, in
the valley, and for the entrance into the Fish Gate, and carried it round
Ophel, and raised it to a very great height; he also put commanders of
the army in all the fortified cities in Judah. And he took away the foreign
gods and the idol from the house of the Lord, and all the altars that he
had built on the mountain of the house of the Lord and in Jerusalem, and
he threw them outside the city. He also restored the altar of the Lord and
offered upon it sacrifices of peace offerings and of thanksgiving; and he
commanded Judah to serve the Lord.

It seems obvious that the Deuteronomist deliberately suppressed this
information, because he wished to blame Manasseh for the final downfall of Judah (cf. 2 Kgs 24.3-4). Chr, on the other hand, cites it from his
source, albeit with some theological interpretation, in order to clear the
air with regard to Manasseh's later behavior.[58]

Josiah. In the description of the temple repairs under Josiah, there
are some details that seem directly related to everyday affairs of

---

56. Thiele, *Mysterious Numbers*, p. 176.
57. A.F. Rainey, 'Manasseh, King of Judah, in the Whirlpool of the Seventh
Century B.C.E.', in A.F. Rainey (ed.), *kinattū ša dārāti Raphael Kutscher Memorial
Volume* (Tel Aviv Occasional Publications, 1; Tel Aviv: Tel Aviv University,
Institute of Archaeology, 1993), pp. 147-64.
58. Japhet, *I & II Chronicles*, pp. 1000-1004.

construction and of administration, and these may very well have been
part of the original source (2 Chron. 34.11-13):

ויתנו לחרשים ולבנים לקנות אבני מחצב ועצים למחברות
ולקרות את־הבתים אשר השחיתו מלכי יהודה: והאנשים
עשים באמונה במלאכה ועליהם ׀ מפקדים יחת ועבדיהו הלוים
מן־בני מררי וזכריה ומשלם מן־בני הקהתים לנצח ...
ועל הסבלים ומנצחים לכל עשה מלאכה לעבודה ועבודה
ומהלוים סופרים ושטרים ושוערים:

And they gave (it) to the craftsmen and to the builders to purchase
quarried stone and timber for binders and beams for the buildings that
the kings of Judah had let go to ruin. And the men did the work faithfully. Over them were set Jahath and Obadiah the Levites, of the sons of
Merari, and Zechariah and Meshullam, of the sons of the Kohathites, to
have oversight ...and over the burden bearers and they were directing all
who work in every kind of service; and some of the Levites were scribes
and officials and gatekeepers.

Military and Geopolitical Affairs

Chr gives numerous examples of military campaigns and geopolitical
events that not only serve his theological purposes but also give a
picture of the role of Judah in its geographical region. It seems hardly
credible that these affairs could be his own invention. To be sure, he
has added his own interpretation, including numerical totals for troops
involved, and so on, which can hardly be accepted as historical. Chr
was, after all, a child of his day, and the use of such exaggerated figures
was commonplace.

Rehoboam. Details about Shishak's campaign, especially the chronological framework (after the list of fortified towns) and the names of the
peoples who took part in the campaign,[59] probably derive from the
original source (2 Chron. 12.2-3):

ויהי בשנה החמישית למלך רחבעם עלה שושק מלך־מצרים
על־ירושלם כי מעלו ביהוה: באלף ומאתים רכב ובששים
אלף פרשים ואין מספר לעם אשר־באו עמו ממצרים לובים
סכיים וכושים:

And it happened in the fifth year of Rehoboam that Shishak king of
Egypt came up against Jerusalem, because they had been unfaithful to

---

59. K.A. Kitchen, *The Third Intermediate Period in Egypt (1100-650 B.C.)*
(Warminster: Aris & Phillips, 1973), pp. 295-96.

the Lord, with a thousand two hundred chariots and sixty thousand horsemen; and the people who came with him from Egypt were without number: Libyans, Sukkim, and Nubians.

Abijah/Abijam. Abijah's successful thrust into the southern districts of Jeroboam's territory and the resultant acquisition of several towns can hardly be an invention of Chr. The Deuteronomist gives Abijah a most cursory treatment, dismissing him as one who 'walked in all the sins of his father before him' (1 Kgs 15.3). This unfair judgment is corrected by Chr, and the story of the battle in the southern hills of Ephraim is his principal proof text; the geographical details in vv. 4 and 19 are such that they could hardly be the result of free invention (2 Chron. 13.3-20).

(v. 4) ויקם אביה מעל להר צמרים אשר בהר אפרים...

(v. 19) וירדף אביה אחרי ירבעם וילכד ממנו ערים את־בית־אל

ואת־בנותיה ואת־ישנה ואת־בנותיה ואת־עפרון [עפרין] ובנתיה:

(v. 4) And Abijah stood up on Mount Zemeraim, which is in the hill country of Ephraim ...(v. 19) And Abijah pursued after Jeroboam and captured towns from him, Bethel and its daughter settlements, and Jeshanah and its daughter settlements, and Ephraim and its daughter settlements.

Asa. The attraction of Israelites from the north to Jerusalem during the reign of Asa (cf. above) was directly related to the celebrations in the aftermath of the victory over Zerah the Cushite (2 Chron. 14.8-14 [EVV, vv. 9-15]).

ויצא אליהם זרח הכושי בחיל אלף אלפים מרכבות שלש

מאות ויבא עד־מרשה: ויצא אסא לפניו ויערכו מלחמה

בגיא צפתה (צפנה = LXX κατὰ βορρᾶν) למרשה:...

(v. 11) ויגף יהוה את־הכושים לפני אסא ולפני יהודה וינסו הכושים:

וירדפם אסא והעם אשר־עמו עד־לגרר ויפל מכושים לאין

להם מחיה כי־נשברו לפני־יהוה ולפני מחנהו וישאו שלל הרבה

מאד ויכו את כל־הערים סביבות גרר כי־היה פחד־יהוה

עליהם ויבזו את־כל־הערים כי־בזה רבה היתה בהם וגם־

אהלי מקנה הכו וישבו צאן לרב וגמלים וישבו ירושלם

And Zerah the Cushite came out against them with an army of a million men and three hundred chariots, and came as far as Mareshah; and Asa went out to meet him and they drew up their battle lines in the valley north (LXX) of Mareshah ...(v. 12) So the Lord smote the Cushites before Asa and before Judah and the Cushites fled. Then Asa and the people who were with him pursued them as far as Gerar, and the Cushites fell and none remained alive, because they were broken before the Lord and before his army, and they carried away very much spoil. Then they smote all the towns around Gerar because the fear of the Lord was upon them; so they plundered all the towns because they contained much spoil. They also smote the tents of the pastoralists and captured small cattle in abundance and camels. Then they returned to Jerusalem.

Disregarding the exaggerated numbers ('a thousand thousands'), one can still see in the geographical names a reasonable description of an attempted invasion of Judah from the southwest. The identification of Zerah (a Semitic name) is fraught with controversy. Because of the reference to Libyans in 2 Chron. 16.8 in the speech of Hanani, it has been assumed that he is Osorkon IV—or more likely his general.[60] If it can be suggested, on the other hand, that these Cushites are the people known in other biblical contexts as coming from the Hejaz (cf. Hab. 3.7; Gen. 10.7; 1 Chron. 1.8-9; 2 Chron. 21.16), then the attack on Judah can be viewed within the context of the ongoing conflict between Judah and her neighbors on the east and on the west for control of the southern caravan routes (note 2 Chron. 21.16, 'the Arabians who are beside the Cushites'). These Cushites were somehow in league with pastoral elements in the western Negeb (Gerar and its surroundings). If there were really Libyans with the Semitic leader Zerah, they were probably taking part as allies of the peoples on the seacoast and in the Gerar district. The connection of Ham and the Hamites with both the Cushites (Gen. 10.6-7; 1 Chron. 1.8-9) and the Gerar area (1 Chron. 4.39-40, LXX) may provide further background for Asa's campaign in the western Negeb (Gerar area). Therefore, in spite of elaboration by Chr, the passage in question most likely preserves the record of a real conflict as recorded in the 'Chronicles of the Kings of Judah'.

Jehoshaphat. Opinions have varied concerning the narrative about an attempted invasion of Judah from the east (2 Chron. 20.1-30). Noth argued that the geographical details must derive from some local tradition; he believed that the background was some otherwise unknown invasion by the Nabateans.[61] Rudolph agreed that there was some source behind the narrative,[62] and Williamson concurs that that account

---

60. Cf. Kitchen, *Third Intermediate*, p. 309 and n. 372.

61. M. Noth, 'Eine palästinische Lokalüberlieferung in 2. Chr. 20', *ZDPV* 67 (1943), pp. 45-71.

62. *Chronikbücher*, pp. 260-61.

may have already been part of Chr's historical source.[63] This is not to deny that Chr has reworked the material to suit his own theological goals.[64]

Chr's chronological sequence is of major importance here: he places the invasion after Jehoshaphat's return from the battle at Ramoth-gilead. His statement ויהי אחריכן, 'And it came to pass after this ...', is more than a literary convention here.[65] Furthermore, the details of the narrative fit just this particular time. The invasion took place in 853 BCE, just after the death of Ahab.[66] It is also significant that Chr refers to the joint nautical venture with Ahaziah in the subsequent verses (2 Chron. 20.35-37). Again the expression אחריכן 'after this' is intentional: it is meant to confirm the sequence of events. The reign of Ahaziah lasted for two official years (non-accession system) but only one calendar year, viz. 853/852 BCE. By placing the attempted Moabite-Ammonite invasion between the death of Ahab and the reign of Ahaziah, Chr enables us to date that campaign to 853/852 BCE.[67]

2 Chron. 20.1-30

ויהי אחריכן באו בני־מואב ובני עמון ועמהם מהעמונים

(*מהמעונים = LXX ἐκ τῶν Μιναίων) על־יהושפט למלחמה:

ויבאו ויגידו ליהושפט לאמר בא עליך המון רב מעבר לים

מארם והנם בחצצון תמר היא עין גדי:...(v. 10) ועתה הנה

בני־עמון ומואב והר־שעיר אשר לא־נתתה לישראל לבוא בהם

בבאם מארץ מצרים כי סרו מעליהם ולא השמידם...

(v. 22) ובעת החלו ברנה ותהלה נתן יהוה מארבים על־בני עמון

מואב והר־שעיר הבאים ליהודה וינגפו:

And it happened after this that the Moabites and the Ammonites and with them some of the Meunites (LXX) came against Jehoshaphat for battle. And they came and reported to Jehoshaphat, saying: 'A great host is coming against you from beyond the (Dead) Sea, at the instigation of Aram; and behold they are at Hazazon-tamar (that is En-gedi)...' (v. 10) 'And now behold, the men of Ammon and Moab and Mt Seir, whom you would not let Israel invade when they came from the land of Egypt, whom they avoided and whom they did not destroy...' (v. 22) And

---

63. Cf. *1 and 2 Chronicles*, pp. 292-93, and other references cited there.

64. Williamson, *1 and 2 Chronicles*, pp. 292-93; Japhet, *I & II Chronicles*, pp. 785-803.

65. *Contra* Japhet, *I & II Chronicles*, p. 785.

66. Thiele, *Mysterious Numbers*, pp. 94-96.

67. Rainey, 'Moabite Invasion'.

when they began to sing and praise, the Lord set ambushers against the
sons of Ammon, Moab, and Mt Seir who had come against Judah, and
they smote one another.

Three points determine the correct interpretation of this passage. First,
the LXX reading ἐκ τῶν Μιναίων is to be preferred and taken to represent an original Hebrew מהמעונים* 'some of the Meunites'.[68] Second,
מארם is not to be amended to מאדם* 'from Edom'.[69] The LXX has ἀπὸ
Συρίας 'from Syria', and the implication is that the Arameans had
incited the Ammonites and Moabites to launch this invasion. This can
be seen as an offensive move designed to avenge Jehoshaphat's
participation in the war against Aram alongside Ahab. Finally, the Mt
Seir in vv. 10 and 22 is not to be sought to the east but rather to the
west of the Arabah Valley.[70] The people of Mt Seir in this passage
are those Meunites from 2 Chron. 20.1 (LXX). They were the pastoral
people living in southern Transjordan, who controlled the caravan
routes across the Sinai desert. Subsequently, they paid tribute to Uzziah
(2 Chron. 26.7, 8; cf. also 1 Chron. 4.41) and still later, to Tiglath-
pileser III.[71] It is not surprising that their misfortune in this attempted
invasion was followed by Jehoshaphat's enterprise on the Gulf of Elath.
He had the upper hand in the southern expanses of his kingdom, and
the Meunites were undoubtedly included among the 'Arabians' who
brought him tribute (2 Chron. 17.11).

The Deuteronomist skipped over this event as well as many other interesting details of the life of Jehoshaphat. Nevertheless, he does allude
to the fact that Jehoshaphat engaged in military activity (1 Kgs 22.46
[EVV, v. 45]). Chr included the narrative of ch. 20, because it served to

68. RSV; Williamson, *1 and 2 Chronicles*, pp. 293-94.

69. Cf. Y. Aharoni, *The Land of the Bible: A Historical Geography* (trans.
and ed. A.F. Rainey; Philadelphia: Westminster, 2nd edn, 1979), pp. 332-33;
Williamson, *1 and 2 Chronicles*, p. 294; *contra* Japhet, *I & II Chronicles*, p. 781.

70. Cf. 1 Chron. 4.42; F.-M. Abel, *Géographie de la Palestine* (Etudes
bibliques; Paris: Gabalda, 1933–38), I, pp. 389-91; J.R. Bartlett, 'The Land of Seir
and the Brotherhood of Edom', *JTS* ns 20 (1969), pp. 1-20; G.I. Davies, 'The
Significance of Deuteronomy 1.2 for the Location of Mount Horeb', *PEQ* 111
(1979), pp. 97-101; Williamson, *1 and 2 Chronicles*, pp. 294-95.

71. ND 400:22; D.J. Wiseman, 'Two Historical Inscriptions from Nimrud', *Iraq*
13 (1951), p. 23, pl. XI; the gentilic is [KUR]Mu-'u-na-a-a = *Mu'ûnāya <
*Ma'ûnāya; with R. Borger and H. Tadmor, 'Zwei Beiträge zur alttestamentlichen
Wissenschaft aufgrund der Inschriften Tiglatpilesers III', *ZAW* 94 (1982), pp. 250-
51; *contra* E.A. Knauf, 'Mu'näer und Mëuniter', *WO* 16 (1985), pp. 114-22.

balance the picture presented in 2 Kings 3 (a narrative from the 'Chronicles of the Kings of Israel'). That latter campaign took place after the death of Ahaziah of Israel, when Joram of Israel took over his brother's throne (852 BCE).[72] The Israelite motivation was revenge for Mesha's revolt and his conquest of towns in the Moabite tableland north of the Arnon (as depicted in the Mesha Inscription). Jehoshaphat's motivation for joining Israel was revenge for the attempted invasion via En-gedi.

Jehoram, King of Judah. Chr's record of this king's reign gives certain crucial details that help to make better sense of the parallel record in 2 Kings. These military and geopolitical events are consistent with the normal course of developments throughout Judean history (the *longue durée*). The defection of Edom is virtually identical in the two accounts (2 Kgs 8.20-22a//2 Chron. 21.8-10a), but the defection of Libnah, a Judean priestly city in the Shephelah (Josh. 15.42; 1 Chron. 6.42 [EVV, v. 57]) is explained by Chr in some detail.

2 Chron. 21.10-11

ויפשע אדום מתחת יד־יהודה עד היום הזה אז תפשע
לבנה בעת ההיא מתחת ידו כי עזב את־יהוה אלהי אבתיו:
גם־הוא עשה־במות בהרי יהודה ויזן את־ישבי ירושלם
וידח את־יהודה:

And Edom defected from Judean control up to this present time; then Libnah defected at that time from his (Jehoram's) control, because he had abandoned the Lord, the God of his fathers, and he also built cult places in the hill country of Judah and caused the inhabitants of Jerusalem to apostatize, and he led Judah astray.

The geographical details of Jehoram's religious activities, 'in the hill country of Judah' and among 'the residents of Jerusalem', show that Libnah's defection was the reaction of a Shephelah strong-point to the king's program. The 'hill country' of Judah would have benefited from the fact that the cultic centers (במות) would attract offerings and gifts to the local economy instead of them all flowing to the central shrine in Jerusalem. The priests of Libnah apparently had strong ties with the Jerusalem temple and resented the harm done to it by the opening of rival sanctuaries.

Jehoshaphat's control of the southern trade routes was rudely

---

72. Thiele, *Mysterious Numbers*, p. 99.

disrupted by joint action on the part of the Philistines and 'the Arabs who are near the Cushites' (2 Chron. 21.16-17).

ויער יהוה על־יהורם את רוח הפלשתים והערבים אשר
על־יד כשים: ויעלו ביהודה ויבקעוה וישבו את כל־הרכוש
הנמצא לבית־המלך וגם־בניו ונשיו ולא נשאר־לו בן כי אם־
יהואחז קטן בניו:

And the Lord stirred up against Jehoram the spirit of the Philistines and of the Arabs who are near the Cushites, and they attacked Judah, and they invaded it and captured all the property in the king's palace as well as his sons and wives so that none were left to him except Jehoahaz, his youngest son.

Joash. The same process of decentralizing the ritual establishment in Judah is also described by Chr with reference to the reign of Joash. During the tenure of Jehoiada, the monarchy favored the central institution in Jerusalem where Jehoiada was high priest. After the death of the king's trusted mentor, the local officials throughout the kingdom sought to revive the network of community cultic centers.

2 Chron. 24.17-18

ואחרי מות יהוידע באו שרי יהודה וישתחוו למלך אז
שמע המלך אליהם: ויעזבו את־בית יהוה אלהי אבותיהם
ויעבדו את־האשרים ואת־העצבים ויהי־קצף על־יהודה וירושלם
באשמתם זאת:

But after the death of Jehoiada, the princes of Judah came and did obeisance to the king; then the king hearkened to them, and they abandoned the house of the Lord, the God of their fathers, and they worshiped the Asherim and the idols. And there was wrath on Judah and Jerusalem because of this, their guilt.

Amaziah. The incident of the hiring of Israelite mercenaries by Amaziah for his Edomite campaign (2 Chron. 25.6) resulted in deep resentment on the part of the disappointed troops. On their return from the mustering point, they opted to despoil certain towns under Judean control as compensation for the spoil they had expected to acquire from Edom.

2 Chron. 25.13

ובני הגדוד אשר השיב אמציהו מלכת עמו למלחמה
ויפשטו בערי יהודה משמרון ועד־בית חורון ויכו מהם שלשת
אלפים ויבזו בזה רבה:

> But as for the members of the contingent that Amaziah sent back from going with him to the war, they attacked the towns of Judah (taken) from Samaria, in the vicinity of Beth-horon, and they smote three thousand (men) from them and greatly despoiled them.

The geography of this passage has caused considerable difficulty to commentators.[73] The expression 'from Samaria' must refer to the northern kingdom, not to the city of Samaria. The expression ועד־ must be another example of Heb. עד = Arabic *'and*.[74] The reference is thus to some settlements in the area of southern Mt Ephraim, along the border between Benjamin and Ephraim, which at that time were under Judean control (cf. 2 Chron. 17.2; 19.4). Therefore, it is not implausible that such a raid was conducted and became the cause for the subsequent conflict between Amaziah and Jehoash of Israel (2 Kgs 14.8-14//2 Chron. 25.17-24), which seems inexplicable in the Deuteronomist's account.

Uzziah. The same interest in Judah's geopolitical domination of the trade routes on the coastal plain and in the south, towards Elath, is reflected in Chr's description of military campaigning by Uzziah and his prestige as far as the Egyptian border. This passage is missing in Kings, but there is nothing about its geographic and ethnographic details to suggest that it is a pure invention by Chr[75] Two corrections from the LXX (supported by other versions as well) are certainly in order. The presence of the Meunites in v. 7 strongly suggests their inclusion in v. 8 (with LXX) instead of the Ammonites (cf. the similar situation in 2 Chron. 20.1 concerning Jehoshaphat's reign, discussed above).

2 Chron. 26.6-8

ויצא וילחם בפלשתים ויפרץ את־חומת גת ואת חומת יבנה
ואת חומת אשדוד ויבנה ערים באשדוד ובפלשתים ויעזרהו
האלהים על־פלשתים ועל־הערביים [הערבים] הישבים בגור
ועל (!) המעונם (LXX καιλ ἐπὶ τούς Μιναίους) ויתנו העמונים
(המעונים = LXX οἱ Μιναῖοι) מנחה לעזיהו וילך שמו עד־לבוא
מצרים כי החזיק עד־למעלה:

---

73. Cf. the discussion in Japhet, *I & II Chronicles*, p. 865.

74. H.L. Ginsberg, 'A Preposition of Interest to Historical Geographers', *BASOR* 122 (1951), pp. 12-14; *idem*, 'Postscript to Bulletin, No. 122, pp. 12-14', *BASOR* 124 (1951), pp. 29-30.

75. Japhet, *I & II Chronicles*, pp. 879-80.

And he went forth and he fought with the Philistines, and he broke down
the wall of Gath and the wall of Jabneh and the wall of Ashdod, and he
built towns in Ashdod and among the Philistines, and God helped him
against the Philistines and against the Arabians who dwell in Gur and
against (!) the Meunites (!). And the Meunites (!) paid tribute to Uzziah,
and his prestige was extended as far as Egypt because he had become
very powerful.

All of this provides the necessary background for understanding how
Uzziah could eventually establish a new fortified presence at Elath
(2 Kgs 14.22 // 2 Chron. 26.2).

Jotham. Judean dominance over the Ammonites is said to have been
achieved during the reign of Jotham. If that had been done during
Jotham's co-regency with his father (750-740 BCE),[76] then the passage
above might really pertain to Ammonite tribute to Uzziah. However, it
seems more plausible to assume that Jotham did not dare to exert
Judean influence in Transjordan until after Pekah had seized power in
Samaria (740 BCE),[77] the same year in which Uzziah died. The three
years during which the Ammonites paid tribute to Jotham were most
likely between 739 and 736 BCE, because after that, Ahaz took over the
reigns of power from Jotham (735 BCE).[78]

2 Chron. 27.5

והוא נלחם עם־מלך בני־עמון ויחזק עליהם ויתנו־לו
בני־עמון בשנה ההיא מאה ככר־כסף ועשרת אלפים כרים
חטים ושעורים עשרת אלפים זאת השיבו לו בני עמון ובשנה
השנית והשלשית

And he fought with the king of the Ammonites, and he overcame them
so that the Ammonites paid him in that year one hundred talents of silver
and ten thousand cors of wheat and ten thousand of barley; this the
Ammonites again furnished him in the second and the third years.

Ahaz. The early years of this king's reign (before his deposed father
died in 732 BCE)[79] were marked by the intense pressure exerted on
Judah by her neighbors because of Ahaz's refusal to join an anti-
Assyrian coalition. Chr gives a considerably expanded version of these

76. Thiele, *Mysterious Numbers*, p. 132.
77. Thiele, *Mysterious Numbers*, p. 129.
78. Thiele, *Mysterious Numbers*, pp. 133-34.
79. Thiele, *Mysterious Numbers*, pp. 133-34.

events, although the series of topics treated is practically the same.[80] Besides the fact that some of the parallels with Kings are formulated differently, the two most outstanding additions are the descriptions of the war with the enemies in the north (2 Chron. 28.5-15) and those in the south and southwest (2 Chron. 28.17-19). The account of the Israelite-Aramean attack on Judah and the prisoners they took is an apparent expansion of 2 Kgs 16.5b, ולא יכלו להלחם ויצרו על־אחז 'and they besieged Ahaz but they were unable to make war'. In fact, this statement in Kings looks more like an abbreviation of material that he wanted to suppress, perhaps the northern outcry against taking prisoners from Judah. The Deuteronomist was not interested in admitting Yahwistic tendencies among the prophets and other leaders of Israel. On the other hand, the reference in Chr's expanded version to the slaying of 'Maaseiyah, the royal prince, and Azrikam, the administrator of the palace, and Elkanah, the king's second in command' (2 Chron. 28.7) has the ring of authenticity. So in spite of the usual exaggerated numbers, a version of the story of the capture and return of Judean prisoners was probably in the original of the 'Chronicles of the Kings of Judah'.

2 Chron. 28.5-15

ויתנהו יהוה אלהיו ביד מלך ארם ויכו־בו וישבו ממנו שביה
גדולה ויביאו דרמשק וגם ביד־מלך ישראל נתן ויך־בו מכה
גדולה: ויהרג פקח בן־רמליהו ביהודה מאה ועשרים אלף
ביום אחד הכל בני־חיל בעזבם את־יהוה אלהי אבותם:
ויהרג זכרי | גבור אפרים את־מעשיהו בן־המלך ואת־עזריקם
נגיד הבית ואת־אלקנה משנה המלך וישבו בני־ישראל
מאחיהם מאתים אלף נשים בנים ובנות וגם־שלל רב בזזו מהם
ויביאו את־השלל לשמרון: ושם היה נביא ליהוה עדד שמו
ויצא לפני הצבא הבא לשמרון ויאמר להם הנה בחמת יהוה
אלהי־אבותיכם על־יהודה נתנם בידכם ותהרגו־בם בזעף עד
לשמים הגיע: ועתה בני־יהודה וירושלם אתם אמרים לכבש
לעבדים ולשפחות לכם הלא רק־אתם עמכם אשמות ליהוה
אלהיכם: ועתה שמעוני והשיבו השביה אשר שביתם
מאחיכם כי חרון אף־יהוה עליכם: ויקמו אנשים מראשי
בני־אפרים עזריהו בן־יהוחנן ברכיהו בן־משלמות ויחזקיהו
בן־שלם ועמשא בן־חדלי על־הבאים מן־הצבא: ויאמרו
להם לא־תביאו את־השביה הנה כי לאשמת יהוה עלינו אתם
אמרים להסיף על־חטאתינו ועל־אשמתינו כי־רבה אשמה
לנו וחרון אף על־ישראל: ויעזב החלוץ את־השביה
ואת־הבזה לפני השרים וכל־הקהל: ויקמו האנשים

---

80. Japhet, *I & II Chronicles*, pp. 895-97.

אשר־נקבו בשמות ויחזיקו בשביה וכל־מערמיהם הלבישו מן־
השלל וילבשום וינעלום ויאכלום וישקום ויסכום וינהלום
בחמרים לכל־כושל ויביאום ירחו עיר־התמרים אצל אחיהם
וישובו שמרון:

So the Lord his God gave him into the hand of the king of Aram so that
he smote him and took captive a large group and brought them to
Damascus. He was also given into the hand of the king of Israel so that
he smote him a great blow and Pekah, son of Remaliah, slew a hundred
and twenty thousand in Judah in one day, all of them men of valor,
because they had forsaken the Lord, the God of their fathers. And Zichri,
the mighty man of Ephraim, slew Maaseiyah, the royal prince, and
Azrikam, the administrator of the palace, and Elkanah, the king's second
in command. So the Israelites captured from their brothers two hundred
thousand women, boys, and girls and a great deal of spoil they also
plundered from them, and they brought the spoil to Samaria. There, there
was a prophet of the Lord, Oded by name, and he came forth to meet the
army that was approaching Samaria, and he said to them, 'Behold,
because of the wrath of the Lord, the God of your fathers, against Judah,
he has given them into your hand, and you have slain them in a rage that
has reached up to heaven. And now you intend to reduce to slavery the
Judahites and the Jerusalemites! Have you not sins of your own before
the Lord your God? So now, heed me and return the captivity that you
have captured from your brothers, because the wrath of the Lord is upon
you.' So there arose from among the heads of the Ephraimites, Azariah
son of Johanan, Berechiah son of Meshillemoth, and Jehizkiah son of
Shallum, and Amasa son of Hadlai against those who were coming from
the army. And they said to them, 'You shall not bring the captivity here,
because you intend to bring upon us guilt against the Lord in addition to
our sins and our guilt, since our guilt is great and there is wrath upon
Israel.' So the advance guard left the captives and the booty before the
officers and all the assembly. And the afore-mentioned men arose and
took charge of the captives, and from the spoil they clothed the naked
among them. They clothed them and shod them and fed them and gave
them to drink and anointed them and led them on asses for all the feeble
among them, and they brought them to Jericho, the City of Palms, to
their countrymen, and they returned to Samaria.

At this point Chr skipped over the reoccupation of Elath by the
Edomites with the active support of Rezin, king of Aram (2 Kgs 16.6).
The passage in Kings begins with בעת ההיא 'at that time', and Chr
copied these same words but then skipped down to the delegation sent
to Tiglath-pileser III (2 Chron. 28.16), which he gives in a much abbreviated form. But then he picks up the narrative with a passage that is
obviously from the original 'Chronicles of the Kings of Judah', namely,

the further aggression of the Edomites and the (most probably coordinated) invasion by the Philistines:

2 Chron. 28.17-19

ועוד אדומים באו ויכו ביהודה וישבו־שבי ופלשתים
פשטו בערי השפלה והנגב ליהודה וילכדו את־בית־שמש
ואת־אילון ואת־הגדרות ואת־שוכו ובנותיה ואת־תמנה ובנותיה
ואת־גמזו ואת־בנתיה וישבו שם

> And the Edomites had come and had smitten Judah and had captured
> captives, and the Philistines had attacked the towns of the Shephelah and
> the Negeb of Judah, and they had captured Beth-shemesh and Aijalon
> and Gederoth and Socho and its villages and Timnah and its villages and
> Gimzo and its villages, and they occupied them.

The Edomite attack was surely a consequence of the seizure of Elath.
The Aramean support of the Edomites was a continuation of the
Damascene policy of always supporting the Transjordanian states
against Judah (cf. the discussion of 2 Chronicles 20 in the reign of
Jehoshaphat above). On the other hand, the Philistine action was a
countermeasure to redress the geopolitical situation created by Uzziah's
former aggressions in the coastal plain and the western Negeb (cf.
2 Chron. 26.6-8 discussed above). The mention of Gimzo (only here in
the Hebrew Bible) adds authenticity to the report: why would Chr
invent a passage with hitherto unknown place names? Since Chr shows
a continued interest in the geopolitical and military status of Judah vis-
à-vis her neighbors to the southeast, south, and west, the omission of
Judah's loss of Elath is remarkable. In fact, it would not be implausible
to suggest that Chr had intended to use the passage—hence his beginning, בעת ההיא 'at that time' in 2 Chron 28.16. From there his eye may
have skipped over the Elath incident. In any event, Chr wanted to stress
the drastic change in Judah's fortunes. Judah had lost control of the
southern and western trade routes, and the Philistines had encroached in
the northern Shephelah, effectively blocking the Valley of Elah, the
Brook Sorek, and the Valley of Aijalon—Jerusalem's lifelines to the
outside world.[81]

Hezekiah. The military preparations of Hezekiah were discussed above.
Neither Kings nor Chronicles gives much detail about the actual course
of the war with Sennacherib. Oddly enough, 2 Kgs 18.8 does refer to

81. Aharoni and Avi-Yonah, *Macmillan Bible Atlas*, pp. 109-10, maps 144-45.

Hezekiah's attack on Philistine territory, especially in the direction of Gaza. This campaign may be reflected in the comments of 1 Chron. 4.39-41 about encroachments into the western Negeb, but since that passage is probably not derived directly from the 'Chronicles of the Kings of Judah', it will not be quoted here. Suffice it to say that neither Kings nor Chronicles admits that the Assyrian monarch drastically reduced the territory of Judah, while increasing its annual tribute payment.[82]

Josiah. The expansion by this king into the northern territories of the former state of Israel has been discussed above. Whatever military action—if any—was required to achieve Josiah's goals has not been recorded in either Kings or Chronicles. Concerning Josiah's attempt to prevent Necho's march northward to Carchemish, the expression על־מלך אשור (2 Kgs 23.29) does not mean '*against* the king of Assyria'.[83] This is a simple case of על replacing אל 'to, towards' (cf. 2 Sam. 15.4), which should be obvious from the very next phrase על־נהר־פרת, which can only mean '*to* the Euphrates River'. After all, Necho was not going to attack the river! There is no contradiction between the Chronicles and the Kings passages.

A drastic difference is observable, however, between the Kings and Chronicles versions of Josiah's political and religious reforms.[84] The Deuteronomist's telescoping of the whole process into one great burst of energy in the eighteenth year of Josiah's reign is hardly credible. Chr's description of a gradual process, beginning in the eighth year of Josiah's reign and progressing through his twelfth year to the eighteenth, makes much more sense. Josiah's activity in the territory of northern Israel has been discussed above. Here note will only be taken of the two dates given by Chr for the early stages of Josiah's reform:

2 Chron. 34.3

ובשמונה שנים למלכו והוא עודנו נער החל לדרוש לאלהי דויד אביו
ובשתים עשרה שנה החל לטהר את־יהודה וירושלם מן־הבמות והאשרים
והפסלים והמסכות:

82. Rainey, 'Manasseh', pp. 149-50.

83. *Contra* J.A. Soggin, *An Introduction to the History of Israel and Judah* (Valley Forge, PA: Trinity Press International, 2nd edn, 1993), p. 259.

84. Japhet, *I & II Chronicles*, pp. 1017-20.

> And in the eighth year of his reign, he being still a youth, he began to
> seek the God of his father, David; and in the twelfth year he began to
> purify Judah and Jerusalem from the cult places and the Asherim and the
> graven and the molten images.

The eighth year would be 633/632, during the time when Josiah's first
two sons were being born. The eldest, Jehoiakim, born during 634/633,
was the son of Zebidah, the daughter of Pedaiah from Rumah (2 Kgs
23.36). But the favorite, Jehoahaz, was born in 633/632, and he was the
son of Hamutal, the daugher of Jeremiah of Libnah. It can hardly be
coincidental that the young king Josiah was influenced by his father-in-
law from the priestly city of Libnah. The twelfth year of Josiah would
be 629/628. At this time, the purification of Jerusalem and Judah was
followed by an extension of the reforms into the northern territory
(discussed above). The king of Judah was daring to seek the allegiance
of people living in Assyrian provinces. It had been suggested that this
coincided with the death of Asshurbanipal.[85] Meanwhile, further
research has shown that this Assyrian king died in 627 BCE, but he
seems to have turned the reins of power over to Asshur-etil-ilani in
630,[86] and it may have taken some months for the implications of that
move, that is, the weakness of the central Assyrian authority (especially
in the west), to be realized in states such as Judah. Therefore, the order
of events in Chronicles makes more sense in every way. There were
always problems with the Deuteronomist's version: for example, how
could Josiah be regarded as such a good king when only after eighteen
years did he remove the foreign cults from his kingdom?[87] The expansion of the reform movement into the north during Josiah's twelfth year
also makes more sense than the way the Deuteronomist has gathered all
these events together in the reform of the eighteenth year. He evidently

85. F.M. Cross and D.N. Freedman, 'Josiah's Revolt against Assyria', *JNES* 12
(1953), pp. 56-58.

86. R. Borger, 'Der Aufstieg des neubabylonischen Reiches', *JCS* 19 (1965),
pp. 59-78; J. Oates, 'Assyrian Chronology, 631-612 B.C.', *Iraq* 27 (1965), pp. 135-
59; W. Von Soden, 'Aššuretellilāni, Sînšarriškun, Sînšum(u)lišer und die Ereignisse
im Assyrerreich nach 635 v. Chron.', *ZA* 58 NS 24 (1967), pp. 241-55; J. Reade,
'The Accession of Sinsharishkun', *JCS* 23 (1970), pp. 1-9; H.W.F. Saggs, *The
Might that Was Assyria* (Great Civilization Series; London: Sidgwick & Jackson,
1984), pp. 117-18; G. Frame, *Babylonia 689-627 B.C. A Political History* (Istanbul:
Nederlands Historisch-Archaeologisch Instituut te Istanbul, 1992), pp. 191-213,
296-306.

87. Japhet, *I & II Chronicles*, p. 1019.

wanted to depict everything as the result of the discovery of the book in the temple compound, while Chr brings in the discovery of the book as a result of the reform in progress.[88] Considering the three precise dates given by Chr, the eighth, the twelfth, and the eighteenth years, there is no reason to assume that he made up the significance of the first two. Thus, it is reasonable to assume that Chr based his description on his source, the 'Chronicles of the Kings of Judah'. Further support for that assumption is the geographical description treated in an earlier section of this paper. Such details can hardly be the result of invention. It is not true that there is an 'absence of any indication of an additional source' for Chr's narrative of the Josianic reform.[89]

Jehoiakim–Jehoiachin. On one final point it may be possible to exonerate Chr of a historical error. The obvious contradiction between Kings and Chronicles about the fate of Jehoiakim has long been a topic of discussion, and various solutions have been proposed.[90] The reference in 2 Chron. 36.6-7 to Jehoiakim's being taken to Babylon is perhaps the basis for the opening verses of Daniel (1.1-2), except that the latter passage places Jehoiakim's being taken to Babylon in 605 BCE (his third year, according to Tishri reckoning).[91] However, according to 2 Kgs 24.1-2 Jehoiakim became the servant of Nebuchadnezzar for three years. One could assume that Jehoiakim was taken to Babylon in 605 and returned to Jerusalem by 604. This would be required by the fact that his son, Jehoiachin, surrendered the city of Jerusalem to Nebuchadnezzar on 2 Adar 597 BCE (Babylonian Chronicle)[92] and was taken captive to Babylon, on 10 Nisan (22 April) 597 BCE (2 Kgs 25.12; Ezek. 40.1). But this was after a reign of only three months and ten days (2 Kgs 24.6, 8; 2 Chron. 36.9).[93] Therefore, Jehoiakim must have been alive and in Jerusalem until 21 Marcheshvan 598 BCE.

The solution, which was proposed several years ago,[94] may be in

---

88. Japhet, *I & II Chronicles*, p. 1020.
89. Japhet, *I & II Chronicles*, p. 1020.
90. Japhet, *I & II Chronicles*, pp. 1065-66.
91. Thiele, *Mysterious Numbers*, p. 183.
92. Thiele, *Mysterious Numbers*, pp. 186-87.
93. Thiele, *Mysterious Numbers*, p. 187.
94. A.F. Rainey, 'The Fate of Lachish during the Campaigns of Sennacherib and Nebuchadrezzar', in Y. Aharoni (ed.), *Investigations at Lachish: The Sanctuary*

assuming that 2 Chron. 36.6b-7 was originally part of the Jehoiachin pericope, but was displaced and later reinserted in the wrong place, namely, in the Jehoiakim pericope. The key phrase that caused the error was simply מלך בבל 'the king of Babylon', which is found as the epithet of Nebuchadnezzar in 2 Chron. 36.6a. In v. 10, the name of the king of Babylon appears but without his title, although the parallel verse, 2 Kgs 24.11 (also in 24.10), has נבכדנאצר מלך־בבל 'Nebuchadnezzer, King of Babylon'. At some point in the early textual history of Chronicles, a scribe's eye jumped from נבכדנאצר in 2 Chron. 36.10 to ויבאהו בבלה 'and he brought him to Babylon' (2 Chron. 36.10b), skipping over the clause that describes how the king of Judah was bound in fetters, etc. The skipped passage was probably later written in the margin, and when the manuscript was recopied, it was inserted wrongly in the Jehoiakim pericope, where נבכדנאצר מלך־בבל 'Nebuchadnezzar, King of Babylon' is found in 2 Chron. 36.6a.

It must also be noted that according to LXX, the passage from 2 Kgs 24.1b-4 also appears in 2 Chron. 36.5a-5d. But the latter part of that passage refers to the downfall of Judah as a result of the sins of Manasseh, an opinion that Chr rejected. Somehow, the misplaced passage from the Jehoiachin pericope (vv. 6b-7) was inserted here in the Jehoiakim pericope. The result is the erroneous statement that Jehoiakim was taken in fetters to Babylon. A hypothetical reconstruction of the original Jehoiakim pericope in the 'Chronicles of the Kings' of Judah, minus 2 Kgs 24.3-4, which is an editorial note by the second Deuteronimistic redactor,[95] might run as follows (based on 2 Chronicles 36; material exclusively from Kings underlined):

וימלך פרעה נכה את־אליקים אחיו על־יהודה וירושלם
ויסב את־שמו יהויקים ואת־יואחז אחיו לקח נכו ויביאהו
מצרימה: בן־עשרים וחמש שנה יהויקים במלכו ואחת עשרה
שנה מלך בירושלם ושם אמו זבודה בת־פדיה מן־רומה: ויעש
הרע בעיני יהוה אלהיו: <בימיו> עלה נבוכדנאצר מלך בבל
(LXX 2 Kgs 24.1b-4) ויהי־לו יהויקים עבד שלש שנים וישב
וימרד־בו וישלח יהוה <בו את־גדודי כשדים ואת־גדודי ארם
ואת ׀ גדודי מואב ואת גדודי בני־עמון וישלחם ביהודה להאבידו
כדבר יהוה אשר דבר ביד עבדיו הנביאים>...<וישכב

and the Residency (Lachish V) (Tel Aviv University, Publications of the Institute of Archaeology, 4; Tel Aviv: Gateway Publishers, 1975), p. 55.

95. R.D. Nelson, *The Double Redaction of the Deuteronomistic History* (JSOTSup, 18; Sheffield: JSOT Press, 1981), pp. 23, 85, 88, 123, 126, 132 *et al.*

יהויקים עם־אבתיו> וימלך יהויכין בנו תחתיו: <ולא־הסיף עוד
מלך מצרים לצאת מארצו כי־לקח מלך בבל מנחל מצרים
עד־נהר־פרת כל אשר היתה למלך מצרים:>

And Pharaoh Necho made his brother Eliakim king over Judah and
Jerusalem, and he changed his name to Jehoiakim, and Necho took
Jehoahaz his brother and brought him to Egypt. Jehoiakim was twenty-
five years old when he began to reign, and he reigned eleven years in
Jerusalem, and he did what was evil in the sight of the Lord his God. In
his days Nebuchadnezzar king of Babylon came up, and Jehoiakim
became his servant three years, but then he turned and rebelled against
him. So the Lord sent against him bands of the Chaldeans and bands of
Aram and bands of Moab and bands of the sons of Ammon, and he sent
them against Judah to destroy it, according to the word of the Lord,
which he spoke by means of his servants the prophets ... And Jehoiakim
slept with his fathers and Jehoiachin his son reigned in his stead. And the
king of Egypt did not come forth from his land anymore, because the
king of Babylon had taken all that had belonged to the king of Egypt
from the Brook of Egypt to the Euphrates River.

Chr's Jehoiachin pericope, with 2 Chron. 36.6b-7 inserted where I conjecture it had originally been, can be reconstructed as follows (2 Chron
36.9-10a, 6b-7, 10b; additions from Kings underlined):

בן־שמנה עשרה שנה יהויכין בלכו ושלשה חדשים ועשרת
ימים מלך בירושלם ויעש הרע בעיני יהוה: ולשובת השנה
שלח המלך נבוכדנאצר >(6b) מלך בבל ויאסרהו בנחשתים
להליכו בבלה,(7) ומכלי בית יהוה הביא נבוכדנאצר לבבל
ויתנם בהיכלו בבב:< ויבאהו בבלה עם־כלי חמדת בית־יהוה
וימלך את־צדקיהו אחיו על־יהודה וירושלם:

Jehoiachin was eighteen years old when he began to reign, and he
reigned three months and ten days in Jerusalem, and he did evil in the
eyes of the Lord. And at the turn of the year, King Nebuchadnezzar, king
of Babylon, sent and he bound him in fetters to bring him to Babylon,
and from the vessels of the house of the Lord Nebuchadnezzar brought
to Babylon and he put them in his palace in Babylon. So they brought
him to Babylon with the choice vessels of the house of the Lord, and he
(Nebuchadnezzar) appointed Zedekiah his brother over Judah and
Jerusalem.

Chr's rejection of the second Deuteronomist's attempt to blame
Manasseh for the final destruction of Judah and his attempt to condense
some other details (e.g., 2 Kgs 24.13-17 about the temple vessels) may
have led to the displacement of vv. 6b-7 and its subsequent insertion in

the Jehoiakim pericope. This suggestion may leave many scholars unconvinced, and the lack of firm external controls in the versions makes it unprovable. It is interesting to note that Chr has the more precise 'three months and ten days', for which there is no tendentious reason to assume that it was simply invented. On the other hand, Chr gives Jehoiachin's age as only eight years (influenced by the reference to Josiah's eighth year?), and he calls Zedekiah the 'brother'—rather than the correct 'uncle' (2 Kgs 24.17)—of Jehoiachin, without mentioning that Zedekiah's former name was Mattaniah.

Chr seems to want to pass over Jehoiachin as quickly as possible. Perhaps he was reacting against the final emphasis in Kings on the release of Jehoiachin from detention at the accession of Evil-merodach. Instead, he skips from the end of Zedekiah's reign to the edict of Cyrus the Great.

Concluding Remarks

The extensive sampling of passages that bear indications of having come from an ancient source do not exhaust the possibilities. That is not to say that Chr did not express his own historiographic predilections. He is concerned to stress certain principles of moral and political life. But he also has an understanding of geopolitical and geographical factors that were basic in the life of the ancient kingdom of Judah. He does not divorce the periods of economic and military strength/ weakness from the religious attitudes and policies of the successive monarchs. Is it not reasonable to suggest that a large measure of that insight derives from his main supplementary source, the 'Chronicles of the Kings of Judah'?

WAS THE CHRONICLER A HISTORIAN?

Isaac Kalimi

In order to understand any literary composition and fully appreciate its value, the reader must understand its precise nature and the author's intention. Was it meant to be fiction or history, literary narrative or historical novel, commentary or theology? One must also know as much as possible about the author and his or her time and place in history. In short, it is helpful to know the author's biography, historical context, and intentions, before studying the composition itself.

If we use the Hellenistic authors as a standard of comparison, we find that most authors of biblical-historical books are quite different from the Hellenistic historians. The latter provide explanatory statements or prefaces to their works and reveal their motives for writing, that is, the nature and purpose of their compositions.[1] For example, Dionysius of Halicarnassus[2] (the second half of the first century BCE) prefaced his work *Roman Antiquities* with some remarks concerning himself and his reasons for undertaking the work and then noted the narratives and records that were used as sources, the periods and subjects of history that he would describe, and the form that he would give to the work. At the close of his preface he introduced himself by revealing his name, his father's name, and his place of birth (*Roman Antiquities*, 1.1.1–8.4).[3]

Unfortunately, this is not so in the case of the Chronicler (Chr), who volunteered no information about himself or his work. Chr did not even

---

1. See, for example, Herodotus, *History*, 1.1; Thucydides, *The Peloponnesian War*, 1.1-2; Dionysius of Halicarnassus, *Roman Antiquities*, 1.1.1–8.4; and Josephus Flavius, *Antiquities of the Jews* 1.1-26.

2. Halicarnassus has been identified as the modern Bodrum on the west coast of Asia Minor.

3. *Roman Antiquities of Dionysius of Halicarnassus* (trans. E. Cary; LCL, 319; Cambridge, MA: Harvard University Press; London: Heinemann, 1937), I, pp. 3-27.

provide a basic preface, such as that of Thucydides (ca. 454–399 BCE) in his history of the Peloponnesian War (1.1): 'Thucydides, an Athenian, wrote the history of the war waged by the Peloponnesians and the Athenians against one another'.[4] Chr preferred to remain absolutely anonymous: he did not tell us his name, his place and time, or anything about the nature and the purpose of his work. Therefore, the modern scholar must carefully study the book of Chronicles, and on the basis of this research, form conclusions about the writer and his setting and about the nature of the work itself, its literary genre, and its purpose. The definition of Chr and his work has direct implications not only for the understanding of the nature of the book and its content but also for the scholar's assessment of the reliability of the information contained within Chronicles and hence for the book's usefulness as a historical source for the history of Israel in the monarchic era.

The Definition of Chronicles and its Author

In the sections that follow, four major views on the nature of Chronicles will be critically reviewed, and then there will be an attempt to set the work within its context of biblical historiography.

Chronicles as Midrash

In his well-known *Prolegomena zur Geschichte Israels*,[5] Julius Wellhausen defined the nature of the Book of Chronicles as midrash, arguing, '...whether one says Chronicles or *Midrash* of the Book of Kings is on the whole a matter of perfect indifference; they are children of the same mother, and indistinguishable in spirit and language, while on the other hand the portions which have been retained verbatim from the canonical Book of Kings at once betray themselves in both respects'.[6]

---

4.   C.F. Smith, *Thucydides with an English Translation* (LCL, 108; Cambridge, MA: Harvard University Press; London: Heinemann, 1928), I, p. 3.

5.   The title, *Prolegomena zur Geschichte Israels*, appeared only on the second edition of Wellhausen's work (see below, n. 6). The first edition of the work appeared as *Geschichte Israels. In zwei Bänden. Erster Band* (Berlin: G. Reimer, 1878).

6.   Wellhausen, *Prolegomena to the History of Ancient Israel* (Gloucester, MA: Peter Smith, 1973), p. 227 (=*Prolegomena zur Geschichte Israels* [Berlin: G. Reimer, 2nd edn, 1883], p. 237).

What is the meaning of 'midrash'—a term that appears only twice in the Hebrew Bible and both times in Chronicles (2 Chron. 13.22; 24.27)? Wellhausen did not leave the question unanswered. He was aware that the meaning of the word in these passages in Chronicles is quite different from its meaning elsewhere. Still he wrote:

> ...but the natural sense suits admirably well, and in Chronicles we find ourselves fully within the period of the scribes. Midrash is the consequence of the conservation of all the relics of antiquity, a wholly peculiar artificial reawakening of dry bones, artificial especially by literary means, as is shown by the preference for lists of names and numbers.[7]

Wellhausen continues with his pictorial description of midrash: 'Like ivy it overspreads the dead trunk with extraneous life, blending old and new in a strange combination'.[8] According to Wellhausen the motive for the midrashic activity stems from a high evaluation of tradition, which leads to a modernizing tendency, but he notes, '...in the process it is twisted and perverted, and set off with foreign accretions in the most arbitrary way'.[9] Here Wellhausen cannot resist making an anti-Judaic remark: 'Within this sphere, wherein all Judaism moves, Chronicles also has had its rise'.[10]

Wellhausen's understanding of Chronicles was adopted by several scholars—for example, by Immanuel Benzinger[11] and Rudolf Kittel[12] in their commentaries—and in 1938, Adam C. Welch took a similar position, observing that 'the Chronicler was not writing history', but the 'essence of his work' was midrash.[13]

There is no doubt that the book of Chronicles includes midrashic elements,[14] but it is inaccurate to conclude from these that the whole

---

7. Wellhausen, *Prolegomena to the History*, p. 227.
8. Wellhausen, *Prolegomena to the History*, p. 227 .
9. Wellhausen, *Prolegomena to the History*, p. 227.
10. Wellhausen, *Prolegomena to the History*, p. 227.
11. I. Benzinger, *Die Bücher der Chronik* (KHCAT, 20; Tübingen: Mohr [Paul Siebeck], 1901), pp. xi-xiii.
12. R. Kittel, *Die Bücher der Chronik übersetzt und erklärt* (HKAT, 6/1; Göttingen: Vandenhoeck & Ruprecht, 1902), p. ix.
13. See A.C. Welch, *The Work of the Chronicler: Its Purpose and its Date* (Schweich Lectures 1938; London: Oxford University Press, 1939), p. 54.
14. See W.E. Barnes, 'The Midrashic Element in Chronicles', *The Expositor* 5th series, 4 (1896), pp. 426-39; I.L. Seeligmann, 'The Beginnings of Midrash in the Books of Chronicles', *Tarbiz* 49 (1979/80), pp. 14-32. On midrashic names,

book is midrash—except for some verbatim passages from the books of
Samuel and Kings. This is not the picture that emerges from the book
in its entirety. The purpose of Wellhausen and his school is clear: to
destroy the credibility of Chronicles as a historical source for pre-exilic
Israelite history. They tried to show that Chr was dependent only on the
earlier canonical books and treated them in a midrashic way, especially
against the background of the priestly code's (P) appearance in the post-
exilic era.[15] Chr also fabricated stories about the Israelite monarchy
based on his fantasy.

Moreover, it seems that Wellhausen and most German, British, and
French historians of the nineteenth century followed Leopold von
Ranke's definition in the 1830s of the task of the historian, that is, to
show 'wie es eigentlich gewesen' ('how it really was'). This motto,
which directed generations of historians, caused, as Edward H. Carr
stated, a 'fetishism of facts' that was 'completed and justified by a
fetishism of documents'.[16] These historians stood for 'factual history'
without any interpretation and evaluation. They approached the 'facts'
and 'documents' 'with bowed head and spoke of them in awed tones'.[17]
Since then our definitions and understanding of historiography have
changed: 'history' definitely is not only 'facts' and 'documents', and the
task of the historian is not limited to show 'wie es eigentlich gewesen',
as will be seen below.

Furthermore, it is hard to ignore that a theological and an anti-Jewish
tendency also guided Wellhausen's definition of Chronicles as midrash.
As mentioned above, according to Wellhausen the whole of Judaism
moves in a midrashic sphere, and it was within such a sphere that the
book of Chronicles grew. Therefore, one may conclude that Wellhausen
thought that 'the new/true Israel' (i.e., Christianity) continues in the

---

see also I. Kalimi, 'Paronomasia in the Book of Chronicles', *PAAJR* 59 (1993),
pp. 29-40, esp. 37-40 (Hebrew; rev. English version: *JSOT* 67 [1995], pp. 27-41,
esp. 37-41).

15. Cf. M.P. Graham, *The Utilization of 1 and 2 Chronicles in the Reconstruction of Israelite History in the Nineteenth Century* (SBLDS, 116; Atlanta: Scholars
Press, 1990), pp. 141-50.

16. E.H. Carr, *What Is History?* (The George Macaulay Trevelyan Lectures
Delivered at the University of Cambridge January-March 1961; New York: Vintage
Books, 1961), p. 15.

17. See Carr, *What Is History*, p. 15.

sphere of ancient biblical Israel, as shown in the books of Samuel and Kings.[18]

The Chronicler as an Exegete

In his monograph, *Die Chronik als Auslegung*, Thomas Willi defines the literary nature of Chronicles as a commentary 'in the best meaning of the word',[19] arguing that the demand of the old sources to be interpreted was the only impulse behind the composition of Chronicles.[20] Willi describes this as follows: 'When the Chronicler intended to surrender to the compulsion to write a history of the pre-exilic period, for this very reason he had but one option, namely, an interpretation of the material of tradition passed on to him, and that meant an interpretation of the Deuteronomistic History.'[21] Moreover, Willi tends to find in Chronicles the application of the rules whereby the Sages interpreted the Pentateuch. Hence, he views Chr as an 'exegete' interpreting the texts of Samuel and Kings. His basic assumption is that Chr viewed the Pentateuch and the Former Prophets as canonical books.[22]

But how should one consider the non-synoptic parts of Chr's work—the passages that 'supplement' Samuel–Kings, on the one hand, and the books of Ezra–Nehemiah, on the other? In the 1970s, the latter complex was still considered by most scholars as part of a comprehensive work by Chr. Willi solves the problem only partially, arguing that Chronicles and Ezra–Nehemiah are two independent works by the same author.[23]

---

18. The idea that Christianity replaced Judaism and at the same time was also a continuation of 'biblical Israel' is deeply embedded in Christian theology. See, e.g., Mt. 8.11-12; Lk. 13.24-30; Acts 15.14-17; 28.28; and cf. R.R. Ruether, *Faith and Fratricide: The Theological Roots of Anti-Semitism* (New York: Seabury, 1974), pp. 84-86.

19. '...*im besten Sinne des Wortes...*': *Die Chronik als Auslegung: Untersuchungen zur literarischen Gestaltung der historischen Überlieferung Israels* (FRLANT, 106; Göttingen: Vandenhoeck & Ruprecht, 1972), p. 66.

20. Willi, *Chronik*, p. 193.

21. 'Wenn der Chronist der Nötigung, Geschichte der vorexilischen Zeit zu schreiben, nachgeben wollte, so blieb ihm schon aus diesem Grunde nur ein Weg: der der Interpretation des überlieferten Materials, mithin der Auslegung des deuteronomistischen Geschichtswerkes': Willi, *Chronik*, p. 54.

22. Willi, *Chronik*, pp. 176ff., 241-44; cf. also pp. 48-66, esp. pp. 53-54, 55-56, 66.

23. Willi, *Chronik*, p. 180. Claims of this kind were already made by W.M.L. de Wette, *Lehrbuch der historisch-kritischen Einleitung in die kanonischen*

Thus, while the nature of Chronicles is 'commentary', Ezra–Nehemiah is 'historiography'. Regarding texts in Chronicles that have no parallels in the Former Prophets, Willi considers most of 1 Chronicles 1–9, 15.2-16, as well as 23.2b–27.34 and several other passages in 2 Chronicles as additions made by one or more later editors.[24] He did not refer to other paragraphs without parallels in the earlier books.

Nevertheless, Willi's position exerted great influence, especially among German-speaking scholars. Rudolf Smend's *Die Entstehung des Alten Testaments*, for example, maintained that the whole complex from Genesis to Kings was used by Chr as a canonical text.[25] Hence, Chr's work 'is first and foremost an interpretation of its predecessor, a predecessor which itself was attaining canonical status'.[26] A similar view of Chr and his work was also reflected in Ingeborg Gabriel's recent study, *Friede über Israel*, in which she writes,

> With the completion of the Pentateuch in the fifth century, there existed for the first time a text that was binding on all who believed in Yahweh. In addition, those writings that interpreted history, namely, the Former and Latter Prophets of the Hebrew canon, also essentially achieved their present form during this period. Hand in hand with these first steps toward a canonization of Old Testament texts, a literature of interpretation emerged. Chronicles, which was later accepted into the canon in its own turn, also belonged to this new literary genre. As an interpretation of earlier historical works, above all of the Deuteronomistic History, it [Chronicles] explains the history of Israel for its own time.[27]

und apokryphischen Bücher des Alten Testamentes (Berlin: G. Reimer, 6th edn, 1845), I, pp. 290-91; *idem, A Critical and Historical Introduction to the Canonical Scriptures of the Old Testament* (translated from the German and enlarged by T. Parker from the 5th German edn; Boston: Rufus Leighton, 3rd edn, 1859), pp. 328-30; C.F. Keil, *The Books of the Chronicles* (Clark's Foreign Theological Library, 4th series, 35; Edinburgh: T. & T. Clark, 1872), pp. 23-25.

24. See Willi, *Chronik*, pp. 194-204.

25. R. Smend, *Die Entstehung des Alten Testaments* (ThW, 1; Stuttgart: Kohlhammer, 1978), p. 228.

26. '...ist zuerst und vor allem Auslegung ihrer in den Rang des Kanonischen einrükkenden Vorgängerin...': Smend, *Entstehung*, p. 229.

27. 'Mit dem Abschluß des Pentateuch im 5. Jhdt. lag erstmals ein Text vor, der für alle Jahwegläubigen verbindlich war. Auch die geschichtsdeutenden Schriften, die früheren und späteren Propheten des hebräischen Kanons, erhielten in dieser Zeit im wesentlichen ihre heutige Form. Hand in Hand mit diesen ersten Schritten in Richtung auf eine Kanonisierung alttestamentlicher Texte ging die Entstehung einer Auslegungsliteratur. Zu diesem neuen literarischen Genre gehörte auch die

This thesis seems inaccurate and based on extremely weak presuppositions. First, although it is probably true that Chr treated the Pentateuch as a canonical book and that the specific texts that he used from this book were generally not altered,[28] the books of Samuel and Kings were by no means canonical for Chr. He did not treat them as immutable, sealed books that one may strive only to explain and comprehend in their given form. On the contrary, these books served him as raw materials for manipulation as he saw fit: he adapted, supplemented, and omitted from them according to his own ideological-theological outlook, applying his literary and historiographical methods, as well as his linguistic and stylistic tastes.

Second, the logical patterns by which the Sages drew their conclusions from the Pentateuch were foreign to Chr's world of thought, and attempts to identify them in Chronicles are anachronistic.[29]

Third, Chr's main purpose was not to exegete earlier books. There are many passages that he transferred verbally from the previous works without alteration, even when these texts required explanation.[30] On the

---

Chr, die später ihrerseits in den Kanon aufgenommen wurde. Als Interpretation früherer Geschichtswerke, vor allem des DtrG, deutet sie die Geschichte Israels für ihre eigene Zeit': I. Gabriel, *Friede über Israel. Eine Untersuchung zur Friedenstheologie in Chronik I 10–II 36* (ÖBS, 10; Klosterneuburg: Österreichisches Katholisches Bibelwerk, 1990), p. 5. Similarly, J. Becker, *1 Chronik* (NEB, 18; Würzberg: Echter Verlag, 1986), p. 6.

28. On the differences between the canonical Torah and the legislation that relates to Chronicles, see I. Kalimi, *Zur Geschichtsschreibung des Chronisten. Literarisch-historiographische Abweichungen der Chronik von ihren Paralleltexten in den Samuel- und Königsbücher* (BZAW, 226; Berlin: de Gruyter, 1995), pp. 336-37. For another opinion, see J.R. Shaver, *Torah and the Chronicler's History Work: An Inquiry into the Chronicler's Reference to Laws, Festivals, and Cultic Institutions in Relationship to Pentateuchal Legislation* (BJS, 196; Atlanta: Scholars Press, 1989), p. 128.

29. Cf. Seeligmann, 'Beginnings', p. 15 n. 3.

30. For example, in 1 Chron. 16.3, Chr transferred the term אשפר from 2 Sam. 6.19 without explanation. Later generations failed to understand the exact meaning of the term; Septuagint, Aquila, and Symmachus on 2 Samuel translated it as 'cake or roll'; RSV, 'a portion of meat' (cf. already *b.Pes* 36b); from among the modern commentators, see for example, F. Stolz: 'einen Dattelkuchen' (*Das erste und zweite Buch Samuel* [Zürcher Bibelkommentare AT, 9; Zürich: Theologischer Verlag, 1981], pp. 213, 217); R.L. Braun: 'a date-cake' (*1 Chronicles* [WBC, 14; Waco, TX: Word Books, 1986], p. 182). Still, though, the etymology and meaning of the term remain elusive. Another example occurs in 2 Chron. 26.21, in which

other hand, almost half of Chronicles has no parallel in the Pentateuch and Former Prophets or in any other biblical book.[31]

Fourth, there are hundreds of literary, stylistic, and linguistic differences between the texts in Chronicles and their parallels in earlier books.[32] These modifications do not fit the category 'commentary'. Indeed, as already pointed out by Rudolf Mosis, sometimes Willi imposed his thesis on the text of Chronicles.[33]

Fifth, Chr omitted many texts from Samuel–Kings and arranged others differently.[34] The classification 'commentary' is unable to explain these phenomena.[35]

Sixth, most of the interpretive and exegetical changes appearing in Chronicles stem primarily (1) from the author's particular usage of earlier books—which occasionally contain difficulties of various types or contradict some other biblical verse[36]—and (2) from Chr's attempt—as a historian—to provide his sources with evaluations and explanations.[37] All of these changes are subsumed within a much larger group of modifications that differentiate Chronicles from the Deuteronomistic History.

Finally, Willi's definition of the literary genre of Chronicles as 'commentary' and its purpose as that of interpreting the canonical books negates completely and necessarily the historical value of Chronicles as

Chr transferred the problematic words בית החפשות (Qere: החפשית) as they appear in 2 Kgs 15.5; on this, see in detail Kalimi, *Geschichtsschreibung*, pp. 104-105. For other examples, see 2 Chron. 10.10 = 1 Kgs 12.10: קטני עבה ממתני אבי; 2 Chron. 23.4-5//2 Kgs 11.5-6: 'neither the arrangements envisaged here nor in 2 Kg. 11:5-7 are entirely clear'; see H.G.M. Williamson, *1 and 2 Chronicles* (NCB; Grand Rapids, MI: Eerdmans; London: Marshall, Morgan & Scott, 1982), p. 316.

31. Cf. R. Mosis, *Untersuchungen zur Theologie des chronistischen Geschichtswerkes* (FTS, 92; Freiburg: Herder, 1973), pp. 12-13.

32. For this, see A. Kropat, *Die Syntax des Autors der Chronik verglichen mit der seiner Quellen: Ein Beitrag zur historischen Syntax des Hebräischen* (BZAW, 16; Giessen: Töpelmann, 1909); Kalimi, *Geschichtsschreibung; idem*, 'Paranomasia', pp. 27-41.

33. See, for example, Willi, *Chronik*, pp. 26, 28; and cf. Mosis, *Untersuchungen*, p. 13.

34. Cf., e.g., 1 Chron. 11.1-47 with 2 Sam. 5.1-10; 23.8-39; and 1 Chron. 13.1-14; 14.1-17 with 2 Sam. 5.11–6.12.

35. Cf. Mosis, *Untersuchungen*, p. 13.

36. See Kalimi, *Geschichtsschreibung*, pp. 35-50, 127-43.

37. See, e.g., 1 Chron. 10.13-14; 14.17; 2 Chron. 12.2, 14; 22.9 (cf. = 2 Kgs 9.28); 24.7.

a source for the pre-exilic period. Although generally information in Chronicles is unreliable,[38] there are a number of valuable texts in the book that contain indispensable historical information, and at least as yet, the accuracy of some of them remains debatable among scholars.[39]

The Chronicler as Theologian

Some scholars consider Chronicles as primarily theological discourse and therefore believe that its author should be regarded as a theologian. Peter R. Ackroyd, for example, suggested that Chr's aim was to present 'a unifying concept of the nature of the Jewish religious community and hence of its theology and the meaning of its rich and varied traditions'. He notes further,

> It points forward to other attempts at unification to be found in later Jewish and Christian writings, and while it would be straining the evidence to describe it as the first 'theology of the Old Testament,' it nevertheless, in its endeavour to be comprehensive and yet true to the tradition, anticipates some more modern essays which have sought the essential centre of Old Testament theological thought...[40]

This understanding of Chronicles was reached independently a few years later by Richard J. Coggins. In the introduction to his commentary he notes that Chr's presentation is 'basically theological' and addressing methodological concerns, he states, 'More important, therefore, than asking questions about historicity, is the attempt to discover the

---

38. Let us not forget, first and foremost, that Chr's history is 'third-hand', while the Deuteronomistic History is 'second-hand', and his sources are believed to include material that came—at least partially—from 'first-hand'. Furthermore, Chr interfered with and made changes to his sources from different viewpoints. Also, the book of Chronicles was written hundreds of years after the events.

39. For example, 1 Chron. 8.1-40; 11.41b-47; 12.1-22; cf. Williamson, *Chronicles*, pp. 83, 103-104, 106.

40. P.R. Ackroyd, 'The Theology of the Chronicler', *LTQ* 8 (1973), p. 108 (= 'The Theology of the Chronicler', *The Chronicler in his Age* [JSOTSup, 101; Sheffield: JSOT Press, 1991], p. 280); cf. also his article, 'The Chronicler as Exegete', *JSOT* 2 (1977), pp. 2-3, 24 (= *Chronicler in his Age*, pp. 312, 343). In the same article (p. 24) Ackroyd also suggests that one consider Chr as a 'conciliator': while he is 'a conciliator between different groups and interests...he portrays Ezra as the conciliator,...he is also a conciliator between different lines of thought...'

underlying theological purpose of the Chronicler.'[41]

It seems that although Chr intended to relate history, he was true to the other biblical traditions and understood that the essence of 'history' was not merely a human activity but first and foremost God's treatment of humans. The world and everything in it belongs to God (1 Chron. 29.11; 2 Chron. 20.6; 25.9), and he is everywhere in the world (2 Chron. 16.9a). He knows everything, and without his knowledge and will nothing happens (1 Chron. 28.9; 29.17; 2 Chron. 6.30; 19.6). God motivates nations to do what they do (1 Chron. 5.26; 2 Chron. 21.16), and nations' kings act as tools in his hands (2 Chron. 36.17-21).[42] God is always involved in human activity, in the making of history—whether directly (e.g., 1 Chron. 14.10, 14, 17) or indirectly (e.g., 1 Chron. 10.13-14).[43] In other words, as a historian Chr's ideological presuppositions guided his historiography. In antiquity, these lines of thought typically converged with the writer's theological convictions.[44] Nevertheless, the main feature of Chr's work is history—not theology—though it is indeed a 'sacred history' and not a 'secular history'. Therefore, Chr is primarily a historian rather than a theologian.

The Chronicler as Historian

The appearance of Chronicles in the LXX among the historical books, immediately after the books of Kings (ἡ βίβλος βασιλειῶν, that is, the books of Samuel and Kings in the Masoretic version), shows that the Greek compilers of the canon considered the book as historiography.

41. R.J. Coggins, *The First and Second Books of the Chronicles* (CBC; Cambridge: Cambridge University Press, 1976), pp. 5-6.

42. Cf. W. Rudolph, *Chronikbücher* (HAT, 21; Tübingen: Mohr [Paul Siebeck], 1955), pp. xviii-xix.

43. On this point, see also Kalimi, *Geschichtsschreibung*, pp. 143-48.

44. This feature is obvious in the biblical literature, but elsewhere, too. In the Mesha Inscription, for example, we read: 'He [Chemosh] saved me from all the kings and caused me to triumph over all my adversaries' (line 4); 'And Chemosh said to me "Go, take Nebo from Israel!"' (line 14; English translation according to W.F. Albright, in *ANET*, p. 320). Similarly, in the Monolith Inscription from Kurkh, Shalmanesser III announces: 'The terror and the glamor of Assur, my lord, overwhelmed [them]...I fought with him upon a trust (inspiring) oracle of Assur and the (other) great gods, my lords...I fought with them (assisted) by the mighty power of Nergal, my lord, by the ferocious weapons which Assur, my lord, has presented to me...' (English translation by A.L. Oppenheim, in *ANET*, p. 277). No one claims that the authors of these inscriptions were theologians!

This placement was followed by the Vulgate and other Christian translations.[45] In medieval times, the Jewish commentators Rabbi David Kimchi (c. 1160-1235) and Don Isaac Abarbanel (or Isaac Ben Judah Abarbanel, 1437–1508) pointed out that the book of Chronicles is in its nature to be considered as history. For example, in the introduction to his commentary on the book of Samuel, Abarbanel says:

והנה ספר דברי הימים נעשה על צד הסיפור המוחלט (היינו היסטוריה־י'ה).
ובעבור זה באו בו דברים על הצד היותר טוב, עם היותם בלתי
הכרחיים, כפי מה שיורה עליו שמו.

In contrast to the book of Samuel, 'As to the book of Chronicles it has been written as a historical narrative as its name דברי הימים implies, its description of events is much better, although some narrative elements are not essential.' In modern biblical scholarship Chronicles was considered similarly, with the exceptions mentioned above. However, to date no one has adequately explained what makes the book of Chronicles historiography. The inclusion of the work among the historical books in the LXX and the fact that the book deals with the monarchic era and is based largely on Samuel–Kings (which all regard as historical books) points to the identification of Chronicles as an example of historiography.

Indeed, a careful study of Chronicles reveals that we are dealing with historiography, and so Chr should be considered a historian. This definition is based, in brief, on the following features that are found in the book: the author deals with the past; he collects material from the earlier books and perhaps additional sources; he selects from the sources, evaluates, and interprets them; he makes connections between the sources; and above all, his work as a whole is imprinted with a unique 'philosophy' of history. Let us turn to these points in detail.

Chr, who apparently wrote in the first quarter of the fourth century BCE,[46] narrated the past of the Israelites from the earliest times until the destruction of the kingdom of Judah. In his writing Chr referred to the

---

45. Cf., e.g., the King James Version, New King James Version, Revised Standard Version, New Revised Standard Version, The New American Bible (Saint Joseph Edition), The New Catholic Study Bible (Saint Jerome Edition), the German edition of Martin Luther, the Zürcher Bibel, etc.

46. On this, see I. Kalimi, 'Die Abfassungszeit der Chronik—Forschungsstand und Perspektiven', *ZAW* 105 (1993), pp. 223-33; *idem*, 'Könnte die aramäische Grabinschrift aus Ägypten als Indikation für die Datierung der Chronikbücher fungieren?', *ZAW* 109 (1997), forthcoming.

earlier books (i.e., of the Pentateuch and the Former Prophets),[47] and he also claimed that he had different sources, which he mentioned repeatedly.[48] Without dealing with the question of whether these sources— part or even all of them—actually existed or were invented by Chr to create an illusion of reliability, we receive the impression that Chr attempted to write a 'history'. Therefore, it seems likely that he understood himself as a narrator of past events, in western terminology, a 'historian'.

Chr selected the material from the earlier books and edited them in the order, context, and form he thought appropriate. His 'exegesis' found expression first and foremost in the definition of the ancient data that was made available at the time of selection. As mentioned already, Chr provided evaluation for his sources, commenting on the meaning and the significant effects of the historical events in the earlier texts.[49] Generally, he also interpreted and explained the difficulties and contradictions that he detected in his sources, although sometimes he even omitted these problematic texts.[50]

Chr made connections between various sources and at times conflated different texts into a single description.[51] He had a unique view of history that informed his composition and found expression both in alterations of earlier texts and in additions to or at the edges of them.[52] As was common among the deuteronomistic, as well as the Hellenistic historians, Chr also articulated his views in the guise of speeches and prayers by the heroes in his narrative.[53] As his writings originated in the first quarter of the fourth century BCE, this left him ample chronological

47. For discussion on this issue, see Kalimi, *Geschichtsschreibung*, pp. 3-6.

48. See 1 Chron. 9.1 (cf. 29.29; 2 Chron. 9.29); 27.24; 28.1; 2 Chron. 9.29; 12.15; 13.22; 16.11; 20.34; 25.26 (cf. 28.26; 32.32); 24.27; 26.22; 27.7; 29.29; 32.32; 33.18, 19; 35.25.

49. See, e.g., 1 Chron. 10.13-14; 14.17; 2 Chron. 32.22-23.

50. See Kalimi, *Geschichtsschreibung*, pp. 37-50, 100-12.

51. E.g., 1 Chron. 3.1-9; 2 Chron. 5.1–7.3. On these examples and others, see Kalimi, *Geschichtsschreibung*, pp. 249-73.

52. On these, see Wellhausen, *Prolegomena*, pp. 165-223; S. Japhet, *The Ideology of the Book of Chronicles and its Place in Biblical Thought* (BEATAJ, 9; Frankfurt am Main: Peter Lang, 1989).

53. See, e.g., 1 Chron. 28.2-10; 29.10-19; 2 Chron. 13.4-12; 20.5-13; 32.6-8; 36.13-21. For detailed bibliography on this issue, see I. Kalimi, *The Books of Chronicles: A Classified Bibliography* (SBB, 1; Jerusalem: Simor, 1990), pp. 81-83, items 469-84.

distance to survey Israel's past from a broad perspective. It seems that he did not sit and 'dream' about the past but studied it in order to learn about the present and perhaps about the future as well.[54]

All these features of Chronicles lead me to consider its author as a historian and to classify his work as late biblical historiography. Nevertheless, it should be emphasized that these features do not make Chronicles a reliable historical composition. The plausibility of the book as a source for the pre-exilic period is an entirely different issue. In any case, it is inappropriate to deny the credibility of the whole book in advance—each case should be evaluated on its own merits. The problem of the reliability of Chronicles should not overshadow the evaluation of the work's literary and historiographical nature. Moreover, even if one considers the book as 'bad history' (i.e., as presenting inaccurate information), it is still historiographical in intent. No one denies that Herodotus has unreliable stories in his *Historia*, but neither does one deny that his book is a history nor that its author should be considered a historian.

Evaluation of Chronicles and its Place in Biblical Historiography

The attitude of the LXX's translator(s)/redactor(s) toward Chronicles was ambiguous, as is suggested by the name given to the book: παραλειπομέων (i.e., 'Omissions' [from Kings]). In other words, the significance of Chronicles lies in its 'additional' materials that are not found in (or are said to be 'omitted from') the books of Samuel and Kings, which it follows in sequence. The Greek name implies that the 'parallel texts' are unimportant in themselves or even 'boring repetitions'. This term (παραλειπομέων) is found also in the Vulgate ('Paralipomenon'), and consequently in a number of Christian translations. A similar attitude may be detected in the writings of commentators and philosophers from various times and places. For example, Don Isaac Abrabanel wrote in the introduction to his commentary on Samuel, 'Why did Ezra the Scribe repeat in Chronicles that which already appears here in Samuel? What was his purpose in reiterating these matters? That which is mentioned here need not have been written

---

54. Many scholars claim that Chr also thought about the future, as exemplified by his expectation of a future Davidic messiah. See, e.g., Mosis, *Untersuchungen*, pp. 15, 89ff.

there, since they all already appear here.'[55] This attitude could be found later in a work by Benedictus de (Baruch) Spinoza (1632–1677), who observed, 'Concerning the two Books of Chronicles...as to their actual writer, their authority, utility and doctrine, I come to no conclusion. I have always been astonished that they have been included in the Bible by men who shut out from the canon the books of Wisdom, Tobit and the others styled apocryphal.'[56]

Nevertheless, a close comparison of the text of Chronicles with the books of Samuel and Kings reveals much more than mere minor linguistic emendations or even textual or theological modifications. Many of Chr's alterations give the earlier texts a new literary aspect, with form and meaning different from those of their parallels in the earlier books. The comparison shows clearly the forms and structures, literary devices and techniques, and methods of historiographical editing and adaptation that Chr applied to the earlier texts.[57] The uncovering of these historiographical methods and literary techniques is of paramount importance in understanding the content, ethos, and full meaning of the text of Chronicles. To cite J. Wolfgang von Goethe: 'Gehalt bringt die Form mit; Form ist nie ohne Gehalt' ('Content includes form; form is never without content').[58] These enable us to determine the precise nature of the changes that Chr made in the earlier texts—his additions, omissions, rearrangements, and editing—and hence the significance and degree of historical credibility of Chronicles. An awareness of Chr's method of writing facilitates the study of other aspects of his book,[59] but above all, it illuminates the author and the nature of his book. Recognition of Chr's literary techniques and historiographical methods shows him in a new light: no longer is he to be viewed either as a

55. *Mikra'ot gedolot* (New York: M.P. Press, 1973/4–1975/6), IV, p. 162-63.

56. See B. de Spinoza, *Tractatus Theologico-Politicus*, Chapter X (at the beginning); *The Chief Works of Benedict de Spinoza* (trans. R.H.M. Eleves; New York: Dover, 1951), I, p. 146. Cf. Kalimi, *Geschichtsschreibung*, pp. 322-24.

57. On this, see Kalimi, *Geschichtsschreibung*, pp. 18-318.

58. See J.W. von Goethe, 'Paralipomena', in *Gedenkausgabe der Werke, Briefe und Gesprache* (ed. E. Beutler; Zürich: Artemis-Verlag, 1949), V, p. 541; cf. also Kalimi, *Geschichtsschreibung*, pp. 319-20.

59. There is the textual aspect, the ideological-theological aspect, and so on. See Kalimi, *Geschichtsschreibung*, pp. 320-26; *idem*, 'The Contribution of the Literary Study of Chronicles to the Solution of its Textual Problems', *Tarbiz* 62 (1993), pp. 471-86 (Hebrew; revised English version: *Biblical Interpretation* 3 [1995], pp. 190-212).

passive scribe-copyist or as a scissors-and-paste 'compiler'. He is not even 'in der Hauptsache nur ein Redaktor' ('in the main only an editor'), as Carl Steuernagel defined him.[60] Based on these comparisons Chr is revealed as a creative artist with a variegated range of literary and historiographical talents—a skilled professional historian with sophisticated writing methods at his disposal, one who not only selects material suitable to his aims from earlier works, but also presents it in a fresh style, rewriting and formulating it in a new literary mode.[61] This, too, may be said of the parallel texts in Chronicles: they are neither a 'pointless copy' nor a 'boring repetition' of what appears in the classical biblical historiography nor a 'review' that is 'useless' for the reader. These are old-new literary historical works, gripping in their form and sophistication.

Contrary to Steuernagel,[62] Chr's description of Israelite history in the monarchic era is not intended to replace earlier historical writings. Actually, we are unable to understand properly the book of Chronicles without knowledge of Samuel and Kings.[63] Moreover, the description in Chronicles is also not simply 'a composition which retells the already known story of the history of Israel', as claimed by Sara Japhet.[64] By no means is the story of 1 Chron. 10.6 ('So Saul died and his three sons and all his house died together', וימת שאול ושלשת בניו וכל ביתו יחדו מתו), a retelling of the earlier story in 1 Sam. 31.6 ('So

---

60. See C. Steuernagel, *Lehrbuch der Einleitung in das Alte Testament* (Sammlung theologischer Lehrbücher; Tübingen: Mohr [Paul Siebeck], 1912), p. 408.

61. Yet it must be emphasized that there remains a lack of systematization in the literary and historiographical adaptation of the early texts in Chronicles. Furthermore, there are certain alterations introduced by Chr in the earlier texts which create dissonance with other passages in his own work or in other biblical books. A few historiographical modifications in Chronicles seem to originate in lacunae in Chr's own knowledge of the historical, geographical, linguistic, and cultural background of Israelite history in the monarchic period. See Kalimi, *Geschichtsschreibung*, pp. 327-47.

62. See Steuernagel, *Einleitung*, p. 389.

63. Cf. Willi, *Chronik*, pp. 56-66; Kalimi, *Geschichtsschreibung*, pp. 172-84.

64. S. Japhet, 'Conquest and Settlement in Chronicles', *JBL* 98 (1979), p. 205. This idea was stated earlier by J.W. Bowker, *The Targums and Rabbinic Literature: An Introduction to Jewish Interpretation of Scripture* (Cambridge: Cambridge University Press, 1969), p. 6 n. 2: 'Chronicles is, in a sense, a "retelling" of Samuel and Kings in order to express the insights and interests of a later generation'.

Saul died and his three sons and his armor-bearer and all his men on the
same day together', וימת שאול ושלשת בניו ונשא כליו גם כל אנשיו ביום
ההוא יחדו). What was told in 1 Chron. 10.14 about Saul ('and he did
not seek Yahweh', ולא דרש ביהוה) is completely contrary to what was
reported in 1 Sam. 28.6 ('And when Saul inquired of Yahweh, Yahweh
did not answer him, either by dreams, or by Urim or by prophets',
וישאל שאול ביהוה ולא ענהו יהוה גם בחלמות גם באורים גם בנביאם).
2 Chron. 8.2 ('... Solomon *rebuilt the cities that Choram had given to
Solomon, and he settled Israelites there*', הערים אשר נתן חורם לשלמה
בנה שלמה אתם ויושב שם את־בני ישראל) completely contradicts the story
in 1 Kgs. 9.11b-13 ('...*Solomon gave to Chiram twenty cities* in the
land of Galilee...', אז יתן המלך שלמה לחירם עשרים עיר בארץ הגליל).
Another example—and there are many—is what was related in 2
Chron. 32.1, 'After these things and this faithfulness Sennacherib, king
of Assyria, came and entered into Judah and encamped against the fortified cities, and thought to win them for himself' (ויאמר לבקעם אליו).
This is certainly no retelling of what one reads in 2 Kgs 18.13 that 'in
the fourteenth year of King Hezekiah, Sennacherib, king of Assyria,
attacked all of Judah's fortified cities and seized them' (ויתפשם).

   The book of Chronicles is an impressive attempt to organize material
into a single comprehensive and systematic work. It focuses above all
on the history of the Davidic dynasty, paying particular attention to the
Jerusalem temple and its services (from the author's own perspective,
of course). According to our knowledge of the sources, it is the first of
its kind. This work would seem to have been sorely needed by its
generation, considering the religious, social, linguistic, and literary
norms that had developed since the composition of Samuel and Kings.
In other words, Chronicles represents the principle of 'each generation
with its own historiography'. The message of Chr was different from
that of the earlier historical works and was directed to a different time
and audience. It was attuned to new historical circumstances. Therefore, the Chronicler's work should be valued as a significant contribution to the dialectic between the historian of the Second Temple era
and the pre-exilic period. Such a dialectic brings with it an evaluation
of Israelite history (especially in the monarchic period) from the
perspective of a historian in the Second Commonwealth era. As one
conditioned by his own time and his place—and no one can ignore
these—Chr evaluated the past from his own historical context and its
norms: he pointed out the priestly codex, the temple, and its services,

and stressed the continuity of the Judean tribes as the real Israelites who survived until his own day. He described the high priest in the kingdom of Judah, as the institution was reflected in his own time in Yehud Madinta.[65]

In closing this article, R.G. Collingwood's comment, related in a manuscript written in 1936, is worth noting to clarify my point:

> St Augustine looked at Roman history from the point of view of an early Christian; Tillemont, from that of a seventeenth-century Frenchman; Gibbon, from that of an eighteenth-century Englishman; Mommsen, from that of a nineteenth-century German. There is no point in asking which was the right point of view. Each was the only one possible for the man who adopted it.[66]

Even if we do not completely agree with Collingwood's conclusion, his basic idea is clear: every generation has its historian, or if you will, its Chronicler!

Conclusion

The literary nature of the book of Chronicles is neither midrash nor commentary nor theology. Therefore, Chr cannot be considered as a 'midrashist' nor commentator nor theologian, as some have done. The literary nature of Chronicles is historiography, and Chr is not simply a 'copyist' but a creative artist, a historian who selected his material from earlier books, reorganizing and editing it in the order, context, and form he found appropriate. He also made connections between the texts; stylized, reshaped, and explained some of them; and harmonized others. Chr also attempted to express his theology and 'philosophy' of history through his composition and so created a literary work that fits well within late biblical historiography.

---

65. See Kalimi, *Geschichtsschreibung*, pp. 127-29, 161-64.

66. This manuscript is quoted by Collingwood's editor, T.M. Knox, in his preface to R.G. Collingwood's *The Idea of History* (London: Oxford University Press, 1946), p. xii.

PART II
ELEMENTS OF THE NARRATIVE

1 CHRONICLES 1–9 AND THE RECONSTRUCTION OF THE HISTORY OF ISRAEL: THOUGHTS ON THE USE OF GENEALOGICAL DATA IN CHRONICLES IN THE RECONSTRUCTION OF THE HISTORY OF ISRAEL

Roddy L. Braun

Introduction

The first point we should note is that the author or authors of 1 Chronicles 1–9 would doubtless have taken exception to the pre-suppositions of the topic as I have framed it. Had he been familiar with our word 'history', he would have protested that what he had written *was* history. Chronicles, together with the genealogical data in Chronicles, *is already a part* of a writing of history. It might not be history as we understand it, or as we would choose to define it. But it is in fact part of a history that is already to a considerable degree a revision of one or several prior histories—a 'revisionist' history, if you will. It is a reminder that what we often mean by the reconstruction of history may be little more than replacing one set of presuppositions with another.

There is a sense in which genealogy, and genealogical records, *are* history. One might argue, for example, that they are history in its purest, most concise form. They are history in outline form. They are history, not just according to the great man theory, but according to the 'every-man' theory. When genealogies are amplified, altered, or abridged, they show the beginnings of what we now think of as historical thinking. They are beginning to interpret the data.

I recall having once argued (unsuccessfully, I believe) that the genealogy at the beginning of Matthew's Gospel should be understood as a kind of historical narrative embodying Israel's history from Abraham to Jesus, because of the phrase 'the book of the genealogy of Jesus Christ...' at the beginning, which recalls the 'these are the generations' (תולדות) of Gen. 2.4 *et al.* I should have supported my argument by calling attention to the inclusion of the four women in Jesus' genealogy, all of less than saintly character. Surely their inclusion was meant to tell a story. Similarly, the construction and division of that genealogy into three segments of fourteen generations indicates that the author wished to give expression to a particular understanding of the course of history.

While some have preferred to question or deny to Chronicles the designation 'history', others are not hesitant to do so. Sara Japhet writes:

> ...Noth (1943) defined Chronicles as a work of history, and studied it along the same guidelines which directed his study of the other comprehensive biblical histories, the Pentateuch and the Deuteronomistic History.[1]

She continues:

> The results of my study bring me closest to the position taken by Noth. A consideration of the work's relevant features, such as aim, plan, form, and method, must lead to the conclusion that Chronicles is a history, an idiosyncratic expression of biblical historiography.... It is a presentation of consequent events, focussed on the fortunes of a collective body, Israel, along a period of time within a defined chronological and territorial setting. The events do not constitute an incidental collection of episodes but are both selected and structured. They are represented in a rational sequence, governed by acknowledged and explicitly formulated principles of cause and effect, and are judged by stringent criteria of historical probability. The Chronicler wrote this history with full awareness of his task, its form and meaning.[2]

The question might remain as to the accuracy, quality, and integrity of that history and of the data that are included within it. But the idea that the scholar could produce a pure, scientific, objective history or report 'events as they really happened' (i.e., events perceived without an interpreter) is in popular disrepute today. In fact, the interpreter of history is seen as so much a part of the event itself that the writing of such a history is sometimes considered impossible.

Nevertheless, the writing of history is based on certain events, 'facts', or 'data' which to our mind's eye correspond to reality. Either X is the father of Y, or he is not the father of Y, as the terms in that

---

1. S. Japhet, *I & II Chronicles* (OTL; Louisville, KY: Westminster/John Knox, 1993), p. 32.
2. Japhet, *I & II Chronicles*, p. 32.

equation are commonly understood. If History A correctly remarks that X is the father of Y, then Historian B can use that same statement with the same meaning in History B and can make logical deductions from that datum in constructing his own historical complex of ideas.

For the purposes of the present essay, we must begin by investigating the accuracy of the data found in the genealogies of 1 Chronicles 1–9 and then proceed to determine their usefulness—and in particular the genealogical information found there—for subsequent historians writing their own histories. In one sense the end of this investigation is quite obvious. The use of genealogies taken from the books of Chronicles in reconstructing history is in general no different than the use of genealogical material from any other source, and the use of genealogical material from Chronicles or elsewhere is no different than the use of any other kind of material in reconstructing history. Thus the conclusion of Wilson is quite apropos:

> All our evidence also indicates that in fact genealogies may contain accurate information and may be potentially valuable sources for the modern historian. In many cases we found agreement in the various versions of a given genealogy and therefore have no reason to question its accuracy... In conclusion, then, we may say that genealogies may be used for historical re[s]earch but that they cannot be used uncritically. Each individual genealogy must be examined, and an attempt made to assess the reliability of each of its components.[3]

Notice that Wilson comments that genealogies '*may contain*' accurate information. But in order to isolate and understand this information correctly, we must apply the same principles of historical and literary criticism to the genealogies and associated materials of Chronicles as we do to other literature. We are thus faced with the basic questions of literary and historical criticism:

1.   What is the nature of the material? Where did it have its origin? What was its *Sitz im Leben?*
2.   What was the history of the material *before* it came into the hands of the present writer? *How* was it handled in stages *before* the current author found it? For what purpose has it been gathered? How might the purpose(s) have influenced the contents of the material transmitted?

---

3.   R.R. Wilson, *Genealogy and History in the Biblical World* (Yale Near Eastern Researches, 7; New Haven, CT: Yale University Press, 1977), p. 200.

3.   How did the author(s) of the document in which the material
     is found deal with the material? What purpose(s) did that
     writer(s) have in transmitting the material?

To these three questions we now turn.

Genealogy: Its Shape and Purpose

The inquiry into the accuracy of the information found in Chr's
genealogies is advanced considerably by arriving at a more precise
understanding of the nature of genealogies in general, and of genealogies in biblical times in particular. What are genealogies like? What
characteristics do they exhibit that would be necessary or helpful for us
to understand if we wish to extrapolate certain 'facts' from them for the
reconstruction of history?

Studies indicate that genealogical information has a special character
and displays unique features that the reader needs to understand as the
data are considered.[4] Here we will only summarize some of the more
relevant points of which the student of Chronicles (and other biblical
genealogies) needs to be aware.

Genealogies are defined as linear (tracing a family line through a
single descendant in each generation) or as segmented (tracing all of the
descendants of a given individual). Linear and segmented genealogies
differ substantially in their functions. The former commonly seeks to
legitimate the position of the last-named person, relating him or her to
an ancestor whose position is accepted as established: hence the various
king lists of the ancient Near East and Old Testament are uniformly
linear in form. The segmented genealogy, on the other hand, has as its
primary function the expression of the relationships existing between
the various branches of individuals named. As such, it points both to a
commonality, in that those named are descended from a single individual, and to a divergence, in that respective branches are derived through
different intermediate ancestors. Johnson points to 1 Chron. 7.20-29 as
an example of confusion arising from the fact that the author understood

---

4.   For details see M.D. Johnson, *The Purpose of the Biblical Genealogies with
Special Reference to the Setting of the Genealogy of Jesus* (SNTSMS, 8; New
York: Cambridge University Press, 1969); and especially Wilson, *Genealogy and
History*.

Numbers 26 to be linear in form rather than segmented.[5]

However, as indicated by Wilson, genealogies may reflect not only blood relationships, but geographical, social, economic, religious, and political realities as well.[6] Genealogies may reflect fluidity, that is, they may change from time to time in response to social changes. Two genealogies may differ, yet each may be correct in that it expresses relationships existing at the time that it describes. Some parts of genealogies may become frozen, after which no significant alteration can occur. An example is the structuring of Israel into twelve tribes, although this may demand the partitioning of Joseph into Ephraim and Manasseh and the inclusion of Simeon after it ceased to exist.[7]

Natural genealogies are rarely more than four or five generations deep. (Most of us know of our grandparents; we may have been informed of our great-grandparents; but it is rare for an individual to recall data beyond that point.)

Finally, the meanings of words in genealogies may diverge from the meanings that we commonly associate with them. Consider, for example, the common words for father and son, which may appear at first to be rather clear in their denotations. However, genealogies may describe a man as the 'father' of a village or of an occupation or trade rather than as the parent of a natural-born son, and in some cases 'son' may be restricted to male descendants, while in others denote children generally, including daughters. In some cases generations may be omitted, so that the relationship really denotes that of grandfather–son rather than father–son.

All of these, and many more features that could be enumerated, raise obvious difficulties for the person who wishes to extrapolate data from a genealogy for purposes of historical reconstruction. It might seem that the difficulties facing one in the use of such data are immense and that many are insuperable. To some extent that is true. There are few controls against which to measure the data. With rare exceptions comparable data are not and will never be available. Nevertheless, it must be said that the genealogies in Chronicles, as stated by Wilson, may be

5.   Johnson, *Purpose*, p. 51; R.L. Braun, *1 Chronicles* (WBC, 14; Waco, TX: Word Books, 1986), p. 2.

6.   Genealogies may be used '...metaphorically to indicate the relationships of individuals and groups in other aspects of social life', R.R. Wilson, 'Genealogy, Genealogies', *ABD* II, p. 931.

7.   Braun, *1 Chronicles*, p. 4.

expected to *contain* accurate and reliable information for historical reconstruction. The careful and honest historian must simply investigate and sift such data with all the tools available and seek to determine how it may best be used. For example, does the genealogy under examination report in precise chronological order the names of family members so that the historian may use this list with the confidence that it accurately reflects biological relationships (i.e., that X is indeed the father of Y)? Alternatively, the scholar may determine that a different reality is reflected in the genealogy, that it preserves, for example, political relationships between neighboring social groups rather than biological relationships among individuals. In yet another instance, it may be that the interpreter determines that the genealogy is wholly the invention of Chr, crafted to advance a certain theological point (e.g., God blessed a family with many descendants because of their faithfulness). In each scenario the genealogy from Chronicles proves useful to the historian's understanding—though in different ways.

Chronicles and Sources

In some cases in Chronicles we can answer initial questions about sources with reasonable certainty. If it is determined that the author(s) took his material from other portions of Scripture,[8] we can say that the one who uses genealogies or genealogical material from Chronicles has an advantage over students of most parts of Scripture. He or she knows at least some of the attitudes of the writer(s) responsible for the current use of these materials and can therefore be alert to ways in which the previous writer(s) might have been interested in utilizing the material available. There remains the prior question, of course, of where the earlier biblical authors found their material. In most cases that information simply is not, and in all likelihood will never be, available to us.

In other cases, the source of Chr's material, either genealogical or otherwise, is simply not known. While references to some such source as 'the books of the kings of...' occur frequently in 2 Chronicles, they appear to be merely adaptations of similar closing formulae from DtrH.[9] As for the material found in Chronicles that has no parallel in

---

8. E.g., J.R. Bartlett, 'The Edomite King-List of Genesis xxxvi. 31-39 and I Chron. I. 43-50', *JTS* NS 16 (1965), pp. 301-14; H.G.M. Williamson, 'A Note on 1 Chronicles VII 12', *VT* 23 (1973), pp. 375-79.

9. On this point, see the recent discussions by Japhet, *I & II Chronicles*,

other biblical books, much of it deals with priests, warfare, or royal building operations, as has often been noted. Could such information then have come from the official archives of the king or of the temple or from some other official or semi-official sources, or might it have been transmitted through oral tradition? Discussion on this point continues, without consensus.[10]

It will become readily apparent that, although the nature of the genealogical material in Chronicles may have distinct qualities, the questions that must be asked about it are no different than those asked about any other material under scholarly examination. They are the primary historical-critical questions.

Genealogies in Chronicles

There is little controversy concerning the general purpose of the genealogies of 1 Chronicles 1–9. Johnson has pointed to no less than nine functions that genealogies serve in the Old Testament. With specific regard to Chronicles, he states:

> Taken as a whole, the Chronicler's genealogical survey of 'all Israel'...
> may be viewed as the attempt to assert the importance of the principle of
> the continuity of the people of God through a period of national
> disruption.[11]

Expressed somewhat differently, and focused more sharply, Weinberg believes that 1 Chronicles 1–9 (and 23–26) '...contains the requisite and decisive foundations of the claims and laws of the postexilic citizen-temple-community'.[12] However, the careful reader will observe

---

pp. 19-23; and W.M. Schniedewind, *The Word of God in Transition: From Prophet to Exegete in the Second Temple Period* (JSOTSup, 197; Sheffield: JSOT Press, 1995), pp. 209-30.

10. See the works cited in n. 9 and in I. Kalimi, *The Books of Chronicles: A Classified Bibliography* (SBB; Jerusalem: Simor, 1990), pp. 77-78.

11. Johnson, *Purpose*, p. 80.

12. '...enthält die notwendigen und ausschlaggebenden Begründungen der Ansprüche und der Rechte der nachexilischen Bürger-Tempel-Gemeinde': J.P. Weinberg, 'Das Wesen und die funktionelle Bestimmung der Listen in I Chr 1-9', *ZAW* 93 (1981), pp. 91-114 (p. 113). Weinberg's sociological analysis has been made far more accessible to English-speaking audiences through the English translations of eight of his essays in *The Citizen–Temple Community* (trans. D.L. Smith-Christopher; JSOTSup 151; Sheffield: JSOT Press, 1992).

with little more than a glance a host of striking features that the genealogies of 1 Chronicles 1–9 exhibit, which affect the understanding of the whole and its various parts. Most obviously, the genealogies are very unequal in their concentration upon the tribes of Judah, Levi, and Benjamin, which formed the nucleus of the restored Judah of post-exilic times. Correspondingly, relatively little attention is paid to the remaining tribes, and in at least one case, the tribe of Dan, either by textual error or perhaps tendentially, the tribe is missing altogether.[13] The focus of the writer(s) who have gathered the data here was reasonably circumscribed.

In Chronicles too we meet cases in which names of people and places seem more-or-less interchangeable (2.42-45) and in which occupational groupings and communities seem coterminous (4.21-23). Each of Hur's three sons, for example, is listed as the father of a well-known city (2.50-52).

Notice also that Chr does not seem to be concerned with providing a complete line of descendants. There are examples of telescoping, as well as the opposite, termed 'lineage growth'.[14] Only nine generations span the period from Judah to David, a number far too small to span the 430 years in Egypt and the 480 years from the Exodus to Solomon.

In addition, one is confronted by obvious cases of doublets and discrepancies that at least suggest to many that one author is not responsible for the total collection. Compare the genealogies of Saul in 8.29-38 and 9.35-44, the double genealogies of Levi (ch. 6) or the divergent names Caleb and Chelubai in 2.18-55; 4.1-7. The Sheshan, who in 2.31 appears as the father of Ahlai, is in v. 34 said to have had no sons. Is it more likely that the original author introduced such a contradiction into his work, or that a later author did so? Examples could be multiplied.

In other instances, Chr's genealogies seem to contradict other biblical material. Compare, for example, the listing of Josiah's sons in 3.15

---

13. A good case can be made that the omission is due to simple textual error. However, the tribe of Dan is also missing in 1 Chron. 6.46, 54 [61, 69], suggesting a tendential omission. G.A. Rendsburg ('The Internal Consistency and Historical Reliability of the Biblical Genealogies', *VT* 40 [1990], pp. 202-203) notes that all six tribes associated with the handmaids of Rachel and Leah and later tribes born to Leah herself are significantly absent from the narrative portions of the Hexateuch, suggesting later accretions. This would certainly include Dan.

14. Rendsburg, 'Internal Consistency', p. 200-201.

with that found in other Old Testament traditions,[15] or the perennial problem of Zerubbabel and Sheshbazzar/Shenazzar (3.17-19; Ezra 1.8, 11).[16] Does this indicate that the forms of the biblical texts available to Chr differed from those available to scholars today or could it have been the case that Chr was not averse to contradicting earlier writings?

There are also cases in which the reading of Chronicles has been influenced for tendentious reasons. Within the genealogy of Judah, for example, David's place has been secured by the inclusion of two genealogical links, neither of which is found in other Old Testament traditions.

> Through the otherwise unknown Ram (2.9-10), a bridge is constructed between Hezron and the age of the Exodus...; through the also unknown Salma a similar linkage is made between Nahshon and the line of Boaz, which concludes with Jesse and David himself (2.10-15).[17]

David is himself named the seventh son of Jesse, while other Old Testament traditions list him as the eighth.[18] Both the Jerahmeelites and the Calebites are connected directly with Judah (2.9). (That this process was not unusual or unique to Chr is apparent from Num. 13.6; 34.39, where P has also made a full-fledged Judahite out of Caleb.) Similarly, Ethan, Heman, Calcol, and Darda are attached to Judahite Zerah (2.5), and Samuel is included in the Levitical genealogy (6.17). A time line is devised so that Zadok is the twelfth priest and that a similar twelve generations extends from Solomon's temple to the priest of the restoration.[19] Finally, it seems clear that Chr has arranged genealogical material by the use of chiasm, concentric ring structure, and other

15. Braun, *1 Chronicles*, p. 51.

16. T.C. Eskenazi, 'Sheshbazzar', *ABD* V, pp. 1207-1209, who points to the current refusal to identify Sheshbazzar with Shenazzar, which occurs only in 1 Chron 3.18, or Zerubbabel.

17. Braun, *1 Chronicles*, pp. 61-62. Cf. also pp. 33-35.

18. Braun, *1 Chronicles*, p. 34. This placement of David lends support to J.M. Sasson's thesis that in the Old Testament 'minimal alterations were made in the inherited lists of ancestors in order to place individuals deemed worthy of attention in the seventh, and, to a much lesser extent, fifth position of a genealogical tree'. 'Genealogical "Convention" in Biblical Chronography', *ZAW* 90 (1978), pp. 171-72. The possibility that the genealogies in Chronicles were influenced by such considerations makes it all the more necessary that the historian proceed with caution in the appropriation of this genealogical material for historical reconstruction.

19. Braun, *1 Chronicles*, p. 86.

literary devices in order to advance certain theological positions regarding the importance of specific persons or groups.[20]

Nevertheless, although no proof of it exists, we may assume that some genealogical information, either accurate or inaccurate, was available to the writer from other sources that are unknown to us. There appears to be no obvious reason, for example, why the writer would have invented the names of various sons of David, since no genealogical connections are then provided through them. As mentioned previously, the many references to warfare within Chr's additions suggest a connection with military records of some sort.

Chronicles and History

The study of Chronicles has often been preoccupied with concern about Chr's reliability as a historian. Japhet is surely correct in her affirmation that the study of Chronicles has for a long time been concentrated upon, if not bogged down in, the question of historical reliability.[21] This may be illustrated abundantly in the case of the genealogical material in Chronicles, where scholars have attempted to restore what is regarded as a corrupt text, acknowledging along the way that 'there may be little that is historical' in the text beyond a few names,[22] or used genealogies to reconstruct the pre-exilic history of Israel and Judah,[23] sometimes in careful coordination with

20. See, e.g., H.G.M. Williamson, 'Sources and Redaction in the Chronicler's Genealogy of Judah', *JBL* 98 (1979), pp. 351-59; and the treatments of the structure of the various genealogies in Chronicles by M. Oeming, *Das wahre Israel: Die 'genealogische Vorhalle' 1 Chronik 1–9* (BWANT, 128; Stuttgart: Kohlhammer, 1990), in which it is argued (chapter 4) that Chr used the genealogies to position Israel at the center of the world.

21. S. Japhet, 'The Historical Reliability of Chronicles: The History of the Problem and its Place in Biblical Research', *JSOT* 33 (1985), pp. 83-107. Cf. also M.P. Graham, *The Utilization of 1 and 2 Chronicles in the Reconstruction of Israelite History in the Nineteenth Century* (SBLDS, 116; Atlanta: Scholars Press, 1990).

22. H.W. Hogg, 'The Genealogy of Benjamin: A Criticism of 1 Chronicles viii', *JQR* 11 (1899), p. 114.

23. M. Noth ('Eine siedlungsgeographische Liste in 1. Chr 2 und 4', *ZDPV* 55 [1932], pp. 97-124), for example, uses Chr's genealogies to argue for the settlement of Judah in areas between the cities of the hill country in Palestine, and D.V. Edelman ('The Asherite Genealogy in 1 Chronicles 7:3-40', *BR* 33 [1988],

archaeological discoveries.[24] In recent years, however, there has been an increasing interest in the message of Chronicles, resulting in something of a flood of articles that seems to have breathed new life into the study of the work.[25]

Developments in the study of Chronicles, as in other biblical books, often proceed simultaneously in different directions. So today one might argue that the fresher study of Chronicles has spilled over into the genealogical sections. Here might be listed most recently the works of Williamson,[26] Rendsburg,[27] and Weinberg,[28] as well as the more extensive studies of Oeming[29] and Kartveit,[30] and in a different sense De Vries[31] and Kegler and Augustin.[32]

In general, these scholars have set about their work heeding the admonition of Wilson quoted above, to review the materials at their disposal critically and hence arrive at what is in their judgment accurate historical data. In fact, Wilson's statement is in large measure a restatement of similar words that can be found in the writings of such distinguished scholars as Albright, Noth, and Rudolph.[33] In sifting through 1 Chronicles 1–9, however, it soon becomes apparent that both wheat

---

pp. 13-23) dates some of Chr's genealogical material concerning Asher to the tenth century, seventh century, and post-exilic period and uses it to reconstruct the political history of the time.

24. In 'The Genealogy of Gibeon (I Chronicles 9:35-44): Biblical and Epigraphic Considerations', *BASOR* 202 (1971), pp. 16-23, A. Demsky attempts to correlate Chr's genealogy of Gibeon with archaeological discoveries (the inscribed jar handles from el-Jib) to illuminate a 'system of administrative record-keeping prevalent in ancient Israel' (p. 23).

25. See the survey in R.L. Braun, 'Martin Noth and the Chronicler's History', in S.L. McKenzie and M.P. Graham (eds.), *The History of Israel's Traditions: The Heritage of Martin Noth* (JSOTSup, 182; Sheffield: JSOT Press, 1994), pp. 63-80, and esp. pp. 70-72.

26. Williamson, 'Sources and Redaction', pp. 351-59.

27. Rendsburg, 'Internal Consistency', pp. 185-206.

28. Weinberg, 'Das Wesen', pp. 91-114.

29. Oeming, *Das wahre Israel*.

30. M. Kartveit, *Motive und Schichten der Landtheologie in 1 Chronik 1–9* (ConBOT, 28; Stockholm: Almqvist & Wiksell, 1989).

31. S.J. De Vries, *1 and 2 Chronicles* (FOTL, 11; Grand Rapids, MI: Eerdmans, 1989).

32. J. Kegler and M. Augustin, *Synopse zum chronistischen Geschichtswerk* (BEATAJ, 1; Frankfurt am Main: Peter Lang, 2nd edn, 1991), pp. 27-62.

33. See Japhet, 'Reliability', pp. 93-97 and associated notes.

and chaff are to be found there, and the sifting and separation of the two is an exceedingly difficult task. All seem to begin, as does Wilson, with the presupposition that at least some historically accurate material is to be found in Chronicles. To seek to validate that position in any given case, however, is extremely difficult in the face of a general lack of evidence, and the matter is complicated further by the fact that the historian may be tempted to use (or reject) data from Chr's genealogies as it suits (or contradicts) the argument being advanced.

Albright, as noted by Japhet,[34] anticipated the support of archaeological materials to shore up biblical history. In the eyes of some, significant advances have been made there. By any accounting, however, advances have been few, and the conclusions drawn disparate. One need only consider, for example, the different use of data from Chronicles in the histories of Noth and Bright.[35]

Critical studies continue to bear witness to the mixed nature of the material. While Rendsburg, for example, seeks to affirm the reliability of the various genealogies by observing that 'All the characters whose lives are depicted in Exodus through Joshua as being coeval with those of Moses and Aaron, and for whom we have genealogies, are three, four, five, or six generations removed from their tribal fathers',[36] he then must exclude Joshua from that observation and notes that both Samuel and Zadok have been given a Levitical genealogy.[37] Moreover, it might appear to some that the difference between three and six generations is not insubstantial. Rendsburg expresses concern that his work may be considered uncritical, but in fact what he affirms is quite critical. Parts of various genealogies are labeled 'suspect and partly artificial', and it is said that 'Zadok's genealogy may be accurate to some extent' and 'There is a large amount of evidence pointing to the unreliability of the Chronicles material especially.'[38]

J.P. Weinberg's thorough study concludes that the materials of 1 Chronicles 1–9 stem primarily from the pre-exilic period and that Chr

---

34. Japhet, 'Reliability', pp. 94-95. See, also, nn. 23 and 24 above.

35. The index to M. Noth's *The History of Israel* (New York: Harper & Row, 2nd edn, 1960) cites twenty-seven texts from 1 and 2 Chronicles, while J. Bright's *A History of Israel* (Philadelphia: Westminster, 3rd edn, 1981) cites eighty-three and makes far greater use of them for the reconstruction of Israel's pre-exilic history.

36. Rendsburg, 'Internal Consistency', p. 189.

37. Rendsburg, 'Internal Consistency', pp. 195-99.

38. Rendsburg, 'Internal Consistency', pp. 197-99.

had four types (*Gattungen*) of pre-exilic texts: '...the registers of officials and mobilization lists, both deriving from the state-temple administration, as well as the "clan tales" and genealogies rooted in the tribal-clan tradition'.[39] That is indeed to say something of the potential value of the material in an independent sense. It is at the same time not to go far beyond the position of W. Rudolph:

> Specifically, those particular reports in which no influence of the key ideas of the Chronicler can be recognized deserve our full confidence and constitute a welcome supplement to our knowledge; yet even where that influence is indeed evident, we are not exempt from examining whether the Chronicler did not make genuine events the bearers of his theological views, even when these [events] are not known to us from another quarter....[40]

That is to say, as I understand it, that while the information itself may be accurate, it may have been placed in its present context by Chr to give expression to his own purposes.

It is obvious then that concern about historical accuracy remains paramount. The end of Japhet's article, which is a kind of epilogue, indicates that interest in substantiating the historical reliability of Chronicles continues to exercise many. That obviously includes Japhet herself, for she then evaluates negatively the conclusions arrived at by Welten (whose methods and conclusions Japhet associates with Torrey!), R. North, and R.W. Klein and expresses concern about this 'new skepticism'.[41] North should probably be considered representative of a previous day of Chronicles study (cf. his commentary on Chronicles,[42] which dates from the 1960s and reflects a failure to appreciate the books on any level). Welten is criticized for failing to

39. '...die der Staats-Tempel-Administration entstammenden Beamten-verzeichnisse und Mobilmachungslisten und die in der Stämme-Sippen-Tradition wurzelnden "Sippensagen" und Genealogien': Weinberg, 'Das Wesen', p.113.

40. 'Namentlich Nachrichten, bei denen keine Einwirkung der chronistischen Leitgedanken zu erkennen ist, verdienen volles Zutrauen und bilden eine Willkommene Ergänzung unseres Wissens, aber selbst da, wo jene Einwirkung zu spüren ist, sind wir nicht der Prüfung überhoben, ob der Chronist nicht echte Ereignisse zu Trägern seiner theologischen Anschauungen macht, auch wenn uns diese anderweitig nicht bekannt sind...': Rudolph, *Chronikbücher* (HAT, 21; Tübingen: Mohr [Paul Siebeck], 1955), p. xvii.

41. Japhet, 'Reliability', pp. 98-99.

42. R. North, '1-2 Chronicles', in R.E. Brown *et al.* (eds.), *The Jerome Biblical Commentary* (Englewood Cliffs, NJ: Prentice-Hall, 1968), pp. 402-38.

find a significant contribution in Chronicles to the history of the monarchical period, and Klein's study of Abijah likewise concluded that
Chr's sources were biblical and nothing more.

It is clear then that the introductory chapters of Chronicles *are* useful
for historical reconstruction. What is not so clear, however, is *how* this
material is useful to the historian (e.g., for the reconstruction of biological, political, or other sorts of relationships or for other purposes). This
determination, my study suggests, will have to be worked out independently for each piece of genealogical material that is examined.
Moreover, a certain amount of humility will be in order for the interpreters, since just as Chr's circumstances and biases influenced the
construction of his work, so these same factors affect the work of
historians today.

NON-SYNOPTIC CHRONOLOGICAL REFERENCES
IN THE BOOKS OF CHRONICLES

William H. Barnes

Previous Treatments of Chronological Data in Chronicles

Interest in the historical accuracy of the various independent traditions in the books of Chronicles (i.e., those found in the portions of Chronicles that are non-synoptic with Samuel–Kings) has been on the increase over at least the last half-century. This is certainly true, for example, in the area of chronological data. In 1945, W.F. Albright published his influential chronology of the kings of the divided monarchy of Israel,[1] in which he relied heavily upon the chronological data in 1 and 2 Chronicles that are independent of the Deuteronomistic material. As he remarked in his prefatory comments to the study:

> In view of the fact that Chronicles contains a considerable amount of original material dealing with the history of Judah which is not found in Kings and that the historical value of this original material is being established by archaeological discoveries, we have no right to disregard the datings by regnal years of the kings of Judah which we find there, especially when they are as consistent and reasonable as, e.g., in the case of Asa.[2]

Indeed, it is these same data, especially the synchronism found in 2 Chron. 16.1 MT, indicating that Baasha was still king of Israel in the thirty-sixth year of Asa, which Albright used as major support for his reduction of the Deuteronomistic regnal totals for a number of Israelite and Judahite kings. As he argued:

1.   'The Chronology of the Divided Monarchy of Israel', *BASOR* 100 (1945), pp. 16-22.
2.   'Chronology', pp. 18-19. The references in question are found in 2 Chron. 15.10, 19; 16.1, 12, 13.

The tendency of ancient chronological numbers to increase with time is very well known; it is unfair, however, to the ancient scholar and scribe not to recognize that it was usually influenced (and often caused) by their efforts to do justice to variants by including them in a new total, either by direct addition or by selecting the higher of any two alternatives.[3]

One significant conclusion resulting from this analysis is Albright's reduction of the years of reign of Rehoboam from seventeen to eight, and his strikingly low date of 922 BCE for the disruption of the united monarchy of Israel.

Another influential chronologist first writing in the 1940s, E.R. Thiele,[4] agreed that Chr's chronological references for Asa were historically significant, but Thiele argued that they actually referred to the years since the disruption of the united monarchy. Only by such an interpretation could these references be harmonized with the regnal totals transmitted in the books of Kings. However, as Albright pointed out in his review of Thiele's book, the disruption of the united monarchy is not otherwise attested as an era of chronological reckoning:

> [I]t is difficult to accept Thiele's involved efforts to show that my original argument for cutting off a decade (or slightly less) from the reign of Rehoboam was wrong...My argument is based on the confrontation of the numbers of Kings with the detailed list of years from Asa's reign, given in II Chron. 15-16, where there are five such dates (fifteenth, thirty-fifth, thirty-sixth, thirty-ninth, and forty-first), all consistent with one another and, if correct, quite at variance with the data in Kings. Thiele does not refer to these dates at all except in polemic with me, and here he proposes attributing them to two different frames, the accession of Asa and the Disruption of the Kingdom (not otherwise recorded as an era).[5]

---

3. 'Chronology', p. 19 n. 12. For an extended analysis of Albright's chronological methods and conclusions, see my *Studies in the Chronology of the Divided Monarchy of Israel* (HSM, 48; Atlanta: Scholars Press, 1991), pp. 4-11.

4. E.R. Thiele first published his chronological work as, 'The Chronology of the Kings of Judah and Israel', *JNES* 3 (1944), pp. 137-86; but it is not until his publication of the first edition of his *Mysterious Numbers of the Hebrew Kings: A Reconstruction of the Chronology of the Kingdom of Israel and Judah* (Chicago: University of Chicago Press, 1951) that his reconstruction concerning 1 Chron. 15.19 and 16.1 is to be found (see pp. 58-59 of the latter work).

5. Albright's review of E.R. Thiele's *Mysterious Numbers of the Hebrew Kings* appeared as 'Alternative Chronology', *Int* 6 (1952), pp. 101-103; the quote is from p. 103.

In 1953, F.M. Cross and D.N. Freedman also drew attention to the independent chronological data in the books of Chronicles, this time in regard to Josiah.[6] Noting the correspondence between the weakening of Assyrian authority after the death of Asshurbanipal in ca. 633 and the strengthening of the Josianic kingdom, they cited Chr's data in 2 Chron. 34.1-7 as attesting independently the results of such Assyrian weakness for the vassal state of Judah. More specifically, they pointed out that in v. 3 Josiah is said in his eighth year to have begun 'to seek the God of his ancestor David', implying thus his repudiation of the gods of the Assyrian overlords immediately following the death of Asshurbanipal (according to the chronological reconstruction of W.H. Dubberstein).[7] Also in v. 3 is the notice that in his twelfth year Josiah began to undertake reform of the Judahite cultus (in clear contrast to the Deuteronomistic account in Kings, which dates all such reform to Josiah's eighteenth year). Of particular interest is the notice in v. 6 about cult reform in the northern provinces, which were nominally under Assyrian control. After discussing the extent of the reform in the north, the authors pointed out:

> Whether Josiah's action is taken as an open break with Assyrian authority or, as seems more likely, as an internal reorganization within the framework of nominal Assyrian suzerainty (i.e., maintaining the legal fiction of Assyrian control, since Josiah was a vassal king), it is clear that a drastic change in the Palestinian situation had taken place. Assyria was losing effective control both of Judah and of the northern provinces; at the same time Josiah was making good the ancient claim of the house of David to these territories.[8]

Finally, after noting the apparent correspondence of the death of Asshurbanipal to the eighth year of Josiah, Cross and Freedman concluded,

> Thus the Chronicler records a progressive sequence of moves for religious—and therefore political—independence in Judah in the years 632, 628, and 622 BC... It may be, of course, that the Chronicler's dates

---

6. F.M. Cross and D.N. Freedman, 'Josiah's Revolt against Assyria', *JNES* 12 (1953), pp. 56-58.

7. That is, 633 BCE; more recently, the probable dating of Asshurbanipal's death has been lowered to 627, according to R.B. Dillard, *2 Chronicles* (WBC, 15; Waco, TX: Word Books, 1987), p. 276, citing J. Oates, 'Assyrian Chronology', *Iraq* 27 (1965), pp. 135-59.

8. Cross and Freedman, 'Josiah's Revolt', p. 57.

are unreliable or have no political significance... Tentatively, however,
the suggested synchronisms tend to confirm both the sequence of events
in Judah and the proposed chronology for the last kings of Assyria.[9]

Such positive appraisals of the historicity of the independent
chronological data found in the books of Chronicles have not met with
universal acceptance, of course. The recent article by Mordechai
Cogan,[10] for example, has focused upon the chronological data in
regard to David's transfer of the ark to Jerusalem (1 Chron.
11–16), Hezekiah's reform (e.g., 2 Chron. 29.3), Josiah's reform (2 Chron.
34.1-8), and the use of 'three years' as a 'typological period' in both
Kings and Chronicles. All these independent chronological references
in Chronicles he characterized as 'pseudo-dating', and he compared
them to the Babylonian Inscription of Esarhaddon, which in the
colophons of all eight extant recensions bear one and the same
impossible date: *šanat rēš šarrūti Aššur-ahu-iddina šar māt Aššur*, 'the
accession year of Esarhaddon, king of Assyria'.[11] As he noted:

> Thus, according to this colophon date, the inscriptions themselves and
> the events they describe are attributed to Esarhaddon's accession year.
> But from what we know about this time period, this date is incon-
> ceivable. The events which surrounded Esarhaddon's rise to the throne—
> the assassination of Sennacherib and the civil war waged against
> Esarhaddon by rival brothers—marked his *rēš šarrūti* as one of much
> turmoil, hardly a time for construction at Babylon on the scale described
> in our inscription...[12]

9. 'Josiah's Revolt', pp. 57-58. J.M. Myers (*2 Chronicles* [AB, 13; Garden
City, NY: Doubleday, 1965], pp. 205-206) accepted Cross and Freedman's historical reconstruction with marked enthusiasm. In addition, both J. Bright (*History of
Israel* [Philadelphia: Westminster, 3rd edn, 1981], pp. 317-18) and S. Herrmann (*A
History of Israel in Old Testament Times* [Philadelphia: Fortress, rev. edn, 1981],
p. 266; see esp. p. 272, n. 4) took seriously Chr's description of an extended period
of time for Josiah's reform. As Bright pointed out, 'the very fact that the Temple
was being repaired when the lawbook was found [in Josiah's eighteenth year]
indicates that reform was already in progress, for the repairing and purification of
the Temple was itself a reform measure' (*History of Israel*, p. 318).

10. 'The Chronicler's Use of Chronology as Illuminated by Neo-Assyrian
Royal Inscriptions', in J.H. Tigay (ed.), *Empirical Models for Biblical Criticism*
(Philadelphia: University of Pennsylvania Press, 1985), pp. 197-209.

11. 'Chronicler's Use of Chronology', p. 200.

12. 'Chronicler's Use of Chronology', Cogan goes on to calculate that
Esarhaddon's *rēš šarrūti* actually lasted only some 22 days!

He then concluded:

> The date in the *Babylonian Inscription* is obviously a pseudo-date, and in
> an inscription we suspect was reedited several times over a span of five
> to six years the utilization of this pseudo-date would seem to have been
> purposeful. It is not hard to suggest the rationale behind this antedating...
> The *rēš šarrūti* date served as testimony to Esarhaddon's early concern
> for Babylon. It was as if to say: From his very first days on the throne,
> the Assyrian monarch, encouraged and supported by the god Marduk,
> turned to the affairs of his lord's city, 'the city (from which) the gods
> supervise the fate (of mankind).' As the inscription was revised over the
> years, all progress on the reconstruction of Babylon which had taken
> place in the intervening years was similarly credited to the accession
> year.[13]

Turning to the Hebrew Bible, Cogan noted the parallel between this
Babylonian 'pseudo-date' and Chr's dating of the reform of Hezekiah
to the first year of his reign (e.g., 2 Chron. 29.3). As he pointed out, no
matter which date one accepts for the accession of Hezekiah,[14] one
cannot coordinate Chr's reform date with what we know about the
events of the late eighth century BCE. Acceptance of the early date (ca.
727), prior to the Assyrian conquest of the northern kingdom of Israel,
leads to difficulties with Chr's subsequent description of Hezekiah's
invitation to the northerners (described in 30.6 as 'the remnant who
escaped out of the hands of the kings of Assyria') to participate in the
celebrations in Jerusalem. But acceptance of the late date (ca. 715)
leads to the necessity of assuming that the invitation to the Israelites of
what is now the Assyrian province of Samaria must have taken place
while the Assyrian authorities were otherwise preoccupied. Cogan therefore rejected both of these options, characterizing Chr's date of 'the
first year of his reign in the first month' as a 'pseudo-date': 'This was
simply the Chronicler's way of saying: The pious Hezekiah concerned
himself with Temple affairs from his very first day on the throne.'[15]

Cogan also suggested that the Josianic account in 2 Chronicles 34 is
likewise suspect. As he argued:

> The neat progression of events and its very rationality raise the suspicion
> that the Chronicler has ordered his data to conform to his conceptions of

13. 'Chronicler's Use of Chronology', p. 201.
14. A vexed issue in and of itself, of course. For an introduction to the
controversy surrounding this issue, see my *Studies in the Chronology*, pp. 73-124.
15. Cogan, 'Chronicler's Use of Chronology', pp. 202-203.

royal piety. Its effect is to have Josiah undertake the reform as soon as he was able to act on his own... The pious king knew from previous exposure to the Lord since age sixteen what was pleasing to Him. By age twenty-six—the age at which Kings has the whole reform take place and six years into Josiah's majority—there was nothing left to do but repair the Temple and learn of the Torah book, whose demands Josiah had already fulfilled. The schematic nature of the Chronicler's chronology and its historiographic underpinnings are readily discernible: they are designed to show the earliness and self-motivation of the king's piety.[16]

As already noted, Cogan also examined Chr's arrangement of the various episodes describing David's transfer of the ark to Jerusalem. Again he concluded that, like the Ninevite scribes in their editing of Assyrian historiographical traditions, Chr saw fit to rearrange the order of presentation to obtain the desired message: 'Care for the Jerusalem cult precedes one's personal desires and ambition. Unattended during Saul's reign, the Ark is taken up by David to his new capital as the first royal act. David's exemplary behavior set the standard by which all future monarchs would be measured.'[17]

Lastly, in regard to the issues of 'three years' as a typological period, that is, 'the end point or the completion of a short span of time', Cogan noted one occasion where Chr did *not* take seriously such a phrase in his Deuteronomistic source. In 1 Kgs 22.1-2, we read of 'three years' of peace between Israel and Aram, followed by Jehoshaphat entering into coalition with Ahab 'in the third year'. But in the closely parallel account in 2 Chronicles 18, we find only the vague reference in v. 2 to 'after some years', or as Cogan preferred to translate, 'toward the end of [Jehoshaphat's] reign'. Cogan argued that Chr's substitution demonstrates his (correct) realization that the references in Kings probably had no chronological significance even for the original Deuteronomistic audience.[18]

16. 'Chronicler's Use of Chronology', pp. 204-205. Cogan cites Tigay's observation that Chr's placement of the reform before the discovery of the Torah book leads to the following incongruity: 'the sudden recognition of guilt which the book prompts is pointless: the sins mentioned by the book had been abolished six years earlier' (p. 204, n. 30).

17. 'Chronicler's Use of Chronology', pp. 206-207. Similarly, Cogan, following Mazar, did not place much confidence in 2 Samuel's order of presentation of the events comprising David's early rule.

18. 'Chronicler's Use of Chronology', p. 207. Cogan also cited two places where Chr in non-synoptic texts (i.e., texts not paralleled in Kings) uses the phrase

Cogan later summarized the results of his study as follows:

> As we compare the dates and order of events in ancient texts, either with
> the sources of those texts or with other information about the events
> themselves, we observe that dates and order were on occasion used as
> literary devices rather than precise historical data. Chronologies were
> malleable.[19]

Toward a New Analysis of Chronological Data in Chronicles

In light of these different appraisals of the historical accuracy of the
non-synoptic chronological notices found in the books of Chronicles, a
re-examination of all such data seems to be in order. Any would-be
historian of the ancient Near East would not wish to ignore or discount
any possible source for the existence of firm chronological data about
the often murky world of the divided monarchy of Israel, but still less
would she or he wish to appropriate uncritically chronological notices
that are intended primarily to further the political/theological agenda of
Chr rather than to represent the precise historical situation under
discussion. I propose, therefore, in the balance of this study to examine
each of the approximately 30 examples of non-synoptic chronological
notices in the books of 1 and 2 Chronicles in some depth, noting especially the likelihood of their historical accuracy and then concluding
with a brief summary concerning the use of such data for historical
reconstruction. My efforts will be comprehensive, erring perhaps on the
side of pedantic completeness rather than that of pithy succinctness.
The necessary corollary of such comprehensiveness—tedium—will be
mitigated somewhat by the list-like nature of the enterprise, allowing
the researcher to skip over material of little relevance to his or her task
at hand and focus on areas of more immediate concern.

At the outset of this study, however, something must be said about
the 'synoptic' chronological data found in the books of Chronicles, that
is, those that find their direct counterparts in Samuel–Kings. The following chart provides a simple table of correspondences between
chronological notices found in the DtrH and their parallels in the books
of Chronicles. As is usual practice in commentaries on Chronicles,
reference should be made to these parallels in the commentaries of

---

'three/third year(s)'—in 2 Chron. 11.7 and in 17.7—both of which are usually
taken to be creations of Chr and probably not chronologically precise.

19. 'Chronicler's Use of Chronology', p. 208.

Samuel–Kings, where discussions concerning the historical background and accuracy of the chronological notice in question may be found. As is well known, for example, the issues concerning the accuracy of the various synchronisms and regnal totals found in the DtrH are far from settled,[20] and in any case, it will be obvious that we cannot be detained here by such matters. I have noted several important literary and/or textual variants between Chronicles and Samuel–Kings in the chart, but in none of the instances do I find the Chronicles' synoptic variant of significant textual or historical value.[21]

Synoptic Parallels to Chronological References in 1 and 2 Chronicles

Reference in 1 and 2 Chronicles	Parallel reference(s) in Samuel–Kings (and elsewhere)[22]
1 Chron. 3.4—[David] reigned in Hebron 7 years and 6 months	2 Sam. 5.5
1 Chron. 29.27—[David] reigned over Israel 40 years; 7 years in Hebron, and 33 years in Jerusalem	1 Kgs 2.11
2 Chron. 3.2—[Solomon] began to build [the Temple] on the (second day [?] of the) second month of the fourth year of his reign[23]	1 Kgs 6.1 (?); the parallel is close but inexact

20. Again, I offer my *Studies in the Chronology* as a recent orientation to this murky subject.

21. The rather transparent nature of the textual variations found between Chronicles and Samuel–Kings supports Albright's observation: 'Once the numbers [i.e., the regnal totals of the kings of Judah and of Israel] were included in the text of the great work of the Deuteronomist, they were transmitted by copyists with astonishing accuracy, as proved by confrontation of the versions' ('Chronology', p. 19, n. 12).

22. For the sake of completeness, the last chronological datum in Chronicles (2 Chron. 36.22 [= Ezra 1.1]), which formally qualifies as a synoptic chronological notice, could have been included in the chart, but this would raise the issue of the relationship of Chronicles to the book(s) of Ezra–Nehemiah—an issue currently quite unsettled in contemporary scholarship, and one that is not critical for the present study (cf. my brief comments below). All chronological data with reasonably close parallels to Samuel–Kings are nonetheless included in the chart.

23. MT is difficult; the phrase בשני השני is probably a dittography (cf. *BHS* note). In any case, the Kings text makes reference only to the second month of the fourth year.

Reference	Parallel
2 Chron. 8.1—at end of 20 years during which Solomon had built the house of Yahweh and his own house...[24]	1 Kgs 9.10
2 Chron. 9.30—Solomon reigned in Jerusalem over all Israel 40 years	1 Kgs 11.42, with somewhat different wording
2 Chron. 12.2—in the fifth year of King Rehoboam... Shishak king of Egypt came up against Jerusalem	1 Kgs 14.25
2 Chron. 12.13—Rehoboam was 41 years old when he began to reign; he reigned 17 years in Jerusalem[25]	1 Kgs 14.21
2 Chron. 13.1-2—In the eighteenth year of King Jeroboam,[26] Abijah (Abijam)[27] began to reign over Jerusalem. He reigned for 3 years in Jerusalem...	1 Kgs 15.1-2[28]
2 Chron. 20.31—[Jehoshaphat] was 35 years old when he began to reign; he reigned 25 years in Jerusalem	1 Kgs 22.42
2 Chron. 21.5—Jehoram was 32 years old when he began to reign; he reigned 8 years in Jerusalem[29]	2 Kgs 8.17

24. In Chronicles the cities are given to Solomon *by* Huram (Hiram), king of Tyre, whereas in the Kings parallel Solomon gives the cities *to* Hiram. For a convincing solution to this discrepancy, see H.G.M. Williamson, *1 and 2 Chronicles* (NCB; Grand Rapids, MI: Eerdmans, 1982), pp. 227-29, who suggests that Chr's *Vorlage* was corrupt at this point.

25. The Kings parallel is quite close (including a reference to the queen mother), but the location of this regnal notice in Chronicles is unexpected and probably secondary (i.e., moved by Chr to its present location). Cf. Williamson, *Chronicles*, pp. 248-49.

26. This is the only example in Chronicles of the characteristic Deuteronomistic synchronisms found throughout 1 and 2 Kings.

27. Alternative names in parentheses represent the version found in the Kings parallel(s).

28. This is one of only three examples in Kings of a Judahite regnal formula without the age at accession given (the others are for Solomon [1 Kgs 11.42] and for Asa [1 Kgs 15.10]). Chr's (somewhat inexact) parallel for Solomon's regnal formula is in 2 Chron. 9.30, as already noted (see above); there is no parallel at all in Chronicles for Asa's regnal formula.

29. Curiously, this regnal formula is repeated almost exactly in v. 20, perhaps as part of a palistrophe. Cf. Dillard, *2 Chronicles*, p. 164; and n. 34 below.

Reference	Parallel
2 Chron. 21.8—In [Jehoram's (Joram's)] days Edom revolted from the rule of Judah, and set up a king of their own	2 Kgs 8.20
2 Chron. 22.2—Ahaziah was 42 [*sic*][30] years old when he began to reign; he reigned 1 year in Jerusalem.	2 Kgs 8.26
2 Chron. 22.12–23.1—Joash hidden for 6 years...in the seventh year Jehoiada took courage...	2 Kgs 11.3-4
2 Chron. 24.1—Joash (Jehoash) was 7 years old when he began to reign; he reigned 40 years in Jerusalem	2 Kgs 12.1-2 [EVV 11.21–12.1]
2 Chron. 25.1—Amaziah was 25 years old when he began to reign; he reigned 29 years in Jerusalem.	2 Kgs 14.2
2 Chron. 25.25—Amaziah...lived 15 years after the death of King Joash (Jehoash) son of Jehoahaz of Israel	2 Kgs 14.17
2 Chron. 26.1—the people...took Uzziah (Azariah), who was 16 years old, and made him king...	2 Kgs 14.21
2 Chron. 26.3—Uzziah (Azariah) was 16 years old when he began to reign, and he reigned 52 years in Jerusalem	2 Kgs 15.2
2 Chron. 27.1—Jotham was 25 years old when he began to reign; he reigned 16 years in Jerusalem[31]	2 Kgs 15.33
2 Chron. 28.1—Ahaz was 20 years old when he began to reign; he reigned 16 years in Jerusalem	2 Kgs 16.2
2 Chron. 29.1—Hezekiah began to reign when he was 25 years old;[32] he reigned 29 years in Jerusalem	2 Kgs 18.2, slightly modified

30. Kings reads '22', a far more plausible figure. As Williamson (*Chronicles*, p. 310) pointed out, Chr's figure would make Ahaziah older than his father! Myers (*2 Chronicles*, p. 125) suggested that the '42' of MT for this verse may represent a conflation of two different traditions (the '20' attested in the major LXX mss. for this verse, plus the '22' of the Kings passage). He then argued that 'originally the numbers were kept separate, e.g., 22 or 20, and only later added together.' Cf. also the comments of Albright, as cited above in the first section of the present study, concerning such scribal practices.

31. Again, there is a curious repetition of this regnal formula in v. 8 (cf. above, n. 29, with regard to Jehoram; see also n. 34 below). In neither case is the regnal formula so repeated in the parallel texts in Kings.

32. The syntax of this first part of the regnal formula (the age at accession) in Chronicles differs somewhat from its parallel in Kings, but there is no compelling reason to see Chr's version as original; it diverges syntactically from the regular

Reference	*Parallel*
2 Chron. 32.24—In those days Hezekiah became sick and was at the point of death	2 Kgs 20.1; also Isa. 38.1
2 Chron. 33.1—Manasseh was 12 years old when he began to reign; he reigned 55 years in Jerusalem[33]	2 Kgs 21.1
2 Chron. 33.21—Amon was 22 years old when he began to reign; he reigned 2 years in Jerusalem	2 Kgs 21.19
2 Chron. 34.1—Josiah was 8 years old when he began to reign; he reigned 31 years in Jerusalem	2 Kgs 22.1
2 Chron. 34.8—In the eighteenth year of [Josiah's] reign...he sent Shaphan son of Azaliah [etc.]...to repair the house of Yahweh his God	2 Kgs 22.3, with somewhat different wording
2 Chron. 35.19—In the eighteenth year of the reign of Josiah this passover was kept[34]	2 Kgs 23.23
2 Chron. 36.2—Jehoahaz was 23 years old when he began to reign; he reigned 3 months in Jerusalem	2 Kgs 23.31
2 Chron. 36.5—Jehoiakim was 25 years old when he began to reign; he reigned 11 years in Jerusalem	2 Kgs 23.36

Judahite formula as found in Kings, but elsewhere Chr also alters his text quite freely as well (note that the rest of the chapter is virtually totally independent of Kings).

33. Interestingly, from this point on there are no queen mothers listed in the regnal formulas found in Chronicles (i.e., for Manasseh, Amon, Josiah, Jehoahaz, Jehoiakim, Jehoiachin, or Zedekiah), even though in every case the name of the queen mother is found in the otherwise closely paralleled regnal formula in Kings. As S.L. McKenzie has argued (following the observations of H.R. Macy, 'The Sources of the Books of Chronicles: A Reassessment' [PhD dissertation, Harvard University, 1975]), the shift here is not evidently tendentious and may simply represent a change in Chr's source for the regnal formulae for these kings: *The Chronicler's Use of the Deuteronomistic History* (HSM, 33; Atlanta: Scholars Press, 1985), pp. 174-75. Cf. my discussion in *Studies in the Chronology*, pp. 141-42; also Dillard, *2 Chronicles*, p. 267.

34. This is now the third time that Chr has designated a Judahite king with a double date formula (cf. 2 Chron. 21.5, 20 for Jehoram, and 2 Chron. 27.1, 8 for Jotham). It hardly seems coincidental that Chr does this for every fifth king after the disruption of the united monarchy (cf. my *Studies in the Chronology*, pp. 142-44). To be sure, as noted in the present chart, Chr's double date formula for Josiah is closely paralleled in Kings and most probably finds its origin there.

Reference	*Parallel*
2 Chron. 36.9—Jehoiachin was 8 [*sic*] years old when he began to reign; he reigned 3 months and 10 days in Jerusalem[35]	2 Kgs 24.8
2 Chron. 36.11—Zedekiah was 21 years old when he began to reign; he reigned 11 years in Jerusalem	2 Kgs 24.18; also Jer. 52.1

Analysis of Non-Synoptic Chronological Data in Chronicles

The following analysis of the approximately 30 'non-synoptic' chronological references in the books of 1 and 2 Chronicles represents the heart of the present study. The references will be arranged in strictly numerical order, grouped under the heading of the appropriate Judahite monarch (alternate names represent the name of the monarch as found in Kings). Although relevant textual analysis will be included as appropriate, the major emphasis of the present analysis will be on literary and historical issues.

David (1 Chronicles 26.31)

The chronological datum found in 26.31 ('In the fortieth year of David's reign search was made, of whatever genealogy or family...'), as well as its larger context (1 Chron. 22.2–29.22a), finds no parallel in the Deuteronomistic literature. The notice of the 'fortieth year' agrees, of course, with the final year of David's reign according to the standard Deuteronomistic regnal formulae (2 Sam. 5.4; cf. 2 Kgs 2.11); the so-called throne succession narrative (2 Sam. 9–20; 1 Kgs 1–2), however, pictures David as evidently quite senile and impotent just before his death (even earlier, if a brief co-regency with his son Solomon is posited). Nonetheless, it is the contention of a number of commentators[36] that this chronological notice may well afford independent evidence as to the minimum length of David's reign. As Myers pointed

---

35. The parallel passage in Kings reads the more plausible 18 years old at the age of accession and a reign of thee months (and no extra days) for Jehoiachin; cf. the textual notes in *BHS* for this verse. Williamson (*Chronicles*, p. 414) characterized the age at accession in Chronicles as the result of a simple scribal error and the regnal total as arising by mistake from a marginal correction of the previous error (cf. also Dillard's textual note and bibliographic citation for the verse [*2 Chronicles*, p. 296, n. 9a, b]).

36. E.g., J.M. Myers, *1 Chronicles* (AB, 12; Garden City, NY: Doubleday, 1965), p. 181; cf. Williamson, *Chronicles*, p. 173.

out, 'This is an interesting reference to the length of his [i.e., David's] reign because it tends to confirm it and points to its correctness, since nothing is served by such a reference.'[37]

Solomon
There are no non-synoptic references.

Rehoboam (2 Chronicles 11.17)
Here we are told that for the first three years of Rehoboam's reign, the priests, Levites, and people from all Israel came to Judah and Jerusalem, making Rehoboam 'secure' for three years, since they 'walked for three years in the way of David and Solomon'. 2 Chron. 11.5-23 is independent of Kings and replete with vocabulary and themes typical of Chr.[38] Verses 5-12 employ one of Chr's favorite themes—building projects as an indication of the prosperity that results from obedience to God; vv. 13-17 emphasize the faithfulness of the religious leaders of all Israel (another favorite theme of Chr), even in the light of Jeroboam's apostasy in the north; and vv. 18-23 discuss Rehoboam's large family, again a sign of blessing. It is not until ch. 12 that Rehoboam is cast in a negative light: his cultic unfaithfulness (12.1) immediately, as it were, leading to disaster (12.2; note that this verse is identical to 1 Kgs 14.25, except for the additional phrase, 'because they had been unfaithful to Yahweh'). Chr's theology of 'immediate retribution' is here well illustrated.[39] As Williamson characterized this section, the writer has 'moulded' his material in order to illustrate the effects, first of unfaithfulness (12.1-11), then of repentance (12.12), all framed in vocabulary characteristic of Chr.[40]

It is in light of this analysis that Williamson's characterization of 11.17 seems apropos: he suggested that the twice-repeated phrase 'for three years' was deduced from 12.1-2, 'which was taken to imply that Rehoboam "forsook the law" in his fourth year'.[41] Again the theology of immediate retribution is to be found: three years of blessing, one year

37. *1 Chronicles*, p. 181.

38. See Williamson, *Chronicles*, pp. 240-45.

39. Williamson, *Chronicles,* p. 245; cf. R.B. Dillard, 'The Reign of Asa (2 Chronicles 14-16): An Example of the Chronicler's Theological Method', *JETS* 23 (1980), pp. 207-18, esp. pp. 208-10.

40. *Chronicles*, p. 245.

41. Williamson, *Chronicles*, p. 244.

of unfaithfulness, and in the very next year (12.2 = 1 Kgs 14.25), military disaster. As Dillard[42] phrased it, one should note the sequence of 'righteousness–blessing, sin–disaster, repentance–restoration' that Chr employs, as well as his introduction of 'a chronological schema to effect the immediacy of these cause-effect cycles' in order to make his theological points.

In conclusion, it will be evident that the above literary analysis strongly argues against the independent historicity of the twice-repeated chronological datum, 'for three years', in 2 Chron. 11.17—the references are almost certainly the result of Chr's theological concerns, rather than examples of an authentic historical reminiscence independent of the DtrH.

Abijah/Abijam
There are no non-synoptic references.

Asa (2 Chronicles 13.23 [EVV 14.1]; 15.10, 19; 16.1, 12, 13)
As already discussed at some length in the introductory section of this study, the strikingly independent nature of Asa's chronological notices in 2 Chronicles 15–16 led Albright to embrace them as original, indeed to base his low date for the disruption of the united monarchy upon them. Few, however, have followed him,[43] most preferring Thiele's approach of dating most of them from the disruption of the monarchy ca. 931.[44] Thus it would seem that, according to either approach, Chr has preserved valuable chronographic data independent of the Deuteronomistic literature, although he may well have misunderstood his own numbers according to Thiele's reconstruction.

Before discussing the important chronological data in chs. 15–16, the notice in 13.23 (EVV 14.1) that 'the land had rest for 10 years' after Asa came to the throne merits some attention. The report replaces the more typical Judahite regnal formula in 1 Kgs 15.9-10, the '10 years' probably representing Chr's secondary calculation in light of the later invasion of Zerah, or as Williamson phrased it, '[the number 10] is

---

42. Dillard, 'Reign of Asa', p. 210.

43. But see, e.g., Bright, *History of Israel*, p. 229, n. 1; and cf. Myers, *2 Chronicles*, p. 93.

44. See the helpful summary in Williamson, *Chronicles*, pp. 255-57; also, Dillard, *2 Chronicles*, pp. 124-25, who noted that 'Thiele was not the first scholar to suggest this approach.'

somewhat arbitrarily chosen, the constraints being simply a round number which is less than fifteen (15.10-11).'[45] Thus, once again, little weight should be placed on the historical veracity of this chronological datum inasmuch as it serves mainly to reinforce Chr's *Tendenz* to link cult reform with military victory.[46]

Now, back to the references in chs. 15–16. In regard to these anomalous data, I formerly adopted what may be termed Thiele's 'harmonistic' approach[47] as seemingly the easiest way to accommodate the figures.[48] Dillard, however, in his provocative *JETS* article[49] gave four reasons why he had come to reject Thiele's approach. First, out of hundreds of examples of such chronological references during the period of the divided monarchy, these would be the only examples of dating from the division of the kingdom itself.[50]

Second, Thiele's reconstruction ignores the plain meaning of Chr's text, which maintains (15.19; 16.1) that these were the thirty-fifth and thirty-sixth years 'of Asa's reign'. As Dillard argued,

> The formulae used for these regnal years are identical to the formulae used throughout Chronicles as well as in Kings and generally throughout the OT to cite the regnal years of individual kings. While it is certainly allowable that the Chronicler used a doublet account to achieve his purposes, it is hard to argue that the Chronicler intended anything other than the thirty-fifth and thirty-sixth years of Asa's reign.[51]

Third, Thiele's reconstruction plays havoc with Chr's argument and theological method: for Thiele argued that the date in 16.12 ('in the thirty-ninth year of his reign Asa was diseased in his feet') should *not*

45. *Chronicles*, p. 259.

46. Cf. Williamson (*Chronicles* p. 258), who cited R. Mosis's observation (*Untersuchungen zur Theologie des chronistischen Geschichtswerkes* [FTS, 92; Freiburg: Herder, 1973], pp. 173-75) of the parallel in 1 Chron. 13–15 of cult reform, again interrupted by war resulting in military victory, as a reward for 'seeking' God.

47. For this terminology, see Dillard, *2 Chronicles*, p. 124.

48. E.g., the tentative comments in my *Studies in the Chronology*, p. 149, n. 29.

49. 'Reign of Asa', pp. 214-15; see also his *2 Chronicles*, p. 124.

50. Albright, of course, had already made this point. See the quotation from his review of the first edition of Thiele's *Mysterious Numbers*, which I cited in the introduction. Cf. also, S. Japhet, *I and II Chronicles: A Commentary* (OTL; Louisville, KY: Westminster/John Knox, 1993), pp. 703-705.

51. Dillard, 'Reign of Asa', p. 215.

be redated from the division of the kingdom. This would leave a 20-year gap between Asa's sin of unbelief in 16.2-10 and Yahweh's sending of the foot disease as retribution. (Of course, if one redates 16.12, as Thiele did 15.19 and 16.1, one must posit that Asa had the foot disease for some 20 years!) Even Williamson,[52] who basically accepted Thiele's chronological reconstruction, had to admit that Chr must have added the phrase 'of the reign of Asa' in 15.19 and 16.1 to support his schematized retribution theology.

Finally, Thiele's methodology fails to reckon with 'the Chronicler's careful introduction of chronological patterns into his accounts of various reigns in order to achieve his theological purposes'.[53] Here Dillard cited both the examples of Chr's treatment of Rehoboam (see discussion above) and Josiah (see below). Once again, the emphasis is to be placed on '*immediate* retribution' (italics mine).

In summary, I am willing to recognize the likelihood that the reference in 15.10 to Asa's covenant renewal ceremony taking place in the third month of his fifteenth year may well have been original (as already noted, it probably provides the basis for the round number in 13.23 [EVV 14.1]).[54] The other four chronological data in chs. 14–15, however, are probably secondary, resulting from Chr's own composition (15.19 flies in the face of 1 Kgs 15.19, and it, as well as 16.1, 12, 13, draws attention to Chr's favorite theme of immediate retribution: war with Baasha not taking place until Asa's thirty-sixth year [15.19; 16.1]; Asa's resultant lack of faith leading to foot disease in his thirty-ninth year [16.12]; and his further lack of faith leading to his death in his forty-first year [16.13]).

Jehoshaphat (2 Chronicles 17.7; 18.2; 20.25-26)
In 2 Chron. 17.7, in the midst of a chapter entirely independent of Kings (except for v. 1a = 2 Kgs 15.24b), we are told, 'In the third year of [Jehoshaphat's] reign, he sent his officials...to teach in the cities of

---

52. *Chronicles*, pp. 256-58.
53. Dillard, 'Reign of Asa', p. 215. He cited (n. 36) some 18 such chronological notices, although his reference to 2 Chron. 12.2 should probably be removed, for it parallels rather closely 1 Kgs 14.25.
54. Cf. Dillard, *2 Chronicles*, p. 123; and Williamson, *Chronicles*, pp. 269-70, who noted the wordplay between the Feast of Weeks (the holiday most likely to have been celebrated in the third month) and the verbal root 'to swear, take an oath' found in vv. 14-15 (Hebrew שבעות and שבע, respectively).

Judah.' As already noted (see above), Cogan understood dates such as this one to indicate 'typological periods' marking the end of a short period of time. Indeed, Cogan[55] took Williamson[56] to task for suggesting that Chr reckoned Jehoshaphat's 'effective rule' as beginning in his third year (cf. 2 Chron. 16.12-13, in the light of which Chr may have reckoned Jehoshaphat a co-regent with his ailing father Asa). In either case, of course, the reference to the 'third year' in 17.7 must be taken as a secondary calculation or literary creation of Chr, devoid of independent historicity.[57]

I have included 2 Chron. 18.2 ('after some years') for the sake of completeness, but I agree with Cogan's characterization of it as a vague summary of the parallel chronological data found in 1 Kgs 22.1-2.[58] Similarly, Williamson noted how, in clear contrast to Chr's chronological treatment of Asa, his chronological references for Jehoshaphat are mostly 'general in the extreme'.[59]

Finally, I have included here as non-synoptic chronological data the references in 2 Chron. 20.25-26 to the 'three days' required for plundering after the victory over 'the Moabites, Ammonites, and with them some of the Meunites',[60] and the etiological reference to the 'fourth day' when they 'blessed Yahweh' in the Valley of Beracah ('blessing'). A number of scholars have linked the battle account in 2 Chronicles 20 with the Deuteronomistic account in 2 Kings 3, where both Judah under Jehoshaphat and Israel under Jehoram campaign against Moab (an account otherwise without parallel in Chronicles). Whatever their original relationship may have been,[61] most recognize once again the heavy hand of Chr in ch. 20, as he composes freely or heavily rewrites his sources. As Dillard noted, one readily recognizes the *Tendenz* of Chr: 'he has concentrated on the epic dimensions of the battle, reported it

55. 'Chronicler's Use of Chronology', p. 207, n. 38.

56. *Chronicles*, p. 282.

57. For a different view, see Dillard, *2 Chronicles*, p. 134, where he followed the chronology of E.R. Thiele, a chronological system that I have criticized in my *Studies in the Chronology*, pp. 12-27.

58. See my discussion above, p. 111.

59. *Chronicles*, p. 278.

60. Concerning this last term, see *BHS* footnote to 20.1. The entirety of vv. 1-24 is without parallel in Kings.

61. Dillard, *2 Chronicles*, pp. 153-55, contains a helpful summary of the major scholarly perspectives.

along lines of his retribution theology, and has emphasized the significance of the cultic personnel to the course of the battle'.[62] Still, I suspect
little weight should be placed on the historical accuracy of the chronological notices found in 2 Chron. 20.25-26.

Jehoram/Joram (2 Chronicles 21.19, 20)

The NRSV translates the chronological notice in 2 Chron. 21.19, which
refers to the death of Jehoram as the result of an 'incurable disease', as
follows: 'in the course of time, at the end of two years'. The MT, however, is difficult; the phrase translated 'two years' would more naturally
be translated 'two days' (ימים שנים), but this seems to contradict the
previous reference to the protracted nature of the disease: 'in the course
of time' (לימים מימים), or as Dillard translated, 'it continued for some
time'.[63] Both Dillard[64] and Williamson[65] suggested the possibility that
the 'two days' of MT refers to the final stages of the illness at the very
end of Jehoram's life (prolapse of the bowels?), but I suspect that,
inasmuch as the Hebrew term ימים elsewhere can mean 'years',[66] a
translation akin to the NRSV can be defended without recourse to
emendation. In any case, inasmuch as Jehoram's illness is clearly meant
to be seen as the direct fulfillment of Elijah's letter (vv. 12-15), a free
composition of Chr in the opinion of most scholars,[67] I suspect that the
chronological notice in v. 19 had a similar origin and is therefore of
dubious historicity.

Verse 20, the repetition of the regnal formula found in v. 5, has
already been cited in the chart, above (see the note accompanying the
reference to 2 Chron. 21.5, where Dillard's palistrophe for Chr's narrative for Jehoram is cited). I suspect that this double regnal formula is
also meant to 'flag' Jehoram as the fifth king in the Judahite king list,
inasmuch as the tenth king, Jotham (see below on 27.8), and the fifteenth king, Josiah (cf. the note for 34.8 in the chart above), also have

---

62. *2 Chronicles*, p. 154. Dillard saw some basis in historical fact, however,
underlying Chr's presentation, as did Williamson (*Chronicles*, p. 293): 'It would
not be surprising...if once again the Chronicler had taken up an originally fairly
insignificant incident and magnified it for didactic reasons.'

63. *2 Chronicles*, p. 163.

64. *2 Chronicles*, pp. 168-69.

65. *Chronicles*, p. 309.

66. Cf. BDB, p. 399 (6.c).

67. Williamson, *Chronicles*, p. 306.

double chronological notices. In any case, the double regnal notice for Jehoram here is again clearly the work of Chr.

Ahaziah

There are no non-synoptic references; see the chart above in regard to the textual variant found in 2 Chron. 22.2.

Joash/Jehoash (2 Chronicles 24.5 [but cf. 2 Kings 12.6], 15)

The curious reference to the phrase 'year by year' in 2 Chron. 24.5 (apparently Chr's interpretation of the reference in 2 Kgs 12.6 to the 'twenty-third year of King Jehoash' when the scheduled temple repairs were still delayed), as indicated above in the heading, possibly should have been included in the synoptic chart above. But, as Williamson suggested with some hesitation, vv. 5b-6 (including the chronological reference) may well represent a later (pro-Priestly?) addition to Chr's work (the anti-Levitical perspective in these verses is particularly noteworthy), drawing the whole account closer to that found in the Deuteronomistic parallel in 2 Kings 12 and softening the criticism of the priesthood found in the earlier version of Chr's work.[68]

The remarkable statement found in v. 15 that the high priest Jehoiada died at the age of 130 is usually taken quite understandably as a sum that is symbolic of God's blessing, rather than a numerically precise age.[69] Williamson characterized the entirety of vv. 15-16 as follows: 'There is no clear evidence to suggest an alternative source for this material, as in his [i.e., Chr's] presentation each item is to be regarded as symbolic rather than necessarily literal.'[70]

Amaziah

There are no non-synoptic references.

Uzziah/Azariah (2 Chronicles 26.5)

In 2 Chron. 26.5 (just after the first four verses that were taken from 2 Kgs 14.21-22 and 15.2-3) Chr presents the following notice: '[Uzziah] set himself to seek God in the days of Zechariah, who instructed him in

---

68. *Chronicles*, pp. 320-21.

69. As Williamson (*Chronicles*, p. 322) pointed out, this age supersedes that of Sarah, Joseph, Aaron, Moses, and Joshua!

70. *Chronicles*, For a more positive assessment of the literal interpretation of this age, see Dillard, *2 Chronicles*, p. 322.

the fear of God; and as long as he sought Yahweh, God made him prosper.' Following this is a lengthy section (vv. 6-15) with no parallel in Kings, enumerating the military accomplishments of Uzziah, and then a section (vv. 16-21) that describes Uzziah's pride and his inevitable downfall. Although these verses are mostly independent of Kings, they have undoubtedly been influenced by the brief notice in 2 Kgs 15.5 that Yahweh 'smote the king so that he was a leper to the day of his death'.

Verse 5, therefore, with its language characteristic of Chr, represents his own introduction to the first half of Uzziah's reign.[71] As the commentators note, the Zechariah' cited in the verse is apparently otherwise unknown, although as Williamson pointed out, 'In view of the Chronicler's practice elsewhere...it is probable that he found a reference to a Zechariah in association with Uzziah in one of his sources.'[72] With so little information, one cannot decide definitively as to the historical accuracy of this brief notice in v. 5, but its characteristically Chronistic language would cast doubt on the independence of the tradition.

Jotham (2 Chronicles 27.5, 8)

Verse 5 discusses a Judahite victory over the Ammonites and the tribute paid for the next three years, part of a section discussing Jotham's achievements (vv. 3b-6) that is independent of Kings. Myers maintained that 'there is no reason to doubt the substantial accuracy of these reports',[73] whereas Williamson was less sanguine. Noting again the characteristic language and style of Chr in vv. 3-4, he suggested that they represent a conscious attempt to develop parallels with the positive period of his father Uzziah's reign.[74] In v. 5, insofar as no other account of Jotham's war with the Ammonites is preserved, Williamson preferred to remain completely agnostic in regard to the historicity of the tradition, a perspective that seems wise to the present author as well.[75]

Verse 8 has already been mentioned in the chart above (see the note accompanying the reference to 2 Chron. 27.1). I suspect that, *contra*

71. Williamson, *Chronicles*, p. 334.
72. *Chronicles*, p. 334; cf. Japhet, *I and II Chronicles*, pp. 878-79.
73. *2 Chronicles*, p. 157.
74. *Chronicles*, p. 342.
75. *Chronicles*, p. 342; but cf. Japhet, *I and II Chronicles*, p. 892..

Williamson,[76] this repetition of the regnal notice in v. 1 is not 'unnecessary', but rather represents the second example of the chronological cipher flagging every fifth king in the Judahite king list.

Ahaz (2 Chronicles 28.6)
This notice, with its reference to 120,000 soldiers killed 'in one day', perhaps does not qualify as a chronological datum inasmuch as it so clearly serves Chr's purpose of emphasizing his theology of 'immediate retribution'.[77] The number of the slain, as given, is impossibly high.[78] The reference to the 'one day' of victory is more plausible, however, at least on the literary level: Douglas Stuart has pointed out that a number of biblical and ancient Near Eastern texts regularly depict a sovereign's victory over the enemy as having taken place in a single day.[79]

Hezekiah (2 Chronicles 29.3, 17; 30.2, 13, 15, 21-23; 31.7)
A cluster of chronological notes peculiar to Chr is to be found in his three chapters devoted to Hezekiah (chs. 29–31), which are nearly totally independent of 2 Kings 18–20 and Isaiah 36–39 (2 Chron. 32 is not in this category). I have already cited the skepticism of Cogan in regard to the dating of Hezekiah's reform to the first year of his reign (see above). It should be noted that all the references listed in the heading to this section (with the possible exceptions of 30.21-23 and 31.7) depend upon the dating of Hezekiah's reform to his first year. So if it is only a 'pseudo-date' as Cogan termed it, the others would have to be placed in that category as well.

Raymond Dillard, among others, has effectively argued that Chr presents Hezekiah as a second Solomon,[80] and I think he was correct to see the chronological reference in 29.3 to Hezekiah's 'first month of the first year' as another example of this comparison (Chr's Solomon likewise was concerned with the temple from the time of his accession).[81]

---

76. *Chronicles.*, p. 343.
77. Dillard, *2 Chronicles*, p. 221.
78. Dillard (*2 Chronicles*, p. 222) cited Y. Shiloh's estimate of the population of Iron Age Judah as rarely exceeding 300,000 persons: 'The Population of Iron Age Palestine in the Light of a Sample Analysis of Urban Plans, Areas, and Population Density', *BASOR* 239 (1980), pp. 25-35.
79. 'The Sovereign's Day of Conquest', *BASOR* 221 (1976), pp. 159-64.
80. *2 Chronicles*, pp. 227-29.
81. *2 Chronicles*, p. 234. Williamson argued similarly: 'The actual chronology

It is probable, therefore, that once again a non-synchronic chronological datum from Chronicles serves to indicate the theological *Tendenz* of the writer, rather than representing a reliable chronological datum independent of DtrH. Thus, the additional references in 29.17 to the process of temple cleansing from the 'first' to the 'eighth' to the 'sixteenth' day of the first month may well be typological—although the notices also help set the stage for the delayed observance of the passover in ch. 30.

All the chronological notices in ch. 30 deal with the celebration of Hezekiah's passover on the fourteenth day of the second[82] month (vv. 2, 13, 15), with seven days of celebration (vv. 21, 22), and indeed seven more days of celebration *à la* Solomon (v. 23; cf. v. 26 [the Solomonic parallel is in 7.8-10]). Williamson noted that the 'joy' of the people in v. 26 surely included the occasion of the reuniting of people from both Israel and Judah (v. 25), an event that again finds its closest parallel in the time of Solomon.[83]

Finally, the references in 31.7 to the 'third' and the 'seventh' months (of the second year?—the text is unclear) for the collection of tithes and other offerings correspond to the time of the grain harvest and of the vine and fruit harvests respectively.[84] In summary, once again the various chronological notices for Hezekiah should not be understood as attesting independent historical recollections, with the possible exception of the passover dated to the second month (30.2, 13, 15); rather,

---

of Hezekiah's accession has been much debated, and the relationship between his reform and the fall of Samaria is of considerable importance to the historian. The Chronicler, however, shows no interest in such an approach, and it would be unwise to use his account as evidence in such discussions.' *Chronicles*, p. 352.

82. This datum may well be historical, inasmuch as it would deviate markedly from common post-exilic practice (but cf. Num. 9.1-14). Myers (*2 Chronicles*, p. 178), in particular, argued enthusiastically for the historical accuracy of this delayed passover: 'At least some of the details [of the passover story] have no meaning apart from the time of Hezekiah.' S. Talmon ('Divergences in Calendar-Reckoning in Ephraim and Judah', *VT* 8 [1958], pp. 48-72) argued that the one month delay in the passover was particularly meant to align the celebration with the northern calendar (see, especially, pp. 58-62 of his article). J.B. Segal, however, understood the one month delay as due to the insertion of an intercalary month: 'Intercalation and the Hebrew Calendar', *VT* 7 (1957), pp. 250-307; see especially p. 257.

83. *Chronicles*, p. 371.

84. Williamson, *Chronicles*, p. 375. He was probably correct to emphasize Chr's challenge to his post-exilic community to do likewise (p. 374).

they illustrate Chr's likening of Hezekiah to Solomon and his urging a post-exilic audience to be as generous with their offerings as Hezekiah's subjects were.

Manasseh
There are no non-synoptic references.

Amon
There are no references.

Josiah (2 Chronicles 34.3 [bis])
Much has already been said in the introductory section concerning the double chronological reference found in 34.3, where we are told that already in the eighth year of his reign Josiah had 'begun to seek the God of his ancestors', and in the twelfth year 'he began to purge Judah and Jerusalem of the high places [etc.]'. It will be recalled that Cross and Freedman suggested that the material from this section (vv. 3b-7) probably came from one of the 'special sources' used by Chr, and they tried to link these chronological references quite specifically to events marking the decline of Assyrian power in the late seventh century BCE. As already noted,[85] a number of commentators have accepted this appropriation of the chronological data, but as also already noted, not all concurred with this approach, especially Cogan, who, as we have seen,[86] described these dates as 'pseudo-dates', devoid of any value for reconstructing the history of the monarchical period. Insofar as we have seen that nearly all of the previous non-synoptic references in the books of Chronicles are probably not historically precise, I suspect the burden

---

85. See above, n. 9. Dillard (*2 Chronicles*, pp. 276-77) also indicated qualified acceptance of this approach; as he pointed out, 'It is possible both to regard the chronological notices as reflecting some accurate sources at his disposal and to appreciate that it may well suit the Chronicler's interests to portray Josiah's piety as stemming from a much earlier point in his reign. The theological interests need not be at the expense of historicity.'

86. See above, p. 110. Williamson (*Chronicles*, pp. 397-98) came to a similar conclusion, arguing that since a literary analysis of the passage gives no reason (other than the two dates in v. 3) to suggest that Chr was following an alternative source, and since elsewhere the dates unique to Chr are to be attributed to his own reckoning, it would therefore be 'illegitimate' to understand these verses as giving us an alternative and more accurate record of the early reign of Josiah than that found in Kings.

of proof would lie with those who would see these Josianic dates as historically accurate. In any case, especially in the light of the more recent shift of dating for the demise of Esarhaddon,[87] I would argue that once again one ought not to place much weight upon these references in 2 Chron. 34.32 for historical reconstruction.

Jehoahaz
There are no non-synoptic references.

Jehoiakim
There are no references.

Jehoiachin
There are no references.

Zedekiah and the Exile (2 Chronicles 36.21, 22)
Little can be said here about either of these two very important chronological references other than to note that they both have been frequently discussed in the scholarly literature.[88] The land 'keeping sabbath to fulfill 70 years' (v. 21) finds literary parallels both in Jeremiah (25.11-12; 29.10; cf. Chr's own reference to Jeremiah earlier in the verse)[89] and in the Torah (Lev. 26.34-35, 43-44), and it is evidently a note of hope as well as of judgment.[90] The reference in v. 22 to 'the first year of King Cyrus of Persia' is of course paralleled in Ezra 1.1, leading many scholars to stress the editorial unity between the two works (i.e., Chronicles and Ezra–Nehemiah). Again, this is not the place to discuss this most important issue. For the purposes of the present study, let it

87. See above, n. 7. Japhet, (*I and II Chronicles*, pp. 1018-20) came to a similar conclusion.

88. Cf. Williamson, *Chronicles*, pp. 417-18, for a helpful overview of v. 21, and pp. 5-11 for a brief but similarly helpful overview of the issues underlying v. 22.

89. The precise chronological reckoning of these 70 years is not certain; possibly a normal life-span is all that is meant (cf. J.A. Thompson, *The Book of Jeremiah* [NICOT; Grand Rapids, MI: Eerdmans, 1980], pp. 513-14, and the references cited there). For the possibility that Chr envisioned a 490-year era of the monarchy, see Williamson, *Chronicles*, p. 418 (also cf. my own hypothesis in *Studies in the Chronology*, pp. 145-49, that the exilic Deuteronomistic editor [or his source(s)] may have envisioned a 480-year period for the Davidic monarchy stretching down to the thirty-seventh year of the exiled king Jehoiachin).

90. Cf. Myers, *2 Chronicles*, p. 223.

simply be emphasized that the chronological accuracy of the verse is not in dispute (it may be closely dated to 538 BCE, the year after the fall of Babylon to the Persians).[91]

Conclusions

This study began with the citation of several influential scholarly studies, published some time ago, that emphasized the historicity of a number of the non-synoptic chronological data found in the books of Chronicles. Further reflection, however, especially concerning more recent literary studies of these books and how the theological *Tendenz* of Chr has thoroughly shaped his work, leads one largely to discount the results of this earlier scholarship, indeed to doubt the independent historicity of nearly all of the 30 or so non-synoptic chronological notices to be found in Chronicles. In fact, I would now submit that only some three separate (non-synoptic) chronological notices may be retained as historically promising: the reference in 1 Chron. 26.31 with its oblique and independent attestation of the minimal length of David's reign; the reference in 2 Chron. 15.10 to the covenant renewal cere-mony that occurred in the third month of the fifteenth year of Asa; and the several references in 2 Chron. 30.2, 13, and 15 that date Hezekiah's passover to the second month of the year (of which year, however, remains uncertain). From a modern historian's point of view, therefore, it seems that Chronicles yields little grist for the historian reconstructing the monarchical period! Nonetheless, it is, of course, not our place to fault the particular historiographic style of Chr (or of any ancient writer or tradent) by using modern historiographical criteria. Whether it be Chr's repeated inclusion of seemingly specific chronological notices of dubious accuracy, or his inflation of the numbers of military troops or the size of temple donations, or his propensity to rearrange the order of the Deuteronomistic traditions (themselves often already tendentiously arranged) for his own political/theological reasons—our task is to understand and then to appropriate his historiographic data, not to con-demn his historiographical method. The suggestions of the older posi-tivistic scholars such as Albright or Thiele, while still insightful, founder on their lack of sensitivity to these issues of literary style and

91. See, e.g., Bright's *History of Israel*, pp. 360-62; also H.G.M. Williamson, *Ezra, Nehemiah* (WBC, 16; Waco, TX: Word Books, 1985), pp. 8-9, and the sources cited there.

theological *Tendenz,* which have so occupied us in the latter section of this study. While on the one hand, it would certainly be unfortunate if researchers returned wholesale to the extreme skepticism of biblical scholarship of the late nineteenth century (e.g., of that of Julius Wellhausen, who once wrote in regard to the issue of historicity in the books of Chronicles: 'it is indeed possible that occasionally a grain of good corn may occur among the chaff, but to be conscientious one must neglect this possibility of exceptions, and give due honour to the probability of the rule');[92] on the other hand, a nuanced approach such as that of Cogan, with its helpful emphasis on contemporary parallels in the ancient Near East, seems essential as a healthy corrective to the naive historical positivism of much recent biblical scholarship. In light of this, it appears appropriate indeed to conclude this study with the final summation that Cogan gave to his:

> One cannot but conclude, on the basis of the cases examined above, that the Chronicler as a chronographer did not follow present-day standards. Modern biblical historians would do well if they studied the ancient Chronicler's work not only as a theological statement based on history— the focus of most major investigations during the last two decades—but also as an example of historiographic writing which mirrors the canons of ancient Near Eastern literature.[93]

---

92. J. Wellhausen, *Prolegomena to the History of Ancient Israel* (Gloucester, MA: Peter Smith, repr., 1973), p. 224. I am indebted to Dillard ('Reign of Asa', p. 207) for this reference.

93. Cogan, 'Chronicler's Use of Chronology', pp. 208-209.

THE CHRONICLER AS A HISTORIAN: BUILDING TEXTS*

Ehud Ben Zvi

The Chronicler presents to the readers of 1 and 2 Chronicles a number of reports about building activities outside Jerusalem. These reports explicitly associate the building activities with particular kings of Judah and with Solomon (see 2 Chron. 8.4-6; 11.5-12; 14.5-6; 16.6; 17.12-13; 26.2, 6, 10; 27.4; 32.29) and likely serve multiple functions in the shaping of the message of 1 and 2 Chronicles for its readers. This thematic article will address the question of how these accounts illuminate both the historiographical work of Chr and the value of Chr's testimony for a critical reconstruction of the history of Judah in the monarchical period. To this purpose, it will first attempt to clarify basic methodological issues and premises underlying the study of these accounts. Then it will address in particular the reports that have no parallel in

---

*   In accordance with an agreement with J. Van Seters, another contributor to this volume, the present contribution will discuss accounts of building activities outside Jerusalem. Activities within Jerusalem will be addressed in his article. This division of work actually reflects the tendency in Chronicles to consider Jerusalem apart from other cities in Judah with regard to royal initiatives such as building and administrative organization. See, for instance, P. Welten, *Geschichte und Geschichtsdarstellung in den Chronikbüchern* (WMANT, 42; Neukirchen–Vluyn: Neukirchener Verlag, 1973), pp. 52-78; N. Na'aman, 'The Date of 2 Chronicles 11:5-10—A Reply to Y. Garfinkel', *BASOR* 271 (1988), p. 76.

As for the term 'Chronicler', it points here, and throughout this article, to the authorial voice construed by the (ancient) readers of the book of Chronicles through their reading of the book. This authorial voice may reflect, in part, that of the actual author or authors (hereafter, author) of the book, yet it should be clearly differentiated from the latter. Moreover, it must be stressed that it is the authorial voice construed by the readers that influences society, for readers only have access to it, rather than to the flesh and blood author. It is the communal and interpersonal reception of the book that construes the discourse of the group and that, in turn, construes the group. Cf. B.O. Long, *1 Kings* (FOTL, 9; Grand Rapids, MI: Eerdmans, 1984), p. 21.

Kings and will advance a proposal concerning the criterion that led to their inclusion in Chronicles. Finally, it will explore the implications of this criterion for the study of Chr's historiography and for the use of Chronicles in the reconstruction of monarchical Israelite and Judahite history.

Methodological Issues

On the surface, the most natural approach to the study of the building accounts and their respective degrees of historical accuracy (as understood in modern historical-critical research; hereafter and simply, accuracy or historical accuracy) is to take them at face-value and then compare their specific claims with relevant archaeological evidence. It is no surprise, therefore, that appeals to archaeology to prove or disprove the historical reliability of Chr have been repeatedly made since the second half of the nineteenth century.[1]

However, the potential results of this method, at least in our case, are somewhat limited. An obvious and substantial limitation of this approach is that it involves the well-known difficulties in dating archaeological findings to the reign of a certain monarch rather than to larger and less well-defined periods, such as 'the seventh century BCE', without relying on the biblical information. If biblical information were used, then such a dating would be another case of circular argumentation, and as such would be unconvincing from a critical perspective.

On the other hand, it is true that archaeological data may undermine

---

1. See M.P. Graham, *The Utilization of 1 and 2 Chronicles in the Reconstruction of Israelite History in the Nineteenth Century* (SBLDS, 116; Atlanta: Scholars Press, 1990), pp. 193-249. The conclusion of one of the most significant of such studies is noteworthy: '...it would follow as a fact that no single use of extrabiblical sources by the Chronicler has ever been proved. From this further follows not the fact but the undeniable possibility that any information communicated to us only by the Chronicler may be due in every case to his own legitimate theological inference or paraphrase from the canonical Scripture.' R.S. North, 'Does Archaeology Prove Chronicles' Sources?' in H.N. Bream *et al.* (eds.), *A Light unto my Path: Studies in Honor of J.M. Meyers* (Gettysburg Theological Studies, 4; Philadelphia: Temple University Press, 1974), pp. 375-401; quotation from p. 392.

For a general survey of the history of research on the question of the historical reliability of Chronicles, see S. Japhet, 'The Historical Reliability of Chronicles: The History of the Problem and its Place in Biblical Research', *JSOT* 33 (1985), pp. 83-107.

the argument in favor of the historical accuracy of the ostensible claims of historical narratives, or even render them unlikely beyond redemption. Such is the case concerning the claim of a single conquest campaign in the book of Joshua. Turning to the building reports in Chronicles, Funk, for instance, maintains that 'on the basis of the archaeological evidence, it is difficult to account for the Chronicler's attribution of the rebuilding of Beth-Zur to Rehoboam'.[2] Funk's conclusion—if correct, and so it seems to be—clearly undermines the argument for the historical accuracy of 2 Chron. 11.7 in particular, and of 2 Chron. 11.5-10 in general.

Moreover, the building reports themselves are not all of one kind. For the purpose of this article, it would be helpful to distinguish between those in which the text of Chronicles follows that of Kings— or its source—as in 2 Chron. 8.4-6 (// 1 Kgs 9.17-19, to a large extent),[3] 2 Chron. 16.6 (// 1 Kgs 15.22), and 2 Chron. 26.2 (// 2 Kgs 14.22), and those accounts that are unique to Chronicles. In the former, since Chronicles rests on Kings—or its source—the issue at stake is that of

2. R.W. Funk, 'Beth-Zur', *NEAEHL* (1993) I, pp. 259-60. See also N. Na'aman, 'Hezekiah's Fortified Cities and the LMLK Stamps', *BASOR* 261 (1986), pp. 6-7 and bibliography cited there. Although a few sherds from the tenth– ninth centuries were found in Kh. et-Tubeiqeh (i.e., Beth-Zur), and their presence may suggest some form of occupation, it seems that Kh. et-Tubeiqeh was not a fortified site during the tenth–ninth centuries. (My thanks are due to Avi Ofer for sharing with me his insights concerning this site.)

3. The *ketiv* תמר in 1 Kgs 9.18 projects an image of Solomon's kingdom as comprising a smaller realm than the *qere* תדמר. For this reason, the *ketiv* is often preferred. See, for instance, G. Gerleman, *Synoptic Studies in the Old Testament* (LUÅ, 44/5; Lund: Gleerup, 1948), pp. 122-23; G.H. Jones, *1 and 2 Kings* (NCB; Grand Rapids, MI: Eerdmans, 1984), p. 216; A.G. Auld, *Kings without Privilege* (Edinburgh: T. & T. Clark, 1994), p. 64; G.W. Ahlström, *The History of Ancient Palestine from the Palaeololithic Period to Alexander's Conquest* (JSOTSup, 146; Sheffield: JSOT Press, 1993), p. 506-507; and the bibliography mentioned in these works; but see, for instance, G.N. Knoppers, *Two Nations Under God: The Deuteronomistic History of Solomon and the Dual Monarchies* (HSM, 52; Atlanta: Scholars Press, 1993), I, pp. 127-28. In any case, it seems questionable that the author of Chronicles was the 'creator' of the reading תדמר here, for it is attested in the ancient versions of Kings—including the Lucianic recension—and 4QKgs[a]. It is likely that here, as in some other instances, the author of Chronicles followed a source different from MT (*ketiv*) Kings (see e.g., Gerleman, *Synoptic Studies,* pp. 122-23).

the accuracy of the information given in Kings.[4] Most significantly, the reports that are unique to Chronicles (i.e., unparalleled in Kings)—with the exception of 2 Chron. 11.5-10, which will be discussed below—are among the building reports least amenable to the 'archaeological approach' in the entire Hebrew Bible because of the vagueness of their claims, as even a cursory reading of these texts shows:

2 Chron. 14.5	ויבן ערי מצורה ביהודה כי ...
2 Chron. 17.12	ויבן ביהודה בירניות וערי מסכנות
2 Chron. 26.6	ויבנה ערים באשדוד ובפלשתים
2 Chron. 26.10	ויבן מגדלים במדבר ויחצב ברות רבים כי...
2 Chron. 27.4	וערים בנה בהר־יהודה ובחרשים בנה בירניות ומגדלים
2 Chron. 32.29[5]	וערים עשה לו ומקנה־צאן ובקר לרב כי...

Furthermore, it is certainly to be expected that, for instance, some towers in the wilderness were built and some cisterns were hewed out in the approximate half-century assigned to the reign of Uzziah (see 2 Chron. 27.10). Of course, the same holds true for many other regnal

---

4. Of course, in principle, the deviations from the source underlying the text in Chronicles may shed light on several aspects of the theological message of Chr and on the issue of how the historical narrative in Chronicles was shaped so as to serve such a message.

In fact, with regard to these accounts the textual divergences between Chronicles and its source are not especially significant, with the clear exception of the report in 2 Chron. 8.4-6. On the latter, see S. Japhet, *I & II Chronicles* (OTL; Louisville, KY: Westminster/John Knox, 1993), pp. 620-23; H.G.M. Williamson, *1 and 2 Chronicles* (NCB; Grand Rapids, MI: Eerdmans, 1982), pp. 229-30 and the bibliography cited there. On the overall theological message of this pericope, see also S.J. De Vries, *1 and 2 Chronicles* (FOTL, 11; Grand Rapids, MI: Eerdmans, 1989), pp. 266-69, esp. p. 269.

The omission of אין נקי in 2 Chron. 16.6 (cf. 1 Kgs 15.22) may reflect uneasiness concerning the king's decree that *no one* be exempt from working on this project.

5. The reading וערים is not certain. Although עשה points to *homo faber* (see DBHE, pp. 591-92) and may be translated here and there as 'build' (e.g., 2 Kgs 20.20), it is not found in relation to cities elsewhere (cf. 1 Kgs 15.23; 22.39). For the proposal to read ועדרים instead of וערים, see W. Rudolph, *Chronikbücher* (HAT, 21; Tübingen: Mohr [Paul Siebeck], 1955), p. 312, and Williamson, *Chronicles*, p. 387; for the view that the MT reading is preferable, see R.B. Dillard, *2 Chronicles* (WBC, 15; Waco, TX: Word Books, 1987), p. 254. The mention of ערים in this pericope (and cf. 2 Chron. 26.6-7, 10) might be reminiscent of the circumstances narrated in Num. 32, where references to מקנה רב and to building ערים are interlinked.

periods in Judah or anywhere in the ancient Near East.[6]

This being so, archaeological evidence pointing to the presence of towers and cisterns in Judah in the first half of the eighth century BCE does not and cannot contribute significantly to our understanding of historiographical aspects in Chronicles, nor even to the issue of the (intended) historical accuracy of Chr, unless one assumes *beforehand* that Chr could not have told the readers of Chronicles about the building of cisterns by Uzziah (and fortresses by Jehoshaphat and the like), unless these activities were described in a historically reliable source that was considered such by the author of Chronicles.[7]

---

6. 'Usually the kings of the ancient Near East were great builders. Government buildings, such as palaces, temples, store cities and fortresses, were expressions not only of a king's duties or of his dreams about power and might; the building programs were at the same time an expression of his position as the god's viceroy, the one who should shepherd the people. In this way the king carried out the god's demands for making his realm organized, strong and grand.' Ahlström, *History*, p. 507. Of course, there were towns, store towns, fortified towns, fortresses, watch-towers, and the like in Iron Age Judah, and certainly most, if not all of them, were built under the royal auspices, but does it prove the historicity of the accounts in Chronicles? See below.

For an attempt to relate, with much qualification, some of the archaeological findings with the accounts in Chronicles, see A. Mazar, 'Iron Age Fortresses in the Judaean Hills', *PEQ* 114 (1982), pp. 87-109.

7. To put it bluntly, archaeological evidence pointing to building and development in southern Judah and the Negev during the eighth century does not and cannot confirm the historicity of Chr's report concerning Uzziah. At best, it may allow for such a historicity. (*Contra*, for instance, Williamson, *Chronicles*, pp. 336-37; cf. Welten, *Geschichte und Geschichtsdarstellung*, p. 26.) This is so not only, or even mainly, because of issues involved in the comparison between precise details in the text and archaeological findings, nor even because of the problematic character of unequivocal correlations between archaeological (relative) datings and precise regnal periods that are based on the biblical narrative. The main reason concerns itself with the recognition of a gap of several centuries between the writing of Chronicles and the events reported. To claim that archaeological findings confirm Chr's *historicity*—rather than that they are not in tension with specific claims of a certain account—represents an unwarranted logical jump, unless one can advance a reasonable argument linking building activities in the eighth century with the historical narrative written several centuries later. Did the author of this narrative know that Uzziah developed the countryside? If so, how?

To state the obvious, an 'inductive' approach aimed at evading the latter question—i.e., to point to such a large number of instances of compelling and unequivocal, positive correlation between archaeological findings and plain narrative

In general terms, the methodological issue at stake here is ultimately that of *ad verecundiam*, that is, concerns with the appeal to authority. In this case, the appeal is to the authority of Chr.[8] Hence, as in any case of an appeal to authority, the weight of the appeal depends on: (1) an understanding of the statement of the authority that is faithful to its intentions and that takes into account the conventions of its discourse, and (2) the competence of the authority on the subject under discussion. It follows, therefore, that the validity of the appeal to the testimony of Chr regarding the accounts discussed here—and for the purpose of

claims in Chronicles, both concerning each Judahite king's actions and lack thereof, so as to make it reasonable to assume that such a link exists, even if it cannot be explained—is doomed to failure from the outset.

Moreover, is a de-contextualized reading of the building report included in the account of Uzziah's reign the best way to reconstruct the most likely *testimony* of Chr concerning Uzziah's actions? In Chronicles, the book read by the intended community of readers, the report is set in a larger context, within which Uzziah is compared and contrasted with other kings. Thus, for instance, neither Manasseh nor Josiah are described in this form, despite the great development in the seventh century. Moreover, Uzziah is the only king—in fact the only person in the Hebrew Bible—described as 'a lover of soil'. But is this 'historical' image of Uzziah due to the fact that 'this ancient historian' knew about specific deeds of Uzziah that set him apart from other Judahite kings?

The answers given to these and related questions have clear implications for the critical use of Chr's testimony for the purpose of a historical-critical reconstruction of monarchic Judah (see below). In any case, such an endeavor must begin with the recognition that the book of Chronicles *is not* and *should not* be considered a primary source for the monarchic period. Cf. E.A. Knauf, 'From History to Interpretation', in D.V. Edelman (ed.), *The Fabric of History: Text, Artifact and Israel's Past* (JSOTSup, 127; Sheffield: JSOT Press, 1991), esp. pp. 51-52.

8. See, for instance, Japhet's discussion of 2 Chron. 11.6-10aα. She maintains that no 'unequivocal literary or archaeological evidence can be brought forward in favour of any one view' concerning the chronological context of the list of fortifications associated with Rehoboam in these verses. Then she writes, 'conclusions ...cannot be definite; but since it seems likely that the new king followed his father's policy in fortifying Judah, I am inclined, pending further evidence, to accept the association of this list with Rehoboam.' See Japhet, *I & II Chronicles*, pp. 665-66. Of course, Japhet does not tend to relate the list to Rehoboam only, or even mainly, on the grounds that it is seems likely that a son follows the footsteps of a father, but because Chr associates the list with Rehoboam, i.e., on an appeal to the authority of Chr, an authority that seems strong enough to decide the balance when no unequivocal argument can be made one way or the other.

reconstructing the history of monarchic Judah—depends on two independent items.

First, it depends on one's understanding of Chr's historical/theological narrative in general, and of the building reports in particular, as texts written under the social and literary (genre) requirement that they should be historically accurate—at least within the limit of Chr's knowledge.[9] Alternatively, at the very least, it depends on the strength of the argument that the mentioned reports, or their basic claims, *had to be anchored* in historical knowledge about specific and concrete actions (or lack of actions) of Judahite kings, both *thought to be historically accurate* by the author of Chronicles and acceptable as such by the reading community for which the book was written.[10]

Second, the appeal to Chronicles as a source for historically reliable information about the pre-exilic period depends on Chr's expertise concerning building projects carried out during the monarchic period, outside Jerusalem; or alternatively, on the existence of sources underlying the relevant reports in Chronicles that fulfill the aforementioned two criteria. Of course, the latter can be considered an option only if a strong argument can be made that (1) these sources really existed, and (2) Chr faithfully (re)presented them.[11]

9. The weakness of such an understanding is often recognized. See, for instance, I. Kalimi, 'Literary-Chronological Proximity in the Chronicler's Historiography', *VT* 43 (1993), pp. 318-38.

10. The alternative is to assume that the historical narrative in Chronicles includes literary, theological, and ideological *topoi*, selected mainly according to their roles in the shaping of the text's message, and whose presence there *may or may not* reflect historical events or at least, historical knowledge thought to be accurate—in the modern sense of the term—by the author and readers. If such is the case, then no critically controlled position concerning their historical accuracy can be taken without the support of independent evidence.

11. Of course, this approach is diametrically opposed to that which claims from the outset that one should accept the historical reliability (and historical referentiality) of Chr's narrative, with the only exception of specific claims that can be convincingly ruled out. Such an approach *presumes* (rather than analyzes) the validity of the appeal to authority of that narrative as an accurate historical source for the monarchic period. It is worth mentioning in this respect that, as Bentzen already noticed decades ago, one may not be in a situation to rule out completely even the claim of *b. B. Bat.* 15a that Jeremiah was the author of Kings. Of course, from this observation it does not follow that one should accept such a claim, unless one presumes the value of an appeal to the authority of *b. B. Bat.* 15a as an accurate source for the history of the late monarchic and early post-monarchic period. (From

It follows, therefore, that the decisive observations about these accounts concern themselves with: (1) the likelihood that there were sources underlying them; (2) if there were, the extent to which they can be reasonably reconstructed from Chronicles; (3) if there were and they can be reconstructed, the issue of how to assess the strength of an appeal to their authority; (4) turning to Chronicles itself, the image of the past conveyed by these accounts and its implications concerning the historiographical craft of the author of Chronicles; and finally, (5) the question of whether Chr's building reports had to be anchored at all in what was regarded as accurate historical knowledge.

That the image of the past conveyed by Chr through these reports need not be accurate is self-evident once one recognizes the relative scarcity of kings mentioned. To illustrate, is it historically likely that Josiah, who reigned for several prosperous decades, never built anything? Should all the development in the seventh century in Judah be associated with Manasseh? It is significant that even if one accepted such a position, Chr does not claim that Manasseh built or rebuilt any town in Judah (see 2 Chron. 33.12-17). In fact, Chr does not report any royal building activity in Judah's countryside after Hezekiah, and the relevant(?) reference to events in Hezekiah's reign is not certain.[12]

It seems difficult to maintain that although the author of Chronicles had no knowledge about construction projects in Judah's countryside since Hezekiah, this writer knew about such projects in the eighth and ninth centuries (i.e., that narrative gaps in Chronicles correspond to source/knowledge gaps). Such a proposal is not only unsupported by evidence, but it is also an unnecessary *ad hoc* hypothesis, whose sole function is to support the view that Chronicles would not have omitted 'historical' information if available, a position contradicted by any close comparison between Kings and Chronicles.[13]

An additional question should then be added to the others: Why did

a methodological viewpoint alone, the two cases are comparable.) See A. Bentzen, *Introduction to the Old Testament* (Copenhagen: Gads Forlag, 1949), II, p. 97.

12. On 2 Chron. 32.29, see above. That a historical narrative does not have to be 'historically' accurate is clearly shown by Kings, as it creates an image of the past in which the Assyrian domination of Judah came to a complete end in the fourteenth year of Hezekiah.

13. Notice, for instance, the difference between their accounts of Solomon's building activities in Jerusalem. On this point, see Japhet, *I & II Chronicles*, pp. 537-38, 549-50, 613-14.

Chr associate building accounts *only* with certain kings,[14] and what can be learned from this fact concerning the aforementioned issues to be assessed?

Building Texts Unique to Chronicles

Turning to the accounts themselves, it is generally accepted that the text in 2 Chron. 11.5b-10 reflects a written source, most likely a list of cities entitled ערים למצור, or perhaps ערים למצור ביהודה.[15] There is no reference to Rehoboam in the reconstructed text that is assumed to reflect the original source, nor is there any indication that the text of the source itself associated the list with Rehoboam. And so, how did the author of Chronicles know that this list belonged to Rehoboam?[16]

A claim that Chr relied on a 'tradition of interpretation' that was passed along with the list, but significantly left no identifiable traces,[17] is not only an *ad hoc* hypothesis but also one that by definition cannot be verified.[18] In addition, one cannot reasonably assume that the author of Chronicles associated the list with Rehoboam, because after careful analysis the writer reached the conclusion that the specific geographical deployment of fortifications suited best the circumstances of that

14. The answer cannot be that 'pious kings' build. As widely recognized in Chronicles, only kings who behave piously may build, but there are kings who are described in such a way and to whom no report about building activities in the countryside of Judah is attached (e.g., Abijah, Joash, Josiah), nor is it simply an issue of building 'parity' between Jerusalem and 'Judah' (e.g., Joash, Manasseh). (In Chronicles, military-related building activities are considered to be an expression of the divine blessing that generally follows righteous behavior. Cf. 1 Chron. 11.8; 2 Chron. 26.9-10; 27.3-4; 32.5. On these *topoi*, see Welten, *Geschichte und Geschichtsdarstellung*, pp. 9-78.)

15. E.g., M. Noth, *The Chronicler's History* (JSOTSup, 50; Sheffield: JSOT Press, 1987), pp. 58-59; Rudolph, *Chronikbücher*, pp. 228-30; Welten, *Geschichte und Geschichtsdarstellung*, pp. 11-15; V. Fritz, 'The "List of Rehoboam's Fortresses" in 2 Chr 11.5-12—A Document from the Time of Josiah', in B. Mazar (ed.), *Y. Aharoni Memorial Volume* (ErIs, 15; Jerusalem: Israel Exploration Society, 1981), pp. 46*-53*; Na'aman, 'Fortified Cities', p. 5; *idem*, 'Date', p. 76.

16. Such a question points to the heart of the argument in favor of the appeal to the authority of Chr as a historian.

17. Should one assume that it was oral?

18. It is needless to say that even if, for the sake of argument, one accepted this hypothesis, the historical reliability of this untraceable tradition would be questionable, and along with it, that of Chr's testimony.

period. In fact, the geographical deployment is such that it does not allow any clear conclusion in this regard, neither on the basis of the Deuteronomistic narratives about monarchic Judah that were available to the author, nor on those of modern historical reconstructions. Moreover, the period of Rehoboam is not necessarily among those most consistent with the data in the list, in either case.[19] One must also keep in mind that biblical writers could and actually did use—knowingly or unknowingly—city lists in (historical) narrative contexts that had nothing to do with their likely historical context, as the lists in Joshua clearly show.[20]

This being so, it seems preferable to rephrase the question, so as to ask *why* Chr related such a list to Rehoboam, rather than *how* the author of Chronicles knew that this list belonged to Rehoboam.

The most secure starting point for this inquiry is the fact that details (and especially detailed lists) serve the general purpose in historical narratives of strengthening the narratives' verisimilitude or their history-likeness. It is obvious that Chr resorts to this rhetorical device quite often. Moreover, recourse to it is widely found in other biblical 'historiographical' works.[21] Taking all this into account, it is noteworthy that there is no list comparable to this fortification list in Chr's account of the monarchic period and that general language characterizes the other reports on building activities outside Jerusalem found in Chronicles but not in Kings. Chr communicates thus a unique emphasis on the history-likeness of Rehoboam's building activities outside Jerusalem, and accordingly on the credibility of the speaker[22] in this special regard.[23] If

19. For example, the list suggests a threat from the west, whereas the immediate literary context in Chronicles is more consistent with a threat from the north.

20. See also E. Ben Zvi, 'The List of the Levitical Cities', *JSOT* 54 (1992), pp. 77-106 and the bibliography cited there.

21. The lists in Joshua provide a 'classic' example. Concerning Chronicles, see also Ben Zvi, 'Levitical Cities', pp. 77-106. The itinerary form in Num. 33.1-49 has the same purpose. See J. Van Seters, *The Life of Moses: The Yahwist as Historian in Exodus–Numbers* (Louisville, KY: Westminster/John Knox, 1994), pp. 161-64. The same holds true also for the list of cities built by the Transjordanian tribes in Num. 32.34-38; cf. Van Seters, *Life*, pp. 446-50.

22. On these issues, see also R.K. Duke, *The Persuasive Appeal of the Chronicler: A Rhetorical Analysis* (Bible and Literature Series, 25; JSOTSup, 88; Sheffield: Almond Press, 1990), pp. 105-38.

23. One may conjecture that the author had no access to additional fortification lists and did not wish to 'fabricate' new ones. Perhaps one may surmise that Chr

so, the question is why Chr considered it necessary to support so strongly the description of Rehoboam as one who builds and fortifies, and at this specific time in his career.[24]

The answer seems to lie in 1 Kgs 12.25 and in its significance within the context of Chr's theological discourse. The text in 2 Chron. 10.1–11.4 follows—with some deviations—that in 1 Kgs 12.1-24; then one finds 1 Kgs 12.25, which reads, ויבן ירבעם את־שכם בהר אפרים וישב בה ... ויבן את־פנואל, and in its place וישב רחבעם בירושלם ויבן ערים למצור ביהודה (2 Chron. 11.5).

The similarities in language and the explicit contrasts between ירבעם, שכם, and בהר אפרים on the one hand, and ירושלם, רחבעם, and ביהודה on the other, are self-evident. Moreover, according to the historico/theological discourse in Chronicles, Jeroboam has just committed one of the most significant sins in Israel's past by revolting against the House of David (2 Chron. 10), whereas Rehoboam and his people have just followed the voice of the Lord as announced by Shemaiah, the man of God (2 Chron. 11.1-4). Since building activities and especially fortifications are usually an expression of divine blessing in Chronicles, the report in Kings suggests (or would have suggested) a 'strange inconsistency' to the (intended) readers of Chronicles: it is not the pious king but the wicked one who is characterized there as a builder (and by probable connotation, as blessed). It seems, therefore, that it is not by chance that the account in Chronicles deviates just at this point in the narrative from the text in Kings. The more so, since it seems obvious that Chr took the language and the contents of the relevant section in Kings as the starting point for the new (unparalleled) narrative but used them so as to construct—in a way that is coherent with Chr's own discourse—a clear contrast among central terms involved in the ongoing theologico/historical narrative that characterize the book of Chronicles.[25] Significantly, Chr claims that Rehoboam built not two,

---

had more than one list but wished to emphasize the case supporting the characterization of Rehoboam as a (main) 'builder' by means of a uniquely detailed account. Both suggestions are essentially unverifiable and, as such, do not advance the discussion. It is better to remain with what can be verified, i.e., that Chr rendered Rehoboam's account unique in this respect and that it is most likely that there was a reason for it.

24. As is well-known, Chr develops Rehoboam's career in three stages.

25. Cf. Rudolph, *Chronikbücher*, p. 227; J. Goldingay, 'The Chronicler as a Theologian', *BTB* 5 (1975), pp. 102-103; Auld, *Kings*, p. 106. On the surface, one

but fifteen[26] cities, and despite that, as a good king he dwells in Jerusalem. Of course, the more significant that 'Jeroboam's rebellion' is in the discourse in Chronicles, the more significant the strength of the characterization of Rehoboam as builder (and blessed) becomes, and accordingly, the stronger the reason to associate a list of fortified cities with Rehoboam.

But was this association thought to be historically accurate by the author of Chronicles? One may indeed conjecture that this writer (ancient historian) extrapolated from what was maintained to be true to what was unknown, in order to reach the 'likely'.[27] So, if as a rule pious kings are more likely than evil ones to build fortifications, then Rehoboam—at this moment in his career—was among the likely candidates for this endeavor, and for reasons that will be explained later, perhaps one of the most likely. Still, this would be a totally unverifiable conjecture; the mind of the author is outside the realm of critical investigation, and it is impossible to assess to what degree an ancient writer thought that his or her work was likely to reflect past historical events.

may argue that Chr could have solved 'the problem' by presenting a text that denied the building activities of Jeroboam, rather than by accentuating those of Rehoboam (and omitting all reference to those of Jeroboam). But such a solution would have been inconsistent with Chr's work, for Chr does not explicitly refute received texts nor make polemical statements about them. Chr, as narratorial voice, prefers to let the events reported speak for themselves, as it were (see Duke, *Persuasive Appeal*, p. 108; M. Fishbane, *Biblical Interpretation in Ancient Israel* [Oxford: Clarendon Press, 1988], p. 382). In fact, omitting references to 'positive' actions of Jeroboam and elevating the character of the lawful king, Rehoboam, was not only the most attractive alternative, but also the one most consistent with the literary and theological conventions guiding the work of the author of Chronicles (cf. also Chr's characterization of Abijah, about whom not all could have been good in the eyes of the author). See D.G. Deboys, 'History and Theology in the Chronicler's Portrayal of Abijah', *Bib* 71 (1990), esp. p. 52.

26. That is seven times more than Jeroboam did, plus one. On seven cities pointing to completeness, see Jdt. 2.28 (C.A. Moore, *Judith* [AB, 40; Garden City, NY: Doubleday, 1985], p. 139); Rev. 1.4. The number fifteen is among the possible candidates of a system based on triads, such as this list.

27. Cf. L.I.C. Pearson, *The Greek Historians of the West: Timaeus and his Predecessors* (Philological Monographs, 35; Atlanta: Scholars Press, 1987), p. 50. Some of these issues were discussed in J. Van Seters, 'Filling in the Gaps: Composition Techniques in Near Eastern and Greek Historiography and in Deuteronomistic History', (a paper presented at the 1994 annual meeting of the SBL).

Hence, it seems more appropriate to focus on the authorial voice in Chronicles, that is, Chr. The latter certainly asks the intended reader to accept the validity and relevance of the reconstruction of the past that is presented in Chronicles, as well as its accuracy. It is surely reasonable to assume that the readers for whom the book was written perceived these narrative claims. However, whether these readers interpreted such claims as necessarily pointing to precise historical referentiality and to historical accuracy in a modern sense, or even thought in such categories, is doubtful.

Turning to the other reports of building activities outside Jerusalem, in sharp contrast to 2 Chron. 11.5b-10, there are no lists of cities in 2 Chron. 14.5-6; 17.2; 26.10; 27.4; and 32.29. Moreover, contrary to expectations associated with the requirements of verisimilitude and credibility, there is almost no detail in these reports: what is described as built is designated only by generic terms such as 'cities', 'fortified cities', 'towers', and the like; and the places where the latter are built are characterized only in the most general terms ('Judah' or its main subregions, such as 'the Judean Hills' or 'the wilderness'). The issue of credibility is solved here—probably less successfully, and likely with less at stake than in 2 Chron. 11.5-12—by striking a balance between the language that is shared among these reports and that serves to convey a sense of patterning and some degree of individuality given to each of them, so as to correspond to the particular actions of each monarch as described in the book. Significantly, Chr does not attribute the same building activities to more than one king. Each monarch is presented, therefore, as somewhat distinctive in this regard, and accordingly, the credibility of the narrative is enhanced.

A few examples must suffice. According to Chronicles, Jehoshaphat built בירניות, as did Jotham, and both built cities. Those of the former, however, are referred to as ערי מסכנות, whereas those of the latter only appear as ערים; the former built ביהודה—as a whole, the latter his בהר־יהודה, ערים; but his בירניות בחרשים. Moreover, Jotham built not only בירניות, but also מגדלים.[28]

Significantly, Asa also set up מגדלים, but in cities (see 2 Chron. 14.6) and as part of city defenses. So the same word, מגדלים points to

---

28. Cf. 2 Chron. 17.12 with 2 Chron. 27.4. Notice also the *qtl–wyqtl* contrast, as well as that between the order 'verb–location–direct object1–direct object2' and the chiastic pattern: 'direct object1–verb–location1 + location2–verb–direct object2-3'.

(watch)towers in one report and to towers in the other.[29] Jotham was not the only king to build מגדלים (watchtowers); Uzziah did the same, but he did so במדבר, unlike Jotham. Moroever, Uzziah's מגדלים (watchtowers) were associated in the text with cisterns, rather than with בירניות, as Jotham's were. Large flocks were the explicit reason given for the aforementioned building projects of Uzziah, but another king, who also has his share of the same blessing, did not build מגדלים nor hew cisterns because of that, but 'made' ערים (see 2 Chron. 26.10; 32.29).

Contrary to the case in 2 Chron. 11.5b-10, the reports in 2 Chron. 14.5-6; 17.2; 26.10; 27.4; and 32.29 do not seem to contain language or expressions that may further the argument that the author of Chronicles was following independent, written sources, each dealing with the specific building projects of a Judahite monarch.[30]

The report in 2 Chron. 26.6 deserves further study. It shows many of the characteristics of the texts mentioned above. It differs from them, however, because it clearly refers to building activities in the (territories) of Yavneh and Ashdod. It has been claimed that this account is based on some external source, on the grounds that 'it [Jabneh] is not otherwise found in literary sources before the Maccabean period, a fact that argues against pure invention here by the Chronicler'.[31] But the same fact, especially when is taken along with the observation that

29. The same contrast between the two referents of this word is found in 2 Chron. 26.9-10. See below.

30. ערי מצורה occurs in 2 Chron. 14.5 and nowhere else in the Hebrew Bible (but see 2 Chron. 11.10, 11, 23; 12.4; 21.3). בירניות is found only in Chronicles (2 Chron. 17.12; 27.4; בירנית [the singular form] occurs nowhere). ערי מסכנות occurs in Exod. 1.11; 1 Kgs 9.19 (// 2 Chron. 8.6); and 2 Chron. 8.4; 16.4; 17.12. Although the word מגדלות is found in 1 Chron. 27.25 and 2 Chron. 32.5, מגדלים occurs four times, namely in 2 Chron. 14.6; 26.9, 10; and 27.4.

It is true that the referent of מגדלים in 2 Chron. 26.9 and 10 is not the same, but this does not necessarily mean that one of them comes from an independent source. On the contrary, one may claim that this is a stylistic device to bind together the two (parallel) reports (see above). In any case, the use of מגדלים in reference to (watch)towers is found in 2 Chron. 26.10 and 27.4 and in reference to the towers of a city wall in 2 Chron. 14.6; 26.9. Hence there is no need to hypothesize a non-chronistic source. For a different approach, see Welten, *Geschichte und Geschichtsdarstellung*, p. 26; Williamson, *Chronicles*, p. 336; De Vries, *1 and 2 Chronicles*, p. 356.

31. Williamson, *Chronicles*, pp. 334-35. For studies in this verse, see De Vries, *1 and 2 Chronicles*, pp. 358-59 and the bibliography cited there.

Yavneh seems to have developed into an important city since the Achaemenid period and onward,[32] is better explained as another case in which the author of Chronicles is influenced by the historical circumstances of the writing,[33] just as in the well-known instance in 1 Chron. 29.7, and likely also in 2 Chron. 28.18, where the list of cities suits better the circumstances of the Achaemenid period than those of Ahaz's day.[34]

If so, and if there is no convincing reason to suppose the existence of sources behind the building reports in 2 Chron. 14.5-6; 17.12; 26.6, 10; 27.4; and 32.29, then for the purpose of this article, the inquiry into these accounts should proceed directly to a study of the issue referred to as (4) above, namely, the image of the past conveyed by these accounts and its implications concerning the historiographical craft of the author of Chronicles. Such an analysis should, of course, take into account the conclusions reached earlier about the reasons that led Chr to include the list of fortified cities in Rehoboam's account, namely, a 'hidden' contrastive dialogue with the information present in Kings, one in which actions in the kingdom of Israel are contrasted with contemporaneous actions in Judah.

All these reports share a call to their readers to include in their image of the past the building activities carried out by specific kings of Judah outside Jerusalem that were not mentioned in the book of Kings.[35]

---

32. See E. Stern, *Material Culture of the Land of the Bible in the Persian Period, 538-332 B.C.* (Warminster; Jerusalem: Aris & Phillips/Israel Exploration Society, 1982), pp. 19-22. Cf. Jdt. 2.28; 1 Macc. 4.15; 5.58; 10.69; 15.40; Strabo 16.2.28 §759.

33. I tend to follow Williamson and others with regard to the date of the composition of Chronicles and so set it within the fourth century BCE.

34. Notice especially the reference to Aijalon and Gimzo. For a different approach to this list of cities, see R.W. Dornemann, 'Archaeology and Biblical Interpretation: Tell el Hesi', in L.G. Perdue, L.E. Tombs, and G.L. Johnson (eds.), *Archaeology and Biblical Interpretation: Essays in Memory of D. Glenn Rose* (Atlanta: John Knox, 1987), pp. 129-46.

It is also worth noting that the textual proximity of יבנה to ויבנה in 2 Chron. 26.6 seems to hold the best explanation for the unusual (long) form of the latter. If so, stylistic considerations may have strongly influenced the text of the report (cf. Zeph. 2.4; see E. Ben Zvi, *A Historical-Critical Study of the Book of Zephaniah* [BZAW, 198; Berlin: de Gruyter, 1991], pp. 150-51). The more the case is so, the more doubtful is the argument for the historical accuracy of the account.

35. The present analysis shows that the book of Kings was included in the repertoire of books read in the society within which (and for which) Chronicles was

These kings are Asa (before his fifteenth year; see 2 Chron. 15.10), Jehoshaphat (certainly before the death of Ahab, according to the narrative), Uzziah, Jotham, and Hezekiah—albeit the inclusion of the latter in the list is debatable.

It is worth stressing that the building activities attributed to Asa that are mentioned only in Chronicles are more or less contemporaneous with the establishment of the second dynasty in Israel (and likely with that of Tirzah as capital). In addition, Jehoshaphat's building activities can be seen as more or less contemporaneous with the reign of Ahab, and within the historical narrative of Chronicles, also with the reign of Omri, who was the founder of the third dynasty of Israel and the builder of Samaria.[36] If one takes into account that Asa's actions are described in strong negative terms since his war against Baasha (see 2 Chron. 16.1-13, and esp. vv. 7-9, 10, 12), then one must conclude that within the discourse of Chronicles, Asa would have been an unlikely candidate for blessing and the construction associated with it, even if these were needed as a counterpoise to the image of Omri as builder in Kings. The job *had*, therefore, to be left to Jehoshaphat.[37]

It is obvious that Uzziah's actions may be seen as coterminous with the heyday of the fourth dynasty of Israel, the reign of Jeroboam II (cf.

written (cf. Auld, *Kings*, p.106). This does not *necessarily* mean that the author of Chronicles had to follow the present text of Kings rather than a forerunner or closely related source. This issue, however, is beyond the scope of the present study.

36. The historical narrative of Chronicles claims that Baasha was still the king of Israel in the thirty-sixth year of Asa (2 Chron. 16.1), and Asa died in the forty-first year of his reign (2 Chron. 16.13). If one accepts this chronology, one has to conclude that Omri must have built Samaria when Jehoshaphat reigned over Judah and Jerusalem.

It is noteworthy that according to 1 Kgs 16.8-11 (with no parallel in Chronicles), Elah, the son of Baasha, began to reign over Israel in the twenty-sixth year of Asa and was murdered, along with all the House of Baasha, in the twenty-seventh year of Asa. Accordingly, the entire reign of Omri is presented as contemporaneous with that of Asa over Judah, despite a certain degree of internal inconsistence in the chronological system of Kings (see 1 Kgs 16.23, 29; and 22.41).

37. It is possible that *one* of the purposes for the 'strange' dating of the war between Asa and Baasha in Chronicles (2 Chron. 16.1) was to let Jehoshaphat, the new pious king, fill the role of Rehoboam over and against the new Jeroboam, Omri. For other comparable elements in Chr's accounts of Rehoboam and Jehoshaphat, see below.

2 Kgs 15.1),[38] but also even with that of Menahem's dynasty (cf. 2 Kgs 15.17),[39] whereas Jotham, within this context, may be related to Pekah (cf. 2 Kgs 15.32).[40]

Thus, it is noticeable and most likely significant that every period that could have been construed as at least a potentially new beginning or renaissance for the kingdom of Israel by a person knowledgeable of the historical narrative of Kings (or a source closely following it) is coterminous with a period described in Chronicles as one of development in the countryside of Judah, by means of accounts that are unique to this book and that seem to rely on no previous source—with the exception of 2 Chron. 11.5b-10. The *misleading* new overtures in the north (Chr considered them all as hopeless, since the very existence of the northern kingdom was an act of defiance against YHWH) are thus compared and contrasted with *actual* divine blessings in Judah and their material expressions, which include among other things, building activities.[41]

Such an implied correspondence between Judah (except Jerusalem) and northern Israel is understandable and actually expected in the discourse of Chr. The latter, along with others, tended to consider Jerusalem apart from other cities in Judah (i.e., from countryside Judah). This being so, northern Israel can be seen as similar in kind only to Judah, certainly not to Jerusalem.

It is worth noting that there is an impressive selection of accounts of correct behavior and 'blessing' *topoi* that appear in close (literary) proximity to the 'building' reports just mentioned.[42] Most of these

---

38. The establishment of the House of Jehu was certainly not a negative event in Chronicles (see 2 Chron. 22.7-8). So it seems appropriate that the Judahite counterpart to a king of this dynasty will be contrasted with the king of this dynasty who was militarily most successful according to Kings, namely Jeroboam II, who, by the way, was considered a sinner, even in Kings.

39. Significantly, the text of 2 Kgs 15.20 seems to imply that there were 60,000 גבורי החיל in Israel in Menahem's days. This number may have evoked an image of wealth—especially agrarian wealth. Cf. Chr's (unique) building account of Uzziah.

40. If Hezekiah is included in this group of kings, he may serve the role of the positive counterpart to Hoshea.

41. E.g., Welten, *Geschichte und Geschichtsdarstellung*, pp. 52-78; Na'aman, 'Reply', p. 76.

42. For instance, concerning cultic reforms or related actions, see 2 Chron. 11.13-16; 14.2-4; 17.6, 7-9; for following the word of prophets, 2 Chron. 11.2-4;

accounts are unique to Chronicles. This observation certainly strengthens the argument developed here that Chr invested much effort in shaping for the audience the image of blessing over Judah at relevant points in their view of the past.[43] This observation also serves to put the building reports in perspective: they are minor elements in a much larger characterization of particularly blessed times. Still, it is worth noting that they appear in all of these instances—unlike other reports—and that they cease to appear, once the northern kingdom vanishes.

A final note: any proposal claiming that Chr sent a single message to the audience in a particular account or set of accounts is inherently weak. Approaches that may be likened to procrustean beds are not conducive to a better understanding of ancient texts that were written to be read and reread by the community, and they are certainly not appropriate for dealing with sophisticated theological voices, such as that of Chr. Many reports, including the building reports, serve multiple purposes, and each of them should be discussed separately with special attention being given to their textual and contextual differences. This article, however, deals mainly with the shared elements of these accounts.

26.5; for building and fortifying Jerusalem, 2 Chron. 26.9, 15; 27.3; for military might or victory, 2 Chron. 14.7-14; 17.14-19; 26.6-7, 11-15; 27.5; for reorganizing and strengthening regional administration and defenses, 2 Chron. 11.11-12, 23; 17.2, 19.

43. One may add that since (1) the audience of the book could not have read it outside any cultural context, and (2) it is most likely that their image of the past was strongly influenced by the historical narratives in Samuel and Kings (see above), then it is actually to be expected that Chr would especially address (potential) turning points in those narratives.

THE FIGHT FOR PEACE: NARRATIVE AND HISTORY IN THE BATTLE ACCOUNTS IN CHRONICLES*

John W. Wright

For a history that understands the absence of war as the ultimate divine blessing,[1] the book of Chronicles abounds in military conflict. Judean victory signals divine favor; defeat, divine judgment. Both usually arise from the theological propriety or impropriety of the king.[2] It is a lesson that appears often in this history of Israel/Judah. Warfare fills the pages of Chr's history.

While battle reports pervade the narrative, perhaps no other area of Chronicles research has recently evoked a wider range of interpretation. Does Chr record otherwise unknown battles from various eras of the history of Judah, or are the accounts only theological constructs? For instance, in recent years scholars have interpreted 2 Chronicles 20 as Chr's embellishment of an actual battle fought during the reign of Jehoshaphat,[3] a non-historical theological tractate calling for theological

* It is an honor to dedicate this essay to the memory of Raymond B. Dillard. Though I was never his student, Ray's encouragement, confidence, and personal interest in me and my scholarship deeply moved me, as I struggled to gain a foot-hold in the discipline as a novice professor and scholar. It was thus with profound sadness that I met the news of Ray's untimely death. Thanks go to Gary Knoppers for reading an earlier draft of this paper and his helpful suggestions for improvement.

1. See I. Gabriel, *Friede über Israel: Ein Untersuchung zur Friedenstheologie in Chronik I 10–II 36* (ÖBS, 10; Klosterneuburg: Österreiches Katholisches Bibelwerk, 1990).

2. Chr applies the doctrine of immediate retribution as well to non-royal figures. See, e.g., 1 Chron. 5.24-26 and 2 Chron. 36.14-20, both treated below. For Chr's doctrine of immediate retribution, see R.B. Dillard, 'Reward and Punishment in Chronicles: The Theology of Immediate Retribution', *WTJ* 46 (1984), pp. 164-72.

3. See, for instance, S. Japhet, *I & II Chronicles* (OTL; Louisville, KY: Westminster/John Knox, 1993), pp. 783-98.

fidelity to seek Yahweh alone,[4] an interpretative midrash on DtrH,[5] and as a battle reflecting the ethnic/social concerns of Chr's own day.[6] The discussion of battle reports in Chronicles, therefore, intersects with the larger understanding of the nature of Chr as a historian.

In pursuit of history, however, scholars have tended to downplay the most obvious feature of Chronicles: its narrative form. Scholars have been prone to isolate the battle accounts from their narrative contexts within the broader narrative of Chronicles in order to isolate the specific theology of Chr and/or to glean historical information independently embedded within the text. Furthermore, attention on battle accounts has likewise focused largely on specifically Chronistic *Sondergut*, passages without parallel in Samuel–Kings. Therefore, again scholars have tended to make historical judgments one passage at a time without proper attention to the larger historical picture that Chr presents.

A brief survey of battle accounts within the Chronistic narrative reveals, however, that battle accounts move the narrative towards or away from a 'historical' norm or ideal for Israel/Judah: honor among the nations and peace may exist for a unified Israel ruled by a Davidic king in conjunction with the proper cultic personnel performing the Mosaic rites in the Jerusalem temple. All that is required is utter theological faithfulness to Yahweh. Chr does not shrink from warfare, nor does he collapse it into cultic practice.[7] When Israel/Judah displays

4. See, e.g., A. Ruffing, *Yahwekrieg als Weltmetapher: Studien zu Yahwekrieg-texten des chronistischen Sondergutes* (SBB, 24; Stuttgart: Katholisches Bibelwerk, 1992), pp. 150-330.

5. K. Strübind, *Tradition als Interpretation in der Chronik* (BZAW, 201; Berlin: de Gruyter, 1991), pp. 177-88.

6. P.R. Davies, 'Defending the Boundaries of Israel in the Second Temple Period: 2 Chronicles 20 and the "Salvation Army"', in E.C. Ulrich *et al.* (eds.), *Priests, Prophets, and Scribes: Essays on the Formation and Heritage of Second Temple Judaism in Honour of Joseph Blenkinsopp* (JSOTSup, 149; Sheffield: JSOT Press, 1992), pp. 43-54.

7. Although the focus of this article takes it away from presenting Chr's theology of war, the reading here given diverges from interpretations of Chr as a proto-pacifist (see, e.g., S. Niditch's *War in the Hebrew Bible: A Study in the Ethics of Violence* [New York: Oxford University Press, 1993]: '1 and 2 Chronicles provide a more extended critique of human participation in the violence of war and a potential for an ideology of non-participation' [p. 139], and 'The Chroniclers... make a breakthrough toward an ideology of peace' [p. 148]), or as collapsing war into liturgical acts (see, e.g., G. von Rad, *Holy War in Ancient Israel* [Grand Rapids, MI: Eerdmans, 1991], esp. pp. 129-31).

theological fidelity, victorious offensive battles bring tribute and wealth to Jerusalem; defensive battles bring divine protection and fear upon Judah's enemies. Peace follows, though peace is only accomplished through battle. In the process of presenting the wars of Judah, Chr radically revises Judean history from its Deuteronomistic *Vorlage*. Battle accounts, both non-synoptic passages and passages taken or revised from Samuel–Kings, divide Judean history into various periods. Yet a program remains clear throughout: Judean battles culminate in peace for Judah under a Davidic monarchy, the faithful of all Israel united in Jerusalem, and cultic personnel performing the Yahwistic rites.

Chr's historical presentation of pre-exilic Judean history, therefore, is deeply affected by the battle accounts, not as isolated events, but as general historical portrayals of different periods within Judean history. Before we critically assess each battle account individually, we must examine them within their narrative contexts and the picture of Judean history that they help project. Therefore, I will briefly analyze the narrative connections of the battle accounts in three sections of Chronicles: the genealogies (1 Chron. 1–9), the David narrative (1 Chron. 10–29), and the time of the divided monarchy (2 Chron. 10–36). The unique Chronistic presentation of Judean history occasionally corresponds to— and occasionally contradicts—our contemporary understanding of that history. What remains consistent, however, is the narrative program that Chr presents. Thus, while it is possibile that Chr had accurate independent knowledge of pre-exilic history from DtrH, the programmatic concern of Chr, expressed within a specific 'historical' narrative, provides a simpler and more adequate explanation of the battle accounts.

Israel and the Land: Battle Accounts in 1 Chronicles 1–9

A generation ago Martin Noth could write, 'The great bulk of that which is now found in 1 Chron 2-9 is a confused and secondary mass of rank textual growth.'[8] Such a position no longer seems tenable. Today scholars are much more prone to see the genealogical material as a significant part of the Chronicles narrative, structured by important

---

8. M. Noth, *The Chronicler's History* (JSOTSup, 50; Sheffield: JSOT Press, 1987), p. 42.

thematic concerns.[9] The question of sources for the genealogical material, however, has not receded into the background.[10] Without seeking to solve the compositional riddle of the genealogies, we may briefly analyze the role of battle accounts within the genealogical preface of Chronicles and the general historical picture that Chr presents.

Stretching from Adam to Saul and his kin, 1 Chronicles 1–9 presents Chr's version of the 'pre-history' of Israel, that is, the time before the Davidic kingship. Military prowess and conflict appear in the first chapter, where Chr introduces Nimrod as a גבור, a mighty warrior (1 Chron. 1.10).[11] Hadad the Edomite, presaging Edom's role as a source of military conflict later in Chronicles, defeats Midian in the first reference to a battle in the book (1.46) .[12] In contrast to the progenitor of the Edomites, Abraham and his heirs appear in the land without a skirmish or conflict. Even in the genealogy of Judah (1 Chron. 4.1-23), Jabez receives land without battle: Jabez merely 'called upon the God of Israel... and God granted what he asked' (4.10). Israel emerges peacefully in the land.[13]

Yet the genealogies do record battles involving the sons of Israel. The first Israelite battle in Chronicles concludes the Simeonite genealogy (1 Chron. 4.41-43). Two Simeonite raids, one against the Meunim (v. 41) and another against the Amalekites at Mount Seir (vv. 42-43), acquire more land for the Simeonites to pasture their flocks. Yet the battles do not occur in a time before the monarchy; the Simeonites emerge in the land in peace. Rather, the text assigns the

9. See, for instance, M.D. Johnson, *The Purpose of Biblical Genealogies* (Cambridge: Cambridge University Press, 1969), pp. 37-76; S. Japhet, 'Conquest and Settlement in Chronicles', *JBL* 98 (1979), pp. 205-18; H.G.M. Williamson, 'Sources and Redaction in the Chronicler's Genealogy of Judah', *JBL* 94 (1979), pp. 351-59; and more recently, M. Kartveit, *Motive und Schichten der Landtheologie in 1 Chronik 1–9* (ConBOT, 28; Stockholm: Almqvist & Wiksell, 1989); and M. Oeming, *Das wahre Israel: Die 'genealogische Vorhalle' 1 Chronik 1–9* (Stuttgart: Kohlhammer, 1990).

10. See recently, D.V. Edelman, 'The Asherite Genealogy of 1 Chronicles 7.30-40', *BR* 33 (1988), pp. 13-23; and N. Na'aman, 'Sources and Redaction in the Chronicler's Genealogies of Asher and Ephraim', *JSOT* 49 (1991), pp. 105-10.

11. Chr here quotes Gen. 10.8, eliminating Gen. 10.9 and thus the possibility of interpreting this term with reference to Nimrod's hunting prowess.

12. Chr draws the battle directly from Gen. 36.35.

13. Nonetheless, Israel emerges very well armed, as in the militia lists given in 1 Chron. 7.

battles to the reign of Hezekiah (v. 41a). They thus portray military expansion that directly corresponds to Chr's unique presentation of Hezekiah.[14]

The Simeonite battles provide a significant narrative connection to ch. 5, the genealogies of the Transjordanian tribes.[15] The Reubenite genealogy contains a brief notice of a Reubenite battle with the Hagrites (1 Chron. 5.9-10). Again, the skirmish takes place during the period of the monarchy, this time during the reign of Saul (v. 10a). Formally, the text parallels the battle notice in 1 Chron. 4.41-43. Both passages conclude tribal genealogies; both record tribal skirmishes otherwise unattested; both provide brief battle accounts without explicit theological commentary; both are preceded by reference to the necessary pasturage to take care of the livestock; both anchor the battles in the reigns of specific kings; both exterminate suspiciously vague or stereotypical foes;[16] and both acquire land to continue their pastoral life. The battle accounts form a 'shared history' between the tribes of Simeon and Reuben.

Battle accounts also unify the genealogical presentation of the three Transjordanian tribes, the sons of Reuben, Gad, and the half tribe of Manasseh in 1 Chronicles 5. The Reubenites are not alone in winning battles. Verses 19-22 briefly depict a victorious battle between these tribes and the 'Hagrites, Jetur, Naphish, and Nodab' (v. 19) at an undisclosed time, because 'they cried to God in the battle, and he granted their entreaty because they trusted in him' (v. 20). Immediately following this account, however, we find the military defeat of this same

14. See Oeming, *Das wahre Israel*, p. 134.

15. Specific Chronistic characteristics fill 1 Chron. 5. The text attributes the Reubenites' genealogical displacement as firstborn to Reuben's sin—his defilement of 'his father's bed' (vv. 1b-2; cf. Gen. 35.22 and 49.3-4), a classic instance of Chr's doctrine of immediate retribution. The passage associates the military census of the Gadites with Jotham and Jeroboam (v. 17), thus foreshadowing the distinctively Chronistic account of the reign of Jotham. Finally, the account of the military muster of the Transjordanian tribes (v. 18) appears in distinctive Chronistic style (see 1 Chron. 12.37). Thus Kartveit's excision of all battle narratives from the *Grundschicht* of 1 Chron. 1–9 (*Motive und Schichten*, pp. 65-69) seems problematic. For a similar interpretation of the passage as Chronistic, see Oeming, *Das wahre Israel*, pp. 135-41.

16. On the Meunim (1 Chron. 4.41), see E.A. Knauf, 'Meunim', *ABD* 4 (1992), pp. 801-802; on the Hagrites (1 Chron. 5.9), see D.F. Graf, 'Hagrites', *ABD* 3 (1992), pp. 24-25.

Transjordanian confederation, because they 'transgressed against the God of their ancestors and prostituted themselves to the gods of the peoples of the land, whom God had destroyed before them,... the God of Israel stirred up the spirit of King Pul of Assyria, the spirit of King Tilgath-pilneser of Assyria, and he carried them away' (vv. 25-26). Military defeat and exile follow theological infidelity, as victory in battle follows invocation of divine aid. As in the reigns of Asa and Amaziah in 2 Chronicles, vv. 18-26 show that Chr's doctrine of immediate retribution may apply positively and then negatively to the same groups.

The battle accounts in 1 Chron. 4.41–5.26 present a certain scheme of Israelite history, a scheme consistent with the narrative that follows the genealogies. First, positive military encounters in his reign foreshadow the reign of Hezekiah—and possibly Jotham. More interesting, however, the battle accounts in 1 Chronicles 5 redefine the neo-Assyrian exile of the northern kingdom of Israel. Instead, Chronicles records a neo-Assyrian exile of the Transjordanian tribes, the Reubenites (5.6), the Gadites (5.22b), and the half-tribe of Manasseh (5.26) by 'Tilgath-pilneser'. While DtrH records the exile of the northern kingdom as a result of the 'sins of Jeroboam',[17] this theme is absent from Chronicles. No general exile of the northern kingdom occurs. 'Tilgath-pilneser' does not wreak havoc on the northern kingdom, but instead 'oppresses' Judah, plundering the temple when Ahaz requests Assyrian aid against the Edomites (2 Chron. 28.16-21). Only 1 Chronicles 5 records an Assyrian exile by Tilgath-pilneser of the Transjordanian tribes.[18]

A brief battle account occurs in the genealogy of Ephraim (1 Chron. 7.21). Found within a 'naming etiology'[19] for Beriah, Ephraim's last son, the account briefly records a raid by the inhabitants of Gath, 'who were born in the land', that kills all the previously born sons of

17. See F.M. Cross, *Canaanite Myth and Hebrew Epic* (Cambridge, MA: Harvard University Press, 1973), pp. 274-89; and G.N. Knoppers, *Two Nations under God: The Deuteronomistic History of Solomon and the Dual Monarchies. II. The Reign of Jeroboam, the Fall of Israel, and the Reign of Josiah* (HSM, 53; Atlanta: Scholars Press, 1994), pp. 13-44, 73-120.

18. 2 Chron. 30.6-9 presumes a partial neo-Assyrian exile for the northern tribes, yet *contra* DtrH, also presumes that a significant remnant persists in the land. Thanks to Gary Knoppers for this observation.

19. S.J. De Vries, *1 and 2 Chronicles* (FOTL, 11; Grand Rapids, MI: Eerdmans, 1989), pp. 79-80.

Ephraim. The battle report in 1 Chron. 7.21 functions consistently to represent the fortunes of Ephraim within Chr's narrative world, where the tribe of Ephraim both is a welcomed member of Israel, yet also 'is isolated as the center of opposition to the true cultus'.[20] Beriah, son of Ephraim, therefore, is a member of Israel, yet appropriately named Beriah 'because disaster has befallen his people' (v. 23b). Thus the passage provides a 'remnant theology' apropos for Chr's view of Ephraim. In 2 Chronicles 25 'a man of God' warns Amaziah not 'to let the army of Israel go with you, for the Lord is not with Israel—all these Ephraimites' (v. 7). Even though Ephraim is mentioned in the report of Hezekiah's passover as the first region that the king's representatives invite to the feast, none initially respond (2 Chron. 30.1, 10-11). Later, however, some from Ephraim do attend the passover—but eat in an unclean state, and are spared from disaster only by the pardon and prayer of Hezekiah (2 Chron. 25.18-20). Ultimately, Hezekiah 'cleanses' the territory of Ephraim from its idolatry, and its people return home in peace (2 Chron. 31.1). The last reference to the Ephraimites in Chronicles depicts them faithfully contributing to the Jerusalem temple (2 Chron. 34.8). Thus the etiological report of Beriah, the movement from the annihilation of the clan to its new beginning, mirrors the movement of Ephraim within the larger Chronistic narrative.

The occurrence of another Beriah in a brief battle account in the Benjaminite genealogy reinforces the coherence of 1 Chron. 7.21 within Chr's narrative. The Benjaminite Beriah (and his brother, Shema) also encounter a military conflict with the inhabitants of Gath. Rather than defeat, however, Beriah and Shema 'put to flight the inhabitants of Gath' (1 Chron. 8.13). Williamson's statement that 'despite the reference to Beriah in this verse and 7:23, no direct association between the incidents alluded to is apparent' seems curious.[21] Given the same name with the same opponent, the most natural reading would perhaps recognize that 8.13 closes the event narrated in 7.23, unless one presupposes that the genealogies originate in historical sources that possess no narrative connection. Once a narrative link is acknowledged, however, one immediately recognizes the *Tendenz* of Chr readily at work: the misfortunes of the ambiguous Ephraimites are reversed by the favored Benjaminites. The battle accounts implicitly function here as they often

20. Johnson, *Purpose*, p. 52; see also 2 Chron. 25.7; 30.11.
21. H.G.M. Williamson, *1 and 2 Chronicles* (NCB; Grand Rapids, MI: Eerdmans, 1982), p. 85.

explicitly function throughout Chronicles: defeat indicates divine displeasure; victory, divine approval.

Narrative links within the genealogies and narratives serve a larger historical scheme within Chronicles. Israel appears in the land without conquest, nearly without any military conflict. Of all the pre-monarchic tribes of Israel, only the sons of Ephraim suffer defeat, and their victors are vanquished by the sons of Benjamin. A Simeonite victory foreshadows the positive reign of Hezekiah. Finally, the Transjordanian tribes end in exile under the neo-Assyrian ruler, Tilgath-pilneser. The Transjordan, though once belonging to Israel, has been forfeited due to theological apostasy.

Battle accounts in the genealogies, therefore, give a unique biblical perspective on the pre-monarchic era. As Japhet has written, 'It is a most distinctive and revolutionary concept: contrary to most established historical traditions of the Pentateuch and the Former Prophets, the Chronicler presents a concept of people and land which is autochthonic in its basic features.'[22] In light of recent research, however, Chronicles here depicts a historical scenario closer to the emergence of 'Israel' in the land of Canaan than the remaining biblical literature.[23] On the other hand, the limitation of the neo-Assyrian exile to the Transjordanian tribes does not correspond with the historical data.[24] Herein lies the quandary of the historical usefulness of Chr's historiography. Occasionally, though not consistently, Chr's narrative and critically reconstructed Judean history converge to depict similar historical images. When inconsistent, as in the geographic limitation of the neo-Assyrian exile to the Transjordanian tribes, the issue is easily solved—we may attribute such a historical discrepancy to the programmatic aim of Chr. Yet does convergence indicate that Chr provides literary evidence for pre-exilic history? The narrative integrity of the battle accounts within 1 Chronicles 1–9 and the broader narrative of Chronicles urge caution

22. Japhet, 'Conquest and Settlement', p. 218. See also S. Japhet, *The Ideology of the Book of Chronicles and its Place in Biblical Thought* (BEATAJ, 9; Frankfurt am Main: Peter Lang, 1989), pp. 363-86, esp. pp. 374-79.

23. For a recent 'state of the question' assessment of Israelite origins in the land of Canaan, see K.W. Whitelam, 'The Identity of Early Israel: The Realignment and Transformation of Late Bronze-Iron Age Palestine', *JSOT* 63 (1994), pp. 57-87.

24. G.W. Ahlström, *The History of Ancient Palestine from the Palaeolithic Period to Alexander's Conquest* (JSOTSup, 146; Sheffield: JSOT Press, 1993), pp. 665-80.

at this point. While it is possible that Chr had access to different traditions about the emergence of Israel in the land (traditions solely
preserved via 1 Chron. 1–9), it seems that we must not move too
quickly to attribute the confluence of narrative and history to Chr's
engagement with pre-exilic, even pre-monarchic, Israelite history.
Rather it may be more prudent to understand both the peaceful
establishment of Israel in the land and the exclusive exile of the
Transjordanian tribes to the broader narrative purpose of Chr. Narrative
interests, not isolated events in the past, seemingly control Chr's presentation of battle accounts in 1 Chronicles 1–9.

The Rise of the Davidic King: Battle Accounts in 1 Chronicles 10–29

Perhaps no other character illustrates Chr's ambiguity about war more
than David. David glories in one victorious battle after another. God's
election and David's faithfulness coalesce in David's military success.
Yet it is precisely his prowess in battle that excludes David from the
honor of building the temple (1 Chron. 22.8).[25] Victory in battle is
good; rest from battle is better. David's reign moves the nation towards
Chr's ideal. David's career, which begins with the Philistine defeat of
Saul, ends with Israel at peace during the final phase of David's reign.

1 Chronicles 10–29 records twenty-one individual or group military
encounters. Interestingly, nineteen of these are paralleled in 1 and
2 Samuel.[26] Only two small skirmishes in 1 Chronicles 12 belong to the
Sondergut of Chronicles.[27] Yet the battle accounts in Chr's David

---

25. 'Great and heroic as David is, ethical and godly, even in the conduct of war,
he is not allowed to build God's holy dwelling on earth, the place where God's
name will rest, because he has shed blood in battle. However noble and necessary
the cause, the killing has disqualified him from constructing the sacred space.'
Niditch, *War*, p. 140.

26. 1 Chron. 10.1-14 // 1 Sam. 31.1-13; 1 Chron. 11.4-9 // 2 Sam. 5.4-9; 1 Chron
11.11 // 2 Sam. 23.8; 1 Chron. 11.12-14 // 2 Sam. 23.9-13; 1 Chron. 11.15-19 //
2 Sam. 23.13-17; 1 Chron. 11.20-21 // 2 Sam. 23.18-19; 1 Chron. 11.22-25 //
2 Sam. 23.20-23; 1 Chron. 14.8-12 // 2 Sam. 5.17-21; 1 Chron. 14.13-17 // 2 Sam.
5.22-25; 1 Chron. 18.1 // 2 Sam. 8.1; 1 Chron. 18.2 // 2 Sam. 8.2; 1 Chron. 18.3-11
// 2 Sam. 8.3-12; 1 Chron. 18.12-13 // 2 Sam. 8.13-14; 1 Chron. 19.1-15 // 2 Sam.
10.1-14; 1 Chron. 19.16-19 // 2 Sam. 10.15-19; 1 Chron. 20.1a // 2 Sam. 11.1;
1 Chron. 20.1b-3 // 2 Sam. 12.26-31; 1 Chron. 20.4 // 2 Sam. 21.18; and 1 Chron.
20.5-8 // 2 Sam. 21.19-22.

27. 1 Chron. 12.8-15, 19-22.

narrative portray a vastly different historical character and scenario than that found in 1 and 2 Samuel. As Niditch has recently written, 'The Chronicler does not want to portray David as a monarch who practices brutality as a regular feature of acquiring and holding power.... David is helped by God in his quest, not by the darker side of his humanity.'[28] Chr transforms the Deuteronomistic military account of David's reign by the careful selection of material taken from his source, organizing its placement within his narrative and using redactional summaries, often at the close of a battle report.

Chr's David narrative begins with the death of Saul in battle against the Philistines.[29] While 1 Chron. 10.1-12 may attest an earlier textual form of 1 Sam. 31.1-13 and thus provide an alternative tradition of Saul's last battle for historical analysis,[30] vv. 13-14 clearly attest Chr's style and *Tendenz*.[31] Verse 14b summarizes 1 Chronicles 10, while guiding the reader directly into the narrative to follow: 'And He [Yahweh] killed him [Saul] and He [Yahweh] turned the kingdom to David, the son of Jesse.' As Zalewski notes,

> the background of the story of the death of Saul is to be explained as representing Saul as being executed directly by the Lord, without any intervention on David's part, and not for a personal reason of David's, nor even as an agent carrying out the Lord's will. It was the Lord himself who put Saul to death and appointed David in his place.[32]

Chr's redactional summary interprets the battle account in two ways. Negatively, the battle indicates divine judgment on Saul for his unfaithfulness. Positively, the battle account opens the way for David to take the throne, not as a usurper, but as the divinely chosen successor to a failed dynasty.

1 Chronicles 11.4-9 recounts the first battle in which Chr's David

28. Niditch, *War*, p. 133.

29. Contrary to R. Mosis (*Untersuchungen zur Theologie des chronistischen Geschichtswerk* [FTS, 92; Freiburg: Herder, 1973]) and many others, I think that Saul's death forms a preface to the David narrative, rather than constituting an independent/typological reign by itself. See S. Zalewski, 'The Purpose of the Story of the Death of Saul in 1 Chronicles x', *VT* 39 (1989), pp. 449-67.

30. C.Y.S. Ho, 'Conjectures and Refutations: Is 1 Samuel XXXI 1-13 Really the Source of 1 Chronicles X 1-12?', *VT* 45 (1995), pp. 82-106.

31. Ho overextends his case by questioning the Chronistic origin of these verses, which clearly bear the stamp of Chr's own hand.

32. Zalewski, 'Purpose', p. 465.

directly participates: the conquest of Jerusalem. While the text parallels 2 Sam. 5.4-9, it substantially diverges from its *Vorlage* both in its narrative position[33] and content.[34] By the time of 2 Samuel 5, David is a shrewd, ruthless, battle-worn veteran in combat against the Philistines and for the Israelite throne. In Chronicles he is a new king establishing a capital with his people as part of his coronation activities. Kalimi observes,

> Such a presentation of the order of events creates the impression that 'all Israel' (xi 1...), who gathered together 'to David unto Hebron and installed him as king over them', went with him immediately after his coronation, and before the celebration of the event, to conquer Jerusalem...[35]

Thus the structural role of the conquest of Jerusalem presents an entirely different historical picture from that found in DtrH.

Joab's role largely distinguishes the Chronicles account of Jerusalem's conquest from its Deuteronomistic predecessor. Rather than receiving his position as military commander through the death of Abner, Joab steps into the center stage in 1 Chronicles 11.[36] The narrative thus begins the significant role that Joab plays in 1 Chronicles and initiates the collection of military leaders who support David as the legitimate king.[37] David and Joab's victory in this battle account bring them both honor and status, David as king with his capital city now named after him, and Joab as David's military chief of staff. 1 Chronicles 11.4-9 distinctively and uniquely prepares for the narrative to follow.

Seven battle accounts occur in 1 Chron. 11.10–12.41.[38] Chr moves 2 Samuel 23 from its place as an appendix to the reign of David and

---

33. See I. Kalimi, 'Literary-Chronological Proximity in the Chronicler's Historiography', *VT* 43 (1993), pp. 320-23.

34. See M. Oeming, 'Die Eroberung Jerusalems durch David in deuteronomistischer und chronistischer Darstellung (II Sam 5, 6-9 und I Chr 11, 4-8)', *ZAW* 106 (1994), pp. 404-20.

35. Kalimi, 'Literary-Chronological Proximity', p. 321.

36. 'The report of the conquest was in this way re-accentuated to the greater glory of Joab.' ('Der Eroberungsbericht wird so *ad maiorem gloriam Joabs umakzentuiert*.'): Oeming, 'Eroberung Jerusalems', p. 418.

37. 1 Chron. 11.6 thus provides the first step in the establishment of David's military officers found in 11.10–12.40.

38. See notes 25 and 26.

transplants and expands it within a narrative detailing how military units voluntarily join David's enthronement.[39] The battle accounts portray the military status and might that David accumulates at his coronation festival. Four battle accounts are drawn nearly verbatim from 2 Sam. 23.8-39, yet project an entirely different historical picture in their new narrative context. While it may simply be a scribal omission,[40] Chr may have shortened the battle report of Eleazar son of Dodo (2 Sam. 23.9-10) and merged it with a battle report of Shammah, son of Agee the Hararite (2 Sam. 23.11-13) in 1 Chron. 11.12-14. By associating Eleazar with David (2 Sam. 23.9b) and then having Eleazar single-handedly defeat the Philistines (v. 10), the passage implies that David was among the 'men of Israel' who 'withdrew' (v. 9b) in Samuel. By excising this, Chr's version has David join Eleazar in alone standing and defeating the Philistines when the rest of their compatriots flee (1 Chron. 11.14). Thus 1 Chron. 11.14b edits the closing verse of the battle account to emphasize his point: 'The Lord saved them [Eleazar and David] by a great victory.'

Two battle accounts arise in *Sondergut* material in 1 Chronicles 12, the only such accounts in the David narrative (v. 15 and v. 21). In each case the battle account concludes the list of those joining David's forces. 1 Chronicles 12.15 highlights the strength of the Gadites who join David. Verse 21, like Chr's redaction of the exploits of Eleazar, associates the victorious military activities of the Manassites with their alliance with David.

Commentators have been quick to posit a source behind these lists, and thus the battle acounts.[41] Before invoking a source, however, one should explore the narrative connections between the accounts and the rest of Chronicles. It is significant that the accounts involve the Gadites and the Manassites, two of the Transjordanian tribes commonly linked in Chronicles (cf. 1 Chron. 5.11-26; 12.37; 26.32). Ties to 1 Chronicles 5 seem especially pronounced. First, all three accounts place the successful military endeavors of the tribes during the reign of

39. As shown by H.G.M. Williamson, Chr frames this redactional effort to emphasize the theme of the establishment of David as king. '"We are yours, O David." The Setting and Purpose of 1 Chronicles 12.1-23', *OTS* 21 (1981), pp. 164-76.

40. Williamson, *Chronicles*, p. 102.

41. For a recent defense of this position, see Japhet, *I & II Chronicles*, pp. 255-59.

Saul. Second, the summaries of the military prowess of the Gadites in 12.8 significantly overlap in terminology with the summary of the Transjordanian tribes in 5.18. Third, the geography and the opponents in the victories of the Gadites and the Manassites in ch. 12 mirror the battles fought in 5.19. It seems, therefore, that Chr uses 1 Chronicles 12 as a chance to detail the successful battle accounts found in 1 Chronicles 5, link them to the person of David, and build the prestige of David through the might of the warriors who had joined him by the time of his coronation in Hebron. Gadite and Manassite military successes come with David; their defeat only at a later time.

The battle accounts in 1 Chron. 11.10–12.22, therefore, seem to have very specific narrative concerns at work in them. By repositioning them after the conquest of Jerusalem, Chr uses the accounts to ascribe military grandeur to the coronation festival of David (1 Chron. 12.38-40), a portrayal vastly different from David's turbulent rise to power in DtrH. Chr consistently uses the battle accounts to legitimate David's smooth acquisition of power.

With 1 Chronicles 14 the nature of the battle reports in the David narrative changes. Rather than establishing his reign, the accounts now serve to defend and extend the boundaries of Israel. The two military encounters in 1 Chron. 14.8-17 (drawn from 2 Sam. 5.11-25) show Philistine aggression and David's successful defense of his divinely given realm. In each David defends his realm against the Philistines according to the divine will. As we have consistently discovered, Chr redacts the accounts in their conclusion. The first encounter ends with David burning the Philistine gods (v. 12), rather than transporting them home as in the Samuel narrative (2 Sam. 5.21). While the divergence could have arisen within the textual transmission of 2 Samuel 5,[42] the end product finds David obeying the holy war ordinances of the book of Deuteronomy.[43] The second account ends with a verse not paralleled in 2 Samuel 5: 'The fame of David went out into all lands, and the Lord brought the fear of him on all the nations' (1 Chron. 14.17). David's victory in these defensive battles leads to worldwide fame and security for Israel! No other battles will occur on Israelite soil during David's reign. The battle accounts serve to establish peace in Israel, united in Jerusalem under the kingship of David.

42. W.E. Lemke, 'The Synoptic Problem in the Chronicler's History', *HTR* 58 (1965), pp. 351-52.

43. Deut. 7.5; see Japhet, *I & II Chronicles*, pp. 289-90.

Finally, 1 Chron. 18.1–20.8 depicts the only offensive battles fought by David and his subordinates, outside the conquest of Jerusalem. Ten separate battles occur, all paralleled in 2 Samuel.[44] In battle David and his representatives expand Israel's realm, collect tribute, and maintain their honor. While space will not permit a detailed redactional analysis, the section reveals well how Chr weaves battle accounts within his broader narrative, producing a widely divergent historical picture from his *Vorlage*.

At least two changes are noteworthy among the ten battle accounts. In 2 Samuel 8 David arbitrarily executes one group of vanquished Moabites, allowing another group to survive. In contrast 1 Chron. 18.2 briefly reports David's victory over Moab and their subsequent tribute brought to him. In the battle accounts in Chronicles, David fights honorably, not according to the code of ruthless expediency that often characterizes him in Samuel.[45] Likewise, tribute received from David's subjected nations does not go for David's personal aggrandizement. Rather it supplies materials later used in Solomon's erection of the temple (1 Chron. 18.8b; cf. 1 Chron. 22.14-16). Thus David's offensive wars anticipate and prepare for the subsequent narrative.

Warfare ceases completely as David's reign enters its final phase.[46] In 1 Chronicles 21 David spares Israel from battle by his personal invocation of divine mercy, willingly and vicariously accepting punishment for a sin not his own (1 Chron. 21.11-13).[47] There are no hints of political and military unrest at the close of Chr's David narrative— Absalom appears only in the genealogy of Judah (1 Chron. 3.2), not within the David narrative proper. After 1 Chron. 22.1, Israel is completely at peace as David prepares his kingdom for the transition to his

---

44. See note 25.

45. As Niditch observes, 'While the heroic tales of David and his men of valor are preserved pretty much in the form of the Deuteronomistic History, portrayals of David as practitioner of the war ideology of expediency have been virtually expunged' (*War*, p. 133).

46. See Gabriel, *Friede*, whose inclusion of 22.1–29.30 with the Solomon narrative, however, does not follow from the fact that David's reign ends in peace in Chronicles. Rather it seems to indicate the close narrative connection between the David and Solomon narratives in Chronicles.

47. J.W. Wright, 'The Innocence of David in 1 Chronicles 21', *JSOT* 60 (1993), pp. 87-105. See, however, the rejoinder by N. Bailey, 'David's Innocence: A Response to J. Wright', *JSOT* 64 (1994), pp. 83-90.

successor, Solomon. David goes to his fathers at rest, spared from military toils in the closing years of his reign.

David in Chronicles, therefore, never fights a losing battle, never fights against fellow Israelites, and never engages in cruel military conduct. The battle accounts produce a progressive development in the David narrative. Initially, they highlight the legitimacy of his rule. David emerges as the divinely elected king, whom all Israel (especially the military) unanimously support. Why should they not? He fought victoriously with them before his reign, thus linking the David narrative to the battle accounts in the genealogical section. Battle accounts next show David as king, defending the boundaries of the land against the incursions of Philistines, resulting in his fame and the protection of Israel from invasion (14.17). Battles of conquest follow. The subsequent wealth moves the narrative towards the building of the temple. David's battles, however, are not without a price. Ultimately they contribute to David's disqualification from building the temple (1 Chron. 22.8). David spends his last year free from battle, preparing for the building of the temple and organizing his kingdom for the transition to the reign of Solomon.

The David narrative, therefore, culminates with Israel at peace under David with the proper priestly and levitical personnel appointed over the cult, preparing for the building of the temple. Though the battle accounts largely originated in Chr's Deuteronomistic *Vorlage*, a shift of narrative contexts, redactional alterations, especially at the conclusion of the accounts, and two brief, unique accounts produce a completely different portrait of 'David, king, and warrior'. As a whole, they contribute to an idealized narrative portrayal of David. Recent historical research based upon material and literary evidence has pictured the 'historical David' as a tribal chieftain, shrewdly holding a fragile tribal coalition together;[48] Chr transforms him more into a 'Hellenistic tyrant'.[49]

Battle accounts in the David narrative therefore function much as they do in 1 Chronicles 1–9. For Chr, narrative demands heavily outweigh historical concerns. Battle accounts in the David narrative move

---

48. See J.W. Flanagan, *David's Social Drama* (JSOTSup, 73; Sheffield: JSOT Press, 1988).

49. See M. Smith, *Palestinian Parties and Politics that Shaped the Old Testament* (New York: Columbia University Press, 1972), pp. 125-47, for an interpretation of Nehemiah as a Hellenistic tyrant.

the 'history' towards Chr's ideal for Israel: a kingdom at peace under
the reign of the Davidic king, with proper priestly and levitical personnel overseeing the Yahwistic cultic rites and properties.

From Peace to Exile: Battle Accounts in 2 Chronicles 10–36

Battle accounts dominate the post-Solomonic Judean history in
2 Chronicles. The accounts, however, differ formally from those in
1 Chronicles. Battles in 2 Chronicles often appear as independent
battles set within long narratives enclosing extensive speeches; in 1
Chronicles battles are generally clustered within the same narrative and
briefly recounted. In contrast to 1 Chronicles, battles often appear in
2 Chronicles without Deuteronomistic parallel or use a brief passage
from Kings as a beginning point to construct a different narrative. Yet
differences between 1 and 2 Chronicles transcend formal characteristics.
A large segment of the narrative, the reign of Solomon (2 Chron. 1–9),
is devoid of any conflict. When wars do break out, battles of individuals
or single tribes end; war occurs as a more national/ethnic phenomenon.
Yet the Davidic kings fight not only Philistines, Edomites, and others,
as in 1 Chronicles; they also fight against their northern kin. For the
first time, civil war occurs within Israel. The narrative progresses, then
regresses. The ideal that the narrative moves towards in David is established in Solomon, and at various times, to various degrees, approached
and forsaken in the battle accounts in 2 Chronicles. As throughout
Chr's history, however, one thing remains constant: victory in battle
still follows faithfulness to Yahweh; defeat follows unfaithfulness.

Recent scholarship has readily analyzed select battle reports in
2 Chronicles from various perspectives.[50] While scholars differ in their
assessments of the value of the passages for the reconstruction of the
history of pre-exilic Israel, a consensus has emerged that, by and large,

50. Three German works published in the early 1970s (P. Welten, *Geschichte
und Geschichtsdarstellung in den Chronikbüchern* [WMANT, 42; Neukirchen–
Vluyn: Neukirchener Verlag, 1973]; T. Willi, *Die Chronik als Auslegung* [FRLANT,
106; Göttingen: Vandenhoeck & Ruprecht, 1972]; and R. Mosis, *Untersuchungen
zur Theologie des chronistischen Geschichtswerkes* [1973]), along with Japhet's
commentary, which defends a basic historical accuracy behind Chronistic *Sondergut*,
largely represent the current competing interpretative paradigms for the battle
accounts of 2 Chronicles. Focus on the individual non-synoptic accounts, however,
has failed to highlight how the battle accounts move the narrative toward and away
from Chr's 'historical' norm of a Davidic-ruled Israel at peace.

Chr's style and concerns shape each battle account in the Chronistic *Sondergut*.[51] The issue of a battle account's historicity, therefore, is whether a passage contains a historical kernel or not, a judgment made usually as a result of a stylistic analysis or on the basis of a hypothetical fit with pre- or post-exilic political-military considerations. Yet the quest for historical kernels has minimalized narrative analysis of the passages within Chr's framework. As in the treatment of 1 Chronicles, I will briefly examine the narrative connections of each passage to discover the general historical picture that Chr grants us. Ultimately, we may then ask whether it is necessary to posit historical materials to explain Chr's narrative.

The absence of war marks Solomon's reign as a high point in Chr's history.[52] Solomon achieves the ideal approached in David's reign: Israel is at peace, united under a faithful Davidic king in Jerusalem with the proper temple personnel overseeing the proper rites at Yahweh's temple. Yet Solomon's peace does not cease with his death; it stretches into the first part of Rehoboam's reign. Although Rehoboam readies himself to do battle with Jeroboam, he obediently follows the divine word spoken by Shemaiah, a man of God, and does not go to battle. This results in a generally positive view of Rehoboam in the first part of his reign, and the narrative only slowly moves away from its ideal. Although Jeroboam divides Israel, those from his kingdom still travel south to 'seek the Lord God of Israel' in Jerusalem (2 Chron. 11.16). Ultimately, it is Rehoboam himself who provokes battle through his apostasy. 'Strengthened' for his rule, Rehoboam nevertheless forsook the law of the Lord (2 Chron. 12.1), and so immediately Shishak, king of Egypt, attacks Judah and Jerusalem (vv. 2-12). In *Sondergut* material Shemaiah the prophet interprets the attack as a result of Judah's theological infidelity (v. 15). Rehoboam and the princes of Israel humble themselves and God grants them 'some deliverance' (כמעט לפליטה, v. 7) especially in Jerusalem. Ultimately, even after Shishak's attack, 'conditions were good in Judah' (v. 12).

Chr's expansion of Shishak's invasion reinforces his presentation of Rehoboam as basically a good king. Though not beyond culpability, Rehoboam faithfully obeys Yahweh when confronted by the prophetic word. As becomes apparent in Abijah's battle against Jeroboam,

---

51. See, e.g., Welten, *Geschichte*; Ruffing, *Yahwekrieg*; Strübind, *Tradition als Interpretation*; and even Japhet, *I & II Chronicles*.

52. Gabriel, *Friede*, pp. 55-101.

responsibility for the schism of Jeroboam does not fall upon Solomon (as in DtrH), but upon Jeroboam.[53] Nonetheless, during Rehoboam's reign Judah has moved several steps away from the norm established during the reign of Solomon. The occurrence of battles highlights the loss of this ideal.

2 Chronicles 12.2-12 is not the only battle account in Rehoboam's reign. 2 Chronicles 12.15b records that hostilities broke out and continued between Rehoboam and Jeroboam. Within the narrative frame work of Chronicles, Abijah's battle against Israel (2 Chron. 13.2-20) concludes this series of military encounters. Entirely Chronistic *Sondergut*,[54] Chronistic ideas fill the passage that explicitly presumes Chr's unique presentation of Rehoboam's reign.[55] As Knoppers has shown, 'The Chronicler shapes the narrative to fit the category of an internal Israelite sacral war.'[56] Despite the strategic wiles of Jeroboam, the army of Judah 'cried to the Lord and the priests blew the trumpets... and God defeated Jeroboam and all Israel before Abijah and Judah' (vv. 14-17). The scene concludes with Abijah taking territory from the realm of Jeroboam. Conflict with Israel ceases and 'in his [Abijah's] days the land had rest for ten years' (2 Chron. 14.1b).

Battle accounts therefore provide the connective thread uniting the reigns of Rehoboam and Abijah. Joining materials found in 1 Kings with non-synoptic materials, battles are not merely isolated events but combine to present a general picture of Judean history. Contrary to DtrH, Jeroboam, guilty for rebelling against the young Rehoboam,

---

53. See the insightful analysis of G.N. Knoppers, 'Rehoboam in Chronicles: Villain or Victim?', *JBL* 109 (1990), pp. 423-40.

54. 'Verse 2b is taken from 1 Kings 51.7b. There, in the original context of a Deuteronomistic summary of Abijah's reign, "war" is to be interpreted as a collective noun, referring to a constant state of conflict throughout the time of Rehoboam and into the reign of his son. The Chronicler takes this word to refer to and introduce a single confrontation, which he now proceeds to describe.' Japhet, *I & II Chronicles*, pp. 688-89.

55. Abijah's war has received an abundance of literary and historical analysis. In addition to the commentaries, see G.H. Jones, 'From Abijam to Abijah', *ZAW* 106 (1994), pp. 420-34; G.N. Knoppers, "Battling against Yahweh": Israel's War against Judah in 2 Chr 13.2-20', *RB* 100 (1993), pp. 511-32; Ruffing, *Yahwekrieg*, pp. 19-79; R.W. Klein, 'Abijah's Campaign against the North (II Chron. 31)— What Were the Chronicler's Sources?', *ZAW* 95 (1983), pp. 210-17; Welten, *Geschichte*, pp. 116-29.

56. Knoppers, 'Battling', p. 525.

ultimately experiences defeat at the hand of Abijah's Judean army, which ushers in a time of peace and prosperity for Judah. Battle accounts do not emerge in 2 Chronicles as a pastiche of independent sources nor as individual typologies linked to the kings of the united monarchy. Chr employs battle accounts to develop a particular narrative that shows the divine election of one Israel, faithful to Yahweh alone, united under a Davidic monarch, worshiping in the temple in Jerusalem. Anything that deviates or distracts from this norm receives condemnation within Chr's narrative, condemnation often encoded within battle accounts. If Chr had access to authentic historical material, he completely subsumed it within his larger narrative purpose.

Asa's reign begins in the peace established by Abijah's defeat of Jeroboam (2 Chron. 14.6). Two battle accounts, however, arise during Asa's reign.[57] First, Asa defends Judah against the invading army of Zerah the Ethiopian in a non-synoptic passage (2 Chron. 14.9-15). In Chronicles Zerah represents the first attack on Judah by a non-Israelite since the Philistine incursion in the early days of David's reign. Asa 'cried to the Lord his God... so the Lord defeated the Ethiopians before Judah' (vv. 11-12). Interestingly, the outcome parallels David's early defensive battles. 'The fear of the Lord' (פחד יהוה) descends upon the Ethiopians, as it did on the nations following David's successful defensive battles (cf. 1 Chron. 14.17). The Judeans plunder the surrounding cities before returning to Jerusalem.

The second battle represents a turning point in the history of Judah (2 Chron. 16.1-6//1 Kgs 15.17-22). The peace between Judah and Israel had enabled faithful from the northern tribe to join the true Israel in Jerusalem under Asa (2 Chron. 15.8-9). This narrative context suggests a different understanding of Baasha's construction of Ramah from what one finds in the Deuteronomistic *Vorlage*. In 1 Kgs 15.17-25, within a pattern of continuing military conflict between Israel and Judah (1 Kgs 15.16), the fortress arises to block traffic. No such conflict exists in Chronicles.[58] Here the fortress functions to block northern pilgrimages from participating in the Jerusalem cult. Asa's alliance with

---

57. In addition to the commentaries, see Gabriel, *Friede*, pp. 112-30; Ruffing, *Yahwekreig*, pp. 80-149; R.B. Dillard, 'The Reign of Asa (2 Chr 14-16): An Example of the Chronicler's Theological Method', *JETS* 23 (1980), pp. 207-18; Welten, *Geschichte*, pp. 129-40.

58. Chr replaces the notice of on-going conflict between Asa and Baasha in 1 Kgs 15.16 with the notice of an era of peace during Asa's reign (2 Chron. 15.19).

Ben-Hadad, king of Syria, in response to Baasha, king of Israel, therefore, seeks to ensure continued access to Jerusalem for the northern tribes. Nevertheless, Asa's actions violate the prophetic exhortation from Azariah to seek aid in Yahweh alone. While the battle strategy works, Asa faces personal divine condemnation as a result of his unfaithfulness (v. 12). The grounds for the peace established after Abijah's victory over Jeroboam are gone. Judean 'history', driven by battle accounts, has moved away from the 'historical' norm established during the reigns of David and Solomon. A need for reform now exists.

This reform comes during the reign of Jehoshaphat,[59] and two battle reports play pivotal roles that move the narrative towards reform. First, Chr borrows the account of Jehoshaphat's alliance and military expedition with Ahab (2 Chron. 18.1–19.4a) from 1 Kgs 22.1-35a. In typical Chronistic fashion, redactional seams occur at the beginning and end of the passage (2 Chron. 18.1-2; 19.1-4a). These 'seams' produce a different historical picture from that provided by 1 Kings 22. In Chronicles the battle arises out of the context of a marriage alliance with Ahab and Ahab's flattery of Hezekiah; in 1 Kings it arises out of continual war between Syria and Israel (1 Kgs 22.1). The Chronicles version focuses on the behavior and redemption of Jehoshaphat, but 1 Kings on the death of Ahab. Finally, Chronicles roundly condemns the alliance between Jehoshaphat and Ahab (cf. 2 Chron. 19.2); 1 Kings presumes its propriety. The renegade tribes of the north are welcome as part of the Davidic, Jerusalem-centered kingdom—but only as subordinates, not equals. The battle account shows that the Davidic king need not form alliances with the illegitimate kings of Israel. Jehoshaphat is saved from defeat only by calling to Yahweh in the midst of battle (v. 31b). Jehoshaphat's combined disloyalty and loyalty to Yahweh, exemplified in the first battle account, continues the state of affairs found at the end of Asa's reign.

This ambiguity dissipates in the second battle account in Jehoshaphat's reign (2 Chron. 20.1-30). This *Sondergut* passage has

---

59. Battles in the reign of Jehoshaphat (esp. 2 Chron. 20) have received much recent attention. In addition to the commentaries, see P.C. Beentjes, 'Tradition and Transformation: Aspects of Innerbiblical Interpretation in 2 Chronicles 20', *Bib* 74 (1993), pp. 258-68; Davies, 'Defending the Boundaries'; G.N. Knoppers, 'Reform and Regression: The Chronicler's Presentation of Jehoshaphat', *Bib* 72 (1991), pp. 423-40; Strübind, *Tradition als Interpretation*; Gabriel, *Friede*, pp. 130-60; Ruffing, *Yahwekrieg*, pp. 150-350; Welten, *Geschichte*, pp. 166-72.

provoked much recent discussion concerning the possible preservation of pre-exilic historical material and has been analyzed as an important source of information about Chr's own perspective.[60] Only brief observations may be made here. First, scholars agree that Chronistic language, forms, and themes fill the passage.[61] Second, the passage records a defensive battle and falls within a certain narrative development that we have seen before. Jehoshaphat and all Judah seek help in Yahweh alone, who delivers Judah without battle. Then Moabites, Ammonites, and Meunites devour each other (vv. 22-23). All the Judeans have to do is collect the spoils of Yahweh's war. As in the defensive battles of David and Asa, the 'fear of God' (פחד אלהים, v. 29) falls upon the surrounding countries and God gives Judah rest from war (2 Chron. 20.30). Yahweh restores the peace of Judah as a consequence of Jehoshaphat's faithfulness to Yahweh alone.

The battle accounts of Jehoshaphat's reign continue a narrative cycle begun in Rehoboam's reign. Judean battles do not increase the boundaries of the realm. Rather, they chiefly preserve the land of Israel, especially Judah and Jerusalem, from outside threats. Northern kings are anathema, unless subservient to the Davidic king and Jerusalem cult. Seeking Yahweh alone in these battles brings victory. In defensive battles, seeking Yahweh alone brings terror upon enemies, and thus peace upon the land. Jehoshaphat restores Judah to its 'natural state' as elected by Yahweh. The result fundamentally alters the historical picture from that of the Deuteronomistic reign of Jehoshaphat.

Narrative concerns and techniques shape Chr's battle accounts in 2 Chronicles 10–20. Yahweh grants victory in battle when the Davidic king seeks him and brings defeat upon the nation when the king acts unfaithfully. Yet this Chronistic 'doctrine of immediate retribution' serves a larger narrative theme. Rest, absence of military conflict, depends upon a Davidic king in Jerusalem ruling over a subordinate Israel loyal to Yahweh, Yahweh's temple, and temple personnel as guided by the prophetic word. Battle accounts move the narrative towards and away from this ideal. From this perspective, after Jehoshaphat's faithful defense of Jerusalem from invaders, only Hezekiah approaches the norm in the remaining narrative of

---

60. See Japhet, *I & II Chronicles*, pp. 780-803.

61. Both Ruffing (*Yahwekrieg*, p. 290), who denies the historicity of the report, and Japhet (*I & II Chronicles*, p. 783), who accepts a pre-exilic historical basis for the account, agree that the passage shows Chr's hand at work.

2 Chronicles. Yet battle accounts continue to serve the same function with the same narrative techniques. The remaining fifteen battle accounts in 2 Chronicles move Judah sometimes towards, but more usually away from, this 'historical' norm.

Rest does not remain long for Judah. Even in Jehoshaphat's reign, his alliance with the north to build a navy forewarns the armada's subsequent destruction (2 Chron. 20.36-37). Two battle accounts in Jehoram's reign show the immediate consequences of theological apostasy as the narrative ideal unwinds. Chr transplants the rebellion of Edom and the consequential rebellion of Libnah (2 Chron. 21.8-10) from 1 Kgs 8.20-22 into his narrative by adding the theological rationale for the rebellion (v. 10b). 'Forsaking the Lord' leads to the unraveling of peace on the fringe of Judah's sphere of influence. Judah's problems, however, intensify. In 2 Chron. 21.16-17, a non-synoptic passage, Judah suffers defeat in an invasion for the first time since Shishak's invasion. Yet Jehoram, unlike Rehoboam, does not repent and loses all his sons, except for Ahaziah (2 Chron. 21.17b).[62]

Battle accounts both move the narrative away from Chr's ideal and reveal the consequences of this movement. Ahaziah enters a military alliance and battles with Jehoram son of Ahab against Syria (2 Chron. 22.4-6 // 2 Kgs 8.28-29). In Chronicles, unlike Kings, the alliance itself is called evil (v. 4), and more importantly, the alliance leads to God's destruction of Ahaziah's sons and then himself (vv. 7-9). Apostasy leads to a defeat so extreme that it removes not only peace, but ultimately Davidic rule of Judah in Jerusalem.[63] With the reign of Ahaziah's mother, Athaliah, Judah moves farther away from the 'historical' norm established several times throughout its 'history'. Only the temple and the faithful priesthood remain.

For the first and only time in Chronicles, battle breaks out between Judeans and begins to move the narrative back towards the ideal. A coup led by Jehoiada the priest re-establishes a Davidic king, Joash, upon the throne (2 Chron. 23.1-15). Chr adapts the battle, largely bloodless (except for the execution of Athaliah), by emphasizing the role that the Levites play in the coup (e.g., 2 Chron. 23.2, 6, 18-19). Joash, under Jehoiada's guidance, leads Judah back towards the ideal in a narrative

---

62. 2 Chron. 22.1b presumes the distinct context of Chr's narrative in 2 Chron. 21.17b, thus anchoring Ahaziah's reign within the events of his father's reign.

63. Ahaziah has moved far from the ideal—and subsequently from the peace of Jehoshaphat, with whom he is compared (v. 9b).

in which battle is noticeably absent. When Jehoiada dies, however, Joash slips into a most serious apostasy—murdering Jehoiada's son, a prophet (2 Chron. 24.22). Contrary to 2 Kgs 17.17-21, Judah and Jerusalem consequently fall to Syria, rather than merely paying tribute: 'the Lord delivered into their [the Syrian's] hands a very great army [of Judah]' (v. 24b). Ultimately Joash's own servants assassinate him 'because of the blood of the son of Jehoiada the priest' (v. 25b, no parallel). Violence suffered by Judah and her kings results from moving away from the 'historical' norm. Chr freely revises his source to make this point clear, even if it means changing the historical picture from DtrH.

Amaziah continues Judah's theological wavering, as 'he did what was right in the eyes of the Lord, yet not with a blameless heart' (2 Chron. 25.2). Two battle accounts illustrate this. First, he acts as a Davidic king loyal to Yahweh alone in sending home the Ephraimites before a victorious offensive battle with the 'men of Seir'.[64] Yet the Ephraimites pillage Judean cities on the way home, and Amaziah accepts the Edomite gods as his own. Amaziah then initiates a parley with Joash, the king of Israel. Idolatry, however, has already sealed his doom (v. 20). Joash responds by defeating the Judean army at Beth-shemesh before moving on to pillage Jerusalem.[65] Judah suffers in the homeland, because they abandoned the Davidic dynasty and failed to remain faithful to God.

The next four battle accounts highlight Judah's move back towards the 'historical' norm and then its abandonment, all in non-synoptic passages. Uzziah fights and wins an offensive war against the Philistines and others because 'God helped him'. As a result, he receives tribute and fame (2 Chron. 26.6-8), all this happening after he set himself to 'seek God' (v. 5). Likewise Jotham defeats the Ammonites, receives tribute, and 'becomes mighty, because he ordered his ways before the Lord his God' (2 Chron. 27.5-6). Ahaz, however, begins his reign with idolatry and suffers defeat not only at the hands of the king of Syria,

64. Chr completely rewrites the passage from his 2 Kgs 14.1-14 *Vorlage*. In addition to the commentaries, see M.P. Graham, 'Aspects of the Structure and Rhetoric of 2 Chronicles 25', in M.P. Graham, W.P. Brown, and J.K. Kuan (eds.), *History and Interpretation: Essays in Honor of John H. Hayes* (JSOTSup, 173; Sheffield: JSOT Press, 1993), pp. 78-89.

65. Chr's conclusion to the battle closely parallels his *Vorlage* (2 Kgs 14.11-14), except for adding the theological rationale for the defeat in v. 20b.

but also before the king of Israel (2 Chron. 28.5-7). Yet God has not abandoned the ideal for Judah; Ahaz's disobedience only interrupts it. In response to the prophetic word, Ephraimite leaders return the spoils of war, both persons and goods, allowing them to return to Judah (2 Chron. 28.8-15).[66]

The leaders of Ephraim display more discernment than Ahaz, who immediately seeks a military alliance with Assyria in response to the continued incursions of the Edomites and a new wave of Philistine battles (28.16-18). Ahaz's tactics backfire. Because the military defeats arose as a result of Ahaz's unfaithfulness, Tilgath-pilneser, king of Assyria, also attacks (vv. 20-21).[67] Ahaz's unfaithfulness leads to defeat in battle after battle and moves Judah farther from its ideal. Yet, even in Ahaz's reign, the ideal is not lost.

The reign of Hezekiah moves Israel directly back towards the 'historical' norm in his cultic reforms and openness to all northerners who will obey his summons. The relative lack of battle accounts high lights this return. The only battle account is a Chronistic version of Sennacherib's seige (2 Chron. 32.1-23). Again, a loyal Davidic king seeks Yahweh in a defensive battle for Jerusalem. The battle account thereby re-established the 'historical' norm for the last time in Chronicles. 'The Lord saved Hezekiah... and gave him rest on every side. And many brought gifts to the Lord to Jerusalem and precious things to Hezekiah king of Judah, so that he was exalted in the sight of all nations from that time onward' (2 Chron. 32.22-23). The Davidic king rules in peace, joined by the faithful from the northern tribes, all united at the Jerusalem temple under the proper temple personnel, while the world honors the might of Judah with gifts.

After the establishment of rest in the reign of Hezekiah, battles in the seventh century remain relatively infrequent. A battle account only briefly interrupts Manasseh's reign, whose idolatry leads to defeat by the Assyrians (2 Chron. 33.11). Like Rehoboam, however, Manasseh repents and quickly is restored in peace to Jerusalem (vv. 12-13). Josiah's reign approaches that of Hezekiah: instead of remaining at peace in Jerusalem, he attacks Shishak in violation of a divine oracle

66. See recently, E. Ben Zvi, 'A Gateway to the Chronicler's Teaching: The Account of the Reign of Ahaz in 2 Chr 28.1-17', *SJOT* 7 (1993), pp. 216-49.

67. The passage thus fills out the narrative briefly described in 1 Chron. 5. See above.

and thus suffers the loss of his life (2 Chron. 35.20-24).[68] Even the deportations of Jehoiakim (2 Chron. 36.6) and Jehoiachin (2 Chron. 36.10) take place without battle. They are merely 'recalled' as Yahweh's reponse to their idolatry. The rest that was established in the reign of Hezekiah does not immediately dissipate.

The final battle account represents the most devastating defeat of Judah in Chronicles: the Babylonian conquest of Jerusalem and the temple. Not only is Zedekiah unfaithful, but for the first time in Chronicles, so is the Jerusalem priesthood (2 Chron. 36.14). All Judean leaders—not just the king—utterly abandon the 'historical' norm of the faithful Davidic king ruling in Jerusalem overseeing the faithful Jerusalem temple personnel in cultic devotion to Yahweh alone. Indeed, they even ignored the prophetic word of Jeremiah (v. 12). True to Chr's doctrine of retribution, the Babylonians devastate Jerusalem and the temple, deporting the people into Babylon (vv. 17-20). Now the land has rest without the presence of a Davidic king or a Jerusalem temple or even priests and Levites. Yet the norm does not seem eclipsed: as David went up to Jerusalem the first time, so Cyrus grants permission for Judeans to return to Jerusalem and rebuild the temple (2 Chron. 36.22-23). The first step in the restoration of the 'historical' norm for Judah is underway.

Battle accounts in 2 Chronicles, therefore, serve a pedagogical purpose within Chr's narrative: they move the narrative both towards and away from a 'historical' norm of peace under a Davidic king, ruling in Jerusalem with the proper temple personnel practicing the proper rites, open to submissive northerners, all seeking faithfulness to Yahweh alone. Battle accounts provide an interpretative scheme for recounting the 'history' of the divided monarchy, dividing it into three eras: Solomon to Jehoshaphat, Jehoshaphat to Hezekiah, and Hezekiah to Zedekiah. Chr can creatively insert Deuteronomistic battle materials into this scheme, extensively revise them (even to the point of changing the outcome), or include non-paralleled material. The result, however, is a 'revisionist' history where Solomon fights no battles: no general neo-Assyrian exile of the north occurs; Sennacherib's siege of Jerusalem results in Hezekiah's prosperity; and Jerusalem suffers only one defeat at the hands of the neo-Babylonians. Whatever the case with each individual battle account in 2 Chronicles, as a whole they portray

68. It is important to note that Judah itself suffers no harm; only Josiah loses his life.

a version of pre-exilic Judean history that, at best, is difficult to harmonize with either DtrH's portrayal or contemporary critical reconstructions.

Conclusion

Battle accounts in Chronicles serve primarily to establish, maintain, and legitimate a 'historical' norm of a united Israel at peace in their ancestral land under a Davidic monarch, with the proper priestly and levitical personnel officiating at the Jerusalem temple. This ideal directly depends upon utter and complete faithfulness to Yahweh alone. In Chronicles 'history' is at the mercy of this 'historical' norm. Thus, Israel emerges in the land in peace. David fights only against the enemies of Israel and ends his reign in peace. War never touches Solomon or his reign. Jeroboam violates the ideal in breaking off from Rehoboam, rendering the kings of the north (and any alliances with them) illegitimate; the northern tribes, however, as part of Israel may voluntarily join the ideal in Jerusalem. There is no neo-Assyrian exile of the northern kingdom, but only of the Transjordanian tribes. The norm is momentarily restored in the reigns of Asa, Jehoshaphat, and especially Hezekiah. Ultimately it is eclipsed, though not extinguished, in the one Babylonian exile due to the apostasy of all Judah, including Zedekiah, the people, and for the first time, the Jerusalem priesthood. In the battle accounts in Chronicles, a desire to interact with historical material is utterly subservient to Chr's narrative ideal. Given the force of this norm in shaping Chr's battle accounts, prudence would seemingly call for extreme caution in moving beyond Chr's battle narratives to historical 'kernels' behind the text to reconstruct pre-exilic Israelite history.

We may obtain a similar conclusion by examining the compositional techniques of Chr in employing battle accounts within his narrative. Battle accounts originate in the narrative by three Chronistic techniques: (1) patching a previously written account into the narrative by constructing narrative 'seams' at the beginning and/or end of the narrative; (2) totally revising, correcting, or expanding a Deuteronomistic account; and (3) seemingly creating accounts to fit his own narrative purposes. One cannot eliminate the possibility that Chr had other sources for information for these accounts, but if he did, he integrated them into the narrative in a radically different way than he did his Deuteronomistic source—never do we discover Chronistic 'seams' patching non-Chronistic *Sondergut* into a larger narrative. Additionally, each case of non-synoptic battle accounts serves a specific narrative function within a general Chronistic scheme of 'history', a scheme that generally differs radically from both the Deuteronomistic depiction and contemporary critical historiography of ancient Israel.

Chr, therefore, does not seem deeply constrained by pre-exilic history in producing his historiography. Yet he does not leave history entirely behind. Chr often found battle accounts in DtrH useful as a basis for his revision of Judean battles through careful editorial replacement. In each case of non-synoptic material, however, Chr's own programmatic narrative sufficiently explains the presence of the battles. While it is possible that Chr may preserve data for pre-exilic battles in the narrative, *in no case is it necessary* to explain the production of the text in its current form. The law of parsimony would, therefore, seemingly exclude such material from critical reconstructions of pre-exilic Israelite history.

Yet the battle accounts could possibly inform us about fourth-century Yehud, not with regard to specific events, but in terms of the particular social and ideological matrix that Chr represents. As the battle accounts serve Chr's narrative, the resultant 'historical' norm itself may possess a 'programmatic' function within Chr's own situation.[69] If so, the battle accounts reveal much about Chr's aspirations. Chr would hope for the restoration of Davidic rule in Jerusalem. Rejecting the legitimacy of the Samaritan government, Chr is nonetheless open to people from the north joining the Jerusalem cultic community—on Jerusalem's terms, of course. Rest—and wealth—will come to Jerusalem once the proper institutions are re-established as a result of international fame following Yahweh's deliverance of Jerusalem from external foes. All of this is predicated on the people's exclusive theological/cultic fidelity to Yahweh as the priests and Levites fulfill their appropriate roles in the temple.

Such a programme never materialized in Chr's day. Nevertheless, the battle accounts in Chronicles may provide important historical information, not for pre-exilic Israel, but for the development of Judaisms in the later Second Temple period. Battle accounts in Chronicles may provide significant material for understanding the historical/ideological

69. The term 'programmatic' is taken from Knoppers, 'Battling against Yahweh', p. 532.

matrix that produced the Maccabean/Hasmonean theology of warfare, texts from Qumran (especially texts such as the War Scroll), and images of war in Jewish apocalyptic literature.[70] This is an entirely different project just beginning to be pursued,[71] yet perhaps is more promising than looking for continuities between Chronicles and pre-exilic history buried in 'historical kernels' behind the narrative of Chronicles.

70. See Welten (*Geschichte*), who raises the issue of the relationship of Chronicles to apocalyptic writings. To my knowledge, however, Welten's suggestion has yet to be pursued in any detail.

71. See, e.g., W.M. Schniedewind, 'King and Priest in the Book of Chronicles and the Duality of Qumran Messianism', *JJS* 94 (1994), pp. 71-78.

History and Historiography: The Royal Reforms*

Gary N. Knoppers

The history of royal reforms can mean at least two different things—the study of the history of royal reforms within Chronicles or the study of royal reforms within Chronicles as a means of writing ancient history. In the first case, one approaches Chronicles as an object in itself, a coherent work of history. In the second case, one approaches Chr's work as an avenue to the past, albeit an indirect one, an aid to reconstruct various incidents either in the history of Judah or in the history of postexilic Yehud.[1] The two approaches are related; indeed, the modern, critical study of Chronicles has often confused them. But they are distinct enterprises.[2] The first approach is a legitimate investigation by

* I am most pleased to dedicate this essay to the memory of Raymond B. Dillard. I first met Ray when he was a visiting professor at my seminary in 1981. The love Ray had both for his students and for his subject matter, Chronicles, were very much in evidence. After receiving my doctorate, I came to appreciate Ray's scholarship, collegiality, and leadership in another setting, the Chronicles, Ezra, Nehemiah Section of SBL.

1. By Chr, I mean the author of Chronicles. Both S. Japhet ('The Supposed Common Authorship of Chronicles and Ezra–Nehemiah Investigated Anew', *VT* 18 [1968], pp. 330-71; 'The Relationship Between Chronicles and Ezra–Nehemiah', in J.A. Emerton (ed.), *Congress Volume: Leuven, 1989* [VTSup, 43; Leiden: Brill, 1991], pp. 298-313) and H.G.M. Williamson (*Israel in the Books of Chronicles* [New York: Cambridge University Press, 1977], pp. 5-70) have forcefully argued against the single authorship of Chronicles and Ezra–Nehemiah. Some of their arguments have been challenged by J. Blenkinsopp (*Ezra–Nehemiah: A Commentary* [OTL; Philadelphia: Westminster, 1988) and D. Talshir, 'A Reinvestigation of the Linguistic Relationship between Chronicles and Ezra–Nehemiah', *VT* 38 (1988), pp. 165-93. I believe that more than one author is responsible for Chronicles, Ezra, and Nehemiah, but I do not deny some connections between them.

2. S. Japhet, 'The Historical Reliability of Chronicles', *JSOT* 33 (1985), pp. 83-107; M.P. Graham, *The Utilization of 1 and 2 Chronicles in the Reconstruction of Israelite History in the Nineteenth Century* (SBLDS, 116; Atlanta: Scholars

itself, because it involves pursuing questions of literary structure, historiographical conventions, and ideology. But pursuing the second approach necessitates giving some attention to the first. Evaluating the historical importance of royal reforms in Chronicles involves understanding Chronicles as a specific kind of literary genre—a history. Chr's history, as a continuous narrative, tells us first of all about the writer's own compositional technique, style, and ideology.[3] The value of this literary work for reconstructing the history of pre-exilic Judah and post-exilic Yehud is, therefore, linked to a knowledge of its structure and *Tendenz*.

In this essay, I will give some attention to both approaches—Chronicles as an example of ancient historiography and Chronicles as an indirect witness to the history of Judah and Yehud. Given the general nature of the assigned topic and the limitations of space, this is not an appropriate occasion to discuss a great variety of individual figures and incidents. I will try to alert readers to relevant scholarly evaluations of particular episodes, but a full discussion of royal reforms would require a book in itself. To do justice to the complexity of the primary material and various secondary treatments, this essay will deal primarily with non-cultic reforms during one particular period, the eighth century.[4]

Chronicles and History

The editors have requested that I address the different ways in which modern scholars have construed the relationship between Chr's portrayal of royal initiatives and history. Before proceeding to a discussion of royal reforms within the eighth century, it will be useful to address these preliminary issues. Reviewing the scholarly treatment of the

Press, 1990); J.W. Wright, 'From Center to Periphery: 1 Chronicles 23–27 and the Interpretation of Chronicles in the Nineteenth Century', in E.C. Ulrich *et al.* (eds.), *Priests, Prophets and Scribes: Essays on the Formation and Heritage of Second Temple Judaism in Honour of Joseph Blenkinsopp* (JSOTSup, 149; Sheffield: JSOT Press, 1992), pp. 20-42.

3.   In maintaining this position, I wish to distance myself from the influential notions that Chronicles primarily tells us about the pre-exilic period or the post-exilic period. What we primarily derive from Chronicles, or for that matter any other historical writing, is what a given author thought about a particular subject.

4.   For issues of cult, see most recently, J.W. Kleinig, *The Lord's Song: The Basis, Function and Significance of Choral Music in Chronicles* (JSOTSup, 156; Sheffield: JSOT Press, 1993).

distinctive nature of royal reforms will illustrate the problems and challenges that one encounters in employing Chronicles to reconstruct ancient history.

The Nature of Royal Reforms in Chronicles

When one studies the nature of royal reforms in Chronicles, one must immediately distinguish these from DtrH's conception of royal reforms. In Kings royal reforms are virtually synonymous with cultic reforms. Non-cultic reforms are occasionally mentioned, but almost as an after-thought. Kings mentions, for example, the cities that Asa built (1 Kgs 15.23 [MT]), the ivory palace and cities that Ahab built (1 Kgs 21.39), and how Hezekiah 'made the pool and the conduit' (2 Kgs 20.20). But in each case, this information is conveyed in the concluding formulae for these monarchs.[5] The main attention of the Deuteronomist lies elsewhere. Assuming a normative (Deuteronomic) mandate for *Kultuseinheit* (cultic unity) and *Kultusreinheit* (cultic purity), the Deuteronomist constructs an elaborate system of religious regression and reform in the histories of the northern and southern monarchies. Two principal Israelite regressions and ten Judahite regressions mark the histories of the two kingdoms.[6] Despite periodic attempts at reform by monarchs, such as Jehu in Israel and Asa, Jehoshaphat, and Hezekiah in Judah, most of these twelve regressions are decisively countered only by the radical measures of Josiah in the late seventh century (2 Kgs 23.4-20). In the Deuteronomistic construction of history, Josiah's enforcement of orthopraxis and removal of heteropraxis redress not only the causes of Israel and Judah's declines, but also the principal reasons for the division itself.[7]

In comparison with the Deuteronomist's interest in cultic regression and reform, Chr exhibits a comprehensive perspective toward the ways

5. In this regard, the formulaic introduction to these notices is relevant, 'The rest of (all) the deeds of RN..., are they not written in the Annals of the Kings of Judah/Israel...?' (1 Kgs 15.23; 21.39; 2 Kgs 20.20).

6. H.-D. Hoffmann, *Reform und Reformen: Untersuchungen zu einem Grundthema der deuteronomistischen Geschichtsschreibung* (ATANT, 66; Zurich: Theologischer Verlag, 1980).

7. G.N. Knoppers, *Two Nations Under God: The Deuteronomistic History of Solomon and the Dual Monarchies. I. The Reign of Solomon and the Rise of Jeroboam* (HSM, 2; Atlanta: Scholars Press,1993); II, *The Reign of Jeroboam, the Fall of Israel, and the Reign of Josiah* (HSM, 53; Atlanta: Scholars Press, 1994).

in which Judahite kings improve conditions within their realm. The shape and contours of royal reforms in Chronicles evince considerable diversity.[8] When one reads Chronicles after having read Kings, one has to redefine 'reform'. Royal reforms in Chronicles are martial, administrative, judicial, geopolitical, and cultic in nature. Having established the united monarchy as the golden age in Israelite history, the time in which normative institutions take shape, Chr pays great attention to how Judah's best kings rejuvenate their nation. If the creation and consolidation of national institutions under David and Solomon establish a normative standard or form for later generations to emulate, the attempts by later Judahite kings to reestablish these institutions constitute reforms. But Chr's reforming kings are not mere conservators of a static ideal; they modify earlier policies, creatively adapt to new circumstances, and introduce new programs. Many, but not all, of Chr's best kings lead their people to recovery and renewal after times of decline and apostasy. Such monarchs renew their domain by building fortified cities, fortifying existing cities, appointing officers, amassing large armies and equipping them, stationing garrisons, constructing towers, and rebuilding city walls.

Chr's independent perspective is all the more surprising, since the Chronicler, as is well known, used a copy of Samuel–Kings to compose his own work. Because Chr's work exhibits broader historiographical interests in narrating the history of the Judahite monarchy than the Deuteronomist's work does, the additional reforms that Chr ascribes to Judah's kings cannot be dismissed for historical reconstruction. This is especially true when one compares both Kings and Chronicles with a variety of ancient Near Eastern royal texts. Chr's keen interest in geopolitical and martial reforms is broadly consistent with the concerns of many ancient Near Eastern royal inscriptions and dedicatory texts.[9] The

8.   R.H. Lowery, *The Reforming Kings: Cult and Society in First Temple Judah* (JSOTSup, 120; Sheffield: JSOT Press, 1991).

9.   Two classic studies on kingship in the ancient Near East are R. Labat, *Le Caractère religieux de la royauté assyro-babylonienne* (Etudes d'assyriologie, 2; Paris: Adrien-Maisonneuve, 1939); and H. Frankfort, *Kingship and the Gods: A Study of Ancient Near Eastern Religion as the Integration of Society and Nature* (Chicago: University of Chicago Press, 1948). See more recently K.-H. Bernhardt, *Das Problem der altorientalischen Königsideologie im Alten Testament* (VTSup, 8; Leiden: Brill, 1961), pp. 67-90; S.N. Kramer, 'Kingship in Sumer and Akkad: The Ideal King', in P. Garelli (ed.), *Le Palais et la royauté (archéologie et civilisation), 19 Rencontre assyriologique Internationale* (Paris: P. Geuthner, 1974), pp. 163-76;

narrow focus on cult in the Deuteronomist's depiction of monarchical history is, therefore, exceptional. King Mesha of Moab boasts:

> I took 200 men of Moab, all of its leaders and I led them to Jahaz. And I took it, adding it to Dibon. I built Qariho, the wall of the Fore[sts], and the wal[l] of the acropolis. I built its gates and I built its towers. I built the palace and I constructed the retaining walls[10] of the reser[voir for the sp]ring in the mid[st] of the city.[11]

Given its particular nature, interests, and date, Chronicles presents a series of literary and historical paradoxes. Its history of the monarchy is heavily dependent upon Samuel–Kings; yet Chronicles is a very different history.[12] Chr narrates what one expects to see Judahite kings doing, given the tenets of ancient Near Eastern royal ideologies; yet Chr writes during the post-exilic period, when that monarchy no longer existed. Chr lavishes attention on military, administrative, and geopolitical affairs; yet there is considerable historical distance between the time of his writing and the events that he portrays. With the exception of the chapter that he devotes to the demise of Saul (1 Chron. 10), Chr's history of the monarchy begins, continues, and ends with an exclusive focus upon the deeds of the Davidic dynasty. Yet Chr writes at least decades, probably centuries, following the collapse of the Davidic kingdom.

and G.W. Ahlström, *Royal Administration and National Religion in Ancient Palestine* (Studies in the History of the Ancient Near East, 1; Leiden: Brill, 1982), pp. 1-25.

10. The masc. pl. construct, כלאי can be understood in two different ways—as 'both' (cf. BH כליאם , Ugaritic כלאת) or as 'confining, retaining things' (cf. BH כלא). In the former case, one would translate, 'the double reservoir for the spring'. K.A.D. Smelik, *Converting the Past: Studies in Ancient Israelite and Moabite Historiography* (OTS, 28; Leiden: Brill, 1992), p. 65.

11. I follow the reconstruction of *KAI* 181.20-24 (כלאי האשוֹ[ח.למֹ]ן); see also H. Eshel, 'The QRHH and the Wall of the Ya'aran in the Mesha Stele', in A. Ahituv and B.A. Levine (ed.), *Avraham Malamat Volume* (ErIsr, 24; Jerusalem: Israel Exploration Society, 1993), pp. 31-33.

12. How much Chr's *Vorlagen* of Samuel and Kings resemble the MT of Samuel and Kings is disputed; see W.E. Lemke, 'The Synoptic Problem in Chronicler's History', *HTR* 58 (1965), pp. 349-63; S.L. McKenzie, *The Chronicler's Use of the Deuteronomistic History* (HSM, 33; Atlanta: Scholars Press, 1985); A.G. Auld, *Kings without Privilege: David and Moses in the Story of the Bible's Kings* (Edinburgh: T. & T. Clark, 1994).

Assessing Chr's Historical Reliability

How, then, does one appraise the historical reliability of Chr's claims about the activities of various monarchs? Modern commentators have approached this question in quite different ways: making inner-biblical comparisons, invoking extra-biblical sources, treating Chronicles as a work of theology or exegesis, applying the criterion of verisimilitude, and appealing to archaeology and epigraphy. Each of these approaches has its strengths and weaknesses. Contrasting Chronicles with various earlier biblical texts, especially Samuel–Kings, calls attention to the particular assumptions and features of each work. One can learn a great deal about Chr's account of Sennacherib's invasion (2 Chron. 32.1-23), for instance, by taking careful notice of how he has abbreviated, edited, rewritten, and supplemented the materials in his *Vorlage* (2 Kgs 18–20).

But comparative biblical analysis also has its shortcomings. To begin with, the application of this approach has been uneven. Comparative studies have often worked to the detriment of Chronicles, because many of its changes over against Samuel–Kings are thought to represent tendentious alterations of an authoritative *Vorlage*. This is unfortunate. Chr does, of course, sometimes alter his *Vorlage*, but comparative studies should pursue broader questions as well. What do the differences between these works say about the compositional technique, historiographical assumptions, and ideology of the respective authors? What do the similarities between the texts say about the composition of history in ancient Judah and post-exilic Yehud? If comparisons are used simply to reflect upon Chronicles, they mystify DtrH—effectively treating this work as history itself, rather than as a narration and explanation of the past. In short, comparisons should teach us how to read both texts.

Second, inner-biblical comparisons are of limited value for historical purposes, because scholars are contrasting one indirect, secondary source with another. The task of historical reconstruction still remains. Moreover, there is much unparalleled material in Chronicles. Some of this additional material may be attributed to Chr's interpretation of his biblical sources.[13] Nevertheless, arguments that much or even all of this

---

13. See, for instance, T. Willi, *Die Chronik als Auslegung: Untersuchungen zur literarischen Gestaltung der historischen Überlieferung Israels* (FRLANT, 106; Göttingen: Vandenhoeck & Ruprecht, 1972); P.R. Ackroyd, 'The Chronicler as Exegete', *JSOT* 2 (1977), pp. 2-32; M.A. Fishbane, *Biblical Interpretation in Ancient Israel* (Oxford: Clarendon Press, 1984); K. Strübind, *Tradition als*

unique material represents Chr's exposition of his *Vorlagen* have not been, in my judgment, successful.[14]

The appeal to extra-biblical sources serves two complementary functions. The supposition of Chr's access to such ancient materials—either unused or unavailable to the Deuteronomists—explains his unparalleled material. Second, because Chr used such putative sources, his history is a reliable witness to pre-exilic realities. However defensible, the invocation of extra-biblical sources also has its limitations. To begin with, commentators sharply disagree about the nature and number of such sources. One has to ask whether a given source employed by Chr was reliable and complete. If so, one has to inquire further whether Chr abridged, rewrote, or supplemented these materials. One has also to determine, inasmuch as this is possible, whether the author has applied a source to the proper historical context. Finally, one has to study how Chr has (re)contextualized the materials that he purportedly uses.[15]

Viewing Chronicles as primarily a work of theology or exegesis shifts the whole question of historical reliability to the post-exilic age.[16] In this line of interpretation, Chronicles does not provide any new and trustworthy information about the pre-exilic period, apart from that which can already be gleaned from Samuel–Kings. If Chronicles can be classified as a history at all, it is a highly paradigmatic history that reflects life in Yehud. The merit in this approach lies in the links that it recognizes between Chr's work and the context in which it was written.

Interpretation in der Chronik: König Josaphat als Paradigma chronistischer Hermeneutik und Theologie (BZAW, 201; Berlin: de Gruyter, 1991).

14. See my review of K. Strübind's *Tradition als Interpretation* in *CBQ* 55 (1994), pp. 780-82.

15. To take one example, most commentators agree that the list of fifteen named, fortified cities built by Rehoboam in Judah and Benjamin (2 Chron. 11.5-10) reflects an extra-biblical source: S. Japhet, *I & II Chronicles: A Commentary* (OTL; Louisville, KY: Westminster/John Knox, 1993), pp. 663-67. But scholars debate whether the listed fortifications should be be attributed to Rehoboam, Hezekiah, or Josiah. On Chr's contextualization of this material, see my 'Rehoboam in Chronicles: Villain or Victim?', *JBL* 109 (1990), pp. 423-40.

16. P.R. Ackroyd, *I & II Chronicles, Ezra, Nehemiah* (TBC; London: SCM, 1973); R. Mosis, *Untersuchungen zur Theologie des chronistischen Geschichtswerkes* (FTS, 92; Freiburg: Herder, 1973). In P. Welten's view, Chronicles anticipates certain features of apocalytic writing: *Geschichte und Geschichtsdarstellung in den Chronikbüchern* (Neukirchen–Vluyn: Neukirchener Verlag, 1973).

Some aspects of Chr's coverage relate more to understanding the author's ideology and post-exilic conditions than they do to understanding pre-exilic history.[17] To take one example, the organization of Uzziah's army (2 Chron. 26.11-13), like Jehoshaphat's (2 Chron. 17.14), is according to a predominately post-exilic social institution: ancestral houses. References to the בית אבות are found only in Chronicles, Ezra, Nehemiah, and the Priestly writing.[18] There are other features of Chr's work that clearly reflect his own ideology. The incredible numbers in the armies of Uzziah and other monarchs, for example, are a meaningful indication of Chr's thought but are not taken by historians as accurate information about either pre-exilic or post-exilic life. Nevertheless, it seems reductive to attribute all of Chr's unique material to literary invention or theological reflection. Not all of Chr's claims about the history of the Judahite monarchy can be shown to mirror post-exilic life or the programmatic interests of the author.

Another criterion of historical credibility is verisimilitude. Some scholars have defended, for example, the (pre-exilic) historicity of Chr's claims about Uzziah's reforms (see below) by pointing to the limited and hence plausible nature of these reforms. Others have pointed to events in the international context of Uzziah's tenure as lending credence to Chr's assertion that Uzziah engaged in some military and geopolitical reforms. The attraction of this criterion is readily understandable.[19] Uzziah's reforms are geographically confined. But the application of verisimilitude can be complicated by other factors. Because the narration of Uzziah's reforms evinces stereotypical Chronistic vocabulary and style, some commentators are skeptical that it has much at all to do with events in the eighth century.

To summarize, there is no doubt that Chronicles betrays the time in

17. G.N. Knoppers, 'Jehoshaphat's Judiciary and "the Scroll of YHWH's Torah"', *JBL* 113 (1994), pp. 59-80.

18. E.L. Curtis and A.A. Madsen, *The Books of Chronicles* (ICC; Edinburgh: T. & T. Clark, 1910), p. 33 (#104). In contrast, the expression בית אב appears only once in Chronicles, Ezra, and Nehemiah (Neh. 1.6). See further J.P. Weinberg, 'Das *beit 'abôt* im 6.-4. Jh. v. u. Z.', *VT* 23 (1973), pp. 400-14; J. Blenkinsopp, 'A Jewish Sect of the Persian Period', *CBQ* 52 (1990), pp. 5-20; P. Dion, 'The Civic-and-Temple Community of Persian Period Judaea: Neglected Insights from Eastern Europe', *JNES* 50 (1991), pp. 281-87.

19. But it is completely rejected by T.L. Thompson, *Early History of the Israelite People: From the Written and Archaeological Sources* (Studies in the History of the Ancient Near East, 4; Leiden: Brill, 1992), p. 388.

which it was written and the particular ideology of its author. But one important question remains: to what extent is Chr's presentation of the monarchy shaped by his own present context, his exposition of Samuel–Kings, and his ideology? Does Chr's history, however much it reflects the ideology of its author, a particular rhetorical structure, and its own time, engage the pre-exilic past? On this matter, scholars are sharply divided. One way to address this question is to turn to the last criterion of historical credibility—the witness of archaeology and epigraphy.

The Appeal to Archaeology and Epigraphy

The advantage of this approach is its focus upon the degree to which Chr's unique claims correspond to our present knowledge of the material remains of pre-exilic Judah, if they indeed correspond at all. Recourse to archaeology and epigraphy does not deny the role of Chr as either a theologian or an expositor. Nor does it exclude the application of other criteria, such as comparative biblical analysis and verisimilitude. Rather, this approach seeks to determine, inasmuch as this is possible, the degree to which Chr's account of a particular reform coheres with information gleaned from ancient Near Eastern epigraphy and archaeology. Although I will be employing this approach in assessing Chr's account of eighth-century reforms, I am well aware that recourse to archaeology and epigraphy also has its problems and limitations.[20] Comparing biblical claims with material evidence is a rather complicated matter. Ancient material remains, unearthed by the archaeologist's spade, are not self-interpreting, and archaeologists differ in their assumptions and methods. In addition, many sites have not been excavated; the identity of others is in dispute; and in dealing with excavated sites, archaeologists can differ in their methods, dating of strata, and interpretation of material finds. To complicate matters

20. R. North, 'Does Archeology Prove Chronicles' Sources?', in H.N. Bream, R.D. Heim, and C.A. Moore (eds.), *A Light Unto My Path: Old Testament Studies in Honor of Jacob M. Myers* (GTS, 4; Philadelphia: Temple University Press, 1974), pp. 375-401; S.L. Dyson, 'From New to New Age Archaeology: Archaeological Theory and Classical Archaeology—A 1990s Perspective', *AJA* 97 (1993), pp. 195-206; W.G. Dever, 'Archaeology, Texts, and History-Writing: Toward an Epistemology', in L.M. Hopfe (ed.), *Uncovering Ancient Stones: Essays in Memory of H. Neil Richardson* (Winona Lake, IN: Eisenbrauns, 1994), pp. 105-17; S. Bunimovitz, 'How Mute Stones Speak: Interpreting What We Dig Up', *BARev* 21/2 (1995), pp. 58-67, 97.

further, archaeological excavations illumine broad periods in Israelite or Judahite history, but they have not attained such technical sophistication that ceramic assemblages can be dated to particular generations. Hence, the material remains from ancient Judah do not easily lend themselves to forming a precise commentary on a biblical author's claims about a given monarch.

Despite these limitations, the use of archaeology and epigraphy may shed some light on the extent to which Chr's depiction of royal enterprises may be used to write the history of pre-exilic Judah and post-exilic Yehud. Because historical reconstruction is linked to a knowledge of the structure and *Tendenz* of a given work, I will first comment upon Chr's presentation of three reforming monarchs. My study will then address how archaeology and epigraphy illumine eighth-century Judahite history and whether the distinctive claims of Chronicles comport with historical reality, as best one can presently construe this.

Eighth-Century Royal Reforms

Chr presents three Judahite monarchs of the eighth century as reformers: Uzziah, Jotham, and Hezekiah. These rulers implement a variety of administrative, geopolitical, and military measures that renew their realms. The detail that Chr accords to non-cultic reforms of Uzziah and Hezekiah, in particular, is remarkable. In contrast, Kings lacks any record of comparable activities for Uzziah and contains only a terse mention of non-cultic reforms for Hezekiah.

Uzziah

The Deuteronomist's brief portrayal of Azariah (Uzziah) presents him as a minor figure (2 Kgs 15.1-7), but Chr presents this monarch as a major reformer, whose fame extended all the way to the entrance to Egypt (2 Chron. 26.8). Uzziah rebuilt 'Elot' and restored it to Judah.[21] Uzziah also 'built cities in (the area of) Ashdod and among the Philistines' (2 Chron. 26.6). If the MT is not corrupt, this building

---

21. The MT of Chronicles consistently reads אֵילוֹת (2 Chron. 8.17; 2 Chron. 26.2), whereas Kings features two forms: אֵילַת (2 Kgs 14.22; 16.6) and אֵילוֹת (2 Kgs 9.26). The LXX of Chronicles has Αἰλάθ. Another issue is the (re)builder of Elat. The subject of 2 Kgs 14.22 is uncertain, but H. Tadmor and M. Cogan argue that the most likely referent is Azariah: *II Kings* (AB, 11; New York: Doubleday, 1988), p. 158.

activity should probably be associated with Uzziah's successes against the Philistines, Arabs, and Meunites (2 Chron. 26.6-8).[22] Chr does not specify which cities Uzziah built.

Most of Uzziah's attention is directed toward the south and south-west, but some of Uzziah's construction activity is directed toward Jerusalem itself. He 'built and fortified towers in Jerusalem by the Corner Gate (שער הפנה), by the Valley Gate (שער הגיא), and by 'the Angle' (המקצוע; 2 Chron. 26.9). Like David, Abijah, Asa, and Jehoshaphat before him, Uzziah commands an enormous army (2 Chron. 26.11-13). Unlike most previous censuses, Uzziah's census mentions those specifically responsible for the muster (2 Chron. 26.11). But as was the case with Jehoshaphat's muster, Uzziah's muster depicts ancestral heads (2,600) as having responsibility for his large army (307,500). Like Rehoboam before him and Hezekiah after him, Uzziah supplies his troops with an arsenal. In addition to 'establishing for them, for all the army, shields, spears, helmets, mail, bows, and sling-stones' (2 Chron. 26.14), Uzziah developed new weaponry by 'making devices, sophisticated devices (to be placed) on the towers and the corners in Jerusalem to shoot arrows and large stones' (2 Chron. 26.15).[23]

Chr's Uzziah also enhances the condition of his royal estates. The subject of royal estates also appears in Chr's depiction of David's reign. 1 Chron. 27.25-31 contains a list of officials (שרי הרכוש), who administer extensive crown properties,[24] and Chr's description of Uzziah's royal estates resonates with the description of David's patrimony, though Uzziah's holdings do not match the variety and extent of those

22. Some commentators favor emending the MT (and LXX) of 2 Chron. 26.6 from ויבנה ערים to ויבו הערים; W. Rudolph, *Chronikbücher* (HAT, 21; Tübingen: Mohr, 1955), p. 282.

23. The MT of 2 Chron. 26.15 has ובאבנים גדולות. The Syriac lacks much of this verse (through גדולות).

24. Y. Aharoni, *The Archaeology of the Land of Israel: From the Prehistoric Beginnings to the End of the First Temple Period* (Philadelphia: Westminster, 1982), pp. 15-16; O. Borowski, *Agriculture in Iron Age Israel: The Evidence from Archaeology and the Bible* (Winona Lake, IN: Eisenbrauns, 1987), p. 28; V. Fritz, *Die Stadt im alten Israel* (Munich: Beck, 1990), pp. 136-37. I view most of 1 Chron. 23–27 as an integral part of Chr's work; see S. Japhet, *The Ideology of the Book of Chronicles and its Place in Biblical Thought* (BEATAJ, 9; Frankfurt am Main: Peter Lang, 1989); and J.W. Wright, 'The Legacy of David in Chronicles: The Narrative Function of 1 Chronicles 23–27', *JBL* 110 (1991), pp. 229-42.

ascribed to David. Commensurate with the geography of his military triumphs, Uzziah's royal properties feature the south and southwest. Uzziah 'built towers in the wilderness (מִדְבָּר) and hewed out many cisterns, for he had large herds in the Shephelah and on the plain (מִישׁוֹר) and vinedressers in the hills and the fertile lands'.[25] Uzziah, Chr explains, was 'a lover of the land' (2 Chron. 26.10).

Jotham

In Kings Jotham is a monarch who is rated positively, but of whom little is said (2 Kgs 15.32-38). Chr also evaluates Jotham positively but adds more material about his reign. In Chronicles Jotham continues the pattern of public works begun by his predecessor, Uzziah. Consistent with his *Vorlage*, Chr asserts that Jotham built the upper gate of the temple (2 Chron. 27.3//2 Kgs 15.35), but Chr attributes other construction and fortification activities to Jotham as well. Like Uzziah, Jotham did not confine his building initiatives to Jerusalem. Jotham built extensively on the wall of the Ophel, established cities in the hill country of Judah, and built fortresses and towers in the wooded areas (חֳרָשִׁים; 2 Chron. 27.3-4). Chr does not specify which cities in the Judahite hill country Jotham established.

Hezekiah

Chr devotes more attention to Hezekiah than to any other king, except David and Solomon. Hezekiah is clearly one (if not the chief) of Chr's favorite monarchs in Judahite history.[26] Although the Deuteronomist's coverage of Hezekiah's reign is also extensive and highly laudatory, the foci of the two accounts diverge considerably. Indeed, it is remarkable how Chr can mention so many major events addressed by his *Vorlage*— Sennacherib's invasion, the speeches of his officers, the prayer of

25. The MT of 2 Chron. 26.10 adds אִכָּרִים (farmers), but I follow the LXX[AB] (*lectio brevior*). On the geography, see Y. Aharoni, *The Land of the Bible: A Historical Geography* (Philadelphia: Westminster, rev. edn, 1979), pp. 345-56. Borowski argues that the towers were most likely built for the protection of agricultural workers and produce in these territories. (*Agriculture*, p. 106).

26. Ackroyd, *Chronicles*, pp. 179-89; Mosis, *Untersuchungen*, pp. 189-92; Williamson, *Israel in the Books of Chronicles*, pp. 119-25; M.A. Throntveit, 'Hezekiah in the Books of Chronicles', in D.J. Lull (ed.), *Society of Biblical Literature 1988 Seminar Papers* (SBLSPS, 27; Atlanta: Scholars Press, 1988), pp. 302-11.

Hezekiah, the intercession of Isaiah, the destruction of the Assyrian camp, Hezekiah's illness and recovery, and the visit of envoys from Babylon—yet present such a different account of Hezekiah's tenure. To begin with, his treatment of these events appears in condensed and varied form. Chr's interests lie more with Hezekiah's reforms and restoration, following the unprecedented evil imputed to Ahaz (2 Chron. 28.1-27).[27] Whereas the Deuteronomist devotes only two verses to Hezekiah's cultic reforms (2 Kgs 18.4, 22), Chr devotes three chapters to the restoration of the temple (2 Chron. 29), the celebration of the passover (2 Chron. 30), and Hezekiah's other cultic initiatives (2 Chron. 31). Only then does Chr deal with an event that dominates the Deuteronomist's coverage: Sennacherib's invasion (2 Chron. 32.1-23). Chr also ascribes to Hezekiah considerably more non-cultic reforms than does the Deuteronomist.[28] Chr situates most reforms to Jerusalem's physical plant before Sennacherib's invasion (2 Chron. 32.3-6) and most royal initiatives in Judah thereafter (2 Chron. 32.27-30). But Chr's chronology of events is not entirely clear.[29]

Consistent with his portrayal of Judah's premier reformers as progressives—kings who uphold the legacy of the united monarchy while successfully enabling their nation to surmount new challenges—Chr presents Hezekiah as a strong leader. Hezekiah explicitly prepared for Sennacherib's campaign against Jerusalem by initiating a program of public works and urban mobilization (2 Chron. 32.1-8). After taking counsel with his officers and mighty men, Hezekiah and a large force stopped the flow of springs outside the city, as well as the wadi that

---

27. E. Ben Zvi, 'A Gateway to the Chronicler's Teaching: The Account of the Reign of Ahaz in 2 Chr 28,1-27', *SJOT* 7 (1993), pp. 216-49.

28. 1 Chron. 4.39-43 also mentions a movement southward by the Simeonites during the reign of Hezekiah.

29. Chr's arrangement of Hezekiah's royal reforms is somewhat schematic (see below). The construction of Hezekiah's conduit, for example, is mentioned in both DtrH (2 Kgs 20.20) and Chr's history (2 Chron. 32.30) after Sennacherib's invasion. But historians unanimously agree that this defensive action must have taken place prior to the siege of Jerusalem. On achronology in ancient Mesopotamian historiography, see H. Tadmor, 'The Campaigns of Sargon II of Assur: A Chronological-Historical Study', *JCS* 12 (1958), pp. 22-40, 77-100; *idem*, 'The Inscriptions of Nabunaid: Historical Arrangement', in H.G. Güterbock and T. Jacobsen (eds.), *Studies in Honor of Benno Landsberger on his 75th Birthday* (AS, 17; Chicago: Oriental Institute of the University of Chicago, 1965), pp. 351-63; J. Van Seters, *In Search of History* (New Haven, CT: Yale University Press, 1983), pp. 61-62.

flowed through the land (2 Chron. 32.3-4).[30] For Chr good government is not only reactive, but also proactive. Hezekiah took strength 'and rebuilt the breached wall and raised towers upon it' (2 Chron. 32.5).[31] Hezekiah's repair and fortification of Jerusalem's wall resemble the actions of two other eighth-century reforming kings: Uzziah and Jotham. But Chr's Hezekiah does not limit himself to rebuilding the old wall. He is also said to have built 'another wall outside it' (2 Chron. 32.5). Another Hezekian public works project consisted of strengthening the millo of the City of David (2 Chron. 32.5).[32] Chr later mentions that Hezekiah also closed the upper outlet of the Gihon spring and directed the waters down to the west of the City of David (2 Chron. 32.30).

There is ac lear logic to this pattern of defensive preparations. Having rebuilt the Jerusalem wall and constructed a new wall outside it, Hezekiah ensured a continuous flow of water for the inhabitants within these walls. He then equipped and mobilized Jerusalem's defenders: 'and he made weapons and shields in abundance' (2 Chron. 32.5). Hezekiah personally organized Jerusalem's defenses by appointing 'battle officers over the people' and by exhorting them to stand firm in the face of 'the Assyrian king and the horde that is with him' (2 Chron. 32.6-8).

In Chronicles Hezekiah's geopolitical initiatives go beyond bolstering Jerusalem's defenses. After providing his much-abbreviated version of YHWH's humiliation of Sennacherib and his forces, Chr depicts additional Hezekian accomplishments and initiatives.[33] Instead of focusing

30. It is unclear precisely what stopping the flow of water in the wadi designates. The most common explanation is that Chr is referring to rivulets in the Wadi Qidron. Thus, Ackroyd, 'Chronicler as Exegete', p. 11; H.G.M. Williamson, *1 and 2 Chronicles* (NCB; Grand Rapids, MI: Eerdmans, 1982), p. 381. The reference to stopping the flow of springs outside the city is usually taken to involve the Gihon: Japhet, *Chronicles*, pp. 982-83.

31. The MT reads, יבן את־כל־החומה הפרוצה ויעל על־המגדלות. The LXX adds καὶ πύργους after הפרוצה, which may be an assimilation toward 2 Chron. 26.9, 15. At the end of the last phrase, the Tg. and Vg. reflect a slightly different and superior version of the Hebrew, עליה מגדלות.

32. In enacting this physical reform, Hezekiah harks back to the time of David (1 Chron. 11.8). Unlike the situation in 1 Kings (9.15, 24; 11.27), Chr does not attribute any (re)construction of the millo to the time of Solomon.

33. 2 Chron. 32.21-22. The reason why Jerusalem survives varies in the sources embedded in the Kings narrative and identified by B. Stade, 'Miscellen 16.

on defensive reforms, Hezekiah is able to pursue broader economic and political initiatives. Prosperous Hezekiah 'made treasuries for himself for silver, gold, precious stones, spices, shields, and every kind of splendid vessel' (2 Chron. 32.27).[34] The king built 'storehouses (מסכנות) for the yield of grain, wine, and oil, as well as facilities for every kind of cattle' (2 Chron. 32.28). In Chronicles royal wealth is an indication of divine blessing, and as a number of commentators have observed, Hezekiah's assets rival those of Solomon.[35] Hezekiah also 'made cities for himself and (enjoyed) flocks and herds in abundance, because God gave to him vast possessions' (רכוש, 2 Chron. 32.29).[36] Chr does not further specify the locations of these treasuries, storehouses, and cities. Nor does he situate Hezekiah's flocks and vast possessions.

We have seen that Chr ascribes reforms to particular monarchs and periods that he wishes to exalt. The scope and nature of these reforms belie some influential conceptions of Chr's work as narrowly religious or theological: 'a cultic history written by cultic functionaries especially for the use of cultic personnel'.[37] All three kings—Uzziah, Jotham, and Hezekiah—are resourceful builders and energetic administrators over Jerusalem and Judah. Each amply uses his resources to enhance the living conditions of his people. Hezekiah, in particular, is lauded for his preparations for and response to a severe international crisis. However

Anmerkungen zu 2 Kö. 15-21', *ZAW* 6 (1886), pp. 172-83. In the B1 narrative (2 Kgs 19.7, 36-37), YHWH causes Sennacherib to hear a rumor and return to his own land, where he is assassinated. In the B2 narrative (2 Kgs 19.35), a מלאך יהוה kills 185,000 Assyrian troops. Chronicles contains short, albeit more vague, references to both: Japhet, *Chronicles*, pp. 988-92.

34. Instead of the MT's מגנים, the LXX has καὶ ὁπλοθήκας. The Vg. reads *et armorum universi generis*. Rudolph reconstructs מגדים: *Chronikbücher*, p. 312.

35. See also 2 Chron. 32.23; Williamson, *Chronicles*, p. 385; R.B. Dillard, 'Reward and Punishment in Chronicles: The Theology of Immediate Retribution', *WTJ* 46 (1984), pp.164-72; *idem*, *2 Chronicles* (WBC, 15; Waco, TX: Word Books, 1987), pp. 252-61; M.A. Throntveit, *When Kings Speak: Royal Speech and Royal Prayer in Chronicles* (SBLDS, 93; Atlanta: Scholars Press, 1987), pp. 121-25.

36. In spite of the textual corruption at the end of 2 Chron. 32.28 (MT, לעדרים; לאורות LXX, καὶ μάνδρας εἰς τὰ ποίμνια), I see no compelling reason to excise ערים at the beginning of 2 Chron. 32.29. *Pace* Rudolph, *Chronikbücher*, p. 312.

37. W. Riley, *King and Cultus in Chronicles: Worship and the Reinterpretation of History* (JSOTSup, 160; Sheffield: JSOT Press, 1993), p. 24; cf. R.L.Braun, 'The Message of Chronicles: Rally "Round the Temple"', *CTM* 42 (1971), pp. 502-14.

one views the nature of Chronicles, this work evinces broad geopolitical and military interests.

Historical Considerations

The past century has witnessed archaeological excavations at various sites, while the last decades have witnessed archaeological surveys of different regions within Judah. It will be useful to compare analyses of the material remains from the eighth century with Chr's account of royal reforms during this same period. Such a comparison yields, I would argue, mixed results. To begin with, it is sometimes unclear what conditions a Chronistic text reflects. The date and nature of the military technology that Uzziah introduces to the wall of Jerusalem can serve as an illustration. If Chr is envisioning catapults, as some scholars think, the reference (2 Chron. 26.15) is anachronistic, because extrabiblical sources do not mention catapults until at least the fifth century BCE.[38] But Yadin argues that Chr is not describing ballistic engines but wooden frames built upon towers and battlements, like those depicted on Sennacherib's reliefs of Lachish, on which defenders could stand to their full height while wielding their bows or casting down heavy stones.[39]

In some cases, comparison between material and written remains plays an important, but penultimate, role in the reconstruction of history. In describing Uzziah's fortification of Jerusalem's wall, Chr may have in mind redressing the damage done by Jehoash of Israel during the reign of Amaziah (2 Chron. 25.23//2 Kgs 14.13), as many commentators claim.[40] But Chr's description of Uzziah's fortification is

---

38. Ackroyd, *Chronicles*, p. 169; S. Herrmann, *A History of Israel in Old Testament Times* (Philadelphia: Fortress Press, 1981), p. 240; D.B. Redford, *Egypt, Canaan, and Israel in Ancient Times* (Princeton, NJ: Princeton University Press, 1992), pp. 327-28. Fourth-century BCE historian Diodorus places catapults in the fourth-century, though Williamson identifies similar devices in Persian sources earlier than the fourth century: *Chronicles*, pp. 337-38.

39. If Y. Yadin's reading of the biblical and iconographic material is correct, there is no chronological problem inherent in Chr's depiction of Uzziah's military technology: *The Art of Warfare in Biblical Lands in the Light of Archaeological Study* (New York: McGraw-Hill, 1963), II, pp. 325-27.

40. Williamson, *Chronicles*, pp. 336-37; Dillard, *Chronicles*, p. 206; A. Mazar, *Archaeology of the Land of the Bible 10,000–586 B.C.E* (ABRL; New York: Doubleday, 1990), p. 446; G.W. Ahlström, *The History of Ancient Palestine from*

difficult to appraise historically, because it resonates with features of Nehemiah's description of Jerusalem's ruined (Neh. 2.13-15) and rebuilt walls (Neh. 3.1-32).[41] As constituent features of Jerusalem's walls, the Valley Gate and the Angle are only mentioned in post-exilic sources,[42] although references to the Valley Gate in the first passage (Neh. 2.13, 15) presuppose the pre-exilic existence of this gate.[43] To complicate matters further, not much is known, archaeologically speaking, about the course and nature of Nehemiah's wall. Nevertheless, the very resonance between the testimony in Nehemiah and Chr's description of Uzziah's modification to Jerusalem's defenses is useful for historical reconstruction. Most scholars agree that Nehemiah's wall, whatever its precise line, encompassed the old City of David and did not surround the Western Hill, which shows no traces of occupation during the post-exilic period.[44] Given the consonance between Chr's description of Uzziah's fortifications and Nehemiah's wall, one can better understand the force of Chr's presentation. Uzziah, Chr tells us, fortified portions of the wall surrounding the City of David. If this understanding of Nehemiah's wall is correct, there is no evidence in Chronicles that Uzziah either built or fortified a wall encompassing the Western Hill.[45]

Not all comparisons result in ambiguous conclusions. Uzziah's expansion to the south and southwest may serve as the first example of how archaeology can illumine a biblical text and contribute positively to the reconstruction of Judahite history. Chr's description of Uzziah's royal estates resonates somewhat with our present knowledge of development in the Judahite Shephelah during the eighth century. The number of towns in the Shephelah during this period was

---

the *Palaeolithic Period to Alexander's Conquest* (JSOTSup, 146; Sheffield: JSOT Press, 1993), pp. 626-27.

41. Welten, *Geschichte*, pp. 63-66; Williamson, 'Nehemiah's Walls Revisited', *PEQ* 116 (1984), pp. 81-88.

42. The Valley Gate appears in Neh. 2.13, 15; 3.13, while the Angle appears in Neh 3.19, 20, 24 (together with הפנה), 25.

43. Williamson, *Chronicles*, p. 336.

44. K.M. Kenyon, *Digging Up Jerusalem* (Nashville: Nelson, 1974), pp. 180-87; *idem*, *Archaeology in the Holy Land* (London: Benn, 4th edn, 1979), pp. 306-308; N. Avigad, *Discovering Jerusalem* (Nashville: Nelson, 1983), pp. 61-62.

45. *Pace* E.-M. Laperrousaz, 'Jerusalem la grande', in S. Ahituv and B.A. Levine (eds.), *Avraham Malamat Volume* (ErIsr, 24; Jerusalem: Israel Exploration Society, 1994), pp. 138-47.

unprecedented. According to recent archaeological surveys, the Judahite Shephelah reached a settlement and demographic peak in the eighth century with about 275 sites, occupying a total of 250 hectares.[46] By contrast, most of the sites in the Judahite Shephelah were destroyed by the end of the eighth century. The most famous example of such massive destruction and depopulation is, of course, the damage inflicted upon Lachish (Stratum III). The surveys indicate that only about 40 built-up sites, occupying a total built-up area of 80 hectares, existed in the Shephelah during the late seventh and early sixth centuries. Hence, the total built-up area of the Judahite Shephelah decreased about 70 percent from the eighth to the seventh and sixth centuries.[47] The assumption is that at the end of the seventh century, as a result of Sennacherib's campaign, this territory was lost to Judah.[48] It is, therefore, highly relevant that Chr mentions an eighth-century monarch as the only king in Judahite history with extensive agricultural interests and holdings within these specific areas. Chr does not make such detailed claims for kings either in the ninth century or in the seventh and early sixth centuries.[49]

A second example of how the material remains, when coupled with Chr's history, can shed some light on pre-exilic history involves the construction activity in Judah ascribed to Uzziah, Jotham, and Hezekiah. Archaeological excavations and surveys disclose a large increase in the number of towns and fortifications in the Judahite hill

46. Y. Dagan, 'The Shephelah during the Period of the Monarchy in Light of Archaeological Excavations and Surveys' (MA Thesis, Tel Aviv University, 1992; Hebrew with English summary); A. Ofer, 'Judah', in E.M. Meyers *et al.* (eds.), *Encyclopedia of Near Eastern Archaeology* (New York: Oxford University Press, forthcoming). I wish to thank Professor Ofer for making a copy of this paper available to me.

47. Ofer, 'Judah'; I. Finkelstein, 'The Days of Manasseh: The Archaeological Background' (unpublished paper read at the annual meeting of the SBL in San Francisco, 1992), p. 5. I wish to thank Professor Finkelstein for making a copy of this paper available to me.

48. For example, I. Finkelstein, 'Environmental Archaeology and Social History: Demographic and Economic Aspects of the Monarchic Period', in A. Biran and J. Aviram (eds.), *Biblical Archaeology Today, 1990* (Jerusalem: Israel Exploration Society, 1993), p. 59.

49. As we have seen, Chr also attributes substantial building projects and wealth to Hezekiah (2 Chron. 32.27-29), but Chr does not specify the geographical locations of Hezekiah's agricultural holdings.

country during the eighth century.[50] Public works projects included walls, water systems, and fortifications.[51] The eighth century also witnessed an impressive increase in the settlement of Judah.[52] Archaeological surveys in the Judahite hill country conducted by M. Kochavi and A. Ofer reveal a peak of 88 sites with a total built-up area of about 85 hectares in the eighth century.[53] Ofer estimates that the total built-up area for all of Judah in the eighth century was 470 hectares.

Given the stylized and generalized nature of Chr's descriptions and the dating of material remains to broad eras rather than to specific generations, archaeological analysis does not prove many of Chr's specific claims about Uzziah, Jotham, and Hezekiah. But there does seem to be at least some congruence between the Chronistic notion of Judahite expansion and fortification in the eighth century and current

50. Y. Shiloh, 'Judah and Jerusalem in the Eighth-Sixth Centuries BCE', in S. Gitin and W.G. Dever (eds.), *Recent Excavations in Israel: Studies in Iron Age Archaeology* (AASOR, 49; Winona Lake, IN: Eisenbrauns, 1989), pp. 97-103. The interpretation of the material remains from a few of these sites is disputed. According to Mazar, Khirbet Abu et-Twain is one of several fortresses and towers in the Judahite hills and Shephelah dating to the eighth and seventh centuries (*Archaeology* [pp. 453-55]). But K.G. Hoglund dates this site to the fifth century: *Achaemenid Imperial Administration in Syria-Palestine and the Missions of Ezra and Nehemiah* (SBLDS, 125; Atlanta: Scholars Press, 1992), pp. 191-94.

51. A. Mazar, 'Iron Age Fortresses in the Judaean Hills', *PEQ* 114 (1982), pp. 87-109; Na'aman, 'Sennacherib's Campaign', pp. 5-21; Y. Shiloh, 'Underground Water Systems in Eretz-Israel in the Iron Age', in L.G. Perdue, L.E. Toombs, and G.L. Johnson (eds.), *Archaeology and Biblical Interpretation: Essays in Memory of D. Glenn Rose* (Atlanta: John Knox, 1987), pp. 203-45; D.W. Jamieson-Drake, *Scribes and Schools in Monarchic Judah: A Socio-Archaeological Approach* (JSOTSup, 109; The Social World of Biblical Antiquity Series, 9; Sheffield: Almond Press, 1991), pp. 81-106; G. Barkay, 'The Iron Age II-III', in A. Ben-Tor (ed.), *The Archaeology of Ancient Israel* (New Haven, CT: Yale University Press, 1992), pp. 332-34, 369.

52. Mazar, *Archaeology*, pp. 438-62; B. Halpern, 'Jerusalem and the Lineages in the Seventh Century BCE: Kingship and the Rise of Individual Moral Liability', in B. Halpern and D.W. Hobson (eds.), *Law and Ideology in Monarchic Israel* (JSOTSup, 124; Sheffield: JSOT Press, 1991), pp. 19-34; Jamieson-Drake, *Scribes and Schools*, pp. 48-73. In this context, the generalizations of Thompson (*Early History*, pp. 409-11) need to be revised.

53. The results of A. Ofer's 'The Highland of Judah during the Biblical Period' (PhD dissertation, Tel Aviv University, 1993; Hebrew with English summary) are conveniently summarized in his 'Judean Hills Survey', *NEAEHL* (1993), pp. 814-15.

analysis of the archaeological record.[54] Such congruence does not make Chronicles merely an important witness for the reconstruction of Judahite history—among the historical books, Chronicles is practically our only witness. Aside from the mention of Hezekiah's water works in Jerusalem, there is no indication in Kings of non-cultic reforms among eighth-century Judahite monarchs.[55]

Chr's account of Hezekiah's reforms in Jerusalem comprises a third example of how Chronicles, when coupled with epigraphic or archaeological analysis, can elucidate ancient Judahite history.[56] A variety of archaeological discoveries pertain to Hezekiah's activity in Jerusalem. The most famous is the Siloam tunnel inscription (*KAI* 189), discovered in 1880, commemorating the completion of this conduit. Both Kings and Chronicles, in different terms, ascribe this engineering feat to Hezekiah (2 Kgs 20.20; 2 Chron. 32.30). Palaeographical analysis of the Hebrew script generally comports with a late eighth-century date but is insufficiently precise to be of more help in dating this inscription.[57] Given the discoveries on the Western Hill (see below), however, one need no longer be skeptical of Chr's unique assertion that Hezekiah brought the waters of the Gihon 'down to the west of the City of David' (2 Chron. 32.30).[58]

Other important archaeological finds, unearthed by Avigad in the

54. More difficult to appraise is Chr's assertion that Uzziah built towers in the wilderness (מדבר 2 Chron. 26.10). Only in the seventh century does one see permanent settlements flourish in the Judean desert. The seventh century is also an important period for the Judahite Negev. When compared with the previous century, the number of sites and total built-up area nearly doubled: Ofer, 'Judah'.

55. Prophetic texts (e.g., Isa. 22.9-11) are another matter.

56. J. Rosenbaum, 'Hezekiah's Reform and Deuteronomistic Tradition', *HTR* 72 (1979), pp. 23-43; Ahlström, *History*, pp. 697-701; Japhet, *Chronicles*, pp. 977-83; B. Halpern, 'Sybil, or the Two Nations? Archaism, Alienation and the Elite Redefinition of Traditional Culture in Judah in the 8th-7th Centuries BCE', in J. Cooper (ed.), *The Study of the Near East in the Twenty-First Century* (Winona Lake, IN: Eisenbrauns, forthcoming). I wish to thank Professor Halpern for making a copy of this paper available to me.

57. Note especially the shape and stance of the *waw, yod, kap, lamed*, and *qop*. See further the three articles by F.M. Cross entitled, 'Epigraphic Notes on Hebrew Documents of the Eighth–Sixth Centuries BC', *BASOR* 163 (1961), pp. 12-14; *BASOR* 165 (1962), pp. 34-46; and *BASOR* 168 (1962), pp. 18-23; and L.G. Herr, *The Scripts of Ancient Northwest Semitic Seals* (HSM, 18; Missoula, MT: Scholars Press, 1978), pp. 79-152.

58. Cf. North, 'Archaeology', pp. 375-79.

Jewish Quarter of the Old City, shed light on the history of eighth-century Jerusalem. One of these is the remains of an ancient city wall, seven meters thick, which Avigad dated to the late eighth century on the basis of stratigraphy and pottery analysis.[59] The discovery of this so-called Broad Wall, as well as a variety of other structures and artifacts, indicate that the settlement of Jerusalem expanded to the Western Hill in the pre-exilic period. These finds also give new credence to the view that at least part of the plateau of the Western Hill was encompassed by a fortified wall.[60] Isa. 22.9-11 and 2 Chron. 32.5 are the only biblical writings referring to two Jerusalem walls.[61] Excavations of ancient Jerusalem and other sites in Judah yield other important evidence. The discovery of למלך jar impressions, 44 of which stem from the Jewish Quarter alone, testifies to significant royal involvement in the administration of Jerusalem and Judah. To be sure, there is ongoing debate about the precise purpose of these jars.[62] But the two-winged sun and four-winged scarab are clearly royal emblems. Hence, the existence and diffusion of these impressions in the late eighth century, continuing to some extent in the early seventh century, bear witness to the influence of a central administrative or military organization. The strongest biblical evidence for such an administrative

59. Avigad, *Jerusalem*, pp. 45-60.

60. Avigad, *Jerusalem*, pp. 31-44; Y. Shiloh, 'Jerusalem', *NEAEHL* 2 (1993), pp. 705-708; H. Geva, 'Twenty-five Years of Excavations in Jerusalem, 1967-1992: Achievements and Excavations', in H. Geva (ed.), *Ancient Jerusalem Revealed* (Jerusalem: Israel Exploration Society, 1994), pp. 5-7.

61. One could argue that Chr employed Isa. 22.9-11 in his construction of Hezekiah's reign, but two features of the Isaianic presentation should be noted before one leaps to such a conclusion. First, Isa. 22 does not explicitly attribute the construction activity to Hezekiah. Second, there are important differences between the two texts in question. Isa. 22.9-11 mentions that the Jerusalem wall was refortified and that a basin was constructed between the walls to collect the water of the old pool (cf. 2 Chron. 32.30). 2 Chron. 32.5 mentions not only the refortification of the city wall, but also the raising of towers upon this wall and the construction of another wall outside the old one. Hence, even if one allows for the possibility that Chr understood Isa. 22.9-11 as alluding to Hezekian activity, this still would not be sufficient to explain the particular details of Chr's presentation.

62. N. Na'aman, 'Sennacherib's Campaign to Judah and the Date of the LMLK Stamps', *VT* 29 (1979), pp. 61-86; *idem*, 'Hezekiah's Fortified Cities and the LMLK Stamps', *BASOR* 261 (1986), pp. 5-21; Avigad, *Jerusalem*, pp. 43-44; Mazar, *Archaeology*, pp. 455-57; Halpern, 'Jerusalem', pp. 23-26.

reorganization and consolidation of power comes, as we have seen, from Chr's presentation of Hezekiah's reign.

The final example of how Chronicles may be used in historical reconstruction involves explaining the surge in Jerusalem's population during the eighth and seventh centuries. The excavations of Kenyon have documented the expansion of Jerusalem on its eastern slopes in the late monarchy, while the excavations of Avigad have documented the expansion of Jerusalem on the Western Hill in the eighth and seventh centuries.[63] Although there is some debate whether this population swell began in the eighth century or somewhat earlier in the ninth century,[64] there is broad agreement that waves of refugees fleeing the Assyrian campaigns against the northern kingdom contributed to the increase of Jerusalem's population.[65] But Kings never mentions any such migration from the north to Jerusalem. In contrast, Chronicles depicts northerners migrating to Judah sporadically throughout the history of Judah (e.g., 2 Chron. 11.13-17; 15.9). Chr also depicts the involvement of northerners in covenant renewals and Jerusalem-centered feasts, most prominently the passovers led by Hezekiah and Josiah (2 Chron. 30.1-27; 35.1-19). Because the reclamation of Israelite people and land is such a clear programmatic interest on the part of the Chronicler, one cannot be sure what historical reality lies behind each of Chr's individual descriptions.[66] But it is remarkable that these descriptions exist at all. In this context, the invitation to the celebration of Hezekiah's national passover is especially relevant (2 Chron. 30.6-9).[67] By appealing to those northerners who survived the Assyrian conquest

63. Kenyon, *Digging Up Jerusalem*, pp. 129-65; Avigad, *Jerusalem*, pp. 54-60.

64. Avigad, *Jerusalem*, pp. 54-55; M. Broshi, 'The Expansion of Jerusalem in the Reign of Hezekiah and Manasseh', *IEJ* 24 (1974), pp. 21-26. Cf. Barkay, 'Iron Age', pp. 364-68.

65. Refugees from the Shephelah and the countryside of Judah probably also contributed to the increase; see Halpern, 'Sybil'. For a dissenting view, see Thompson, *Early Israel*, pp. 410-11.

66. G.N. Knoppers, 'A Reunited Kingdom in Chronicles?', *PEGLMBS* 9 (1989), pp. 82-84; 'Reform and Regression: The Chronicler's Presentation of Jehoshaphat', *Bib* 72 (1991), pp. 504-24; '"Battling against Yahweh": Israel's War against Judah in 2 Chr 13:2-20', *RB* 100 (1993), pp. 511-32.

67. Japhet, *Ideology*, pp. 189-91, 318-20; Williamson, *Israel*, pp. 110-31; Dillard, *Chronicles*, pp. 252-61. I disagree with Williamson, Throntveit, and Dillard, however, that Hezekiah's measures permanently reunify the (former) northern and southern kingdoms: 'A Reunited Kingdom', pp. 74-88.

to journey to Jerusalem, Hezekiah's message effectively counters the repeated assertion of Kings that the northern population was either killed or exiled (2 Kgs 17.6, 18, 20, 23; 18.11), only to be replaced by Assyrian sponsored emigrants (2 Kgs 17.24-33). Chr's very wording of Hezekiah's appeal presupposes that some Israelites survived the Assyrian campaigns and remained in the former northern kingdom. Inasmuch as historians wish to support with textual evidence the notion that some northerners survived the Assyrian conquest and that others contributed to Jerusalem's growth, they must turn to the indirect witness of Chronicles.

We have seen a number of instances of correspondence between administrative and geopolitical reforms during the eighth century and current archaeological and epigraphic analysis of this era. Given the great skepticism that characterizes much scholarly discourse on the relationship of Chr to the pre-exilic age, these correlations are significant. It would misrepresent the data, however, to suggest that such resonance tells the whole story. Archaeological and epigraphic analysis not only illumines, but also greatly complicates the use of Chronicles as a source for reconstructing Judahite history. In his description of Hezekiah's reign Chr, like the Deuteronomist, narrates a miraculous deliverance of Jerusalem. My primary interest is not the divine spectacle, which presents its own set of historical and metaphysical issues, but the impact of the Assyrian campaign upon Judah.

Both the Assyrian western campaigns and Hezekiah's response to those campaigns profoundly affected the social life of Judah.[68] Sennacherib's campaign, in particular, inflicted great damage on many of Judah's cities.[69] He asserts that he decimated '46 of his [Hezekiah's] strongwalled cities, as well as the small cities in their environs, which were without number'.[70] Similarly, according to 2 Kgs 18.13, 'Sennacherib, king of Assyria, came up against all of the fortified cities

68. F.J. Gonçalves, *L'expédition de Sennachérib en Palestine dans la littérature hebraïque ancienne* (Ebib, ns, 7; Paris: Librairie Lecoffre, 1986); J.M. Miller and J.H. Hayes, *A History of Ancient Israel and Judah* (Philadelphia: Westminister, 1986), pp. 353-63; Halpern, 'Sybil'.

69. See Gonçalves, *L'expédition*, pp. 102-36; Halpern, 'Jerusalem', pp. 34-49; Ahlström, *History*, pp. 665-707, and the references listed in these works.

70. D.D. Luckenbill, *The Annals of Sennacherib* (OIP, 2; Chicago: University of Chicago Press, 1924), pp. 32-34.

of Judah and captured them'. The Assyrian king's invasion is associated with the systematic destruction of Judahite border fortresses.[71] Mazar credits Sennacherib with taking Lachish (III), Ramat Rahel (VB), and Timnah (Tell el-Baṭash [III]), and perhaps also Beer-Sheba (II), Gezer (IIB), and Tell Beit Mirsim (A2).[72] The Assyrian king was apparently also responsible for the marked depopulation of many parts of Judah at the end of the eighth century, either through devastation or deportation.[73] Ofer's recent archaeological surveys suggest that Sennacherib killed or exiled most of the inhabitants of the Shephelah and about 50-70 percent of the inland residents. Because of the systematic destruction and deportation, Stohlmann speaks of a 'Judaean exile after 701 BCE'.[74]

The impression of devastation caused by Sennacherib's campaign, gleaned from archaeological and epigraphic sources, contrasts sharply with the picture offered by Chronicles. Chr frames his version of Sennacherib's campaign (2 Chron. 32.9-21) with material that presents Hezekiah's reign in a very positive light. In addition to detailing Hezekiah's extensive preparations for a defensive war (2 Chron. 32.1-8), Chr portrays the aftermath of Sennacherib's invasion as a time of rest (2 Chron. 32.22). In Kings and the Annals of Sennacherib, Hezekiah renders hefty tribute to Sennacherib. But in Chronicles tribute for YHWH flows to Jerusalem, as do precious objects for Hezekiah (2 Chron. 32.23). The Chronicler also adds material describing Hezekiah's impressive public works and riches (2 Chron. 32.25, 23, 27-30). For Chr, wealth, tribute, and rest are sure signs of divine blessing.[75] Given that Sennacherib only encamps against the fortified cities

71. Aharoni, *Archaeology*, pp. 253-69; Tadmor and Cogan, *II Kings*, pp. 223-51.

72. The date and cause of the destruction at some sites, such as Beer-Sheba (II), Gezer (IIB), Tell Beit Mirsim (A2), Arad (X-VIII), Tell Halif (VIB), and Bet Shemesh (IIC), are disputed; see Aharoni, *Land*, pp. 387-94; Mazar, *Archaeology*, pp. 416-40; Ben Tor, 'Iron Age', p. 328; Ahlström, *History*, pp. 707-16.

73. Aharoni, *Archaeology*, pp. 253-66; Mazar, *Archaeology*, pp. 544-47; Halpern, 'Jerusalem', pp. 30-34. Sennacherib's own deportation figure is fantastic: 200,150 (Luckenbill, *Annals*, p. 33).

74. S. Stohlmann, 'The Judaean Exile after 701 BCE', in W.W. Hallo, J.C. Moyer, and L.G. Perdue (eds.), *Scripture in Context II: More Essays on the Comparative Method* (Winona Lake, IN: Eisenbrauns, 1983), pp. 147-75.

75. J. Wellhausen, *Prolegomena to the History of Ancient Israel* (Edinburgh: A. & C. Black, 1885), pp. 203-10; Japhet, *Ideology*, pp. 150-76; Dillard, 'Reward and Punishment', pp. 164-70; R.L. Braun, 'Solomon, the Chosen Temple Builder: The

of Judah, 'thinking that he would capture them' (2 Chron. 32.1), Chr's Sennacherib does little, if any, real damage to Jerusalem and Judah. Hezekiah and his people weather the Assyrian storm extremely well.

By comparing Chr's presentation with other sources, one can see the degree to which Chr's programmatic interests affect his description of Hezekiah's reign. The author's particular brand of royalism leads him to include various notices about Hezekiah's reforms and prestige, but this same impulse also leads him to present a completely one-sided account of Sennacherib's invasion. Like the Deuteronomists, Chr accentuates Jerusalem's survival, the annihilation of Sennacherib's forces, and the humiliation and death of Sennacherib himself. But the Chronicler, even more than the Deuteronomists, draws a veil over the depopulation and massive transformation of Judah at the end of the eighth century. In describing this aspect of Hezekiah's legacy, the author of Chronicles occludes the pre-exilic past. Chr's presentation of Judah's history during the Assyrian crisis tells us much more about Chr's ideal of Davidic kingship than it does about the immense transformations that occurred in the demography of Judah at this time.

Conclusions

To return to the issues raised at the beginning of this essay, Chronicles is historically important in two different ways—as an example of history and as an indirect means of reconstructing history. The first should not be underplayed or underestimated. Chr's history provides commentators with insight into how someone, who was much closer to the period in question than modern authors are, construed the history of Judahite royal reforms. How a civilization takes account of itself is important evidence on its own terms. As to the question of which history—pre-exilic or post-exilic—Chronicles reflects, the answer may not be a case of eithor/or, but both/and. Chr's history inevitably reflects a certain rhetorical structure, the author's own post-exilic context, and the author's programmatic interests. Writing about the past is never done in a vacuum but is always influenced by the witness's own circumstances. Chr's account of royal reforms has to be approached cautiously and critically. It is also clear, however, that the unique evidence of Chronicles, when compared with archaeological or epigraphic evidence,

Significance of 1 Chronicles 22, 28, and 29 for the Theology of Chronicles', *JBL* 95 (1976), pp. 581-90.

is occasionally of some value for historical reconstruction. Chronicles is not a treasure trove of information about pre-exilic history, but it does interact with pre-exilic history.

In this regard, one of the advantages of Chronicles for historical reconstruction—that it relates to both the pre-exilic age and the post-exilic age—is also a disadvantage. Chronicles as a post-exilic construction of the pre-exilic past complicates the history of both Judah and Yehud. Such complexity does not justify, however, scholarly neglect or ignorance. In approaching Chr's account of royal reforms, commentators need to be aware of a variety of issues—their own assumptions and commitments, the limitations of their methods, relevant literary questions (form, structure, style, the author's *Tendenz*), and historical matters (possible relationships of Chronicles to other sources, inscriptional evidence, archaeological remains). But scholars should engage the witness of this extensive ancient history. A discriminating understanding of Chronicles enables contemporary scholars to write more sophisticated, nuanced, and balanced histories of both ancient Judah and post-exilic Yehud.

PROPHETS AND PROPHECY IN THE BOOKS OF CHRONICLES

William M. Schniedewind

One distinctive feature of the books of Chronicles is the broad range of prophetic activities encountered. There are well-known traditional prophetic figures such as Isaiah in texts that are borrowed (i.e., synoptic) from DtrH.[1] There are also non-synoptic texts involving prophets known from DtrH (e.g., Shemaiah). Perhaps more interesting, though, are the non-traditional prophetic roles and figures that we find in Chronicles. For example, the prophets (and 'seers') are cited as historical sources, and alongside traditional prophets we find non-traditional figures—including an Egyptian pharaoh, priests, Levites, and even a soldier—who receive prophetic inspiration. How are we to understand these *ad hoc* prophetic figures? Should we include them among the 'prophets'? This essay will argue that the forms and functions of the prophetic narratives draw a sharp distinction between traditional prophets and the *ad hoc* inspired figures or 'messengers'. This observation has important implications for the Chronicler's view of prophecy, the history of prophecy itself, as well as the purpose of Chr's work.[2]

---

1.   The problem of the *Vorlage* of the books of Chronicles remains an open question. The Qumran discoveries first raised the possibility that the textual tradition of Samuel–Kings that the Chronicler used was different from the Masoretic tradition. More recent studies raise the possibility that Chr's main source for his work may have been an earlier redaction of Samuel–Kings; cf. S.L. McKenzie, *The Chronicler's Use of the Deuteronomistic History* (HSM, 33; Atlanta: Scholars Press, 1985); and A.G. Auld, 'Prophets Through the Looking Glass: Between Writings and Moses', *JSOT* 27 (1983), pp. 3-23. H.G.M. Williamson has a modest proposal: 'The Death of Josiah and the Continuing Development of the Deuteronomic History', *VT* 32 (1982), pp. 242-47.

2.   By 'Chr' I refer only to the author of the books of Chronicles; cf. S. Japhet, 'The Supposed Common Authorship of Chronicles and Ezra–Nehemiah Investigated Anew', *VT* 18 (1968), pp. 330-71; H.G.M. Williamson, *Israel in the Books of Chronicles* (Cambridge: Cambridge University Press, 1977), pp. 5-70.

The Problem of Chr's Prophets and Post-exilic Prophecy

Chr's prophetic narratives properly belong in a study of post-exilic prophecy. On the one hand, Chronicles is a historical work that describes the classical period of the ancient Israelite monarchy. Yet on the other hand, Chr writes in the post-exilic period, and this new context permeates his narrative compositions, and in particular, his description of prophecy. As a result, this survey must begin by placing the prophetic narratives in Chronicles within the broader context of post-exilic prophecy.

Post-exilic Prophecy

Although prophecy has been a topic of intense interest in biblical studies, post-exilic prophecy has suffered from some neglect. This may be traced to Wellhausen's influential *Prolegomena zur Geschichte Israels*,[3] which presented the monarchical period as the classical era of Israel and held that post-exilic Judaism was 'an artificial product' and post-exilic prophecy only a shadowy reflection of its illustrious predecessor. Wellhausen based this harsh evaluation of post-exilic Judaism on his analysis of Chronicles.[4] Consequently, the post-exilic period in general and post-exilic prophecy in particular have been neglected in scholarship until quite recently, when they have begun to break out of the negative assumptions of the Wellhausean analysis.[5]

The authorship of Chronicles remains a lingering question among some scholars; cf. D. Talshir, 'A Reinvestigation of the Linguistic Relationship between Chronicles and Ezra–Nehemiah', *VT* 38 (1988), pp. 165-93; J. Blenkinsopp, *Ezra–Nehemiah: A Commentary* (OTL; Philadephia: Westminster, 1988), pp. 47-54.

3. ET, *Prolegomena to the History of Ancient Israel* (New York: Meridian, repr., 1957). See R. Rendtorff, 'The Image of Postexilic Israel in German Bible Scholarship from Wellhausen to von Rad', in M.A. Fishbane, E. Tov, and W.W. Fields (eds.), *'Sha'arei Talmon': Studies in the Bible, Qumran, and the Ancient Near East Presented to Shemaryahu Talmon* (Winona Lake, IN: Eisenbrauns, 1992), pp. 165-73.

4. *Prolegomena to the History of Ancient Israel*, pp. 224, 421.

5. See the survey by R. Mason, 'The Prophets of the Restoration', in R.J. Coggins, A. Phillips, and M.A. Knibb (eds.), *Israel's Prophetic Tradition: Essays in Honour of Peter R. Ackroyd* (Cambridge: Cambridge University Press, 1982), pp. 137-54.

Discussion of post-exilic prophecy has often focused on the 'decline', 'demise', or 'end' of prophecy. A decline of prophecy depends on a particular definition of prophecy. From a sociological perspective, the theory of the demise of prophecy stands on shaky foundations. Thomas Overholt notes, 'We cannot correctly say that prophecy ended with the exile, either in the sense that it ceased or that it was transformed into something else'. Rather, he suggests, 'We ought to conceive of prophecy as a continuing potentiality in a given society'.[6] Sociological approaches to prophecy point to an inherent *continuity* in prophecy throughout history. In ancient Israel this continuity is underscored by the post-exilic prophetic compositions (e.g., Zechariah, Haggai, Malachi). Still, the perception of a *distinction* between pre-exilic and post-exilic prophecy is not a scholarly invention.

Rabbinic literature recognizes an end in prophecy. For instance, *t. Sot.* 13.2-3 expresses this idea categorically:

> After the first temple was destroyed, kingship ceased from the house of David, the Urim and the Thummim ceased. After Haggai, Zechariah, and Malachi—the latter prophets—died, the Holy Spirit departed from Israel; nevertheless they were informed by the *Bat Qol.*[7]

The destruction of the First Temple brings with it the end of kingship, cultic intermediation, and prophecy. These phenomena define prophecy in terms of the temple and the monarchy, that is, in terms of the institutions that characterize the First Temple period. This perspective describes the end of *classical prophecy*, that is, prophecy associated

6.　T.W. Overholt, *Channels of Prophecy: The Social Dynamics of Prophetic Activity* (Minneapolis, MN: Fortress Press, 1989), p. 161. Similar opinions are expressed by S.B. Reid, 'The End of Prophecy in Light of Contemporary Social Theory', in K.H. Richards (ed.), *Society of Biblical Literature 1985 Seminar Papers* (SBLSPS, 24; Atlanta: Scholars Press, 1985), pp. 515-23; and D.L. Petersen, 'Israelite Prophecy: Change Versus Continuity', in J.A. Emerton (ed.), *Congress Volume: Leuven, 1989* (VTSup, 43; Leiden: Brill, 1991), pp. 190-203.

7.　All translations are my own unless otherwise stated. Cf. *m. Sot.* 9.12; *b. Sanh.* 11a; *2 Bar.* 85.1-3. The end of the classical prophetic age is also implicit in 1 Maccabees: 'until there should come a prophet' (4.46), 'the prophets ceased to appear' (9.27), and 'until a prophet should arise' (14.41). This same periodization of history is also implicit in *m. Ab.* 1.1. See further references in F.E. Greenspahn, 'Why Prophecy Ceased', *JBL* 108 (1989), pp. 37-49. E.E. Urbach points out that there was an expectation of prophets and prophecy throughout the Second Temple period: 'When Does Prophecy End?', in M. Weinfeld (ed.), *A Biblical Studies Reader* (Jerusalem: Bialik, 1979), pp. 58-68 [Hebrew].

with the classical period of Israel's history. Prophecy ceases when that sociopolitical context ends.

A decline in prophecy has some basis in exilic and post-exilic literature. For example, Ps. 74.9 apparently expresses a widely held view in the Second Temple period: 'We do not see our signs, there is no longer any prophet; And, no one among us knows for how long!' This psalm, although difficult to date precisely, apparently speaks about the period of the Babylonian exile (cf. vv. 1-8). In the book of Zechariah, the term 'the former prophets' appears in relation to the prophets who foretold the end of the monarchy and the exile (Zech. 1.4; 7.7, 12). The 'former prophets' belonged to a time 'when Jerusalem and her towns were peopled and peaceful' (Zech. 7.7). It is significant that the last of the 'latter prophets', Malachi, is never called a 'prophet' but only a 'messenger' (cf. Mal. 2.7; 3.1). Additionally, the prophet Haggai is called 'messenger of YHWH' (Hag. 1.13). The emergence of 'messenger' as a term for 'prophet' in these post-exilic books already suggests some distinction between the pre-exilic and post-exilic prophets.

A form of the prophetic voice does continue after the classical prophetic age. Admittedly, the prophetic office wanes, but the scribes and sages are also inspired. Ezra is guided by the 'hand of YHWH' (Ezra 7.6, 28; Neh. 2.8), and Baruch becomes the inspired scribe *par excellence*. The *Tosefta* passage cited above suggests that the sages continued to receive authoritative inspiration for their teaching by the *Bat Qol*, which may be understood as a diminished reflection or 'echo' of classical prophecy.[8] Although Josephus acknowledges that the 'exact succession of prophets' had ended in the Persian period (*Apion* 1.41), he affirms that prophets could still arise and individuals could still prophesy.[9] These texts reflect both a *distinction* between prophecy in

8.   See, e.g., J. Neusner, *The Tosefta: Nashim* (New York: Ktav, 1979), *ad loc.* This translation follows the comment of Rabbi Meir Abulafia in the Palestinian Talmud, which explains the *Bat Qol* as a 'reverberating sound, echo (הברת קול)' (see S. Lieberman, *Hellenism in Jewish Palestine: Studies in the Literary Transmission, Beliefs and Manners of Palestine in the I Century B.C.E.—IV Century C.E.* [Texts and Studies of the Jewish Theological Seminary of America, 18; New York: Jewish Theological Seminary of America, 2nd edn, 1962], pp. 194-99).

9.   On the exact succession of prophets, see S.Z. Leiman, 'Josephus and the Canon of the Bible', in L.H. Feldman and G. Hata (eds.), *Josephus, the Bible, and History* (Detroit: Wayne State University Press, 1989), pp. 55-56. On the continuation of prophecy in Josephus, see D.E. Aune, 'The Use of ΠΡΟΦΗΤΗΣ in

pre-exilic and post-exilic periods and a *continuity* in the prophetic voice.

Following the lead of W.F. Albright,[10] several studies have attempted to explain post-exilic prophecy by the close relationship between classical prophecy and monarchy. Frank Moore Cross, for example, observes, 'It is fair to say that the institution of prophecy appeared simultaneously with kingship in Israel and fell with kingship'.[11] An organic relationship between kingship and prophecy thus becomes a working premise behind several studies of post-exilic prophecy.[12] Cogent objections have been raised against the supposed organic relationship between monarchy and prophecy. Rex Mason, for example, points out that the prophets naturally were concerned with the monarchy but also with many other national, social, and religious issues.[13] This undermines an integral relationship between king and prophet. Moreover, as Robert Wilson points out, prophecy likely existed in Israel even before the rise of the monarchy.[14] If prophecy existed before the monarchy, then it was interested in issues outside of monarchy, and it is unlikely that the end of monarchy was accompanied by an end to prophecy.

Several scholars suggest that prophecy declined because it in some way failed'. Aubrey Johnson argues that false prophecy and the

Josephus', *JBL* 101 (1982), p. 420; J. Blenkinsopp, 'Prophecy and Priesthood in Josephus', *JJS* 25 (1974), pp. 239-62.

10. See W.F. Albright, 'Samuel and the Beginnings of the Prophetic Movement', in *Archaeology, Historical Analogy and Early Biblical Tradition* (Rockwell Lectures; Baton Rouge, LA: Louisiana State University Press, 1966), pp. 42-65.

11. F.M. Cross, *Canaanite Myth and Hebrew Epic* (Cambridge, MA: Harvard University Press, 1973), p. 223; also see I.L. Seeligmann, 'Die Auffassung von der Prophetie in der deuteronomistischen und chronistischen Geschichtsschreibung (mit einem Exkurs über das Buch Jeremia)', in J.A. Emerton *et al.* (eds.), *Congress Volume: Göttingen, 1977* (VTSup, 29; Leiden: Brill, 1978), pp. 271; J. Blenkinsopp, *A History of Prophecy in Israel* (Philadephia: Fortress Press, 1983), pp. 182-84.

12. Most significantly, P.D. Hanson, *The Dawn of Apocalyptic: The Historical and Sociological Roots of Jewish Apocalyptic Eschatology* (Philadephia: Fortress Press, rev. edn, 1979); O. Plöger, *Theocracy and Eschatology* (Richmond, VA: John Knox, 1968); D.L. Petersen, *Late Israelite Prophecy: Studies in Deutero-Prophetic Literature and in Chronicles* (SBLMS, 23; Missoula, MT: Scholars Press, 1977).

13. 'Prophets of Restoration', p. 140.

14. R.R. Wilson, *Prophecy and Society in Ancient Israel* (Philadephia: Fortress Press, 1980), pp. 89-90.

resultant distrust of the prophetic enterprise precipitated the demise of prophecy.[15] James Crenshaw argues that prophecy declined because it was unsuccessful and emphasizes the prophets' failure to face the disparity between theology and experience. Apocalyptic and wisdom replaced prophecy, because they dealt more directly and successfully with daily experience.[16] Robert Carroll applies the psychological theory of 'cognitive dissonance' and comes to a similar conclusion, suggesting that both prophetic hermeneutics and apocalyptic arise from the dissonance between prophecy and fulfillment.[17] Rex Mason, on the other hand, proposes that prophecy died because it *succeeded*, and he makes the compelling observation: 'It is strange that, if earlier prophecy were regarded as having proved such a "failure", the post-exilic period should have been the time when the present prophetic collections were formed and invested with increasing authority.' Thus, 'prophecy began to die, or change, after the exile, not because of its failure but because of its "success". The judgment of the exile was seen as confirmation of the predictions of those prophets who had not cried "peace" when there was no peace...'[18] Precisely because the prophets were right, their oracles were collected and these collections gradually increased in authority. The success of the prophets is seen in the very preservation of their words. Ironically then, the authority of these prophets was now found in written documents that supplanted the 'living' word. For this reason, living prophecy was replaced by the study and interpretation of earlier prophetic texts.[19] Joseph Blenkinsopp gives a spatial rather than temporal analysis to the transition in prophecy, suggesting that prophecy did not end but was merely relocated. After the fall of the monarchy, the temple filled the vacuum left by the monarchy and consequently prophecy was absorbed into the cult.[20] This analysis

15. A.R. Johnson, *The Cultic Prophet in Ancient Israel* (Cardiff: University of Wales Press, 2nd edn, 1962), pp. 66-75.

16. J.L. Crenshaw, *Prophetic Conflict: Its Effect Upon Israelite Religion* (BZAW, 124; Berlin: de Gruyter, 1971), pp. 93-94.

17. R.P. Carroll, *When Prophecy Failed: Cognitive Dissonance in the Prophetic Traditions of the Old Testament* (New York: Seabury, 1979).

18. 'Prophets of Restoration', pp. 141-42.

19. On the prophetic reinterpretation of texts, see M.A. Fishbane, *Biblical Interpretation in Ancient Israel* (Oxford: Oxford University Press, 1985), pp. 443-505.

20. *A History of Prophecy in Israel*, p. 253. Also see J. Blenkinsopp, *Prophecy and Canon: A Contribution to the Study of Jewish Origins* (Studies in Judaism and Christianity in Antiquity, 3; Notre Dame, IN: University of Notre Dame Press,

accords well with the rabbinic dictum that prophecy was taken from the prophets and given to the sages (cf. *b. B. Bat.* 12a).

Each theory that tries to explain the so-called decline in prophecy focuses upon *the* catastrophic event in Israel's history—the Babylonian exile. The Babylonians not only exiled the people: they also destroyed their institutions. Post-exilic prophecy then is a reflection of new realities and new priorities. There is both an end to and a continuation of prophecy. Clearly, post-exilic literature perceived the decline from the classical prophets, yet there is also a continuation of the prophetic voice. The prophetic narratives in Chronicles give a unique glimpse into this transitional period. They are, on the one hand, *an interpretation of classical prophecy* and, on the other hand, *a reflection of post-exilic prophecy itself.*

Prophecy in Chronicles
A few studies have addressed isolated aspects of prophecy in Chronicles. Yet because the issue of historical reliability has shaped the agenda for the investigation of the book of Chronicles,[21] studies on the prophetic narratives in Chronicles have been quite limited. They have addressed the issues of the form of prophetic narratives, levitical prophecy, royal prophecy, and the prophetic source citations, but they have not attempted a synthetic treatment of prophecy in Chronicles. General studies of prophecy have largely ignored the book of Chronicles. John Sawyer's *Prophecy and the Prophets of the Old Testament*[22] for example, includes a discussion of prophecy in DtrH but no comparable section on prophecy in Chronicles. Klaus Koch's two-

1977), pp. 128-38; Petersen, 'Israelite Prophecy', pp. 190-203. Most recently, W. Riley (*King and Cultus in Chronicles: Worship and the Reinterpretation of History* [JSOTSup, 160; Sheffield: JSOT Press, 1993], p. 204) has observed, 'The Chronicler is indeed interested in the promise to David, but sees that promise to have its enduring reality in the Temple and cultic community of God's post-exilic people.'

21. The surveys by S. Japhet, 'The Historical Reliability of Chronicles: The History of the Problem and its Place in Biblical Research', *JSOT* 3 (1985), pp. 83-107; M.P. Graham, *The Utilization of 1 and 2 Chronicles in the Reconstruction of Israelite History in the Nineteenth Century* (SBLDS, 116; Atlanta: Scholars Press, 1990).

22. J.F.A. Sawyer, *Prophecy and the Prophets of the Old Testament* (Oxford Bible Series; Oxford: Oxford University Press, 1987).

volume survey, *Die Propheten*, makes frequent reference to DtrH, but Chr's view of prophecy is almost completely overlooked.[23] A recent study by Joseph Blenkinsopp, *A History of Prophecy in Israel*, contains only a short section on 'Temple Prophecy' where the book of Chronicles is featured.[24] Thus, much work remains to be done on Chr's view of prophecy.

The first seminal contribution to research on the prophetic narratives in Chronicles came in an indirect form. Gerhard von Rad's classic essay, 'Die levitische Predigt in den Büchern der Chronik',[25] investigates the speeches in Chronicles that he claims form a distinctive *Gattung* characterized by the quotation of an ancient source, its application to some past situation, and an exhortation to faith and action. Von Rad believed that the 'levitical sermon' reflected standard levitical homiletic practice and assimilated the style of inspired prophetic utterance. He argued that these speeches were intended primarily to support the prophetic claims of the Levites and thus were motivated by political and institutional interests.[26]

Adam Welch's monograph, *The Work of the Chronicler*, anticipates the more recent studies that link classical prophecy and kingship.[27] Welch believed that Chr conceived of prophecy as a charismatic institution: the spirit came upon certain individuals and they prophesied. At the same time, he maintained that prophets held a recognized position in the royal court. Unfortunately, Welch too easily

---

23. K. Koch, *Die Profeten* (Urban-Taschenbücher, 280-81; Stuttgart: Kohlhammer, 1978–80); ET, *The Prophets* (Philadelphia: Fortress Press, 1983–84).

24. Blenkinsopp, *A History of Prophecy in Israel*.

25. ET, 'The Levitical Sermon in I and II Chronicles', in *The Problem of the Hexateuch and Other Essays* (London: SCM, 1966), pp. 267-80.

26. 'The Levitical Sermon in I and II Chronicles', pp. 269-72.

27. A.C. Welch, *The Work of the Chronicler: Its Purpose and its Date* (Schweich Lectures, 1938; London: Oxford University Press, 1939), p. 42. Willi supports the connection between the king and the prophet: 'Therefore, the association of king and prophet has no historical basis, but rather emerges simply from the thematic nature of Chronicles as a history of the Davidides: just as the king represented Israel, so is the prophet the one representing God in the history of Israel' ('Die Zuordnung von König und Prophet hat also keine historischen Gründe, sondern ergibt sich einfach aus der Thematik der Chronik als einer Davididengeschichte: wie der König Israel vertritt, so ist der Prophet der Repräsentant Gottes in der Geschichte Israels'): *Die Chronik als Auslegung* (FRLANT, 106; Göttingen: Vandenhoeck & Ruprecht, 1972), p. 223.

dismissed the tension between the charismatic and traditional functions. The apparent contradiction between a charismatic institution and an official royal institution derives from the variety of 'prophetic' figures in Chronicles.

Several studies have taken up von Rad's form-critical discussion of the prophetic speeches. While those studies by James Newsome and David Petersen rely on von Rad's claim that the 'levitical sermons' support the Levites' claims to prophetic authority,[28] Rex Mason and Dietmar Mathias have seriously challenged the existence of von Rad's *Gattung*. Mason objects that the formal *Gattung* is not present in Chronicles—only 'elements' of a preaching style are found in Chronicles. Mason's criticism qualifies von Rad's proposal of a formal *Gattung*, yet still allows that the speeches in Chronicles reflect the 'method of preaching and teaching among the temple community'.[29]

A chorus of scholars has suggested that the prophetic speeches function to warn the king. Sara Japhet, for instance, argues that Chr's prophets follow in the steps of the prophet-priest Ezekiel, 'the watchman of Israel' (Ezek. 3.16-17; 33.1-9). The prophets' role is to call to repentance, because God does not punish Israel without warning. For this reason, Chr inserts the prophets at crucial points in his history to warn and summon to repentance. In this respect, Japhet compares Chronicles to rabbinic literature, where warning is crucial to God's dealing with his people.[30]

Scholars have also begun to recognize the importance of the prophetic narratives in Chronicles for the study of early biblical interpretation. For instance, Thomas Willi emphasizes the role of Chr's prophets

28. J.D. Newsome, 'The Chronicler's View of Prophecy' (PhD dissertation, Vanderbilt University, 1973), p. 78; *idem*, 'Toward a New Understanding of the Chronicler and his Purposes', *JBL* 94 (1975), pp. 201-17; Petersen, *Late Israelite Prophecy*, pp. 55-87.

29. R. Mason, 'Some Echoes of the Preaching in the Second Temple Period? Tradition Elements in Zechariah 1–8', *ZAW* 96 (1984), pp. 233; also see Mason, *Preaching the Tradition: Homily and Hermeneutics after the Exile, Based on the 'Addresses' in Chronicles, the 'Speeches' in the Books of Ezra and Nehemiah, and the Post-exilic Prophetic Books* (Cambridge: Cambridge University Press, 1990); D. Mathias, ' "Levitische Predigt" und Deuteronomismus', *ZAW* 96 (1984), pp. 23-49.

30. Japhet, *Ideology* pp. 176-91. Also see G. Fohrer, 'Propheten Erzahlungen', in *Die Propheten des Alten Testaments* (Gütersloh: Gerd Mohn, 1977), VII, pp. 36-37; Seeligmann, 'Die Auffassung von der Prophetie', p. 283.

as interpreters and suggests that Chr's prophets function as exegetes and expositors, who advance Chr's *überlieferungsgeschichtliche Konzeption*.[31] Along these lines, Michael Fishbane is quite correct in pointing out the contemporary aims of Chr that influenced his use of prophetic speech: Chr addresses the post-exilic community via the mouth of a prophet who cites and aggadically transforms Scripture.[32]

The last two decades have seen a flurry of work on prophecy and the prophetic narratives in Chronicles. Although these studies have not integrated all aspects of Chr's view of prophecy, they have raised critical issues: the form-critical aspects of the prophetic speeches, Chr's use of earlier traditions, the 'prophetic' role of the Levites, the relationship between the prophet and the king, and the prophetic references in the source citations. Yet, these studies have not paid adequate attention to the roles of different kinds of prophets, the different types of inspiration, and the functions that these prophetic narratives play in the book of Chronicles.

The Scope and Content of the Prophetic Narratives in Chronicles

The book of Chronicles displays great variety in its prophetic narratives. For example, Chronicles uses prophets and seers to warn kings of impending judgment. Chr refers to levitical singers as 'seers' who 'prophesy' with musical instruments, and priests and Levites receive divine inspiration and prophesy. A foreign king such as Pharaoh Neco acts and speaks by divine inspiration, and even David and Solomon receive divine revelation.

Although a version of Samuel–Kings was apparently the main source of Chr's history, most of the prophetic narratives in Chronicles have no parallel in Samuel-Kings. The obvious reason for this is that the prophetic narratives in Samuel–Kings mostly concern the *northern* kingdom. For example, from 1 Kings 12 to 2 Kings 17 (the period of the divided monarchy) every prophetic narrative concerns a northern prophet or the northern kingdom. Since Chr wrote a history of the

---

31. Willi, *Die Chronik als Auslegung*, pp. 215-44. See also R. Micheel, *Die Seher- und Prophetenüberlieferungen in der Chronik* (BBET, 18; Frankfurt: Peter Lang, 1983), p. 67; Seeligmann, 'Die Auffassung von der Prophetie', p. 273; Y. Amit, 'The Role of Prophecy and Prophets in the Theology of the Books of Chronicles', *BethM* 93 (1983), p. 133 [Hebrew].

32. See Fishbane, *Biblical Interpretation in Ancient Israel*, pp. 386-92.

southern kingdom, there was little for Chr to borrow. There must have been stories of Judaean prophets, but we do not have them in the book of Kings. What then was the source of Chr's prophetic narratives? Did Chr freely compose or borrow from a prophetic source? There is scant evidence to prove that Chr used any written collection of prophetic stories for his prophetic narratives. The prophetic speeches reflect Chr's own language and theology,[33] and in this respect, the prophetic narratives are a first-hand reflection of Chr's views of prophets, prophecy, and inspiration.

In order to limit the scope of this study of prophetic narratives, we must first ask the question, 'Who is a "prophet" according to Chr?' The answer should be quite simple: those figures whom Chr calls 'prophets' are prophets. Unfortunately, previous studies have included everyone from the Davidic kings to the Levites under the label 'prophet'. Certainly these figures may contribute to understanding Chr's view of prophecy, but they are not prophets *per se*.

Chr gives prophets one of the four traditional prophetic titles— 'prophet' (נביא), 'seer' (חזה), 'seer' (ראה), and 'man of God' (איש האלהים). Using these titles as our criterion, we find seven figures who deliver non-synoptic speeches and are labeled with prophetic titles in Chronicles: Shemaiah, Hanani, Jehu, Elijah, Oded, and two anonymous figures in 2 Chronicles 25.[34] To these I would add only Eliezer. Although Eliezer is not given a prophetic label by Chr, the use of the verb התנבא (2 Chron. 20.37), usually translated 'to act as a prophet', indicates that Eliezer was acting as a נביא, even though the title is not explicitly applied to him. Adding Eliezer to our list then, we have eight traditional prophets in Chronicles.

We must add to this first category of prophets a second category of prophetic speakers or 'inspired messengers'. These are those figures

---

33. S.J. De Vries shows that Chr's non-synoptic material differs in form and function from the synoptic, and so he claims that Chr invented both the prophets and the messages: 'The Forms of Prophetic Address in Chronicles', in *Biblical and Other Studies: Tenth Anniversary Volume* (HAR, 10; Columbus, OH: Department of Judaic and Near Eastern Languages and Literatures, Ohio State University, 1987), pp. 15-36.

34. Although he is called 'man of God', I have omitted David from this list, because he is first a king, and only secondarily is the title 'man of God' applied to him. See a full discussion in my monograph, *The Word of God in Transition: From Prophet to Exegete in the Second Temple Period* (JSOTSup, 197; Sheffield: JSOT Press, 1995).

who are inspired by God to speak to the people and should be included in a discussion of Chr's prophetic narratives. I have chosen the term 'messenger' because of its use in 2 Chron. 36.15-16 and because it becomes a term for the post-exilic prophets.[35] I have called them 'inspired', because although they are not given prophetic titles, their speeches are still divinely inspired. Their claims to divine inspiration are made by *ad hoc* inspiration formulas that precede the speeches. The inspired messengers include the soldier Amasai (1 Chron. 12.18), Azariah son of Oded (2 Chron. 15.1-8),[36] the levitical singer Jahaziel (2 Chron. 20.14-20), the priest Zechariah (2 Chron. 24.20), and the interesting case of Pharaoh Neco (2 Chron. 35.20-22).

Formal Aspects of the Prophetic Narratives

Until recently little attention had been paid to differences in the form and function of the prophetic narratives in Chronicles. For example, Mark Throntveit observed in his study of royal speech that 'attempts to analyze the speeches contained in the book of Chronicles have tended to place indiscriminately all the occurrences of direct discourse together in one category, or at best, to differentiate only between speech and prayer'.[37]

Inspiration Formulas

The inspiration formulas can be separated into three categories: intermediary formulas, messenger formulas, and possession formulas. The 'intermediary formula' describes the prophet as a divine intermediary, as in the expression, 'the word of YHWH came to X'. This formula is common in the classical prophets but is found only once in Chr's non-synoptic speeches. The second or messenger formula is the

---

35. See N. Cohen, 'From *Nabi* to *Mal'ak* to "Ancient Figure"', *JJS* 36 (1985), pp. 12-24.

36. Azariah's father, Oded, is called a prophet in v. 8, but this reference is undoubtedly a later gloss. Chr's genealogies (cf. 1 Chron. 5) and 1 Kgs 4.2 would suggest that Azariah was the name of the high priest in the time of Asa; so perhaps this Azariah was the high priest. Note the versions and see the full discussion in my dissertation, 'Prophets, Prophecy, and Inspiration: A Study of Prophecy in the Book of Chronicles' (PhD dissertation, Brandeis University, 1992), pp. 76-78.

37. M.A. Throntveit, *When Kings Speak: Royal Speech and Royal Prayer in Chronicles* (SBLDS, 93; Atlanta: Scholars Press, 1987), p. 127.

most well known and is common in the prophetic books: כה אמר יהוה (usually translated, 'Thus says the Lord').[38] It occurs 291 times in the Hebrew Bible; 185 of these are in Isaiah and Jeremiah. In Ezekiel, we often find the variation, 'Thus says the Lord God', which occurs over 120 times. The messenger formula is found 66 times in DtrH but only 10 times in the Pentateuch (mostly in the plague narratives; cf. Exod. 4.22; 5.1; 7.17, 26; 8.16; 9.1, 13; 10.3; 11.4; 32.27). Clearly then, the messenger formula is typical of classical biblical prophecy. The last formula, the 'possession formula', refers to the 'spirit (רוח)' moving upon an individual and inspiring that individual to prophesy.

Inspiration Formulae in the Prophetic Speeches

PROPHETS

Name	Reference	Title	Inspiration Formulas
Shemaiah	2 Chron. 12.5, 7	נביא	thus says YHWH
			the word of YHWH came to
Hanani	2 Chron. 16.7	ראה	—
Jehu	2 Chron. 19.1	חזה	—
Eliezer	2 Chron. 20.37	נביא	he acted as a prophet
Elijah	2 Chron. 21.12	נביא	thus says YHWH
Anonymous	2 Chron. 25.7	איש האלהים	—
Anonymous	2 Chron. 25.15	נביא	—
Oded	2 Chron. 28.9	נביא	—

INSPIRED MESSENGERS

Name	Reference	Title	Inspiration Formulas
Amasai	1 Chron. 12.19	officer	spirit enveloped
Azariah	2 Chron. 15.1	none	the spirit of God was upon him
Jahaziel	2 Chron. 20.14	Levite	the spirit of YHWH was upon him
			spirit enveloped
Zechariah	2 Chron. 24.20	priest	the spirit of God enveloped
			thus says God
Neco	2 Chron. 35.21	Pharaoh	and God said

38. See J.T. Greene, *The Role of the Messenger and Message in the Ancient Near East: Oral and Written Communication in the Ancient Near East and in the Hebrew Scriptures: Communicators and Communiqués in Context* (BJS, 169; Atlanta: Scholars Press, 1989), pp. 183-86.

There are two outstanding features that are illustrated in the chart. First, in the eight speeches of the traditional prophets, five use no inspiration formulas whatsoever. Evidently, the authority of the prophet's word was implicit in the fact that he is called a prophet by Chr. This underscores the fact that there is little concern about false prophecy in the books of Chronicles, whereas in DtrH false prophecy is a major concern. This is illustrated by the recontextualization of the Micaiah story in 2 Chronicles 18 so that the emphasis is on foreign alliances instead of false prophecy (note especially the new introduction in v. 1). It is also noteworthy that where inspiration formulas are used by the prophets in the speeches of Shemaiah and Elijah, they are the messenger and intermediary formulas that are so well known from classical prophecy. This brings me to my second major observation: four of the five messenger speeches use possession formulas. The spirit comes upon the military officer, the Levite, and the priest, and they are inspired to speak by the spirit. The expressions used here (רוח לבשה and היתה עליו רוח) are atypical of classical prophecy, and the notion of the spirit coming upon a prophet is quite restricted in the Hebrew Bible. In fact, in his classic article, 'The "Spirit" and the "Word" in the Pre-exilic Reforming Prophets', Sigmund Mowinckel writes,

> A study of the conception of the spirit of YHWH in the Old Testament has resulted in the to me surprising conclusion that the pre-exilic reforming prophets never in reality express a consciousness that their prophetic endowment and powers are due to the possession by or any action of *the spirit of YHWH, rû*^{a}*h yahweh.*[39]

The studied avoidance of the 'spirit' in classical prophecy might be explained by the close association between the spirit and ecstatic prophetic practices.

The question that arises then is, if these possession formulas are not typical of classical prophecy, then where do we find them? They usually occur in military contexts. For example, Judg. 6.34 says, 'The spirit of YHWH clothes (לבשה)' Gideon, and Gideon proceeds to lead Israel out to battle against the Midianites. In Judg. 3.10, the spirit comes upon Othniel and he rescues Israel. In Judg. 11.29, the spirit of

---

39. S. Mowinckel, '"The Spirit' and the 'Word' in the Pre-exilic Reforming Prophets', *JBL* 53 (1934), p. 199. G. von Rad also notes the curious absence of the spirit in the prophet's ministry: *Old Testament Theology* (New York: Harper & Row, 1962–65), II, pp. 56-57.

YHWH comes upon Jephthah, marking his rise to leadership over the tribes of Israel. But the most prominent example of the importance of the spirit for military leaders is in Saul's rise and fall from power (cf. 1 Sam. 10.10; 11.6). The spirit comes upon Saul at the beginning of his reign, and the departure of the spirit from Saul marks the beginning of David's rise to power. In light of this, we must conclude that Chr's use of possession formulas for messengers clearly and consciously distinguishes them from the traditional prophets. Chr, on the one hand, supports the observation of Mowinckel, since none of his traditional prophets are inspired by the spirit. On the other hand, the use of possession formulas reflects a different type of prophecy with its new emphasis on the spirit.

Audience

The distinction in the inspiration formulas is paralleled by the different audiences that prophets and messengers address.

Audience of the Prophetic Speeches

PROPHETS

Name	Reference	Title	Inspiration Formulas	Audience
Shemaiah	2 Chron. 12.5, 7	נביא	Messenger, Intermediary	king, officers
Hanani	2 Chron. 16.7	ראה	none	king
Jehu	2 Chron. 19.1	חזה	none	king
Eliezer	2 Chron. 20.37	נביא	none	king
Elijah	2 Chron. 21.12	נביא	Messenger	king
Anon.	2 Chron. 25.7	איש האלהים	none	king
Anon.	2 Chron. 25.15	נביא	none	king
Oded	2 Chron. 28.9	נביא	none	northern army

INSPIRED MESSENGERS

Name	Reference	Title	Inspiration Formulas	Audience
Amasai	1 Chron. 12.19	officer	Possession	David
Azariah	2 Chron. 15.1	none	Possession	all Judah
Jahaziel	2 Chron. 20.14	Levite	Possession	all Judah
Zechariah	2 Chron. 24.20	priest	Possession	people
Neco	2 Chron. 35.21	Pharaoh	and God said	king

Claus Westermann suggests that all the prophetic speeches in Chronicles (both by traditional prophets and inspired messengers), 'with one exception [i.e., 2 Chron. 24.20], are actually prophetic speeches directed to the king'.[40] Chr's prophets would therefore follow a classical model of the judgment speech to an individual. However, in his eagerness to make Chronicles fit this pattern, Westermann has overlooked other exceptions: the messenger speeches of Amasai, Azariah, Jahaziel, and Zechariah focus not on the person of the king but on the people as a whole. For example, Jahaziel the Levite addresses his speech to 'all Judah, the inhabitants of Jerusalem, and King Jehoshaphat' (2 Chron. 20.15), and Azariah addresses his speech to 'Asa, all Judah, and Benjamin' (2 Chron. 15.2). Although the king is mentioned as part of the audience, the king is not *the* audience. On the other hand, the prophet Jehu's speech typifies the traditional prophets' speeches; in this instance, the prophet specifically speaks to the king: 'And Jehu, the seer went out to meet Jehoshaphat and said to the king...' (2 Chron. 19.2). A pattern can clearly be seen here, and the two exceptions to this pattern are easily explicable. Pharaoh Neco, an inspired messenger, speaks to King Josiah because he is Pharaoh's peer. The northern prophet Oded does not speak to the king, because in Chr's view there was no legitimate northern king to address (cf. 2 Chron. 13.4-12). Once we have carefully defined who is a prophet in Chronicles, Westermann's observation is correct. The traditional prophet does address the king. However, the inspired messenger speaks to the people. It should not be surprising that the best examples of von Rad's 'levitical sermon' genre come not from the traditional prophets, but from the inspired messengers (as well as from the royal speeches).

Function of Prophetic Figures
The different audiences of the prophets and messengers are naturally reflected in a third category, the functions of the speeches.

---

40. C. Westermann, *Basic Forms of Prophetic Speech* (London: Lutterworth; Philadelphia: Westminster Press, 1967), p. 166.

Function of the Prophetic Narratives

PROPHETS			FUNCTIONS	
Speaker	*Title*	*Interprets*	*Warns*	*Exhorts*
Shemaiah	נביא	yes	secondary	
Hanani	ראה	yes	secondary	
Jehu	חזה	yes		
Eliezer	נביא	yes		
Elijah	נביא	yes		
Anon.	איש האלהים		yes	
Anon.	נביא	yes	yes	
Oded	נביא	yes	yes	

INSPIRED MESSENGERS			FUNCTIONS	
Speaker	*Title*	*Interprets*	*Warns*	*Exhorts*
Amasai	soldier			yes
Azariah	none			yes
Jahaziel	Levite			yes
Zechariah	priest		yes	secondary
Neco	Pharaoh		yes	yes

The prophets' speeches explain and interpret narrative events. In these speeches, we find that a central purpose is to explain how God has acted, is acting, or will act in history. Chr places the prophets in his narratives to answer the historical questions that result from his doctrine of 'retribution theology'. Thus, for example, the prophet Shemaiah explains why Shishak invaded Jerusalem, and the seer Hanani explains why King Asa had a war with Baasha and why he had diseased feet (2 Chron. 16.7-10). The seer Jehu explains why Jehoshaphat's military expedition with Ahab failed, and the prophet Eliezer explains Jehoshaphat's failed shipping venture. Typical of the prophets' speeches are explanation or motive clauses that begin with the conjunction כי ('because ...'). In some cases, the narrative function is painfully clear when compared with the book of Kings. For example, when we compare Shishak's invasion in Kings and Chronicles, we find that Chr introduces an explanation for Shishak's invasion into the Kings narrative, using a framing repetition. The repeated statement, 'And Shishak, king of Egypt, invaded Jerusalem', in 2 Chron. 12.2 and 9 frames the prophet's explanation of Shishak's invasion. In light of this role of the prophets in Chr's narratives, it is not surprising that we find them mentioned in the source citations of Chronicles. The prophets' role as annalists corroborates and even authenticates their role as interpreters of historical events in the narrative.

On the other hand, we find no priests nor Levites in Chr's source citations, even though—according to later Jewish tradition—both priests and prophets were credited with the writing of sacred history.[41] Rather, the priests, Levites, and other inspired messengers serve a function appropriate for their particular audience. They do not explain how God acts but exhort the people, telling them how they should act. It is in the context of these exhortations to the people that we see the extensive appeal to and citation of Scripture. For example, the spirit comes upon the levitical singer Jahaziel, and he enjoins all Israel to 'stand and see the salvation of God' (2 Chron. 20.17), citing Moses' exhortation to the children of Israel at the Red Sea in Exod. 14.13. Although the speech of Zechariah does not quote Scripture, it appeals to the Torah: inspired by the spirit, Zechariah asks the people, 'Why are you violating the *commandments of Yahweh* (מצות יהוה)? You will not prosper because you have forsaken Yahweh!' (2 Chron. 24.20). In another example, the spirit of God comes upon Azariah and gives a long address to the people that ends with the exhortation: ''Now be strong! Do not be disheartened, because there is a reward for your labor' (2 Chron. 15.7). Various scholars have pointed out that Azariah's speech depends heavily upon Scripture. However, what also needs to be emphasized is the directive tone of the speech. Azariah concludes, using verbs in the *imperative* mood, and his speech exhorts people to trust God. The use of imperative verbs—the mood of exhortation—is typical of the messenger speeches and distinguishes them from the traditional prophets' speeches.

The function of the messenger speeches invites a comparison between the inspired messengers and the post-exilic priest, Ezra. According to Ezra 7.6, Ezra is a scribe wise in the Torah, because 'the hand of YHWH was on him'. The hand of YHWH essentially authorizes Ezra's interpretation of Torah and authenticates his exhortations to the people. He performs a function much like Chr's inspired messengers.

The Purpose of the Prophetic Narratives in Chronicles

The differences that have been laid out here have a number of significant implications, not least of which is that we should be more careful

41. See 1 Macc. 16.23-24; Josephus, *Apion*, 1.29.

about our use of the term 'prophet'. Moreover, it is unlikely that priests, Levites, or Davidic kings were regarded by Chr as 'prophets'. Chr's prophets, those whom he calls 'prophets', undoubtedly reflect his view of pre-exilic classical prophecy. Chr portrays the prophet as a spokesman to the king. The prophet interprets historical events for the king and chastises the king, but without the king, there is no role for the prophets. Chr's description of the traditional prophet implies an end to the prophetic office and so echoes the view of rabbinic sources. However, Chr also allows for a new kind of prophecy, a prophecy not by prophets, but by *ad hoc* inspired messengers, who come not only from the cultic ranks but also include a military officer and a foreign king. The appeal to and citation of authoritative traditions in these inspired messengers' speeches suggest that Chr's inspired messengers are the forerunners of the inspired text interpreters of Second Temple Judaism. In this context, it is interesting to note that in Qumran literature the Teacher of Righteousness is not called a prophet, but the spirit nevertheless inspires him, and God makes known to him 'all the mysteries of the prophets' (cf. 1QpHab. 2.8-9; 7.5).

It is quite possible that Chr saw himself in a role similar to his inspired messengers. Chr speaks primarily to the people, that is, to the post-exilic community. The various aspects of Chr's composition— speeches, narrative style, and theology—all serve a homiletic function. And, in particular, the prophetic narratives in Chronicles cannot be understood simply by the context of their First Temple period referents; they are primarily directed toward the post-exilic community. We may take, as an example, the prophet Shemaiah's speech:

> They have humbled themselves so I will not destroy them, but I will grant them a remnant and my wrath shall not be poured out on Jerusalem by Shishak. Nevertheless, they shall be his servants so that they may know the difference between serving me and serving the kingdoms of the world (2 Chron. 12.7-8).

Although this speech is ostensibly explaining a tenth-century historical event, the language of Shemaiah's speech is remarkably similar to a sermon that Ezra delivers to the post-exilic returnees (Ezra 9.6-9), and its references to a 'remnant' and 'serving the kingdoms of the world' have more relevance to the post-exilic community than to the historical context of Shishak's invasion. In another example, Jehoshaphat enjoins the people, drawing on the words of Isa. 7.9: 'Believe in the Lord and you will be established; believe his prophets' (2 Chron. 20.20).[42] Jehoshaphat's speech obviously has two audiences, the narrative audience and Chr's post-exilic community. The exhortations that typify the inspired messenger speeches fit easily into the context of an exhortation to the post-exilic returnees.

The homiletic character of Chr's work is not just in the prophetic speeches, but the narratives as a whole also serve as a sermon to the post-exilic community. It has been observed, for example, that Chr's narratives are arranged around the theme of retribution theology. This theme is not just a theological abstraction but speaks to the heart of the situation of the post-exilic returnees. The case of Manasseh is perhaps the best example (2 Chron. 33.1-19), where Chr rewrites his *Vorlage*, a version of the book of Kings (cf. 2 Kgs 21.1-18), so that Manasseh is warned by seers about his apostasy (v. 18) but refuses to repent. Consequently, he is taken in chains to *Babylon* and finally in slavery he seeks the Lord, repents, and is returned to *Eretz-Israel*. It takes little imagination to see that Manasseh is a type of the post-exilic community.[43] Chr's retribution theology thus is used as an explanation to the post-exilic community of the exile and return to Zion. Likewise, Chr's emphasis on the temple is not primarily concerned with the First Temple, but rather justifies and legitimates the building of the Second Temple and the restoring of its cultic service. For example, David's parting words to Solomon to keep the commandments and build the temple are ultimately intended for the post-exilic community (cf. 1 Chron. 28.1-10). It is no coincidence then that the First Temple began construction on the second day of the second month, just as the Second Temple also began construction on the second day of the second month (cf. Ezra 3.8 and 2 Chron. 3.2).[44] The erection and maintenance of the temple is part and parcel of the commandments and what it means to seek the Lord. Chr's narratives thus explain what is required to seek the Lord and what happens when one seeks the Lord, as King David did (cf. 2 Chron. 34.3). Conversely, Chr elaborates the consequences for those who do not seek the Lord, as in the case of Saul (1 Chron. 10.13-14). In both the prophetic narratives and Chronicles as a whole then, Chr's voice addresses his post-exilic audience.

42. See Fishbane, *Biblical Interpretation in Ancient Israel*, pp. 386-87.

43. See R. Mosis, *Untersuchungen zur Theologie des chronistischen Geschichtswerkes* (FTS, 92; Freiburg: Herder, 1973), pp. 192-94; also 41-43, 186-88.

44. See A.-M. Brunet, 'Le Chroniste et ses Sources', *RB* 61 (1954), pp. 349-86.

In sum, Chr's purpose is exhortation. In style, the book of Chronicles approximates the function of Chr's spirit-inspired messengers, indicating that Chr viewed his own work as exhortation to the people, not an interpretation of the deeds of the kings. It was the role of the prophet to interpret historical events for the kings and to write *midrash* (or 'history'), but the prophets belonged to the former generation. Chr was a messenger exhorting a new generation by using the history of Israel for examples in his extended historical sermon. There are obvious analogies to Chr's use of history. The historical psalms recount long sections from Israel's history not from 'antiquarian interests' but for the exhortation and encouragement of the community. Similarly, Moses recites Israel's history before entering the land (Deut. 1–4), a tradition that Chr draws upon in another context.[45] So also, the passover in Israel is not remembered in the book of Exodus as a historical event, but 'as a sign and a reminder' so that Israel would remember the teaching of the Lord, to seek God, and to observe his commandments (cf. Exod. 13.8-10). Chr also uses history as a sign and a reminder to his post-exilic community.

---

45. M.A. Fishbane, *The Garments of Torah: Essays in Biblical Hermeneutics* (Indiana Studies in Biblical Literature; Bloomington, IN: Indiana University Press, 1989), pp. 15-16.

THE CHRONICLER'S SPEECHES AND
HISTORICAL RECONSTRUCTION

Mark A. Throntveit

> After all these facts, we may conclude the Introduction to the books of
> the Chronicle, feeling assured of the result, that the books, in regard to
> their historical contents, notwithstanding the hortatory-didactic aim of
> the author in bringing the history before us, have been composed with
> care and fidelity according to the authorities, and are fully deserving of
> belief.
>
> C.F. Keil[1]

> One might as well try to hear the grass growing as attempt to derive
> from such a source as this a historical knowledge of the conditions of
> ancient Israel.
>
> J. Wellhausen[2]

Something of the range of opinion regarding the historical reliability of
the Chronicler (Chr) may be seen in the juxtaposition of these quota-
tions from two of his early interpreters. While the debate concerning
the historicity of Chronicles continues to rage in our time as well,[3] the
place of Chr's speeches in this regard seems to enjoy some consensus.
First expressed by Graf, this consensus holds that, 'they have been so
reworded by Chr that it is no longer possible to find a historical kernel.
As such they are unhistorical.'[4] Towards the end of the nineteenth

---

1.   C.F. Keil, *The Books of the Chronicles* (Clark's Foreign Theological
Library, 4th series, 35; Edinburgh: T. & T. Clark, 1872), p. 45.

2.   J. Wellhausen, *Prolegomena to the History of Israel* (Edinburgh: A. & C.
Black, 1885), p. 215.

3.   For an exhaustive treatment of the debate in the last century with reflections
on the current state of research, see M.P. Graham, *The Utilization of 1 and
2 Chronicles in the Reconstruction of Israelite History in the Nineteenth Century*
(SBLDS, 116; Atlanta: Scholars Press, 1990).

4.   K.H. Graf, *Die geschichtlichen Bücher des Alten Testaments: Zwei*

century, Driver concluded his analysis of the speeches by stating: 'It would have been interesting to point out how the speeches peculiar to Chr reflect, in almost every case, the interests and point of view of Chr himself; but space has obliged me to confine myself to the linguistic argument.'[5] Of those investigations solely devoted to the speeches, only von Rad's form-critical analysis, which led him to deny their origin to Chr, broke ranks with this emerging consensus, and he, nevertheless, credited Chr with placing these sermons from the 'post-exilic cultic officials' in the mouths of kings and prophets.[6] Noth's investigations solidified the view that Chr was responsible for the speeches themselves, and Plöger established their chronistic placement at strategic points in the narrative.[7] These pioneering works in the area of Chr's speeches have been enhanced by the more recent work of Braun, Newsome, Saebø, Mathias, Throntveit, Duke, and Mason, all in basic agreement regarding the function, use, and historicity of these addresses.[8]

Parallel studies of this rhetorical usage of speeches in classical and ancient Near Eastern literature, as well as the book of Acts, have arrived at similar results, namely the discovery of the common historiographical procedure of composing speeches and placing them upon the

---

historisch-kritische Untersuchungen (Leipzig: Weigel, 1986), p. 187, quoted in Graham, *Utilization*, p. 132.

5.   S.R. Driver, 'The Speeches in Chronicles', *The Expositor* 1 (5th series, 1895), pp. 241-56; the quote is found on p. 255, n. 2.

6.   G. von Rad, 'The Levitical Sermon in I & II Chronicles', in *The Problem of the Hexateuch and Other Essays* (New York: McGraw-Hill, 1966), pp. 267-80.

7.   M. Noth, *The Chronicler's History* (JSOTSup, 50; Sheffield: JSOT Press, 1987); O. Plöger, 'Reden und Gebete im deuteronomistischen und chronistischen Geschichtswerk', in *Aus der Spätzeit des Alten Testaments: Studien* (Göttingen: Vandenhoeck & Ruprecht, 1971), pp. 50-66.

8.   R.L. Braun, 'The Significance of 1 Chronicles 22, 28, and 29 for the Structure and Theology of the Work of the Chronicler' (ThD dissertation, Concordia Seminary, 1971); J.D. Newsome, 'The Chronicler's View of Prophecy' (PhD dissertation, Vanderbilt University, 1973); M. Saebø, 'Taler og bønner hos Kronisten og I Esra/Nehemja-boken: Noen bemerkninger til et aktuelt tema', *NorTT* 83 (1982), pp. 119-32; D. Mathias, '"Levitische Predigt" und Deuteronismus', *ZAW* 96 (1984), pp. 23-49; M.A. Throntveit, *When Kings Speak: Royal Speech and Royal Prayer in Chronicles* (SBLDS, 93; Atlanta: Scholars Press, 1987); R.K. Duke, *The Persuasive Appeal of the Chronicler: A Rhetorical Analysis* (JSOTSup, 88; Sheffield: Almond Press, 1990); R. Mason, *Preaching the Tradition: Homily and Hermeneutics after the Exile* (Cambridge: Cambridge University Press, 1990).

lips of important personages to express the author's views.[9]

Speaking as one concerned to uphold the historical reliability of Chr,[10] Japhet's balanced conclusion regarding the speeches and prayers is all the more illuminating:

> Throughout the historical account, these rhetorical passages of the Chronicler's own creation are put in the mouths of prophets and kings. They tie in with the historical background and flow of the narrative but are not integral to the description. Added speeches and prayers therefore provide a clear and unequivocal expression of the writer's views.[11]

It is the task of this essay to look more closely at Chr's royal speech, prophetic speech, priestly speech, and the speech of others[12] in light of this consensus position regarding their value for historical reconstruction. It will be shown that the consensus position is entirely justified and that Chr does indeed function as theologian—not historian—in these addresses.

Royal Speech in Chronicles

Mason has isolated fifteen royal addresses in the books of Chronicles that do not appear in the synoptic material of Samuel–Kings.[13] There is some consensus that these addresses constitute the material that needs to be examined in discussions of Chr's royal speech, with the possible

---

9. For the classical and ancient Near Eastern material, see M. Weinfeld, *Deuteronomy and the Deuteronomic School* (Oxford: Clarendon Press, 1972) pp. 51-58; and J. Van Seters, *In Search of History: Historiography in the Ancient World and the Origins of Biblical History* (New Haven, CT: Yale University Press, 1983), especially pp. 67, 230, 292, 304, 358. For Acts, see M. Dibelius, 'The Speeches in Acts and Ancient Historiography', in H. Greeven (ed.), *Studies in the Acts of the Apostles* (New York: Charles Scribner's Sons, 1956) pp. 138-85; and M.L. Soards, *The Speeches in Acts: Their Content, Context, and Concerns* (Louisville, KY: Westminster/John Knox, 1994), especially p. 16, n. 53, where he denies the possibility of finding definitive answers to questions of sources, methods of composition, or historicity in speech material.

10. See S. Japhet, 'The Historical Reliability of Chronicles: The History of the Problem and its Place in Biblical Research', *JSOT* 33 (1985), pp. 83-107.

11. S. Japhet, *The Ideology of the Book of Chronicles and its Place in Biblical Thought* (BEATAJ, 9; Frankfurt: Peter Lang, 1989), pp. 9-10.

12. The categories are those used in Mason's recent monograph, *Preaching the Tradition*.

13. *Preaching the Tradition*, pp. 133-35.

Relative Placement of the Non-Synoptic Speeches in Chronicles

Royal	Prophetic	Priestly	Others
			I 12.18
I 13.2-3			
I 15.2, 12-13			
I 22.6-16			
I 22.17-19			
I 28.2-10			
I 28.20-21			
I 29.1-5, 20			
(possibly secondary)			
	II 12.5-8		
II 13.4-12			
II 14.7			
	II 15.1-7		
	II 16.7-9		
	II 19.2-3		
II 19.6-7, 9-11			
		II 20.14-17	
		(possibly prophetic)	
II 20.20			
	II 20.37		
	II 21.12-15		
	II 24.20-22		
	(possibly priestly)		
	II 25.7-9		
	II 25.15-16		
		II 26.17-18	
	II 28.9-11		
			II 28.12-13
II 29.5-11, 31			
II 30.6-9			
		II 31.10	
II 32.7-8			
II 35.3-6			
			II 35.21
			II 36.23 (possibly
			secondary)

single exception of David's final address (1 Chron. 29.1-5), which seems to be redactional.[14] The remaining fourteen addresses are divided among the kings as follows: David, six speeches (1 Chron. 13.2-3; 15.2, 12-13; 22.6-16; 22.17-19; 28.2-10; 28.20-21); Abijah, one speech (2 Chron. 13.4-12); Asa, one speech (14.7); Jehoshaphat, two speeches (19.6-7, 9-11; 20.20); Hezekiah, three speeches (29.5-11, 31; 30.6-9; 32.7-8); and Josiah, one speech (35.3-6).

Saebø has suggested that a primary function of the speeches which has not received the attention it deserves, is to invest the speakers with authority.[15] Judging by the distribution of these speeches one would have to agree. It is immediately apparent that only Chr's favorites deliver royal addresses, and if that king is presented in both a favorable and an unfavorable light, his speech will take place during the pious portion of his reign.[16]

Examination of the royal speeches with regard to matters of form and content leads to other useful observations. The initial form-critical classifications of Braun and the present author (edict, oration, and rationale) now appear to be much too rigid.[17] Mason has grouped nine of the fourteen instances of royal speech under the more general heading of 'Encouragement for a Task', which includes 'a call to a specific enterprise, a reason for undertaking it and/or grounds of encouragement which make the task a hopeful one'.[18] David's last five speeches found in 1 Chronicles dominate here and set the pattern for future instances among his heirs. The task that is encouraged is the preparation for Solomon's building of the temple—a primary concern in Chr's

---

14. For the redactional character of all of 1 Chron. 29.1-19 see R. Mosis, *Untersuchungen zur Theologie des Chronistischen Geschichtswerkes* (FTS, 92; Freiburg: Herder, 1973), pp. 105-107; and my partial support in Throntveit, *When Kings Speak*, pp. 89-96.

15. 'Taler og bønner', p. 125.

16. Mason, *Preaching the Tradition*, pp. 134-35.

17. Braun, 'Significance', pp. 225-49; Throntveit, *When Kings Speak*, pp. 20-50. The same may be said for the classification of S.J. De Vries, *1 and 2 Chronicles* (FOTL, 11; Grand Rapids, MI: Eerdmans, 1989).

18. *Preaching the Tradition*, p. 18. The speeches include those of: David (1 Chron. 15.2, 12-13; 22.6-16; 22.17-19; 28.2-10; 28.20-21), Asa (2 Chron. 14.7), Jehoshaphat (19.6-7, 9-11), and Hezekiah (29.5-11; 32.7-8). Cf. Plöger, who speaks of 'Ermunterungsreden' with regard to David's speeches: 'Reden und Gebete', p. 57.

portrayal of David.[19] The remaining five addresses are more difficult to assign. Plöger has suggested that the speeches of Abijah and Hezekiah (2 Chron. 13.4-12 and 30.6-9) are *Umkehrreden*, 'calls to return' addressed to the northern kingdom.[20] Jehoshaphat's brief speech in 2 Chron. 20.20 appears to be an exhortation, as does Josiah's (35.3-6). David's initial address is seen as an 'overture' by Mason.[21]

In terms of content, three themes are represented. Cultic considerations predominate in all of David's addresses, Josiah's address to the Levites, and two of Hezekiah's speeches (2 Chron. 29.5-11, 31 and 30.6-9). Hezekiah's other address (32.7-8), the speeches of Abijah and Asa, and Jehoshaphat's second address (20.20)[22] are mainly concerned with the theme of faithfulness in war. Only Jehoshaphat's other speech (19.6-7, 9-11) falls outside these two thematic areas, and it is concerned with judicial reform.

Several inferences may be drawn from this information. It was mentioned above that the Davidic addresses were uniformly cast as encouragements for a task and that they had to do with David's encouragement of Solomon in the building of the temple. On other grounds there seems to be a broad consensus that David and Solomon are to be seen as linked together in Chr's conception as 'einen zusammenhängenden Akt'.[23] The unity of purpose revealed in these speeches serves to further this understanding and argues for their employment by Chr as part of his theological agenda.

Two pairs of speeches suggest other possibilities of a structural nature. The *Umkehrreden* of Abijah and Hezekiah provide an *inclusio* around the period of the divided monarchy, thereby establishing the three major divisions of Chr's presentation: the united monarchy of David and Solomon, the divided monarchy following the death of

---

19. W. Riley, *King and Cultus in Chronicles: Worship and the Reinterpretation of History* (JSOTSup, 160; Sheffield: JSOT Press, 1993).

20. 'Reden und Gebete', pp. 57-58.

21. *Preaching the Tradition*, p. 18.

22. The virtual quotation of Isa. 7.9 in this address by a king who lived nearly 100 years before Isaiah would seem to argue for Chr's invention of this (and other?) speech(es).

23. Plöger, 'Reden und Gebete', p. 56. See also, Williamson, 'The Accession of Solomon in the Books of Chronicles', *VT* 26 (1976), pp. 351-61; Throntveit, *When Kings Speak*, pp. 114-15; and especially Braun, 'Solomonic Apologetic in Chronicles', *JBL* 92 (1973), pp. 503-16.

Solomon, and the resumption of the united monarchy with Hezekiah.[24] We will see in the next section that Jehoshaphat's exhortation (2 Chron. 20.20), strategically placed in the center of the divided monarchy, serves as an interpretive key to all of Chr's instances of prophetic address. David's initial speech (1 Chron. 13.2-3), with its concern for the disposition of the ark, forms an *inclusio* around all of Chr's royal addresses, when taken in conjunction with Josiah's similar concern for the ark (2 Chron. 35.3-6). Since Chr tells us that the ark had been placed in the temple during Solomon's reign (2 Chron. 5.4-7) and there is no mention of its subsequent removal, Josiah's command to 'Put the holy ark in the temple', is difficult. A common suggestion, translating תנו 'leave the ark in the temple', would resolve this matter with reference to David's second address (1 Chron. 15.15-16). Regardless of one's decision in this matter, concern for the ark as a levitical duty has been altered. Whereas David had established the levitical practice of carrying the ark in the first two royal addresses, Josiah emphasizes the levitical duty of service and ministry, now that the carrying of the ark is no longer necessary.[25]

This leaves the unusual address of Jehoshaphat (2 Chron. 19.6-7, 9-11) unaccounted for in terms of structural or theological placement. The juridical reforms of Jehoshaphat pose serious historical problems. Though dismissed by Wellhausen as based upon the fortuitous nature of the king's name ('Yahweh is judge'),[26] others have seen at least a core of historical material in Chr's report.[27] Against this, however, is the judicious suspicion of Mason:

> ...some very characteristic Chronicler words and phraseology, and the interesting bringing together of high priest and governor in what might be termed the ecclesiastical court, may well reflect efforts in the post-

---

24. Throntveit, *When Kings Speak*, pp. 36-38, 113-20; Williamson, *Israel in the Books of Chronicles*, (Cambridge: Cambridge University Press, 1977), pp. 110-18; Plöger, 'Reden und Gebete', p. 60.

25. See S.J. De Vries, 'Moses and David as Cult Founders in Chronicles', *JBL* 107 (1988), p. 639, for the suggestion that the anachronistic command regarding the ark fulfills the ideal first expressed in David's initial speeches.

26. *Prolegomena*, p. 191.

27. See the bibliography and discussion provided by Mason, *Preaching the Tradition*, pp. 272-73, n. 82; and especially G. Knoppers, 'Jehoshaphat's Judiciary and "The Scroll of YHWH's Torah"', *JBL* 113 (1994), pp. 59-80.

exilic period to translate pre-exilic procedures of the monarchical period
into the new situation of a later time.[28]

Knoppers, in his recent, exhaustive investigation of Jehoshaphat's
reforms, warns against simplistic assumptions on both sides. Chr mirrors neither 'history' nor his own contemporary situation as he draws
on both past tradition and present reality to forge a new entity: a
depiction of Jehoshaphat's reforms that 'ultimately reflects what he
believes justice should be'.[29] The situation is indeed as complex
as Knoppers maintains. Nevertheless, this address remains the best
example of possible historical information as recorded in the royal
addresses.[30]

Brief mention might also be made regarding Chr's royal prayers.
These, too, are best explained in terms of Chr's overall structure and
intent to highlight important aspects of the narrative. David's prayers
(1 Chron. 17.16-27//2 Sam. 7.17-29, though greatly altered, and 29.10-
19, though with some redactional elements) effectively frame David's
participation in the process of planning for the building of the temple.[31]
As such, they enhance Chr's picture of David as supremely concerned
with the establishment of the cult in conjunction with David's addresses. The prayers of Asa (2 Chron. 14.10 [EVV 11]) and Jehoshaphat
(20.5-12) are prayers before battle that hearken back to Solomon's
programmatic prayer at the dedication of the temple (2 Chron. 6.12-40;
especially vv. 34-35) taken over from 1 Kgs 8.22-53. Hezekiah's prayer
(2 Chron. 30.18-19) is of an intercessory nature but also recalls
petitions from Solomon's prayer (especially 6.20). As such, they are
rhetorical instances of Chr's repeated demonstration of answered
prayer (2 Chron. 13; 18.31; 25.5-13; 32.20-22).

Prophetic Speech in Chronicles

Only five prophetic addresses in Chronicles have corresponding parallels in Samuel-Kings: those of Nathan (1 Chron. 17//2 Sam. 7), Gad

---

28. *Preaching the Tradition*, p. 63.

29. Knoppers, 'Jehoshaphat's Judiciary', p. 80.

30. For a more positive assessment of the material with a brief discussion of the
scholarly literature, see S. Japhet, *I & II Chronicles* (OTL; Louisville, KY:
Westminster/John Knox, 1993), pp. 770-74.

31. Plöger, 'Reden und Gebete', p. 60. The placement of the first prayer also
effectively divides David's concern with the ark in his first two speeches from his
concern with the temple in his subsequent addresses.

(1 Chron. 21//2 Sam. 24), Shemaiah (2 Chron. 11//1 Kgs 12), Micaiah ben Imlah (2 Chron. 18.4-27//1 Kgs 22.5-28), and Huldah (2 Chron. 34.22-28//2 Kgs 22.14-20). As such they need not detain us further.

Those instances of prophetic address that have no parallel in Samuel–Kings, however, are much more interesting for our concerns: Shemaiah (2 Chron. 12.5-8), Azariah (15.1-7), Hanani (16.7-9), Jehu ben Hanani (19.2-3), Eliezer (20.37), Elijah's letter to Jehoram (21.12-15), Zechariah (24.20), an anonymous 'man of God' (25.7-8), an anonymous 'prophet' (25.15-16), and Oded (28.9-11). All these prophetic addresses are replete with the characteristic linguistic and stylistic hallmarks of Chr and, as will be discussed below, serve to infuse the narratives in which they occur with Chr's own theological evaluation of the particular king in question in terms of the theology of retribution.

Not only are the addresses unknown to us from other sources, the speakers themselves are also unique. Three possible exceptions to this statement require comment at this point. First, Elijah's letter (2 Chron. 21.12-15) presents difficulties of chronology and geography. With regard to chronology, one would assume from the implicit chronology found in 2 Kings that Elijah could not have been present, having been taken to heaven (ch. 2) before the reign of Jehoram (ch. 3). There is no suggestion in the text that Elijah wrote the letter prior to his departure or that it was sent from heaven.[32] This argument, of course, renders moot the geographical question of whether Elijah, whose ministry consisted of defending Yahweh against the incursion of Ba'al in Ahab's court, carried out an ancillary calling in the south. Virtually all recent commentators have questioned the historicity of Elijah's epistolary encounter.

Second, a Jehu ben Hanani was active in the north during the reign of Baasha (1 Kgs 16.1, 7). This northern location as well as the fact that his prophetic activity took place some fifty years prior to the time of the Jehu ben Hanani mentioned in Chronicles would seem to argue against the common identity of these two individuals. It is also impossible to ascertain whether the father of the Jehu in Chronicles, Hanani, is in fact the prophetic figure found in 2 Chron. 16.7-10.[33]

---

32. As some harmonizing attempts have suggested, cf. Rudolph's list and comments, *Chronikbücher* (HAT, 21; Tübingen: Mohr [Paul Siebeck], 1955), p. 267.

33. 'While there is in principle no apparent reason to deny his authenticity, the prevalent scholarly view is that he was not historical. His figure should be viewed in the perspective given explicit expression in rabbinic literature. Post-biblical

Third, Shemaiah is known to us from his first address (2 Chron. 11.3-4//1 Kgs 12.23-24) and thus, while his later addresses are not paralleled in Kings, he and Elijah are the only prophets who give addresses that are at least not unknown to Chr's audience regardless of the historicity of their messages.

Four of these prophetic addresses are examined as part of von Rad's so-called 'levitical sermons'.[34] In his article von Rad sought to identify a new literary *Gattung* in Chronicles with the following characteristics:

> The first part sets out clearly and precisely the conditions on which God is prepared to give his help—i.e. the doctrine. The second part looks back into history, showing that God's nearness is not to be taken for granted, and that there are whole periods of history in which he was far removed—i.e. the application. The third part is a call to faith with the promise of reward—i.e. the exhortation.[35]

Thus the addresses are 'sermons' with the quotation of or allusion to a text, followed by an application and an exhortation. But von Rad's rather negative appraisal of Chr ('But he really is quite the last person whom we should credit with the creation of anything, let alone a new literary form!')[36] forces him to look to Deuteronomic circles and the traditions of the levitical priests for the *Sitz im Leben* of these addresses. Von Rad's views, however, while initially embraced,[37] have

---

sages, in an attempt to explain irregularities in the presentation of biblical prophets, coined the axiom "every prophet whose patronym is recorded—both he and his father were prophets" (Leviticus Rabbah 6.7). "Hanani" is of course the father of "Jehu", a prophet appearing in Israel in the time of Baasha (I Kgs 16.1, 7), and according to Chronicles also active under Jehoshaphat (II Chron. 19.2; 20.34). Although this principle is articulated only in rabbinic literature, the very appearance of the prophet "Hanani" in the time of Asa may be regarded as its earliest intimation; of course the historicity of "Hanani" is then strongly suspect.' Japhet, *I & II Chronicles*, p. 734.

34. 2 Chron. 15.2-7; 16.7-9; 19.6ff.; 25.7ff. Also discussed are 1 Chron. 28.2-10; 2 Chron. 20.15-17; 20.20; 29.5-11; 30.6-9; 32.7-8a. Von Rad, 'Levitical Sermon', pp. 267-80.

35. 'Levitical Sermon', p. 271.

36. 'Levitical Sermon', p. 277.

37. As seen in the commentaries of J.M. Myers, *II Chronicles* (AB, 13; Garden City, NY: Doubleday, 1965); P.R. Ackroyd, *I & II Chronicles, Ezra, Nehemiah*, (TBC; London: SCM, 1973); and R.J. Coggins, *The First and Second Books of the Chronicles*, (CBC; Cambridge: Cambridge University Press, 1976), among others. H.G.M. Williamson goes so far as to say that Chr's 'work as a whole thus takes on

recently come under serious criticism, and it has been shown that these addresses are neither 'levitical' nor 'sermons'.[38]

Westermann, on the basis of his form-critical comparison of these addresses with earlier prophetic speech, has expanded von Rad's insights to defend the position that these southern prophets who appear in Chronicles were not inventions of Chr, 'but that they were also present all through the whole history of the kingship in the Southern Kingdom'.[39] This evidence would provide some support, on the basis of Chr's speeches, for those wishing to argue for the presence of southern prophets in the monarchical period, a presence omitted by Dtr, though Westermann proceeds to state that 'it is clear that the real interest of the Chronicler in including the prophetic speeches was to give divine authority to his interpretation of history'.

A further objection to von Rad's work concerns the scope of his investigations. Some of these 'levitical sermons' are made by kings, some are rather to be classified as prayers, and other instances of prophetic address are not taken into account. Investigation of the ten non-synoptic prophetic addresses found in Chronicles as a body suggests that they all share a common function: validation of the theme of retributive justice. J.D. Newsome has convincingly argued that four of these addresses have been added by Chr to the narrative of his source in Kings with just this purpose in mind.[40]

First, 2 Chron. 12.2-12 faithfully reproduces 1 Kgs 14.25-28 with the addition of vv. 2b-9a, which provides Chr's interpretation of Shishak's invasion in a dialogue between Shemaiah the prophet and Rehoboam and the princes of Judah. Both the disaster of the Egyptian invasion and God's deliverance of Judah following Rehoboam's repentance are attributed to God's retributive justice.

Second, 2 Chron. 16.7-10 consists of a prophetic address from

---

the parenetic purpose of a "Levitical sermon", warning and encouraging his contemporaries to a responsive faith which may again call down the mercy of their God': *1 and 2 Chronicles* (NCB; Grand Rapids, MI: Eerdmans, 1982) p. 33.

38. Especially Mathias, 'Levitische Predigt'; R.L. Braun, *I Chronicles* (WBC, 14; Waco, TX: Word Books, 1986), pp. xxiv-xxv; and R. Mason, 'Some Echoes of the Preaching in the Second Temple?', *ZAW* 96 (1984), pp. 221-35; *idem*, *Preaching the Tradition*, especially pp. 257-59.

39. C. Westermann, *Basic Forms of Prophetic Speech* (London: Lutterworth, 1967), pp. 162-68. The quotation is from p. 166.

40. Newsome, 'Prophecy', pp. 235-38.

Hanani that seeks to explain Asa's illness (1 Kgs 15.23b) as a result of his alliance with Ben-Hadad of Syria and cruel treatment of the prophet; again Chr's source is silent about the cause of Asa's illness. If we accept Rudolph's proposal that we read, 'the army of the king of *Israel* (with the Lucianic recension of LXX, instead of 'Syria') will escape...',[41] then Chr has also totally transformed Dtr's account of Israelite victory into one of defeat in the interests of his doctrine of retributive justice.

Third, Jehu ben Hanani's address in 2 Chron. 19.1-3 gives the appearance of restoring the character of one of Chr's favorites, Jehoshaphat, who had entered into alliance with Ahab, but who had also destroyed the Asherahs and set his heart to seek God. As noticed by the commentaries, these three verses totally recast the previous Micaiah ben Imlah narrative (1 Kgs 22.1-40//2 Chron. 18) that had ended with the fulfillment of the prophetic word in the death of Ahab. Chr omits this reference to prophetic fulfillment and adds Jehu ben Hanani's address, couched in terms of retributive justice, to emphasize the necessity of avoiding foreign alliances.[42]

Finally, 2 Chron. 20.35-37 is Chr's complete reworking of the brief narrative concerning Jehoshaphat's naval expedition to Ophir (1 Kgs 22.44, 48-50). In Kings, Ahaziah proposes that Jehoshaphat join him in an expedition *after* the ships to be used in the venture have been destroyed in the harbor, a proposal that Jehoshaphat refuses. Chr alters (or restores!) the order of events so that *Jehoshaphat* initiates the alliance, and the ships are destroyed at sea after the prophetic address of Eliezer (lacking in Kings). This drastic reworking of the text would be stronger evidence for Newsome's contention that Chr has, at times, inserted prophetic addresses to voice his theology of retributive justice, were it not for the fact that the Kings account makes practically no sense as it stands. We must assume that Chr has restored the proper order of alliance followed by disaster. This concession, however, leaves unresolved the questions of who initiated the alliance and whether Jehoshaphat succumbed. Furthermore, Chr has still inserted a prophetic address that clearly provides his own theological evaluation of the

41. Rudolph, *Chronikbücher*, p. 248.
42. R.B. Dillard, *2 Chronicles* (WBC, 15; Waco, TX: Word Books, 1987), p. 139.

proceedings.[43] Newsome summarizes his findings with the following brief description:

> The point here is that, for the Chronicler, prophets provide a voice with which to proclaim the retributive justice of God. Because on these occasions they appear in those situations where the Chronicler's known source did not have them, the suspicion is aroused that they have been introduced into the story, not for purposes of historical accuracy, but for the purposes of theological emphasis.[44]

Newsome's suspicion seems well founded. I have argued elsewhere[45] that Chr's non-synoptic prophetic addresses all proclaim a consistent message: blessing and reward for those (especially those kings) who 'seek God' (דרש, בקש) and 'humble themselves' (כנע), judgment and disaster for those who do not (in addition to negative formulations of דרש, כנע, and בקש, their antonyms, עזב ['abandon, forsake'] and מעל ['be unfaithful, rebellious'] serve as the linguistic carriers of Chr's portrayal).[46]

The placement of these addresses also argues for their theological function in the narrative. Of the ten non-synoptic prophetic addresses, nine occur in the period of the divided monarchy.[47] As we have already seen, this is the period that Chr has framed with two of his royal addresses, the *Umkehrreden* of Abijah (2 Chron. 13.4-12) and Hezekiah (30.6-9). In Chr's periodization of history this middle period of the divided monarchy, flanked by the united monarchy of David and Solomon and the re-united monarchy of Hezekiah, is a critical moment for Judah. The north had fallen due to the unfaithfulness of its kings, as Chr's biblical sources repeatedly assert. The only hope for the south lay

---

43. For a closely reasoned attempt to maximize the historiographical significance of this and similar passages where Chr rewrites stories from his source, see Japhet, *I & II Chronicles*, p. 803.

44. Newsome, 'Prophecy', pp. 237-38.

45. Throntveit, *When Kings Speak*, pp. 127-29. I have since been convinced that Jahaziel's address (2 Chron. 20.14-17) is properly a priestly speech, though with decided prophetic overtones. See the discussion below under 'Priestly Speech in Chronicles', and Mason, *Preaching the Tradition*, pp. 134-35.

46. For a discussion of Chr's retributive justice and a cataloging of these terms, see Dillard, *2 Chronicles*, pp. 76-81.

47. Azariah, 2 Chron. 15.1-7; Hanani, 16.7-9; Jehu, 19.2-3; Eliezer, 20.37; Elijah's epistle, 21.12-15; Zechariah, 24.20; 'a man of God', 25.8; 'a prophet', 25.15-16; and Oded, 28.9-11.

in the faithful leadership of its rulers. As Jehoshaphat, Chr's paradigmatic king for this period, had dramatically proclaimed in a royal
address in the center of this period, 'Listen to me, O Judah and
inhabitants of Jerusalem! Believe in the Lord your God and you will be
established; believe his prophets (and you will succeed)!'[48] The call to
faith was to belief in God *and his appointed messengers the prophets.*
Since all but one of those messengers have been placed in this period of
crisis, the suggestion arises that they have been so situated for theological impact as voices for Chr's own agenda rather than for historical
precision.[49]

The same may be said for the one prophetic address appearing before
the period of the divided monarchy, that of Shemaiah (2 Chron. 12.5-8).
That Shemaiah's address serves Chr's theme of retributive justice is
clear and widely acknowledged.[50] Of interest here, are the reasons for
its particular location in the narrative at the time of the schism and as
the first of Chr's prophetic addresses. At least two aspects of this passage set it apart from the other prophetic addresses. First, it is couched
in the form of a dialogue, which is rare in Chronicles in general but
especially unusual in the non-synoptic material.[51] More significantly,
though, it is a two-staged encounter between the prophet and Rehoboam
and the princes of Judah. In the first stage (vv. 5-6) Shemaiah tersely
explains that Shishak's triumph was due to Rehoboam's sin, 'Thus says
the Lord: You abandoned me, so I have abandoned you to the hand of
Shishak.' In response, Rehoboam and the leaders humbled themselves
and said, 'The Lord is in the right.' The second stage (vv. 7-8) presents
Yahweh's assurance of 'some deliverance' (in response to their repentance) and a warning.

Japhet has convincingly argued that Chr's doctrine of retributive
justice consists of both call to repentance *and* warning, under the

---

48. I cannot explain the NRSV's curious omission of the phrase included within
the parentheses.

49. For further discussion on Chr's periodization of history, see Throntveit,
When Kings Speak, pp. 109-25. For a detailed discussion of Chr's depiction of
Hezekiah as a new David and Solomon, see Throntveit, 'Hezekiah in the Books of
Chronicles', in D.J. Lull (ed.), *Society of Biblical Literature 1988 Seminar Papers*
(SBLSPS, 27; Atlanta: Scholars Press, 1988), pp. 302-11.

50. See Dillard, *2 Chronicles*, pp. 76-81.

51. Throntveit, *When Kings Speak*, p. 12 (cf. esp. nn. 1, 2, and 3).

general principle of 'no punishment without warning'.[52] In addition to a saturation of Chr's preferred vocabulary of retribution, all these characteristics of the prophetic addresses appear in this short encounter: retributive justice as the theological explanation for a particular situation (here, both judgment as seen in Shishak's victory in response to sin, and deliverance, though qualified, in response to repentance) and prophetic warning. Thus, the pericope functions as a paradigmatic introduction to the prophetic addresses that will follow.

That Shemaiah's paradigmatic address stands at the close of Chr's depiction of the united monarchy, indeed, during the transitional reign of Rehoboam that will result in the divided monarchy of the following period, should also not be overlooked. The united monarchy, characterized by Chr's glowing picture of David and Solomon, had required no prophetic messengers of retributive justice. That ideal situation now lay in the past and Rehoboam seems to set the pattern, for both good and ill, of future kings. With Shemaiah's address Chr sets the tone for his subsequent theological critique.

Priestly Speech in Chronicles

Mason has drawn the category of priestly address to our attention by isolating four such pieces in the narrative, all of them unique to Chr's presentation: Jahaziel (2 Chron. 20.14-17), Zechariah (24.20-22), Azariah (26.17-18), and Azariah, the high priest (31.10).[53] The classification of two of these addresses is problematic, as can be seen in Mason's references to four priestly addresses (pp. 133, 139), three priestly addresses (p. 134), and two priestly addresses (p. 135), at different times in his discussion. The problem centers on the first two speeches. Though Jahaziel is designated a 'Levite' (the only such Levite to have an address in Chronicles, a factor that seriously damages von Rad's designation of all these speeches as *levitical* sermons), his speech displays strong prophetic overtones. It is introduced with a prophetic narrative ('The spirit of the Lord came upon him', 2 Chron. 20.14) and includes the prophetic messenger formula (כה־אמר האלהים ['Thus says the Lord'], 20.15).

Zechariah is not designated a priest; rather, he is said to be delivering an address from his dead father, Jehoiada, the priest. He, too, is

---

52. *Ideology*, pp. 176-91. The quote is found on p. 188.
53. *Preaching the Tradition*, pp. 133-44.

introduced with the prophetic sounding, 'Then the spirit of God clothed itself with Zechariah' (2 Chron. 24.20a), and his address includes a variation on the prophetic messenger formula (כה־אמר יהוה ['Thus says God'], 24.20b).[54]

Since Jahaziel is clearly designated a Levite by Chr and delivers an address that only vaguely resembles the prophetic speeches with their overt declarations of Chr's theology of retributive justice, it seems best to include his speech as one of the priestly addresses. Zechariah, on the other hand, is only designated as Jehoiada's son. Since his brief speech is clearly of a piece with Chr's other prophetic addresses, it seems best to group him with the prophets, leaving the speeches of Jahaziel, Azariah, and Azariah the high priest as Chr's priestly addresses.

It is hazardous to derive general conclusions regarding the value of Chr's priestly addresses for historical reconstruction when—unlike the sections on royal and prophetic speech—we have only three such addresses to examine. Perhaps a few brief comments on the individual speeches may be ventured for the sake of completeness.

The battle report in which Jahaziel's address appears is a contemporary battleground in the scholarly debate regarding the historicity of Chr, as well.[55] Three factors arise from the speech itself or its narrative introduction. His unusual genealogy, in which he is designated a Levite and traced back to Asaph, the chief singer in David's time, links him with the quasi-prophetic temple singers, a common chronistic theme (e.g., 1 Chron. 25.1-8; 2 Chron. 20.18-21).[56] This linkage, coupled with the symbolic nature of his unique name, Jahaziel ('he who sees God'), prompts Japhet to argue for 'the "literary" nature of his figure', and his address as 'a Chronistic composition'.[57] Although the formal cate gory of the address is elusive,[58] and so probably composite, the predominance of themes associated with the 'priestly salvation oracle',

---

54. Mason draws attention to these inconsistencies as well, *Preaching the Tradition,* pp. 134, 139-40.

55. See P. Welten, *Geschichte und Geschichtsdarstellung in den Chronikbüchern* (WMANT, 42; Neukirchen–Vluyn: Neukirchener Verlag, 1973), pp. 140-53.

56. Dillard, *2 Chronicles,* p. 158.

57. Japhet, *I & II Chronicles,* p. 793.

58. E.g., 'sermon' (von Rad, 'Levitical Sermon', pp. 272-73); 'oracle of mercy' (D.L. Petersen, *Late Israelite Prophecy: Studies in Deutero-Prophetic Literature and in Chronicles* [SBLMS, 23; Missoula, MT: Scholars Press, 1977], p. 72); 'priestly salvation oracle' (Williamson, *1 and 2 Chronicles,* pp. 297-99; see also Welten, *Geschichte,* p. 150; and Dillard, *2 Chronicles,* pp. 154-55).

which follow Josiah's clear example of a national or communal lament (2 Chron. 20.5-12), provides us with 'one of the very few likely examples of this form in a specifically liturgical context, even though on other grounds it has been frequently invoked by scholars to explain the sudden change of mood in a number of the Psalms of lament in the Psalter'.[59] Thus, while we must remain agnostic concerning the historicity of the address in question, Chr's schematic presentation suggests the historical existence of this form-critical category, which may be of some value in the reconstruction of the context of Israel's liturgical practice.

Azariah's denunciation of Uzziah for burning incense (2 Chron. 26.17-18) is generally regarded as a construction of Chr, who has utilized the priest to present post-exilic arguments for priestly authority, already familiar from the Priestly legislation of the Pentateuch. One's prior views regarding the date and composition of the Pentateuch weigh heavily in one's assessment of this passage, though, as Dillard reminds us, views regarding the Priestly legislation may be irrelevant here, as the presence of such regulations in Chronicles might 'well reflect a reliable tradition regarding an action of Uzziah'.[60] The large number of priests ('eighty priests of the Lord who were men of valor', v. 17), however, remains problematic and somewhat suspicious.

The same may be said for the high priest Azaraiah's address (2 Chron. 31.10). He is not mentioned in the list of high priests recorded by Chr (1 Chron. 5.29-40 [EVV 6.3-15]), and matters of chronology would seem to eliminate the possibility that this is the same Azaraiah that denounced Uzziah some forty years before. Japhet proposes the interesting solution that the unique appellative, 'of the house of Zadok', recalled a similar reference to 'Azariah(u) the son of Zadok...the priest' of Solomon's time (1 Kgs 4.2), which she suggests may argue for the literary—rather than historical—character of this figure.[61] If she is right in this assessment, we may have yet another instance of Chr's attempt to portray Hezekiah as a new David *and* Solomon, who instituted the re-united monarchy on the basis of his illustrious forebears.[62]

It is perhaps not too hazardous to notice, as a closing remark, that each of these three priestly addresses deals with an aspect of priestly

59. Williamson, *1 and 2 Chronicles*, p. 297.
60. Dillard, *2 Chronicles*, p. 210.
61. *I & II Chronicles*, p. 966.
62. See Throntveit, 'Hezekiah' for additional instances of Chr's utilization of this theme.

duty. Jahaziel's salvation oracle is the appropriate priestly response to Josiah's national lament. The concern of Azariah and the eighty priests regarding the usurpation of priestly prerogative by Uzziah is also understandable from a priestly perspective, as is Azariah's announcement of God's blessing as a result of the people's willingness to support the temple.

The Speech of Others in Chronicles

Four other non-synoptic speeches in the books of Chronicles have been isolated by Mason: the address of the army officer, Amasai (1 Chron. 12.19 [EVV 18]); the Ephraimite leaders' support of Oded's prophecy (2 Chron. 28.12-13); the injunction of Neco, the Egyptian king, to Josiah (35.21); and Cyrus's decree, which comes at the very end of the book (36.23).[63] A glance at the accompanying chart of Chr's non-synoptic speeches suggests that each of these addresses occurs at a crucial juncture in the narrative. Thus, these speeches take on an importance that belies their number.

The address of Amasai (1 Chron. 12.19 [EVV 18]) enjoys pride of place in this regard. Its position as the first of Chr's non-synoptic speeches invites us to look for programmatic insights into Chr's presentation, and we are not disappointed. Though very similar to that of Zechariah ('the spirit of God clothed Zechariah' [2 Chron. 24.20a]; elsewhere, only in Judg. 6.34), the narrative introduction functions here, as well, to invest another, otherwise unknown, non-prophetic figure with prophetic status. The message itself is a brief poetic blessing upon David and those who rally to his cause with an explicit theological statement that it is God who helps David. Ackroyd has insightfully suggested that the real significance of Amasai's address is found in its repudiation of the people's response to Jeroboam's call for rebellion against David and his house (2 Chron. 10.16).[64] This suggestion, by linking Amasai's address to the disaster of the schism, seems to strengthen the programmatic nature of the speech and justifies Mason's conclusion that:

---

63. *Preaching the Tradition*, pp. 133-44. 'Non-synoptic' in this context refers to having no parallel in Samuel–Kings. The Cyrus Edict, of course, is paralleled in the opening verses of Ezra.

64. *I & II Chronicles, Ezra, Nehemiah*, p. 55. See also Williamson, *1 and 2 Chronicles*, p. 108.

It acts as a summons to all true 'Israelites' to align themselves with the well-being of the Davidic line by showing that active support which places them within the divine purpose. Equally significantly, it associates 'peace' with David, that peace which will later characterise his continuing line and the temple. All God's purposes for peace, prosperity and success centre on David. Amasai is the herald of this theology which is to be at the heart of the Chronicler's interpretation of history.[65]

While we cannot use this address for purposes of historical reconstruction, its theological and programmatic function in Chr's presentation, by dint of its strategic placement as well as its content, is evident.

The positive response of the Ephraimite leaders (2 Chron. 28.12-13) to Oded's prophetic address (28.9-11), the last of Chr's prophetic addresses, also appears at a strategic juncture in the narrative.[66] Williamson has convincingly demonstrated that the entire chapter is best seen as a reworking of the account of Ahaz in 2 Kings 16 and effectively reverses the relationship that obtained between Israel and Judah at the time of the schism (2 Chron. 13).[67] Thus, the section concerned with the divided monarchy ends as it had begun, with rebellion and apostasy. This time, though, it is the south, rather than the north, that has abandoned the ideals of David, as epitomized in the actions of Ahaz, which duplicate the sins of the north chronicled in Abijah's address (13.4-12).

These two rhetorical passages—the prophecy of Oded and the supportive comments of the Ephraimite leaders, which function as a veritable confession of sin—constitute the centerpiece of Chr's presentation. In the past, these positive portrayals of northerners have usually been dismissed as contrary to Chr's so-called 'anti-Samaritan polemic'. But seen in conjunction with the presentation in 2 Chronicles 13, especially in light of the emphasis on the captives being 'brothers' (vv. 5, 11 [in Oded's address], and 15), it becomes apparent that Chr uses these speeches to make the point that all Israel, north and south, is and has been the people of God.

---

65. *Preaching the Tradition*, p. 16.

66. 'The Chronicler's account of the reign of Ahaz is of considerable strategic importance in his treatment of the history of Judah. It was the period during which the Northern Kingdom went into exile; though the Chronicler is silent on that subject, it paved the way for his portrayal of a reunited Israel under Hezekiah.' Dillard, *2 Chronicles*, p. 219.

67. *Israel,* pp. 114-18; cf his summary with further comments in *1 and 2 Chronicles*, pp. 343-49, as well as that of Dillard, *2 Chronicles*, pp. 219-20.

This strategic placement of the speech and the attendant implications of the chapter's relationship to 2 Chronicles 13, of course, only point to the theological significance of the passage and cannot help us with the thorny historical problems that arise from a comparison of Chr's radically different portrayal of the Syro-Ephraimite war with other Old Testament tradents.[68]

The last two addresses in Chronicles are unusual in that both are ascribed to foreign rulers.[69] Depending upon one's understanding of the extent of the work, either one may be seen as the last of Chr's addresses.

The address of Pharaoh Neco (2 Chron. 35.21) occurs in an account for which we have some extra-biblical support.[70] Nevertheless, as Japhet rightly concludes, the function of the address is to carry the *theological* burden of the passage, not the historical.[71] The ignoble death in battle of pious Josiah, despite Huldah's prophecy to the contrary (a prophecy that Chr records from Kings), was explained in terms of Chr's doctrine of retributive justice—the result of Josiah's failure to heed God's warning as delivered by Neco.

There is a broad range of scholarly opinion regarding the authenticity and function of the Cyrus Edict (2 Chron. 36.22-23), undoubtedly due to its appearance at the beginning of Ezra. Space considerations prevent discussion of this vexing problem[72] beyond the passing mention of two recent interpretations.[72]

Among those scholars who favor its retention, Japhet has suggested that these verses allow the book to conclude in the way it began, with

68. For an extended treatment of the conflicting Old Testament interpretations in Isaiah, Hosea, 2 Kings, and 2 Chronicles, see M.E.W. Thompson, *Situation and Theology: Old Testament Interpretations of the Syro-Ephraimite War* (Prophets and Historians Series, 1; Sheffield: Almond Press, 1982), who concludes his section on 2 Chronicles with the words, 'in fact he "used" the incident for his own theological purpose. Clearly, he wishes us to read the story of Ahaz...in a very different way from those enjoined by earlier historians, theologians and prophets' (p. 102).

69. Though Chr has reproduced the message of Sennacherib to Hezekiah from his source with some modification (2 Chron. 32.10-17//2 Kgs 18.28-35), these two addresses are the only non-synoptic instances.

70. For bibliographic references, see De Vries, *1 and 2 Chronicles*, p. 419.

71. *I & II Chronicles*, p. 1056.

72. For strong arguments against authenticity, see Williamson, *Israel*, pp. 7-10. For strong arguments for the authenticity and theological function of this passage, see Riley, *King and Cultus*, pp. 149-56. I remain convinced that Chr ended his account at v. 21.

the citation of an existing source and the inauguration of a new era. She concludes her commentary:

> We find here a salient feature of the Chronicler's historiography, viewing the course of history as moving in extremes of thesis and antithesis, in a constant swing of the historical pendulum. The edict of Cyrus is the beginning of a new era in the history of Israel, pointing with hope and confidence toward the future.[73]

W. Riley takes a different tack. Seeking to show that Chronicles 'is, in effect, a representation of the formative monarchical period of Israel's history as viewed especially through the cultic lens',[74] he sees the rule of Cyrus as terminating the Davidic dynasty. This termination serves the dual purpose of freeing the post-exilic community from the false hope of a Davidic restoration under Persian rule and inviting them to recognize the hope and promise offered in David's true legacy, the restoration of the temple, as announced by Cyrus.[75]

Both of these recent attempts to deal with the final form of the text have much to commend them. Yet, the implications for historical reconstruction remain overshadowed by the theological perspective of Chr that governs the very argumentation that they adopt.

Mason concludes his examination of these addresses with the following statement of their purpose:

> It is noticeable that the résumé of their themes and their theological contents reads remarkably like a précis of the theology of the Chronicler, i.e. of the Books of Chronicles more or less in the form in which we now have them. This must suggest that the 'addresses', and their attribution to those who, the Chronicler tells us, uttered them, serve primarily as a mouth-piece for the Chronicler himself.[76]

In the final analysis, while Chr's speeches, both in terms of the theological material they contain as well as their strategic placement in the narrative, are a primary source of information about the thoughts, ideas, and theological perspectives of Chr himself, they are of considerably less value for the important, if extremely difficult, task of historical reconstruction.

---

73. *I & II Chronicles*, p. 1077.
74. *King and Cultus*, p. 36.
75. *King and Cultus*, pp. 149-55.
76. *Preaching the Tradition*, p. 143.

'YOU CAN'T PRAY A LIE':
TRUTH *AND* FICTION IN THE PRAYERS OF CHRONICLES

Samuel E. Balentine

The citation in the title of this essay is from Mark Twain's *The Adventures of Huckleberry Finn*. In the midst of their wondrous journey down the Mississippi, Huck Finn and Jim, the runaway slave, had once again fallen into trouble. Jim had been captured, and his captors were preparing to claim the reward that had been placed on his head by returning Jim to slavery, in accordance with the laws of the land, unless Huck intervened to save him. The situation created a dilemma for Huck. Should he accede to the law, admit that he had been wrong to steal a slave, and so betray the friend who needed him most? Or should he violate the law, remain true to his deeper loyalties to his friend, and come to Jim's rescue? In a paroxysm of guilt, Huck decided to pray. He would confess to God his miserable ways and promise to reform, the first evidence of which would be his complicity in the plan to return Jim to slavery.

Having knelt to pray, however, Huck discovered that the words would not come. With a moment's reflection, he knew why. It was because he was 'playing double', trying to make his mouth say words that his heart could not accept as true. He could not tell God that he was giving up on sin by returning his friend to slavery, because Huck knew, and he knew that God knew, that a trumped-up prayer is the biggest sin of all. In his moment of decision, Huck saw the matter very clearly: 'Deep down in me I knowed it was a lie, and He knowed it. You can't pray a lie—I found that out.'[1]

In Huck Finn's simple discovery, Mark Twain has proposed a truth about the nature of prayer that captures nicely one of the critical issues that this article has been commissioned to consider. To state the general

---

1. M. Twain, *The Adventures of Huckleberry Finn* (New York: Signet Classic, 1959), p. 209.

question in its simplest form: Are the prayers recorded in Chronicles to be evaluated as statements of truth or fiction? Do they preserve verifiable experiences of heart-felt piety, or are they only trumped-up words that convey someone's imaginative ideas about what might have been or should have been prayed in a given situation?

I have admittedly stated the issue in rather stark terms, positioning the interpretation of prayers in Chronicles between the two extremes of truth and fiction. I have done so because until relatively recently, the scholarly assessment of the Chronicler's prayers has by and large settled for just these kinds of choices. In the main, the prayers in Chronicles have been regarded as either unthinking, verbatim copies of source material in Samuel–Kings or tendentious compositions of Chr himself. In either case, faced with the regnant choices between evaluating these prayers as truth or fiction, most scholars settled for the latter.

Happily, the assessment of these prayers has now begun to enlarge. In light of recent studies, the simple evaluation of a prayer text as either truth or fiction can no longer do justice to the sophisticated historiographic skills of Chr. In the pages that follow, I will pursue these matters by addressing: (1) the use of prayer within the genre of historiography, (2) the recorded prayers in Chronicles and Chr's exegetical techniques, and (3) the function of prayer in presenting both the history and the theology of these books. Finally, I will offer some concluding reflections on Mark Twain's proposal.

Prayer and the Genre of Historiography

It is not necessary to review here the history of the general debate concerning Chronicles as a historical source. That discussion will be center stage in other essays in this volume. It is pertinent to note, however, that from the outset of the debate the rhetorical passages interspersed throughout Chronicles—especially the various prayers, speeches, and sermons—have presented a major challenge to its credibility as a reliable historical source.

At one extreme, some who found Chronicles to be little more than a 'mass of fictions' argued that 'made-up' prayers provided corroborating evidence that Chr had twisted Israel's authentic history into nothing more than 'lies spoken in the name of the Lord'.[2] At the other extreme,

---

2. J.W. Colenso, *Lectures on the Pentateuch and the Moabite Stone* (London: Longmans, Green, 1873), p. 344. The description of prayer as 'made-up' refers to

some conceded that Chr's primary purpose was not historical documentation but theological reflection.[3] Within this perspective, G. von Rad,[4] M. Noth,[5] and O. Plöger[6] argued that Chr had effectively inserted speeches and prayers at strategic points in order to construe the presentation in accordance with his own theological views. In sum, if the prayers could not be appreciated as history, they might at least be salvaged as theology.

In recent years, increasing attention to the sophisticated historiographic traditions in both biblical and non-biblical literature has provided a new orientation to the prayers in Chronicles. Two aspects of this matter are of particular importance. The first concerns prayer as a regular feature in biblical and non-biblical historiography, and the second is the question whether recorded prayer is merely a literary convention or an accurate reflection of actual practice.

As for the first aspect, Noth and Plöger demonstrated—albeit in different ways—that prayers and speeches played a significant role in the two most prominent examples of Israelite historiography: DtrH and

1 Chron. 16.8-22, the prayer of David that has been composed from 'pieces of later psalms' (p. 341). Colenso's general evaluation of Chr's work is evident in the title to the chapter in which this description occurs, 'The Fictions of the Chronicler' (pp. 333-46), a chapter that concludes with the citation from Zech. 13.3, 'lies spoken in the name of the Lord' (p. 346).

3.   Cf. G. von Rad, *Das Geschichtsbild des chronistischen Werkes* (BWANT, 54; Stuttgart: Kohlhammer, 1930). See, for example, von Rad's concluding comments on pp. 133-34.

4.   G. von Rad, 'Die Levitische Predigt in den Büchern der Chronik', *Festschrift Otto Proksch* (Leipzig: Deichert, 1934), pp. 113-24 (= *Gesammelte Studien zum Alten Testament* [Munich: Chr. Kaiser Verlag, 1958], pp. 248-61). The English translation is 'The Levitical Sermon in the Books of Chronicles', in *The Form Critical Problem of the Hexateuch and Other Essays* (London: Oliver & Boyd, 1966), pp. 267-80.

5.   M. Noth, *Überlieferungsgeschichtliche Studien I* (Halle: Niemeyer, 1943). The second part of this monograph deals with Chr and has been translated as *The Chronicler's History* (JSOTSup, 50; Sheffield: JSOT Press, 1987). For Noth's discussion of the speeches and prayers, see *The Chronicler's History*, pp. 75-81.

6.   O. Plöger, 'Reden und Gebete im deuteronomistischen und chronistischen Geschichtswerk', in W. Schneemelcher (ed.), *Festschrift für Günther Dehn* (Neukirchen: Kreis Moers, 1957), pp. 35-49 (= *Aus der Spätzeit des Alten Testaments: Studien* [Göttingen: Vandenhoeck & Ruprecht, 1971], pp. 50-66). All references in this paper are to the essay as published in *Festschrift*.

Chr's history.[7] Subsequent studies have confirmed that in their use of such rhetoric biblical writers were in fact operating well within the normal boundaries of ancient historiography.

The most extensive evidence has been collected by J. Van Seters, who has argued that neither in the ancient Near East nor in Israel was the tradition of history writing meant to be judged solely in terms of historical reliability.[8] To the contrary, throughout the ancient Near East and in early Greece, speeches were routinely used in historiographic traditions to introduce, summarize, and reflect on historical events and experiences.[9] The fact that biblical writers imparted their own perspectives on historical events through composed speeches and prayers is therefore insufficient ground to dismiss their work as poor history. In view of the standard historiographic practices throughout the ancient world, it should not be considered remarkable to discover that 'All Hebrew historiography...is written from a theological perspective.'[10]

If prayer was a regular feature of both biblical and non-biblical historiography, a second issue may be raised: What did prayer, as a distinct literary form, contribute to the enterprise of writing history? Was the inclusion of a recorded prayer in a historical presentation merely a literary convention for theologizing, or did the prayer as reported correlate with actual practice?

A number of recent studies on prayer bring important information to bear on this issue. At the outset it should be conceded that all prayer texts are literary productions. The literary formulation of a prayer, as well as the decision to position it at a certain place in the presentation, clearly reflects the conscious choice of authors and editors. But as M. Greenberg has shown, the fact that a prayer is part of a literary

7. See below, pp. 259-60.

8. J. Van Seters, *In Search of History: Historiography in the Ancient World and the Origins of Biblical History* (New Haven, CT: Yale University Press, 1983). See further M. Cogan, who has shown that even 'historical' information (e.g., dates, chronologies) is typically 'malleable' in biblical and non-biblical history writing ('The Chronicler's Use of Chronology as Illuminated by Neo-Assyrian Royal Inscriptions', in J.H. Tigay [ed.], *Empirical Models for Biblical Criticism* [Philadelphia: University of Pennsylvania Press], 1985, pp. 197-210).

9. Van Seters deals with 'speeches' as a designation for the general literary genre that includes prayers. See, for example, the discussion of royal inscriptions and prayers in Mesopotamian historiography on pp. 60-61. For his discussion of such rhetoric specifically in DtrH see pp. 230, 358-59.

10. Van Seters, *In Search of History*, p. 361.

enterprise does not mean that it is therefore inauthentic. In his words, 'Even if it is granted that prayers are not veridical, that does not foreclose their being verisimilar.'[11] Indeed, in Scripture the latter may be of more value than the former, for as Greenberg notes, recalling the observation of Aristotle, artistic creation has the capacity to present 'something more philosophic and of graver import than history'.[12]

Both Greenberg and Gerstenberger[13] have probed the verisimilitude of prayers in the Hebrew Bible by demonstrating that there is a genetic affinity between the religious language of prayer and the social language of interhuman discourse. All major types of prayer—prayers of petition, confession, and thanksgiving—utilize patterns of speech that are analogous to the common forms of speech between humans.[14] Such congruence between the language and circumstances of prayer and the discourse of everyday experience does not suggest that biblical narrators freely invented prayers that had no correlation with actual practice. Indeed, Greenberg concludes that in such prayers 'We have as faithful a correspondence as we might wish to the form and practice of everyday, nonprofessional, extemporaneous verbal worship in ancient Israel.'[15]

To summarize, recent advances in understanding the genres of historiography and of prayer have laid the foundation for a new approach to Chr's presentation. It is no longer adequate either to dismiss Chr's prayers as merely fictional or to embrace them as purely theological.

---

11. M. Greenberg, *Biblical Prose Prayer as a Window to the Popular Religion of Ancient Israel* (Taubman lectures in Jewish Studies, 6th series; Berkeley, CA: University of California Press, 1983), p. 8.

12. *Biblical Prose Prayer*, p. 8. Greenberg takes the reference to Aristotle from *Poetics*, 9.

13. E.S. Gerstenberger, *Der bittende Mensch: Bittritual u. Klagelied d. Einzelnen im Alten Testament* (WMANT, 51; Neukirchen–Vluyn: Neukirchener Verlag, 1980).

14. Gerstenberger focuses primarily on petitionary prayer (*Der bittende Mensch*, pp. 17-63; on interhuman petitions and petitions to God, see especially pp. 18-20). For Greenberg's analysis of the analogy between social language and the language of prayer, see *Biblical Prose Prayer*, pp. 19-37. See further R.N. Boyce, *The Cry to God in the Old Testament* (SBLDS, 103; Atlanta: Scholars Press, 1988), pp. 27-40.

15. Greenberg, *Biblical Prose Prayer*, p. 37. Greenberg's focus is on prose prayers, which he regards as providing a more direct access to actual piety than psalmic prayers. But it is also plausible to suggest that psalmic prayers, no less than prose ones, are genetically connected to traditional expressions of piety grounded in actual practice. See further A. Aejmelaeus, *The Traditional Prayer in the Psalms* (BZAW, 167; Berlin: de Gruyter, 1986), pp. 90-91.

Recorded prayers are a regular feature in biblical and non-biblical historiography. It is certainly the case that prayers are particularly suitable rhetorical means for theologizing on history. However, if prayer is a means for theological reflection, this does not mean that what is communicated in a prayer text bears no correlation with actual practice. Rather, both the speech and the practice conveyed through literary prayers are congruent with the social conventions of normal interhuman discourse.

The Recorded Prayers and the Chronicler's Exegetical Technique

The focus in this essay will be on *recorded* prayers, that is, on the texts where the words of a prayer are reported. There are 17 such prayers in 1 and 2 Chronicles, and the following table illustrates their distribution.[16] It will be seen from the table that the total is made up of one ancestral prayer (1 Chron. 4.10), ten royal prayers, and six psalmic prayers.

Several general observations may be offered concerning these recorded prayers. First, the prayers are distributed unevenly throughout Chronicles, with a proportionately heavier concentration (11 of 17, approximately 65%) occurring in the chapters devoted to David and Solomon. Second, ten of the 17 prayers (approximately 59%) are 'royal prayers', that is prayers articulated by kings. Of these ten, five prayers are assigned to David (1 Chron. 14.10; 17.17-29; 21.8; 21.17; 29.10-29), two to Solomon (2 Chron. 1.8-10; 6.14-42), and three to post-Solomonic kings (Asa, Jehoshaphat, and Hezekiah). Third, in addition to the royal prayers, one prayer is assigned to an ancestor of Judah (Jabez), and five are presented as hymnic praise sung by specially appointed levitical priests and/or the people in general (1 Chron. 16.8-36; 2 Chron. 5.13; 7.3; 7.6; 20.21). Fourth, of the 17 prayers, six correlate with synoptic material in Samuel–Kings, six utilize hymnic language found in the

16. In addition to the recorded prayers, there are numerous cases where the text indicates that a prayer or an address to God that may be likened to prayer (e.g. a 'cry' [זעק]) or a 'call' [קרא]) has occurred, but the words have not been provided (cf. 1 Chron. 5.20 [זעק]; 14.14 [שאל]; 21.26 [קרא]; 2 Chron. 13.14-15 [צעק]; 18.31 [זעק]; 20.26 [ברך]; 31.8 [ברך]; 32.20, 4 [פלל]; 33.12 [חלה פני]; 33.13 [פלל]). Although these texts indicate something of Chr's general interest in prayer, they offer comparatively little in the way of substantive information. For present purposes these unrecorded prayers may be omitted from the discussion.

Psalter, and five are without parallel in their present form outside Chronicles.

Distribution of Recorded Prayers in Chronicles

1 Chron. 1–9 (Genealogies)	*1 Chron. 10–2 Chron. 9* (David–Solomon)		*2 Chron. 10–36* (Post-Solomon)
	1 Chron. 10–29 (David)	*2 Chron. 1–9* (Solomon)	
4.10 (Jabez)	14.10 [= 2 Sam. 5.19]	1.8-10 [= 1 Kgs 3.6-9]	14.11 (Asa)
	16.8-36* [= Pss. 105; 96; 106]	5.13*	20.6-12 (Jehoshaphat)
	17.16-27 [= 2 Sam. 7.18-29]	6.14-42 [= 1 Kgs 8.22-53]	20.21*
		[vv. 40-42* = Ps. 132.8-10]	
	21.8 [= 2 Sam. 24.10]	7.3*	30.18-19 (Hezekiah)
	21.17 [= 2 Sam. 24.17]	7.6*	
	29.10-19		

*psalmic prayers

Beyond these general observations, it is useful to focus on the different techniques that Chr utilizes in handling these prayers. Four general methodologies may be identified, along with the respective prayers to which they apply.[17] It is important to acknowledge here that a full discussion of the issues involved in these exegetical techniques goes far beyond the scope of this essay. For present purposes I limit myself simply to describing Chr's methods. Later in this article I will explore further how these exegetical tactics serve Chr's interests in the overall presentation.

The Chronicler as Editor

Chr's technique as editor is manifest in two basic ways of handling prayers that have been taken over from source materials. This editorial work is directed broadly towards modification of the source *text* and modification of the source *context*.

First, in two cases (1 Chron. 17.16-27; 2 Chron. 6.14-42) Chr faithfully transfers an existing prayer from its source context to the same context in Chr's own account, but he alters the text of the prayer in

---

17. I had already worked out these categories in their essentials, when I discovered a similar effort by H.N. Bream ('Manasseh and his Prayer', *Lutheran Theological Seminary Bulletin* 66 [1986], p. 10). Although Bream's schematization serves different objectives than mine, I am indebted to him for clarifying my own thinking on these matters.

significant ways to achieve a distinct presentation. In 2 Chron. 6.14-42, for example, Chr's version of Solomon's prayer at the dedication of the temple substantially replicates both the context and the wording of 1 Kgs 8.22-53. In vv. 40-42, however, Chr introduces an important alteration in the prayer by replacing 1 Kgs 8.50-53 with his own version of Ps. 132.8-10. The issues involved in this change are complex and cannot be pursued here.[18] We may note simply that the net effect of Chr's editing is to change the basis for Solomon's appeal to God. In Kings, Solomon petitions God to be attentive to the prayers of the people because of the memories of divine election and compassion invoked by the exodus traditions (vv. 51, 53). In Chronicles, Solomon's appeal is that God 'remember the steadfast love of David your servant' (v. 42).[19]

A second area in which Chr's work as editor may be discerned is in the (re)contextualizing of a source prayer. In three of the recorded prayers (1 Chron. 14.10; 21.8, 17; 2 Chron. 1.8-10) Chr has made relatively insignificant changes in the wording of an existing prayer but has nonetheless achieved a distinctive presentation by positioning the prayer in a new context. Brief comments on two of these texts must suffice as illustration.

In 1 Chron. 14.10 David's inquiry of God is substantially a verbatim account of the prayer recorded in 2 Sam. 5.19. In Chr's presentation, however, the prayer has been dislodged from its original context in the narratives concerning David's capture of Jerusalem (2 Sam. 5.1-25) and

18. Virtually every line of Ps. 132.8-10 has been altered in some way in Chr's presentation. Chr's alterations are conveniently laid out in S. Japhet, *I and II Chronicles* (OTL; Louisville, KY: Westminster/John Knox, 1993), p. 602; and in M. Throntveit, *When Kings Speak: Royal Speech and Prayer in Chronicles* (SBLDS, 93; Atlanta: Scholars Press, 1987), pp. 60-61.

19. A critical issue in this text is whether the phrase לחסדי דויד should be rendered as an objective genitive (i.e., 'steadfast love *for* David'; so NRSV) or as a subjective genitive (i.e., 'steadfast love *of* David'; so REB, JPS). Williamson argues for the former interpretation, based among other things on the use of the same phrase in Isa. 55.3 ('The Sure Mercies of David: Subjective or Objective Genitive?', *JSS* 23 [1978], pp. 31-49). In my judgment, however, a stronger case can be made for the latter rendering (cf. R.B. Dillard, *2 Chronicles* [WBC, 15; Waco, TX: Word Books, 1987], pp. 51-52; Japhet, *I and II Chronicles*, pp. 604-605). Irrespective of the relative strengths of either of these arguments, it remains the case that in Chr's version of Solomon's prayer an emphasis on the exodus traditions has been replaced with an emphasis on David.

has been relocated in the interval between the first, failed effort to transfer the ark from Kiriath-jearim (1 Chron. 13) and the second, successful effort to transfer the ark (1 Chron. 15–16). In this new position the prayer serves not only to report David's successful military campaign against the Philistines, but to call attention to David's act of piety as one of the catalysts for the transition from a failed effort to establish Jerusalem as the residence of God to a successful one.

2 Chron. 1.8-10, an abbreviated version of the source prayer in 1 Kgs 3.6-9,[20] has also been significantly recontextualized. In Kings, Solomon's prayer for wisdom follows the candid description of his complicity in the murders of Adonijah, Joab, and Shemei (1 Kgs 2.12-46) and precedes his judicious handling of the situation presented him by the two prostitutes (1 Kgs 3.16-28). In this context, the prayer affords an opportunity to reappraise Solomon's qualifications for ruling his people.[21] In Chronicles the events reported in 1 Kings 1–2 are omitted; so also the account of the two prostitutes. Solomon's prayer for wisdom is now presented as the first public act of the king's reign. In Chr's arrangement of the events, the wisdom to rule, which God grants to Solomon, along with his wealth and prosperity, are directly linked not to the administration of justice but to the building of the temple (2 Chron. 2–8).

The Chronicler as Collator
There are a number of psalmic inserts in Chr's narrative,[22] but of primary interest for the task at hand is the psalmic medley in

---

20. Most of Chr's omissions represent only minor orthographic or stylistic alterations. The textual differences in the prayer as presented in Kings and Chronicles are conveniently laid out by Throntveit, *When Kings Speak*, p. 55. For further discussion, see Japhet, *I and II Chronicles*, pp. 530-31.

21. Cf. S.E. Balentine, *Prayer in the Hebrew Bible: The Drama of Divine-Human Dialogue* (Minneapolis, MN: Fortress Press, 1993), pp. 56-60.

22. I have already mentioned Chr's use of Ps. 132.8-10 at the end of Solomon's prayer in 2 Chron. 6.40-42. Note further the repeated insertion of the doxological refrain '(for he is good,) for his steadfast love endures forever' (1 Chron. 16.34, 41; 2 Chron. 5.13; 7.3, 6; 20.21), a refrain that is frequent in the Psalms (cf. Pss. 100.5; 106.1; 107.1; 118.1, 2, 3, 4, 29; 136.1-26 [26×]; 138.8). In addition to the standard commentaries, see the recent discussions of this refrain by R.M. Shipp, '"Remember His Covenant Forever": A Study of the Chronicler's Use of the Psalms', *ResQ* 35 (1993), pp. 30-32; and J.W. Watts, *Psalm and Story: Inset Hymns in Hebrew Narrative* (JSOTSup, 139; Sheffield: JSOT Press, 1992), pp. 157-58, 197.

1 Chron. 16.8-36. Throughout this text there are signs that Chr has edited his source materials, much as in the texts discussed above, to bring them into conformity with his own purposes. But the principal exegetical work of Chr in this text focuses more on the technique of collation than editing. The sources for the prayer in 1 Chron. 16.8-36 are three different canonical psalms: Ps. 105.1-15 for vv. 8-22; Ps. 96.1-13 for vv. 23-33; and Ps. 106.1, 47-48 for vv. 34-36. In Chr's presentation these three psalms have been collated and structured into one unified prayer, which has in turn been fully integrated into a new literary context.[23]

Verses 8-14 (cf. Ps. 105.1-7) provide an introduction by bringing to the fore three principal celebratory activities that Chr associates with the return of the ark to Jerusalem: 'give thanks' (ידה, v. 8), 'praise' (הלל, v. 10), and 'remember' (זכר, v. 12). This language provides a 'connective echo'[24] of the activities ascribed to the Levites in v. 4, thus firmly anchoring this psalmic insert to its immediate narrative context. Moreover, these same three activities correlate with the three major structural divisions that define the remainder of the prayer.[25] Verses 15-22, a recitation from Ps. 105.8-15 of God's covenantal commitments to the ancestors, serves as the 'remember' section of the prayer (cf. v. 15: 'remember [זכר] his covenant forever...'). Verses 23-33, a hymn celebrating God's kingship taken from Psalm 96, constitutes the 'praise' section of the prayer (cf. v. 25: 'praised' [מהלל]). Finally, vv. 34-36, introduced with the refrain from Ps. 106.1 ('give thanks [ידי] to the Lord'), concludes the prayer with a 'give thanks' section.

The practice of collating several existing psalms into a single new composition is not unique to Chronicles, nor is the technique of inserting psalmic texts into narrative settings in order to advance compositional goals. Both practices occur elsewhere in biblical and non-biblical material.[26] Moreover, Fishbane has noted that in historiographic

---

23. On the prayer's structural coherence and narrative relations, see T.C. Butler, 'A Forgotten Passage from a Forgotten Era (1 Chr XVI 8-36)', *VT* 28 (1978), pp. 142-50; A.E. Hill, 'Patchwork Poetry or Reasoned Verse? Connective Structure in 1 Chronicles XVI', *VT* 33 (1983), pp. 97-101; Shipp, 'Remember His Covenant Forever', pp. 29-39; Watts, *Psalm and Story*, pp. 155-68.

24. Hill, 'Patchwork Poetry or Reasoned Verse?', p. 99.

25. See especially Shipp, 'Remember His Covenant Forever', pp. 35-37.

26. Cf. Japhet (*I and II Chronicles*, p. 312), who notes that the practice of synthetic psalm composition is evidenced already in the book of Psalms itself, as

traditions it is not uncommon for a tradent to make an 'exegetically derived' connection between a historical event and an appropriate prayer.[27] In this respect, the collation that produces the prayer in 1 Chronicles 16 is more than just a technical procedure.[28] It is a means for exercising important theological and historical judgments. We will return to these issues in the next section.

The Chronicler as Author
Five prayers in Chronicles are not found in other canonical sources (1 Chron. 4.10; 29.10-19; 2 Chron. 14.11; 20.6-12; 30.18-19). Although these prayers make use of earlier Scriptures, they generally appear to be Chr's own creations or at least to reflect a practice of prayer or a tradition about prayer that was current in Chr's own time.

For example, the anecdotal reference to the prayer of Jabez (1 Chron. 4.10) conceivably derives from some ancient source, but there is insufficient evidence to decide finally on its historicity.[29] It can be demonstrated, however, that the prayer's sentiment accords with Chr's overall concern to show the importance of prayer for the descendants of Judah. Similarly, the prayers of Asa (2 Chron. 14.11) and Jehoshaphat (2 Chron. 20.6-12) are both situated in the context of war accounts. In both cases Chr has provided tidbits of geographical and chronological information that have in turn invited numerous efforts to link these accounts to historical episodes. Jehoshaphat's prayer, for example, has been associated with events either in the time

well as in the Psalms Scroll from Qumran. On psalmic inserts in narrative contexts, see especially Watts, *Psalm and Story*.

27. M.A. Fishbane, *Biblical Interpretation in Ancient Israel* (Oxford: Clarendon Press, 1984), p. 400. Fishbane refers to the aggadic technique of exegesis by 'conjunction' (סמוכין), a practice whereby received materials are recontextualized and recombined to yield new exegetical correlations. Although he does not connect this practice specifically to the prayers in Chronicles, Fishbane does point to the historical superscriptions in the Psalms (pp. 403-407), where the technique of connecting historical narrative and prayer is clearly similar to that in 1 Chron. 16. See further Watts, *Psalm and Story*, pp. 182-85.

28. Cf. Japhet, *I and II Chronicles*, pp. 312-13.

29. Japhet, *I and II Chronicles*, pp. 105-106.

of the monarchy[30] or in Chr's own time.[31] But whatever evidence may be garnered in support of the historicity of these wars, in Chr's presentation the victories turn not on military strategy or historical happenstance, but on a decisive act of piety: the king's prayer. The view that war can be averted or won only with God's help is also consonant with Chr's overall views.[32]

Much the same situation applies to the prayers of David (1 Chron. 29.10-19) and Hezekiah (2 Chron. 30.18-19). Both make use of language and traditions that locate these prayers in the cultic situations of temple dedication and passover respectively, although there is no record of these prayers in the source materials from Samuel–Kings. The intent may be to fill in the existing record concerning the actual practices of David and Hezekiah. It is more likely, however, that Chr is simply reflecting the liturgical traditions that were current in his time.[33] In either case, as the following section will show, Chr has composed and positioned these prayers within the larger presentation so as to communicate something of both historical and theological significance.

The Chronicler as Excisor

In addition to editing, collating, and 'authoring' prayers, it should not go unnoticed that in at least two instances Chr omits prayers contained

30. Cf. W. Rudolph, *Chronikbücher* (HAT, 21; Tübingen: Mohr, 1955), pp. 258-59; H.G.M. Williamson, *1 and 2 Chronicles* (NCB; Grand Rapids, MI: Eerdmans, 1982), pp. 291-93; Dillard, *2 Chronicles*, pp. 153-55.

31. M. Noth, 'Eine palästinische Lokalüberlieferung in 2 Chr 20', *ZDPV* 67 (1943), pp. 45-71.

32. Cf. P. Welten, who has linked the prayers of Asa and Jehoshaphat to a quintet of successful war stories (2 Chron. 13.3-20; 14.8-14; 20.1-30; 26.6-8; 27.5-6) that convey Chr's theological message to the community of his own day (*Geschichte und Geschichtsdarstellung in den Chronikbüchern* [WMANT, 42; Neukirchen–Vluyn: Neukirchener Verlag, 1973], pp. 115-72).

33. For example, Hezekiah's petition that God pardon 'all who set their hearts to seek God', even though they may have violated the laws of purity, may be an attempt to reconcile disparate views in the post-exilic community concerning the proper celebration of passover. See further Williamson, *1 and 2 Chronicles*, pp. 360-73, 403-408; J.R. Shaver, *Torah and the Chronicler's History Work: An Inquiry into the Chronicler's References to Laws, Festivals and Cultic Institutions in Relation to Pentateuchal Legislation* (BJS, 196; Atlanta: Scholars Press, 1989), pp. 110-18; T.L. Eves, 'The Role of Passover in the Book of Chronicles: A Study of 2 Chronicles 30 and 35' (PhD dissertation, Annenberg Research Institute [formerly Dropsie College], 1992), pp. 243-55.

in the parallel texts from Kings. Such is the case in Chr's presentation of Hezekiah where the synoptic passage records the words of two prayers for Hezekiah (2 Kgs 19.15-19; 20.3) that are not reproduced by Chr (cf. 2 Chron. 32.20, 24).

Whether Chr's excision of these prayers is merely part of an overall desire to create a simpler, more unified account[34] or a specific effort to bring the existing record into line with his own perspectives is difficult to decide.[35] In view of Chr's use of prayer throughout his presentation, however, including the addition of a prayer for Hezekiah in 2 Chron. 30.18-19, it is difficult to believe that the omissions here are intended to convey a negative assessment of prayer's importance.

Prayer in the Chronicler's Presentation of History and Theology

The preceding description of Chr's exegetical techniques demonstrates that the prayers can no longer be judged merely as verbatim copies of source material or tendentious compositions of pure fiction. As editor, collator, 'author', and excisor, Chr engages in a number of important literary decisions: What prayers will be included, added, or omitted in the presentation? Where will they be located? How will they be integrated into the narrative? Such issues are necessarily linked to other considerations that are both historical and theological in nature: What is the purpose of the presentation? If all Hebrew historiography is theological, as Van Seters argues, then we may conclude that Chr intends not only to impart the *facts* of history (who, what, when, where), but also the *meaning* of history (why), that is, what history says about the way the world works.[36] The question for this article is then: how do the

34. Cf. Japhet, *I and II Chronicles*, p. 989.

35. It is widely recognized that in the portrait of Hezekiah Chr reverses the emphases of the synoptic texts. In Chronicles the emphasis is on Hezekiah's reform efforts (2 Chron. 29–31; cf. 2 Kgs 18.1-6), not on the confrontation with Sennacherib (2 Chron. 32; cf. 2 Kgs 18.13–20.21). In this context, perhaps the omission of the recorded prayers marks Chr's desire to minimize the mediatorial role accorded to the prophet Isaiah in the source texts (cf. Dillard, *2 Chronicles*, pp. 255-56; Japhet, *I and II Chronicles*, p. 989).

36. On the function of historical narratives in presenting and promoting a world-view, see R.K. Duke, 'A Model for a Theology of Biblical Historical Narratives: Proposed and Demonstrated with the Books of Chronicles', in M.P. Graham, W.P. Brown, and J.K. Kuan (eds.), *History and Interpretation: Essays in Honour of*

recorded prayers serve Chr's larger compositional goals?

The subject here is a complex one. At present, there is no hypothesis that claims majority support. In general, the salient issues were brought into focus in the seminal studies of Noth and Plöger. The former recognized that prayers were important rhetorical devices to 'enliven and develop the details' of Chr's story, but he discerned no structural significance in their overall distribution within the composition.[37] Plöger disagreed, and suggested that in at least some cases Chr had strategically placed prayers at certain points in order to structure the presentation in intentional ways.[38]

Recent efforts have generally followed the leads of Noth and Plöger. Some have viewed prayers as important literary and/or theological devices, but find no governing strategy behind their placement within the composition.[39] Others have seen prayers not only as rhetorical devices but also as important structuring vehicles within the overall presentation.[40] Although these studies do not result in a consensus about Chr's use of prayer, they do suggest important avenues for exploration. I will seek to incorporate these into several observations that reflect the emphases of this study and that may in turn invite further reflection.

First, the distribution of prayers in Chronicles follows the general

John H. Hayes (JSOTSup, 173; Sheffield: JSOT Press, 1993), pp. 65-73; cf. Van Seters, *In Search of History*, pp. 4-5.

37. Noth, *The Chronicler's History*, p. 76. See further pp. 80-81.

38. Although he did not pursue the matter in detail, Plöger noted that the prayers in 1 Chron. 17.17-29 and 1 Chron. 29.10-19 served as a structural frame for Chr's presentation of David's participation in the building of the temple ('Reden und Gebete', p. 45).

39. Cf. Throntveit, *When Kings Speak*, pp. 51-75; Japhet, *I and II Chronicles*, pp. 36-38; R.K. Duke, *The Persuasive Appeal of the Chronicler: A Rhetorical Analysis* (JSOTSup, 88; Sheffield: Almond Press, 1990), p. 50.

40. R.L. Pratt has argued that royal prayers are a structural key to Chr's concern for the Jerusalem cult, and specifically with Zerubbabel's program to rebuild the temple ('Royal Prayer and the Chronicler's Program' [ThD dissertation, Harvard University, 1987], pp. 271-327). Pratt's thesis will not likely gain widespread support, if only because most will not adopt such an early dating of Chronicles to a period before the completion of the second temple. In this connection W. Riley, with a majority of scholars, situates Chr's work in the late Persian period and also notes the role of prayer in relation to Chr's concern for cultic faithfulness (*King and Cultus: Worship and the Reinterpretation of History* [JSOTSup, 160; Sheffield: JSOT Press, 1993]).

compositional priorities that define the books as a whole. Chronicles presents the story of Israel from Adam to the edict of Cyrus in 65 chapters. The presentation is divided unequally into three major sections: 1 Chronicles 1–9, the genealogies from Adam to Saul, comprises roughly 14 percent of the whole; 1 Chronicles 10–2 Chronicles 9, the reigns of David and Solomon, roughly 43 percent of the whole; and 2 Chronicles 10–36, post-Solomonic kings, 40 percent of the total composition. Thus, in the account of the history of Israel from the beginnings of humankind to roughly 538 BCE, Chr singles out the reigns of David and Solomon for particular emphasis. Moreover, within the focus on David-Solomon, Chr is keenly concerned with the preparation and building of the temple: 11 of the 19 chapters about David (1 Chronicles 13–16; 21–29) and approximately six of the nine chapters about Solomon (2 Chron. 2.1–7.22) are focused on just this concern.[41] Chr's arrangement reinforces the impression that everything prior to David–Solomon and the temple is prolegomena; everything that follows is the result or the continuation of this critical period in Israel's history.

The recorded prayers in Chronicles are distributed in keeping with these compositional priorities. As previously noted, 11 of the 17 prayers (roughly 65 percent) occur in the chapters dealing with David–Solomon. David receives particular emphasis by being allotted five prayers, more than any other person in Chronicles. Outside the David–Solomon account, there is one prayer recorded in the genealogy section and four (including one psalmic refrain) in the post-Solomonic period. Chr thus locates prayer as one especially important feature in what for him is the most critical period in Israel's history, the period singularly defined by David and Solomon and the building of the temple.

Chr's decision to prioritize the events of Israel's history around David–Solomon and the temple recalls the similar priorities in the final arrangement of the Pentateuch. In this account of Israel's story from creation to the plains of Moab, roughly 42 percent of the total is allotted to the Sinai pericope (Exod. 19–Num. 10).[42] From the Torah's perspective, the 11-month sojourn at Sinai under the leadership of Moses is constitutive for Israel's formation as both a covenant

41. Cf. Riley, *King and Cultus*, pp. 54-66, 76-87.

42. Cf. R.P. Knierim, 'The Composition of the Pentateuch', in K.H. Richards (ed.), *Society of Biblical Literature 1985 Seminar Papers* (SBLSPS, 24; Atlanta: Scholars Press, 1985), p. 396.

community (Exod. 19–24) and a worshipping community (Exod. 25–31; 35–40; Lev. 1–27). Everything that precedes Sinai is important preparation for this formative encounter with God. Everything that follows Sinai focuses on the community's successes and failures in realizing its charter commission to become a 'priestly kingdom and a holy nation' (Exod. 19.6). In sum, the priorities of Chr and of the Pentateuch invite the reader to understand that the temple and worship are at the center of Israel's most formative experiences in history.[43]

Second, if the distribution of prayers in Chronicles accords with a general emphasis on David–Solomon and the temple, then we may probe further to see if there is special significance in the placement of these prayers within the compositional whole. We may begin by observing that the prayers are located at the beginning (genealogy), middle (David–Solomon), and end (post-Solomon) of Chr's history. From a structural standpoint, these prayers function in their respective contexts (1) to establish the vision of the world in which Chr's history has meaning; (2) to facilitate the description of how this vision is implemented in the concrete world of David and Solomon; and (3) to suggest how this vision may be sustained in the period after Solomon. Each of these functions may be elaborated briefly as follows.

The genealogies in 1 Chronicles 1–9 serve as the 'genesis' of Chr's history. Much as in the book of Genesis, these lists trace the story of Israel from Adam to the present (post-exilic) community in Jerusalem. Woven into these genealogical lists, however, are a number of statements that assert that Israel's history cannot be recorded simply as a matter of biological procreation. In this history God is an active participant, intervening on behalf of those who call out in trust (e.g., 5.20), delivering up to punishment or death those who are unfaithful (for example, 2.3; 5.25-26; 9.1).

Among these evaluative insertions into the genealogies is the recorded prayer in 1 Chron. 4.10. An ancestor of Judah, named Jabez (v. 9: יעבץ) because his mother bore him in pain (בעצב), prays to God that the destiny portended in his name might be averted (v. 10: 'so as not to hurt me [עצבי]'). God responds positively. Whether this account

---

43. On this point, see J. Blenkinsopp's observations concerning the structural emphases in the Pentateuch. In the pentadic arrangement of the final composition, it is Leviticus that stands as the central panel, thus emphasizing worship as the goal of creation. *The Pentateuch: An Introduction to the First Five Books of the Bible* (ABRL; New York: Doubleday, 1992), pp. 47, 221, *et passim*.

about Jabez, who is otherwise unknown in the Judean genealogy, derives from some historical source or is the creation of Chr, it serves Chr's larger interests well. The story of Jabez asserts that one who felt doomed to misery reversed his fortunes by praying to God. It is the world of Jabez, the world where prayer connects one to God in ways that change life against all odds, that is the subject of Chr's history.[44]

The world in which prayer plays such a vital role takes on concrete shape for Chr in the history of David and Solomon. An underlying unity in the David-Solomon materials has often been noted, especially with respect to their common focus on the construction of the temple in Jerusalem.[45] Within this context, it may be noted further that Chr has surrounded the Davidic-Solomonic concern for the temple with the most concentrated collection of prayers in the entire composition. The diagram below illustrates this more clearly.

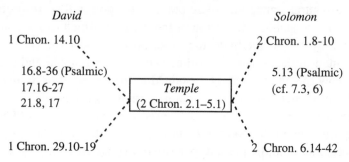

	David			*Solomon*	

1 Chron. 14.10 ⟍ ⟍ ⟍ ⟍ ⟍ ⟍ ⟋ ⟋ ⟋ 2 Chron. 1.8-10

16.8-36 (Psalmic)   ⟍   ⟋   5.13 (Psalmic)
17.16-27   ⟍   ┌──────────┐   ⟋   (cf. 7.3, 6)
21.8, 17   ⟍ ╱│ *Temple* │╲ ⟋
                │(2 Chron. 2.1–5.1)│
              ╱ └──────────┘ ╲

1 Chron. 29.10-19 ⟋ ⟋ ⟍ ⟍ ⟍ 2 Chron. 6.14-42

In the placement of these prayers Chr has drawn a parallel between

---

44. Cf. Duke, *Persuasive Appeal*, pp. 54-56. See further W.L. Osborne, who suggests that Chr's purpose in 1 Chron. 4 is to present the whole tribe of Judah in a series of concentric circles, such that the innermost assume first responsibilities for the protection of the whole. Such an arrangement, he suggests, is like a tribal 'alarm system' ('The Genealogies of 1 Chronicles 1–9' [PhD dissertation, Dropsie University, 1979], pp. 245-47). It is interesting that in such an arrangement, the clan of Hur (Jabez) is the second group mentioned.

45. Cf. R.L. Braun, 'Solomonic Apologetic in Chronicles', *JBL* 92 (1973), pp. 503-16; *idem*, 'Solomon, the Chosen Temple Builder: The Significance of 1 Chronicles 22, 28, and 29 for the Theology of Chronicles', *JBL* 95 (1976), pp. 581-90. See further P. Welten, who has suggested that Chr's presentation of David–Solomon may be viewed in essence as a theological elaboration of Ps. 132.1 ('Lade-Tempel-Jerusalem: Zur Theologie der Chronikbücher', in A.H.J. Gunneweg and O. Kaiser [eds.], *Textgemäss: Aufsätze und Beiträge zur Hermeneutik des Alten Testament. Eine Festschrift für E. Würthwein* [Göttingen: Vandenhoeck & Ruprecht, 1979], p. 181).

David's preparations to build the temple and Solomon's faithful completion of David's initiatives. David's first act after his accession is to initiate the retrieval of the ark (1 Chron. 13.1-14), the successful completion of which comes only after his first recorded prayer for divine assistance (1 Chron. 14.10). David's final act of preparation for the temple is the prayer of blessing and benediction in 1 Chron. 29.10-19. Similarly, Solomon's first act as king is to seek the tent of meeting (2 Chron. 1.2-6), in association with which his first prayer petitions God for divine assistance in accomplishing the task at hand. Following the completion of the temple, Solomon brings his official duties to a close, like his father David before him, with a prayer of doxology and petition (2 Chron. 6.14-42).

It may be recalled from the review of Chr's exegetical techniques that these prayers appear to be intentionally positioned and shaped for these strategic places in the narrative. Through recontextualizing (1 Chron. 14.10; 2 Chron. 1.8-10), editing (2 Chron. 6.14-42), and composing (1 Chron. 29.10-19), Chr has assigned to a series of royal prayers a major role in the successful completion of the temple. Inasmuch as the reigns of David and Solomon are defined by their commitment to building the temple, their record of faithful prayer emerges as a principal factor in their success.[46]

If the prayer of Jabez articulates the primordial vision for the world that Chr wishes to impart, and the prayers of David–Solomon concretize this vision in the building of the temple, then it remains for those in the post-Solomonic period to sustain the vision and insure its legacy to subsequent generations. From Chr's perspective the kings who follow Solomon succeed or fail in direct proportion to their faithfulness to God. Such faithfulness is recorded in a variety of ways, but particularly in relation to the king's responsibility to seek God.

---

46. It is also likely that Chr's handling of these prayers is designed to do more than simply mark the beginning and ending of the temple's construction. It is interesting to speculate on the significance of the several psalmic pieces woven into this pericope. Japhet suggests that the association of psalmody with levitical singers and prayers with lay people (including the king) reflects the liturgical practice in the Second Temple (*I and II Chronicles*, e.g. pp. 504, 601). Beyond this, Chr may also be addressing a dispute about the relationship between the sacrificial cult, music, and prayer. By incorporating aspects of all three liturgical practices in the Davidic-Solomonic temple, Chr may be seeking to resolve and/or authorize the contemporary practice. On these matters, see further Watts, *Psalm and Story*, pp. 164-68.

Indeed, the only kings in the post-Solomonic era who are granted prosperity and success are those who faithfully seek (דרשׁ) God: Asa (2 Chron. 14.6), Uzziah (2 Chron. 26.5), Jehoshaphat (2 Chron. 20.3), and Hezekiah (2 Chron. 31.21).[47] Within this context the prayers assigned to Asa, Jehoshaphat, and Hezekiah underscore the piety of these kings, which Chr has woven into their overall portraits. They become models of faithfulness for the community, and their prayers, like those of David and Solomon before them, a testimony to the royal task *par excellence*.[48]

Finally, we may compare Chr's compositional priorities with the emphases of the source material in Samuel–Kings. DtrH assigns a variety of responsibilities to the king in the general areas of political, economic, and religious administration. This same range of responsibilities is present in Chronicles, but with a decided emphasis on the king's religious duties, as is widely recognized.[49] This is particularly clear in Chr's emphasis on the king's role in establishing and maintaining temple worship.

The construction and maintenance of the temple is clearly important in DtrH also, but it is presented with a surrounding hue of polemic. David desires to build a temple but is forbidden to do so by Nathan the prophet, herald of the prophetic opposition to the monarchy that repeatedly surfaces in this account. Solomon builds the temple, but the construction is viewed as an exceedingly costly enterprise, both economically and politically. On the one hand it leaves Solomon with such debt, he must hand over to Hiram twenty cities in Galilee as payment (1 Kgs 9.10-11). On the other, harsh labor practices in the construction of the temple plant the seeds for a rebellion against Solomon's successor, which ultimately fractures the kingdom (1 Kgs 12.1-19).

---

47. On the connection between 'seeking God' and prosperity and success (צלח), see Welten (*Geschichte und Geschichtsdarstellung*, pp. 17-18, 50-51, *et passim*). On the theme 'seeking God' generally, see G.E. Schaefer, 'The Significance of Seeking God in the Purpose of the Chronicler' (ThD dissertation, Southern Baptist Theological Seminary, 1972); C.T. Begg, '"Seeking Yahweh" and the Purpose of Chronicles', *LS* 9 (1982), pp. 128-41.

48. Cf. Riley (*King and Cultus*, p. 167), who conceives the king's primary task as cultic faithfulness.

49. For the general discussion, see Riley (*King and Cultus*, pp. 157-68), who notes in this connection that Chr's portrayal of kingship as 'cultic vocation' is consonant with ancient Near Eastern ideology. See further A.S. Kapelrud, 'Temple Building, a Task for Gods and Kings', *Or* 32 (1963), pp. 56-62.

Add to these notes the fact that the Kings account provides comparatively little information about the structural details of the temple or the worship that takes place there, and one is tempted to conclude that DtrH has exercised a measure of self-imposed censorship in limiting the monarchy's role in relation to the temple.[50]

In Chronicles the picture is very different. Not only does Chr structure the presentation of David–Solomon to focus on the temple, he also provides a wealth of new information that expands upon the monarchy's important role in the maintenance of religious life. Like Moses, David receives a plan (תבנית) from God for the design of the holy place and its furnishings (1 Chron. 28.11-19; cf. Exod. 25.9). Moreover, David oversees the collection of the building materials, recruits the workers (cf. 1 Chron. 22), and organizes the temple personnel (cf. 1 Chron. 23–26). As Joshua succeeds Moses and completes what he had initiated, so—Chr suggests—Solomon succeeds David[51] and places the construction of the temple at the center of his royal responsibilities.[52]

From a theological perspective, the books of Chronicles suggest that something was lacking in the Samuel–Kings account of Israel's royal history. To recall the LXX's title for these books, *without* the negative connotations often associated with this designation, Chronicles is a record of the 'things left out' (*paralipomena*). From Chr's perspective, what was omitted, but has now been provided, has to do principally with God's 'plan' for worship as the center of Israel's identity and mission. The plan was present with Moses, whose leadership at Sinai made it the central platform in the constitution of a covenant people. And the plan was present in Zion, with David and Solomon who centered the kingdom on the temple and its constant summons to seek God with wholehearted devotion.[53]

50. Cf. M. Barker, *The Gate of Heaven: The History and Symbolism of the Temple in Jerusalem* (London: SPCK, 1991), pp. 20-22.

51. On Moses–Joshua as a paradigm for David–Solomon, see Braun, 'Solomon, the Chosen Builder', pp. 586-88; H.G.M. Williamson, 'The Accession of Solomon in the Books of Chronicles', *VT* 26 (1976), pp. 351-56; *idem, 1 and 2 Chronicles*, pp. 155-56; Dillard, *2 Chronicles*, pp. 3-4.

52. For the chiastic arrangement of 2 Chron. 1–9 that places the temple at the center of the Solomon materials, see Dillard, *2 Chronicles*, pp. 5-7.

53. Cf. S. Japhet, *The Ideology of the Book of Chronicles and its Place in Biblical Thought* (BEATAJ, 9; Frankfurt: Peter Lang, 1989), pp. 247-65.

In this view of Israel's story, Chr proposes that it is *God's plan*, not mere historical contingency, that calls Israel into meaningful existence. It is God's plan that determines history, not vice versa.[54] From this perspective, Chr assigns an important role to prayer as one of the principal acts of piety that secures and sustains God's vision of Israel's destiny. Chr articulates the charter for Israel's future most succinctly in 2 Chron. 7.14: 'If my people who are called by my name humble themselves, pray, seek my face, and turn from their wicked ways, then I will hear from heaven, and will forgive their sin and heal their land.'[55] With the assurance of such a vision, sustained and enlivened with such fervent prayer, Chr's history, like all good histories, promotes a truth that transcends historical data: 'Israel may yet be what it is'.[56]

Prayer as Truth and Fiction

I conclude with a brief reflection on Mark Twain's proposal that in real life 'you can't pray a lie'. For Huck Finn the truth of this observation is clear. One cannot mouth words to God that feign truth but harbor lies. Huck will not return Jim to slavery, no matter the laws of the land. Pray as he might, he cannot pray against his heart's convictions.

Biblical narrators share Twain's sense of propriety where prayers are concerned, for by and large they show no interest in inventing prayers that could not or would not be comprehended as both appropriate and true to the circumstances they report.[57] But they do *report* prayers, and there is no measure of historical sophistication that can verify beyond a doubt that the words they have recorded are precisely the words as they were uttered. They do *create* prayers, sometimes, so far as our sources allow us to see, out of whole cloth.

---

54. Japhet, *Ideology*, pp. 230-32.

55. On the importance of this text for Chr's theology, particularly with respect to the theme of retribution, see H.G.M. Williamson, 'Eschatology in Chronicles', *TynBul* 28 (1977), pp. 149-54; *idem*, *1 and 2 Chronicles*, pp. 30-33, 225-26; Dillard, *2 Chronicles*, pp. 76-81.

56. I take this suggestive quote from S.J. De Vries, who applies it to Chronicles in a somewhat different, though not unrelated, way than I have done: *1 and 2 Chronicles* (FOTL, 11; Grand Rapids, MI: Eerdmans, 1989), p. 20.

57. For cases where biblical narrators use prayer to caricature or parody a person's status, see Balentine, *Prayer in the Hebrew Bible*, pp. 64-79. In such cases it is the very incongruity between the piety expressed in the prayer and the actions of the prayer to which the narrator wishes to call attention.

But the prayers of the Bible are not designed to mislead or distort. Instead, they are modeled on language and practice that faithfully mirror the actual experience of people. As such they *are* designed to communicate a truth about what can and should transpire in the discourse between heaven and earth. This truth is consistent with historical occurrence, but beyond the reach of historical verification. It may be fiction, but it is no lie. If Chr felt compelled to defend himself against Twain's observation, he might well respond with something like the following, 'Yes, you can't pray a lie, and you can't tell the truth about history without (sometimes composing) a prayer'.

PART III
SPECIALIZED STUDIES

HOW MANY IN A THOUSAND?

Ralph W. Klein

According to the Chronicler, Abijah, accompanied by an army of 400,000, attacked the army of Jeroboam, which was 800,000 strong, and inflicted some 500,000 casualties (2 Chron. 13.3, 17). Abijah's successor, Asa, supported by an army of 580,000, was able to stave off an invading horde from Ethiopia numbering 1,000,000 (2 Chron. 14.8). These and similar large numbers in Chronicles have seemed exaggerated, idealistic, or even absurd to nineteenth- and twentieth- century scholars.[1]

While demographic studies of ancient Israel remain at a low level of sophistication, the population of Israel and Judah was surely not large enough to supply the 1,200,000 troops for the Abijah–Jeroboam war, let alone to resist a million invading Ethiopians. W.F. Albright estimated the total population of Judah in the eighth century at about 250,000,[2] and Roland de Vaux[3] speculated that fewer than 1,000,000 people comprised the population of both kingdoms in the same century.

---

1. H.G.M. Williamson (*1 and 2 Chronicles* [NCB; Grand Rapids, MI: Eerdmans, 1982], p. 251) lists two options—without indicating his preference—for the numbers relating to Abijah. They are symbolic, indicating the full effort of the invading Jeroboam and the magnitude of the south's eventual victory, or they are understood rationalistically with the word 'thousand' being reinterpreted as military unit or a fully armed soldier. S. Japhet (*I & II Chronicles: A Commentary* [OTL; Louisville, KY: Westminster/John Knox, 1993], p. 697) takes the numbers in the Abijah–Jeroboam war 'typologically'. The two-to-one ratio illustrates that this is a confrontation between the righteous few and the hosts of evildoers. In her view, these numbers may also reflect some actual military advantage of Israel over Judah.

2. W.F. Albright, *The Biblical Period from Abraham to Ezra* (New York: Harper & Row, 1963), p. 105, n. 118.

3. R. De Vaux, *Ancient Israel: its Life and Institutions* (London: Darton, Longman & Todd, 1961), p. 66.

More recently, Yigael Shiloh[4] and Israel Finkelstein[5] have pursued the same questions but with greater precision. The 500,000 casualties inflicted by Abijah are about the same as the number of deaths on both sides in the American Civil War and equal to all American deaths in World War II. Armies of 400,000, 800,000, or 1,000,000 are totally out of line with what we know about ancient military forces. When Ramesses II and the Hittite king Muwattalis fought, the latter may have had as many as 30,000 troops.[6] At the battle of Qarqar in 853 BCE, Ahab contributed only 2,000 chariots and 10,000 infantry, according to the Assyrian Royal Annals (*ANET*, pp. 278-79), and these records are not known for their understatement.

The view that the numbers in Chronicles are exaggerated has been challenged on the basis of a different understanding of the word אלף, proposed by George Mendenhall in an attempt to interpret the census lists of Numbers 1 and 26.[7] Building on Flinders Petrie's proposal that the Hebrew word אלף means both 1,000 and a subsection of a tribe (cf. Judg. 6.10), Mendenhall argued that during the period of the tribal federation אלף meant both a tribal subsection and the military unit that went to war from this subsection. Numbers 1, in his view, referred originally not to 603,550 fighting men, but to 598 fighting units, numbering 5,550 men. He thereby achieved a 90 percent reduction in the grand total, as well as in the figures for the individual tribes. Similarly, the figures in Numbers 26 were reduced by him from 601,730 to 596 fighting units and a total of 5,750 individuals.[8] More briefly, he proposed a similar interpretation for 1 Chronicles 12, the list of people who came to make David king at Hebron. While the MT suggests that 340,822 men made their way to Hebron, Mendenhall reduced the number to 329 units and a total of about 15,290.

---

4. 'The Population of Iron Age Palestine in the Light of Sample Analysis of Urban Plans, Areas and Population Density', *BASOR* 239 (1980), pp. 25-35.

5. *The Archaeology of the Israelite Settlement* (Jerusalem: Israel Exploration Society, 1988).

6. J. Bright, *A History of Israel* (Philadelphia: Westminster, 3rd edn, 1981), p. 113.

7. G.E. Mendenhall, 'The Census Lists of Numbers 1 and 26', *JBL* 77 (1958), pp. 52-66.

8. B.A. Levine rejects Mendenhall's proposal, since the word 'thousand' alternates with the word 'hundreds' and with other numbers. *Numbers 1–20* (AB, 4A; New York: Doubleday, 1993), p. 139.

In Mendenhall's view, this system, in which each tribe provided a certain quota of men for the army, broke down with the rise of the monarchy. The royal standing army had units of a full 1,000, presided over by an officer (שׂר) appointed by the king. This royal system was later read back anachronistically into early lists, that is, the military unit designed as an אלף was interpreted as 1,000 fighting men, and so the gigantic figures of Numbers 1 and 26 and of 1 Chronicles 12 are due to a mistaken understanding of the word אלף. These lists, while garbled in the present text of the Bible, were held to rest ultimately on archaic documents containing realistic figures.[9] Norman Gottwald accepted Mendenhall's original hypothesis and gave it plausible sociological grounding in *The Tribes of Yahweh*.[10]

Mendenhall's hypothesis has been extended to the numbers in Joshua and Judges,[11] to 1 and 2 Samuel,[12] and to 1 and 2 Chronicles.[13] This extension, however, has been by no means limited to the Anchor Bible.[14]

In this essay I will evaluate the proposed extension of this hypothesis

9. In a similar reinterpretation J.W. Wenham argues that many of the references to אלף are actually to be read אלוף and translated as chiliarch or captain, the com—mander of a folk אלף, a professional, fully armed soldier, or officers in general. See 'Large Numbers in the Old Testament', *TynBul* 18 (1967), pp. 19-53 and especially p. 25. Wenham's opinions will be cited from time to time with critical comments.

10. N.K. Gottwald, *The Tribes of Yahweh: A Sociology of the Religion of Liberated Israel, 1250–1050 B.C.E.* (Maryknoll, NY: Orbis, 1979).

11. R.G. Boling, *Joshua* (AB, 6; Garden City, NY: Doubleday, 1980); *Judges* (AB, 7; Garden City, NY: Doubleday, 1975).

12. P.K. McCarter, Jr, *I Samuel* (AB, 8; Garden City, NY: Doubleday, 1980); *II Samuel* (AB, 9; Garden City, NY: Doubleday, 1984).

13. J.M. Myers, *I Chronicles* (AB, 12; Garden City, NY: Doubleday, 1965); *II Chronicles* (AB, 13; Garden City, NY: Doubleday, 1965).

14. J.B. Payne, 'The Validity of the Numbers in Chronicles', *BSac* 136 (1979), pp. 109-28, 206-20, 285-88; C. Schedl, 'Biblische Zahlen—unglaubwürdig'? *TPQ* 107 (1959), pp. 58-62; Wenham, 'Large Numbers'. Commenting on 2 Chron. 13.3, R.B. Dillard (*2 Chronicles* [WBC, 15; Waco, TX: Word Books, 1987], pp. 106-107) finds the interpretation of אלף as 1,000 or as a reference to 'commanders' unsatisfactory, a judgment he also applies to the hyperbolic interpretation. He takes the numbers in 2 Chron. 14.7-8 as hyperbolic (p. 120). While Roddy Braun concedes that the author of 1 Chronicles 12 may no longer have understood the original connotation of all of the terms, he attributes the huge size of the numbers to hyperbole or to the theological principle that 'all Israel' supported David in his kingship: R.L. Braun, *1 Chronicles* (WBC, 14; Waco, TX: Word Books, 1986), p. 170.

to the books of Chronicles and the implications for Chr's historical accuracy. The following limitations and/or complexities of Mendenhall's hypothesis—or its revision by Gottwald—even for an understanding of Numbers 1 and 26 must be recognized.[15]

1. Mendenhall believed that these two chapters reflected the period of the tribal federation or, perhaps, the earliest days of the monarchy. A dating to the Mosaic period is out of the question for him.

2. The Priestly redactor of Numbers 1 and 26 clearly understood the noun אלף as a designation for 1,000. This is shown by the totals provided in Num. 1.46 and 26.1.[16]

3. A passage such as Num. 1.33 is usually translated, 'Those enrolled of the tribe of Ephraim were forty thousand five hundred' (NRSV). If the narrator had wanted to say what Mendenhall and Gottwald propose, there would be a clearer way to cast the sentence in Hebrew.

4. Gottwald argued that אלף and משפחה are virtually synonymous, but this causes tension in Numbers 26, where the names of the משפחות for each tribe are given, ranging from one for the smallest tribe (Num. 26.8) to eight for the largest (Num. 26.29-32). The reconstructed אלפים range from twenty-two for Simeon to seventy-six for Judah. Gottwald questioned the scope and integrity of the names of the משפחות in ch. 26, but this means that the present text of ch. 26 is even farther removed from history.[17]

5. Gottwald has created an additional problem because of his insistence that the schema of twelve tribes does not antedate the time of David. Hence he must argue that the twelve tribe format in Numbers 1 and 26 is also late and inauthentic.[18]

I do not view these five difficulties as raising insuperable problems, but

---

15. Wenham ('Large Numbers', p. 29) points out that the tribes with many אלפים should have many מאות, but that is not the case. Simeon has 59 אלפים and 3 מאות, whereas Gad has 45 אלפים but more than twice as many מאות.

16. Gottwald (*Tribes of Yahweh*, pp. 272-73) misunderstands the significance of the discrepancy between the Priestly totals and the reconstructed numbers of the tribal units.

17. *Tribes of Yahweh*, pp. 267-76.

18. Gottwald, *Tribes of Yahweh*, pp. 358, 267.

they should warn us that even for the earliest period of Israel's history this proposed understanding of אלף is by no means unproblematic. To understand אלף as a tribal or military unit in a post-exilic document like Chronicles—composed in light of Israel's long tradition of a standing army, with its units of 100 and 1,000, presided over by the שׂרי of 1,000, etc.—would seem to be a doubtful hypothesis at best. These anticipated difficulties multiply when the actual figures in Chronicles are examined.

Numbers Already in Samuel–Kings

Many of the numbers in Chronicles were present already in its *Vorlage*, the books of Samuel and Kings. In these cases, of course, we can be certain that Chr was not manufacturing exaggerated numbers. The meaning of these figures is an exegetical problem primarily for commentators on the Deuteronomistic History.[19]

Numbers Differing Only Slightly from Samuel–Kings

In certain cases, slight differences between Chronicles and the Deuteronomistic *Vorlage* allow us to conclude that Chr understood these figures as true thousands and not as military units. According to 2 Sam. 10.6, the Ammonites hired 20,000 foot soldiers from the Syrians of Beth-rehob and Zobah, 1,000 from the king of Maacah, and 12,000 men of Tob. Chr paraphrases this as 32,000 chariots, plus the king of Maacah with his army (1 Chron. 19.7). Surely he meant 32,000 thousand chariots (the sum of 20,000 and 12,000 from his Samuel *Vorlage*), and not thirty-two 'units' of chariots.

A feature in David's census list also seems to indicate that Chr construed the word אלף as 1,000. According to 2 Sam. 24.9, David

---

19. I refer to such numbers as the 18,000 whom Abishai killed in Edom (1 Chron. 18.12//2 Sam. 8.13), the 22,000 whom David smote in Aram (1 Chron. 18.5//2 Sam. 8.50), the 70,000 who fell in the plague following David's census (1 Chron. 21.14//2 Sam. 24.15), the 180,000 troops mustered by Rehoboam from Judah and Benjamin (2 Chron. 11.1//1 Kgs 12.21), and the 10,000 casualties in Amaziah's war against Edom (2 Chron. 25.11//2 Kgs 14.7). We might note in passing that the information about the 70,000 who fell in the plague is the least ambiguous. It does not seem plausible that the plague wiped out only 70 military units of the 1,300 in the entire census, leaving all other units untouched.

numbered 800,000 in Israel and 500,000 in Judah, but in 1 Chron. 21.5 all Israel numbered 1,100,000. The difference between 1,100,000 and the total of 1,300,000 for Israel and Judah in 2 Samuel 24 is that the tribes of Benjamin and Levi were not included in the census as Chr reports it (1 Chron. 21.6). Chr seems to have calculated that the number 1,300,000, implied in his *Vorlage*, was the product of thirteen tribes (twelve secular tribes plus Levi) times 100,000. Since Levi and Benjamin were not included in the census according to Chr, he reduced the total for all Israel by exactly 200,000.[20]

The notice in 2 Chron. 2.1 and 2.17 that Solomon appointed 70,000 men to bear burdens, 80,000 to quarry stone, and 3,600 to act as their overseers is based on 1 Kgs 5.29-30 (EVV. 15-16). In my judgment the figures in both Kings and Chronicles are not easily interpreted as military units. Chr makes clear his own understanding of these figures in an additional verse (2 Chron. 2.16), which reports that all these laborers were drawn from aliens within Israel. Chr notes further that all these workers totalled 153,600, the sum of 70,000, 80,000, and 3,600, and *not* a figure to be parsed as 153 units, consisting of 600 men each.[21] If Chr meant us to understand that Solomon had a workforce of 153,600, consisting entirely of aliens, should we be surprised if he informs us elsewhere of armies in the hundreds of thousands?

Numbers for Non-Human Objects

Chr reports non-human objects in multiple thousands, in contexts where it is not possible to understand the word אלף as a unit of fighting men. The hyperbolic quantities of non-human objects suggests that we also ought to understand אלף when used of people as the word for 1,000, however unrealistic or unhistorical such figures may be.

I have already mentioned the 32,000 chariots that the Ammonites

20. Originally 'Israel' designated the whole country in this passage. When a figure for Judah was added by a later hand, it was reduced by 30,000 (from 500,000 to 470,000) to make allowance for the non-inclusion of Benjamin. Wenham ('Large Numbers', pp. 33-34) reconstructs original figures of 80,000 untrained men of military age and 30 professional soldiers (אלופים) for Israel and 40,000 men of military age and 70 professional soldiers (אלופים) for Judah. 80,000 became 800,000 by the unexplained addition of a zero, and the 30 אלופים became 30,000 by a new understanding of the noun, and then increased to 300,000 by the unexplained addition of a zero. He uses similar calculations to explain the numbers in 2 Sam. 24.9.

21. Contra Myers, *II Chronicles*, p. 10.

hired against David (1 Chron. 19.7), a number sixteen times the number of chariots Ahab contributed to the battle of Qarqar. Chr notes that the Ammonites paid 1,000 talents of silver for them (1 Chron. 19.6), an amount calculated by Jacob Myers as 37.5 tons.[22] Before his death (1 Chron. 22.14) David gathered for the house of the Lord 100,000 talents of gold (3,775 tons) and 1,000,000 talents of silver (37,750 tons).[23] Wilhelm Rudolph informs us that the gold would be nine times the world production in 1900.[24] The figures in 1 Chron. 29.4 (3,000 talents of gold and 7,000 talents of silver) and 29.7 (5,000 talents of gold, 10,000 darics, 18,000 talents of bronze, and 100,000 talents of iron) confirm that Chr meant thousands when he used the word אֶלֶף of precious metals, and that he did not shrink from reporting highly unrealistic amounts.[25]

Equally astronomical is the number of animals donated at the time of Hezekiah and Josiah for passover celebrations. According to 2 Chron. 30.24, Hezekiah and his princes gave 2,000 bulls and 17,000 sheep, while Josiah and various officials contributed 3,800 bulls and 37,600 lambs and kids (2 Chron. 35.7-9). At the dedication of the temple 22,000 oxen and 120,000 sheep were sacrificed (2 Chron. 7.5).[26]

One of the most significant animal numbers appears in 1 Chron. 5.21. This chapter describes a war between the two-and-one-half Transjordanian tribes and a people called the Hagrites. The Israelite tribes captured 50,000 camels, 250,000 sheep, 2,000 donkeys, and—most significantly—100,000 men.[27] Why should this final figure be read as 100 units of men, consisting of an unspecified number per unit, if Chr

22. *I Chronicles*, p. 136.

23. Myers, *I Chronicles*, p. 152.

24. W. Rudolph, *Chronikbücher* (HAT, 21; Tübingen: Mohr, 1955), p. 151, n. 2, quoting Kugler.

25. Wenham ('Large Numbers', p. 49) proposes that one, two, or even three zeroes need to be removed from these figures. By such textual manipulations he attempts to defend the basic historical accuracy of Chr himself.

26. Wenham ('Large Numbers', p. 49) calculates that the celebration at the dedication of the temple would require 20 sacrifices a minute, 10 hours a day, for 12 days. Therefore, he suggests that 2,200 oxen and 12,000 sheep would be more plausible. He concedes that the numbers for Hezekiah and Josiah are probably also too high. Williamson (*1 and 2 Chronicles*, p. 406) observes that the numbers for Josiah were 'exaggerated for effect'.

27. Myers (*I Chronicles*, p. 38) concedes that these numbers are 'fantastically large'.

in the same breath informs us about 302,000 captured animals?

Numbers for Pre-Monarchical or Early Monarchical Times

According to Mendenhall, אֶלֶף referred to a military tribal unit only in pre-monarchical or early monarchical times. He assigned the census lists of Numbers 1 and 26, as we have seen, to the period of the tribal league or the early monarchy. 1 Chronicles 12 deals with the anointing of David at Hebron—hence it could also be from the early monarchy. In his article for the Wright memorial volume, Mendenhall spoke of the census lists as reflecting the military organization of the league inherited by Saul and continued by David.[28] In his earlier article he had already written:

> Army commanders are now [sc. under the monarchy] *śārīm*, and it seems likely that the *śārīm* actually commanded a unit whose normal strength was a thousand men. The old tribal subdivisions disappear eventually under the impact of fiscal reorganization under David and Solomon...[29]

These views correspond with the majority opinion that the monarchy, perhaps beginning with Solomon, had standing armies, whose recruits were not drawn from the tribal units. It is inappropriate, then, for Myers to use the אֶלֶף = unit equation to interpret numbers during the much later times of Abijah, Jeroboam, Asa, Jehoshaphat, Amaziah, and Pekah. Chr frequently uses the expressions 'captains of thousands' and 'captains of hundreds' in monarchical contexts.[30] If the captain of a hundred during the monarchy commanded 100 men, is it not likely that the captain of a thousand commanded 1,000 men, regardless of what the word אֶלֶף may have meant during the time of the tribal league?

Numbers for the Tribal Period

This leaves only the numbers dealing with the tribal period in 1 and 2 Chronicles as possible occasions for understanding אֶלֶף as a military unit. The first such context is the war of the two-and-one-half Trans-

28. 'Social Organization in Early Israel', in F.M. Cross, W.E. Lemke, and P.D. Miller Jr. (eds.), *Magnalia Dei: The Mighty Acts of God* (Garden City, NY: Doubleday, 1976), p. 148.

29. 'Census Lists', p. 57.

30. 1 Chron. 26.26; 27.1; 29.6; 28.1; 2 Chron. 1.2; 25.5; cf. 17.14.

jordanian tribes against the Hagrites. According to Chr, the Israelite tribes numbered 44,760 (1 Chron. 5.18). While it might be possible to parse this as 44 military units consisting of 760 men, we have already seen that Chr has other figures in the same context that are clearly to be understood as thousands, namely, the 50,000 camels, 250,000 sheep, 2,000 donkeys, and the 100,000 men (v. 21).

A second context is the list of warriors for the tribes of Issachar, Benjamin, and Asher in 1 Chronicles 7. Of the seven numbers given, four do not match Mendenhall's hypothesis. The sons of Bela of Benjamin, for example, number 22,034 (1 Chron. 7.7), but it is meaningless to speak of twenty-two military units with an average number of soldiers per unit of 1.5 men. For three additional groups, the numbers are given in whole thousands (36,000 in 1 Chron. 7.4; 87,000 in 1 Chron. 7.5; and 26,000 in 1 Chron. 7.40). While the other three numbers could theoretically be interpreted according to Mendenhall's hypothesis,[31] this seems quite improbable in light of the fact that the numbers for the other four names contradict the hypothesis. Hence, in all seven numbers, we should understand אלף as equal to 1,000.

Even greater complications appear in the third context, 1 Chronicles 12, which Mendenhall himself considered analogous to Numbers 1 and 26. This chapter lists the people from the twelve tribes and a priestly contingent who came to anoint David at Hebron. The validity of Mendenhall's hypothesis here faces major obstacles.[32]

1. To get units of people for all twelve tribes, Mendenhall had to split up the numbers given for Reuben, Gad, and the half tribe of Manasseh. Hence, instead of 120,000 men, he read 40 units for each of the three tribes. In order to limit the tribes to twelve, he had to count the two parts of Manasseh as one tribe and ignore the data for Levi and the priests.

2. Of the twelve tribes in his list, only four (Judah, Simeon, Ephraim, and Dan) contain figures for both the units and the actual fighting men. For seven of the other eight (Benjamin, Zebulun, Naphtali, Asher, Reuben, Gad, and Manasseh), his reconstructed list contains only a total for units with the actual number of men lacking. For the eighth, Issachar, only 200

31. 22,600, v. 2; 20,200, v. 9; 17,200, v. 11.

32. Wenham ('Large Numbers', pp. 44-45) believes that this chapter originally represented a list of 1,925 captains of thousands and captains of hundreds.

chiefs are listed, neither units nor men.

3. Naphtali, according to Mendenhall's interpretation, has only 37 units consisting of an unspecified number of men, but it has 1,000 officers or 27 for each unit![33]

4. Mendenhall excludes the figures for the Levites (4,600 or four units of 600 men), for Jehoiada (3,700 or three units of 700 men), and for Zadok, who was accompanied by twenty-two commanders.

5. Mendenhall did not insist on the attribution of this list to the time of David's coronation, but he did believe that it came from a time early in the united monarchy. But why should Judah be represented by 6,800 men (or 6 units) while the vastly less significant tribe of Zebulun had 50,000 men (or 50 units), and the Trans-jordanian tribes had 120,000 men (or 120 units)? Mendenhall found no pattern in this list and the lists from Numbers 1 and 26 and therefore believed them to be historical. But when in Israel's history would such proportions—Zebulun nearly eight times the size of Judah—make historical sense?

I believe that these difficulties are so severe that the 'unit interpretation' of 1 Chronicles 12 must be given up. Mendenhall had to divide Reuben, Gad, and Manasseh into three tribes, ignore the figures for the priests and other cultic officials, and combine the two halves of Manasseh into one in order to get twelve tribes. But if we include the Levites and other priestly officials as one division, and if we leave Reuben, Gad, and Manasseh undivided, as they are in the biblical text, twelve divisions appear in the present biblical text. Moreover, the number of men in each of these twelve units seems to be schematic and fits well the united, all Israel interpretation for which Chr always strives.

Naturally, Judah, Simeon, Levi, and Benjamin are there—but they are there in relatively small numbers, ranging from 3,000 to 7,100. The tribes from the heartland of the old northern kingdom are there, too: 18,000 men from Manasseh and 20,800 men from Ephraim, three to six times as many as the tribes like Simeon, Levi, and Judah. But the most remote tribes had the greatest representation: Dan 28,600; Naphtali 37,000; Asher 40,000; Zebulun 50,000; Reuben-Gad-Manasseh—from

33. Mendenhall tries to remove this difficulty by conjectural emendation: 37 officers of 'military units' ('Census Lists', p. 62).

across the Jordan—120,000, while Issachar brought its whole tribe! The principle seems to be, the more remote the tribe, the larger its delegation at David's coronation. The fringe tribes had the greatest numbers.

I propose keeping the twelve tribal designations given by Chr and interpreting his numbers as symbolic indices of popular enthusiasm for the kingship of David and the unity of Israel. Ephraim and Manasseh were more enthusiastic than Judah. The remotest tribes were the most enthusiastic of all.[34]

A fourth tribal context is provided by the list of the commanders of the monthly divisions in 1 Chronicles 27. According to this list, each of the twelve officers provided 24,000 men for his assigned month. If אלף is to be understood as a military unit here, each officer would have to provide twenty-four units in his month. Actually the officers are not historical since they are demonstrably drawn from a list in 1 Chron. 11.11-47//2 Sam. 23.8-39. The number 24,000 is schematic and probably reflects the notion that an officer would provide for two relays of two weeks each, with 12,000 men in each relay.

Numbers that Cannot Fit the 'Tribal Unit Principle'

Finally, a few of the numbers interpreted according to the אלף = tribal unit principle simply do not work. King Uzziah's army, for example, is set at 307,500 (2 Chron. 26.13). If this is read as 307 units consisting of 500 men, we wind up with fewer than two people per unit.[35] When Pekah killed 120,000 (2 Chron. 28.6) and Israel took captive an

---

34. Japhet (*I & II Chronicles*, pp. 258-59) believes that the geographical outlook and the comprehensive view of all Israel fit well with Chr's attitude, but she finds a tension between the numbers—especially for Judah—and the proposal that Chr was the author of this pericope. She believes, therefore, that the list was based on a source, whose nature and delimitation can no longer be determined, but she acknowledges that the extant list is not an authentic reflection of a particular historical situation. Williamson (*1 and 2 Chronicles*, p. 110) believes that the 'curious relations between the tribes as regards the numbers' makes it unlikely that this list was a fabrication of Chr. He lists three choices for אלף: a military unit (Mendenhall), the expected contingent from each clan (often less than 1,000), or chief/armed troops (Wenham).

35. Myers (*II Chronicles*, p. 150) interprets the number as 300 units consisting of 7,500 men. Wenham ('Large Numbers', p. 51) emends 307,500 to 37,500 and compares that with the population of military age in Judah in David's time. I assume that he meant to emend to 30,750, but in any case his methodology seems arbitrary.

additional 200,000 (2 Chron. 28.8), the text surely cannot be interpreted to mean that Pekah killed 120 units or that Israel took captive 200 units.[36] Note that the captives include women, sons, and daughters.

Conclusion

The results of this survey of the numbers over 1,000 in Chronicles contradict the hypothesis that אלף = a military unit in interpreting these books. Differences from the *Vorlage* in Samuel–Kings, analogies with large numbers for precious metals and animals, the monarchical setting of many of the numbers, and the failure of the hypothesis to offer an adequate interpretation for the tribal numbers suggest that Mendenhall's thesis should not be extended to Chronicles, whatever its validity for earlier periods or earlier documents. Now, as before, the high numbers in Chronicles cannot be taken as reflecting historical reality. Rather, the interpreter's goal should be to see how these numbers are a part of Chr's message or of his theological agenda.

Sometimes the large numbers may have been used to emphasize that victory over Israel's enemies was to be attributed to the power of Yahweh and not to the nation's own military power. Abijah's victory over the north was in spite of the latter's two-to-one military superiority. Similarly, 44,760 Trans-jordanian tribal members captured 100,000 Hagrites, who outnumbered them by more than two-to-one. Pious Asa won a victory over a million invaders from Ethiopia.

How Chr arrived at these numbers is still unknown except in a few cases. In 2 Chron. 2.16 (EVV.17) we notice that he replaced the 30,000 men of the Israelite levy (1 Kgs 5.27 [EVV 13]) with 153,000 aliens. The components of this number (70,000; 80,000; 3,600) were drawn from a related context in 1 Kgs 5.29-30 (EVV 15-16). Secondly, the size of Abijah's and Jeroboam's armies was probably related to numbers drawn from the Davidic census (1 Chronicles 21//2 Samuel 24). Thirdly, the round number of 1,000,000 Ethiopians is considerably larger than the 580,000 men available to Asa, though how the latter figure was calculated still escapes us.

---

36. Wenham ('Large Numbers', p. 51) interprets the 120,000 as 120 valiant men (אלוף = אלף) and continues: 'The Israelites fed their captives and where necessary provided them with clothes and transport and sent them back south. Their number might have been 200 or 2,000, but not 200,000.' Here he drops two zeroes or three, that is, he divides the MT's number by 100 or 1,000.

Our understanding of these numbers should not lead us to disparage Chr's value or to denigrate his theological importance. But neither should we try to force his data into a historical genre. Rather, Chr, like other writers in Israel, used what *we* would call 'inflated numbers' to give texture and impact to his presentation of Israel's theological story.

THE CHRONICLER'S ACCOUNT OF SOLOMON'S TEMPLE-BUILDING: A CONTINUITY THEME

John Van Seters

A fundamental purpose of ancient historiography was to establish continuity of identity, ideology, and institutions. For the Chronicler, the temple in Jerusalem stood at the heart of the true community of Israel, the people of God, and his concern was to establish this sense of continuity through his treatment of the building of the temple by Solomon. The sheer quantity of space given to this subject in his work is ample testimony to the importance he attributed to the temple as the foundation of this community. At the same time, the demonstration of continuity for Jerusalem's temple underscores a discontinuity for rival sanctuaries and communities and their respective claims to represent the true Israel, as in the case of the Samaritan temple community of Gerizim.[1]

Some years ago P.R. Ackroyd discussed the subject of the temple vessels and their survival after the destruction of Jerusalem and the temple as a 'continuity theme'.[2] This theme cuts across work by several biblical authors, both those in the Deuteronomistic tradition, as reflected especially in the book of Jeremiah, and in Chronicles and Ezra–Nehemiah. The survival of the temple vessels, however, is only one aspect of the continuity theme. Of equal importance, and a vital counterpart to it, is the manufacture of the 'original' vessels and of the temple to which they belonged. It is Chr's concern to establish the

---

1. The dating of the Samaritan schism and the construction of the temple on Gerazim are debated. Yet there must have been some cultic continuity in the province of Samaria from the time of the northern kingdom onward. See R.J. Coggins, *Samaritans and Jews: The Origins of Samaritanism Reconsidered* (Growing Points in Theology; Atlanta: John Knox, 1975), pp. 60-74.

2. P.R. Ackroyd, 'The Temple Vessels: A Continuity Theme', in *Studies in the Religion of Ancient Israel* (VTSup, 23; Leiden: Brill, 1972), pp. 166-81.

credentials of the vessels and the temple and indeed the whole cultus that they represented, and to do so by means of the accounts of cult foundation and temple-building under David and Solomon.

The continuity theme in Chr is intended to establish, first of all, the divine source and foundation of the temple under David and its construction according to divine requirements under Solomon. But the temple's continuity also reaches back to the Mosaic tabernacle to make the identity and legitimation complete. This means that the description of the temple taken over from Kings is modified to accommodate features that are distinctive to the tabernacle or 'tent of meeting' of the wilderness period. This has been clearly demonstrated by R. Mosis,[3] who states:

> He (Chr) repeatedly attributes to and intersperses the report of the building of the temple in his *Vorlage* with elements of texts from the Priestly Source about the tent of meeting, thereby giving to both the report of the building of the temple and to the Solomonic temple itself the sense of a repetition of the Mosaic sanctuary.[4]

Consequently, any discussion of Chr's temple-building account must take seriously this second source.

At the same time it is this ideal Solomonic temple that is linked with Chr's own Second Temple so that some of the innovations of the latter are reflected in his description of the former. It is vital to Chr's continuity theme, reflected not just in the restoration of the temple vessels and in the temple cultus, but also in the building itself. This means that the three basic 'sources' for Chr's temple description are clear. They are the Kings' account of Solomon's temple construction,

---

3. R. Mosis, *Untersuchungen zur Theologie des chronistischen Geschichtswerkes* (FTS, 92; Freiburg: Herder, 1973). See esp. pp. 136-46.

4. 'Er unterlegt und durchsetzt den Tempelbaubericht seiner Vorlage immer wieder mit Elementen der priesterschriftlichen Texte über das Zelt der Begegnung und gibt dadurch dem Tempelbaubericht und dem salomonischen Tempel den Sinn einer Wiederholung des mosaischen Heiligtums': *Untersuchungern*, p. 136. And again: 'That is, the Chronicler alters the building report of the temple such that the temple clearly is paralleled with the tent of meeting' ('Der Chr verändert nämlich den Baubericht des Tempels so, daß der Tempel deutlich mit Zelt der Begegnung parallelisiert wird'): *Untersuchungen*, p. 130. Mosis sees the 'tent of meeting' as present in, and therefore replaced by, the Solomonic temple and the continuity of the cult of the Bezalel altar in Gibeon (2 Chron. 1.2-6) with the sacrifices of Solomon's temple.

the Priestly description of the making of the tabernacle (Exod. 25–31, 35–40), and the temple that existed in Chr's own time.[5]

In spite of this concern for continuity, there is also the need to suggest some discontinuity between the temple of Chr's own day and Solomon's temple in terms of the greater glory of the latter. This is reflected in the story of the laying of the foundations of the Second Temple, as set out in Ezra 3.10-13. Although it was regarded as an occasion of great joy, there was also an element of sadness: 'But many of the priests and Levites and heads of father's houses, old men who had seen the first house, wept with a loud voice when they saw the foundations of this house being laid, though many shouted aloud for joy.' The idea that at no time could the Second Temple ever equal the magnificence of the first temple is a theme that continues in later Jewish historiography as well.[6]

It is not my intention to deal with the whole of the temple-building story from David's planning to Solomon's dedication, although a full treatment of the theme would require this. Instead, I will focus attention on the account of actual construction in 2 Chronicles 3–4. I will compare Chr with his primary source in 1 Kings 6–7 and discuss the nature and significance of his departure from this source in the interest of the other two sources, especially as it has to do with the theme of continuity.

The Vorlage *of Kings*

Before addressing the specific comparisons between Kings and Chronicles regarding the details of temple description, it is necessary to deal with some major omissions from Chronicles and the bearing these might have on the particular *Vorlage* of Kings used by Chronicles. Do these omissions point to a different, earlier form of Kings from that represented by MT? There have been some recent attempts to suggest

---

5.   In his effort to establish the importance of the second, Pentateuchal source, Mosis seems too dismissive of the influence of the third source, the temple of Chr's own time.

6.   See Th.A. Busink, *Der Tempel von Jerusalem, von Salomo bis Herodes: Eine archäologisch-historische Studie unter Berücksichtigung des westsemitischen Tempelbaus* (Studia Francisci Scholten memoriae dicata, 3; Leiden: Brill, 1970), I, pp. 26-28, for sources.

that Chronicles used an early form of DtrH,[7] or even as Auld has argued, a pre-Dtr text.[8] Some of the abridgments and differences of treatment of particular items can be put down to a matter of Chr's style. Thus Japhet sets down as a matter of principle concerning Chr's dependence on Kings:

> These chapters are therefore characterized by a drastic abridgment and literary restructuring, whereby the Chronicler, while basically faithful to his source in Kings, extracts only the main points, rephrasing them in his own, much shorter, presentation.[9]

There are also specific additions and changes that are attributable to Chr's use of P's description of the tabernacle.[10] These general principles, however, are not those used by Auld to account for the rather major omissions in Chronicles. So it is to some of his arguments that we turn now.

In arguing for a *Vorlage* of Kings, used by Chr, that differs from the text of MT, Auld lays down the following guidelines:

> In most portions of Kings/Chronicles it is apparently easy to reconstruct the text common to the two books; for, in the great majority of instances, that shared text has been modified, usually by being added to, in only one of the familiar books. In such cases the 'original' can be 'restored' by simply giving preference to *the shorter text*.[11]

7. See S.L. McKenzie, *The Chronicler's Use of the Deuteronomistic History* (HSM, 33; Atlanta: Scholars Press, 1985).

8. See A.G. Auld, *Kings without Privilege: David and Moses in the Story of the Bible's Kings* (Edinburgh: T. & T. Clark, 1994), pp. 22-29.

9. *I & II Chronicles: A Commentary* (OTL; Louisville, KY: Westminster/John Knox, 1993), p. 549. See also the extensive discussion of Chr's literary style in T. Willi, *Die Chronik als Auslegung: Untersuchungen zur literarische Gestaltung der historischen Überlieferung Israels* (FRLANT, 106; Göttingen: Vandenhoeck & Ruprecht, 1972), pp. 78-175. While many of Willi's observations on style have been accepted, his characterization of Chronicles' method as 'exegesis' has been criticized. See H.G.M. Williamson, *1 & 2 Chronicles* (NCB; Grand Rapids, MI: Eerdmans, 1982), pp. 21-23.

10. See Mosis, *Untersuchungen*, p. 130; also H.G.M. Williamson, *1 & 2 Chronicles*, p. 203. On this point also see Williamson's review of McKenzie's *The Chronicler's Use of the Deuteronomistic History* in *VT* 37 (1987), pp. 107-14, esp, p. 111: 'Again, it is well known that a number of points in the description of the temple are the result of the influence of tabernacle typology.' Williamson has in mind the work of Mosis that McKenzie has neglected. The same criticism applies to Auld.

11. *Kings without Privilege*, pp. 12-13 (italics mine).

This principle of comparison, however, is highly problematic. It certainly does not apply to the Synoptic Gospels, in which Mark is the *longest* version of the text shared with Matthew and Luke. Assyrian royal inscriptions also regularly abridge common material drawn from earlier texts in order to add new material.[12] The relationship of Chronicles to Kings seems to fit this general practice exactly, and the search for a different *Vorlage* of Kings is quite unnecessary.

In making use of his principle, Auld places great weight on the fact that the description of the palace in 1 Kgs 7.1-12 is missing in Chronicles and that it also has the appearance of being a later addition (along with 6.37-38) to the text of Kings. Now it may be freely acknowledged that the text of 1 Kings 6–7 has received a number of additions, and in my view these are all post-Dtr. But some additions to Kings, regarded by many as the latest, are used by Chronicles, and it will therefore be argued in my synoptic analysis that Chronicles is using the latest version of Kings, which is substantially the text reflected in MT. Consequently, the question of whether the palace text is a later addition to the earliest text of Kings is not entirely relevant. Furthermore, Chr knows of Solomon's palace building and the length of time needed to build it (2 Chron. 8.1), and he refers to the palace and its furnishings in 2 Chron. 9.13-20, which parallels 1 Kgs 10.14-21. In my view it is doubtful that the latter text could exist without the prior description of the palace's construction.[13]

The major question then becomes, 'Why does Chr omit mention of the palace here when he repeats later statements about the palace in another place?' The reason for the omission of the palace building seems entirely ideological. First, the palace had nothing to do with the continuity theme in Chronicles. It did not exist in his day, and its description in this place was a distraction within his treatment of the temple as the center of the Second Temple community. Second, the description of the temple in Kings suggests that the palace was closely connected with the temple, within the great court that encompassed the inner temple court. This was not part of Chr's temple ideal, in which his system of courts is quite different, being influenced by the description of the tabernacle (see below). Ezekiel's temple does not have a

12. J. Van Seters, *In Search of History: Historiography in the Ancient World and the Origins of Biblical History* (New Haven, CT: Yale University Press, 1983), p. 62.

13. Contra Auld, *Kings without Privilege*, pp. 26-27.

palace attached to it either—and for similar ideological reasons—but he does interrupt his description of the temple in Ezek. 41.12-15a by a few remarks about a building on the west side of the temple, in a way similar to the inclusion of the palace in the Kings account.

Chr's omission of the oracle in 1 Kgs 6.11-13 is best explained as a matter of economy and abridgment. It interrupts the focus on the temple construction and adds nothing new to the larger account. The theme is dealt with in a similar way in 1 Kgs 9.4-5, which Chr does repeat in 2 Chron. 7.17-18 so that little is lost by its omission. The remark about the fact that no metal instrument was used in the temple area, in 1 Kgs 6.7, was probably omitted for the simple reason that it contradicted the frequent reference to metalwork in the temple construction, including Chr's specific remark about the use of golden nails (2 Chron. 3.7). To suggest that nails could be used without a hammer would be ridiculous.

Chr also ignores the details about the windows or side chambers of 1 Kgs 6.4-6, 8-10. This cannot be because they are not a part of his *Vorlage*, or that they were unknown in the Second Temple. He seems to be aware of these and other structures associated with the temple, because he mentions them elsewhere in his account.[14] It is clear from Ezek. 41.5-11 that the description of the side chambers was a part of the version of Kings used by this author.[15] It is hard to imagine a scenario in which Chr used a version of Kings that is older and shorter than that used by the author of Ezekiel 40–42. The reasons for his abridgment of the description, therefore, must be something other than a lack of these details in his version of Kings.

Consequently, I see no reason to depart from the well-established position that the *Vorlage* of Kings used by Chr is substantially the text reflected in MT.

The Temple Edifice

Chr's introduction to the building activity in 2 Chron. 3.1 immediately departs from that of Kings. The statement in 1 Kgs 6.1a: 'In the four hundred eightieth year of the Israelites' exodus from the land of Egypt',

---

14. See 1 Chron. 28.11-12, where he suggests a temple plan that is much more elaborate than the one described in 2 Chron. 3.

15. See W. Zimmerli, *Ezekiel 2* (Hermeneia; Philadelphia: FortressPress, 1983), pp. 374-81.

gives the event of temple-construction a *temporal* location within the larger historical continuity of Israel's existence. It is clearly one literary strategy that the author uses to set off the founding of the temple with a special importance. It is a date within an era marked by the founding event of the nation and suggests that a new era with the founding of the temple has now begun.

Chr, by contrast, gives to the temple a *spatial* location that makes its legitimation in Jerusalem at precisely this spot completely secure. It is the place 'where Yahweh had appeared to David his father, at the place that David had appointed, on the threshing floor of Ornan the Jebusite'. This relates back to the episode in 1 Chronicles 21, which reports David's purchase of the site from Ornan—but more particularly, his building of an altar there that was divinely approved (vv. 18-30) and his instruction: 'Here is to be the house of Yahweh God and here the altar for burnt offering for Israel.'[16] The further identification of this site with Mount Moriah and Abraham's sacrifice there, together with God's appearance and promise to the patriarch (Gen. 22.1-19), gives to the place both a spatial and a temporal continuity even greater than that of the exodus of 1 Kgs 6.1. Chr's treatment reflects a major concern with the legitimation of place, perhaps in the face of rival claims, a concern that is much more specific than reference to the historical continuity of 1 Kgs 6.1, or even than Dtr's theme of the divine choice of Jerusalem in the Kings account.[17]

The dating formula in 2 Chron. 3.2 is an abbreviated version and late reformulation of the one in 1 Kgs 6.1aβ. The latter is often regarded as itself a later version of the one in 6.37, but there are good reasons to believe that all such dates in 1 Kgs 6.1, 37-38 are secondary additions to the original Dtr account. The closest parallels in form and language are those found in Phoenician and Punic texts of the Persian and Hellenistic periods.[18] Chr, therefore, uses the latest version of Kings,

---

16. There is no such connection made in 2 Sam. 24, nor do I think that it is intended. Cf. K. Rupprecht, *Der Tempel von Jerusalem: Gründung Salomos oder jebusitisches Erbe?* (BZAW, 144; Berlin: de Gruyter, 1977), pp. 5-17.

17. See Japhet, *I & II Chronicles*, pp. 550-52.

18. See V. Hurowitz, *I Have Built You an Exalted House: Temple Building in the Bible in the Light of Mesopotamian and Northwest Semitic Writings* (JSOTSup, 115; Sheffield: JSOT Press, 1992), pp. 227-33. See also my article, 'Solomon's Temple: Fact and Ideology in Biblical and Near Eastern Historiography', *CBQ*, forthcoming.

not the Dtr original, because DtrH did not yet include any dates in its version of the account.

The measurements for the main part of the temple, as given in 2 Chron. 3.3-4, are confusing and defective. For the 'house' the two ground dimensions of 60 × 20 cubits are given but not the height of 30 cubits, as in 1 Kgs 6.2. The dimensions of the vestibule 'across the width of the house' are given as 20 cubits (as in 1 Kgs 6.3), but the depth is omitted. The height, however, is given as 120 cubits, which many scholars take as a corruption. Nowhere is any other height for the rest of the temple given. This means that Chr does not even supply the basic measurements for the temple. Consequently, it is not his intention to present a reconstruction of the Solomonic temple, as in Kings, because he lives in the time of the second temple. He does not need all the details as guides for a future temple. He only needs enough to establish a sense of continuity.

Chr omits all the material in 1 Kgs 6.4-14, including the side chambers around the temple (as discussed above). Since, as we shall see below, he is concerned with those parts of the temple that correspond most directly with the tabernacle of Moses, he omits a description of any other part of the temple that does not suit his purpose.[19] This brings him, in 1 Kgs 6.15, to the internal panelling with wood, which in Kings is cedar but in 2 Chron. 3.5-6 is cypress, covered with gold and carvings of palms and chains, and adorned with precious stones. This treatment in Chronicles conflates elements in 1 Kgs 6.15, 18, 21-22 and 29 in a much abridged and confusing form.[20] The omission of 1 Kgs 6.4-14 means that the decoration of the interior of the nave follows directly the measurements of the vestibule. This leads Chr to add a covering of gold also to the vestibule (v. 4), about which nothing is said in Kings.

Chr's treatment of the construction of the 'most holy place' in 3.8-9 is quite different from that of 1 Kgs 6.16-17, 19-20. Kings makes it quite clear that the דביר ('inner sanctuary')[21] is a structure built within

---

19. The other chambers are mentioned in the 'plan' in 1 Chron. 28.11-12.

20. It is very likely that 1 Kgs 6.21-22 represents a late addition to the original Dtr account in order to add more gold gilding to the temple interior. See E. Würthwein, *Die Bücher der Könige. 1 Könige 1–16* (ATD, 11/1; Göttingen: Vandenhoek & Ruprecht, 2nd edn, 1985), p. 61, n. 12. This is a tendency also followed by Chr.

21. The explanatory gloss, 'for the most holy place', is a later addition.

the nave, 20 × 20 cubits, so that the nave itself is 40 cubits long. The height of the דביר is also given as 20 cubits, and extensive remarks about its construction are included. Chr describes the construction of the 'most holy place'[22] similarly to the vestibule (cf. v. 4 and 1 Kgs 6.3) giving only the two dimensions of length and width, 20 × 20 cubits. But this creates the impression that the sanctuary is an extension to the nave ('house') in the same way as the vestibule. It only becomes clear from Kings that the measurements of the most holy place are to be included in the 60 cubits of the length of the 'house of God' (3.3).

Chr further states that the most holy place was overlaid with gold (v. 8b; cf. 1 Kgs 6.20) and elaborates on the amount of gold (600 talents!) and the gold nails used to fasten it. This must presuppose Kings' detailed description of the wooden construction of the דביר.[23] Chr's treatment of the inner sanctuary clearly demonstrates his technique of abridging his source with his own ideological elaboration. This cannot go back to a different early *Vorlage*.[24]

Chr mentions (v. 9) the gilding of the 'upper chambers' with gold. Nothing is said about this structure in Kings, but it is mentioned in 1 Chron. 28.11 as part of the temple plan given to Solomon by David. Busink has suggested that the reference to such a structure is an anachronism that relates to the Second Temple and may be as late as the time of the high priest Simon (ca. 200 BCE), who was known for his renovations and beautification of the temple.[25] This addition of an upper story may be why Chr avoids any reference to the height of the temple itself.

Up to this point Chr has followed his *Vorlage* of Kings as his primary source. Even so, he has been influenced by the account of the tabernacle construction in certain ways. From the construction of the most holy place to the temple furnishings and the courts in 3.8–4.10, there is a series of twelve tasks all set out with the verb ויעש. This is

22. Chr clearly prefers the Priestly term, קדש הקדשים and uses דביר only in direct quotes of his Kings source (4.20; 5.7, 9, 11).

23. Japhet (*I & II Chronicles*, p. 555) suggests that the description of the large quantity of gold applies to the whole temple and was misplaced from v. 7. That is possible but highly speculative. The result would be an elaborate treatment of the nave ('house') while the most holy place would receive no more attention than the vestibule (v. 3).

24. *Contra* McKenzie and Auld.

25. See Busink, *Der Temple von Jerusalem*, II, p. 825.

also the case with Moses' construction of the tabernacle in Exodus 36-40.[26] Both accounts are structured in the same way. Furthermore, similarities can also be seen in such details as the extensive use of gold (3.7-8; cf. Exod. 26.29; 36.34) and in the use of golden nails (3.9), whose only function seems to be as a counterpart to the gold hooks of the tabernacle (Exod. 26.32, 37; 36.36).[27]

The Furnishings of the Temple

Chr takes up in 3.10-13 the description of the cherubim in 1 Kgs 6.23-28, omitting the remarks in 1 Kgs 6.20b, 22b about the altar of cedar and the inner altar of gold.[28] Thus the cherubim follow directly the remarks about the most holy place in which they are placed. The description of the cherubim is given with some rewriting and abridgment, omitting any mention of their height, which is given in Kings. There is only the curious addition in v. 13b, 'They stood upon their feet, their faces towards the nave ("house").' Japhet notes that this is probably intended to distinguish these two cherubim from those on the ark, as described by the Priestly writer in Exod. 25.18-20 in which they face each other and are mounted on the covering of the ark and are not free-standing.[29] It is not clear, however, how Chr intended to accommodate the Priestly ark and the 'mercy seat' with its cherubim to the free-standing cherubim of Kings. In the placement of the ark in the temple, Chr simply follows Kings verbatim (2 Chron. 5.7-9; 1 Kgs 8.6-8).

The reference to the veil in 2 Chron. 3.14, as the means of separation between the inner sanctuary and the nave, is a direct contradiction of 1 Kgs 6.31-32, which refers to wooden doors. This is clearly an anachronism from the Second Temple, which had such a veil.[30] The description, however, is derived, with slight modification, from Exod. 26.31; 36.35.[31] Yet there is a problem with the mention of the veil in that Chr

26. See Mosis, *Untersuchungen*, p. 140.

27. Mosis, *Untersuchungen*, pp. 142-43.

28. Chr does refer to the golden altar in 4.19 in the summary taken over from 1 Kgs 7.48-50. Since the latter text and that in 6.21-22 may be later additions, it is not clear whether more than one altar is intended in Kings.

29. Japhet, *I & II Chronicles*, p. 556.

30. On the veil in the second temple, see Busink, *Der Tempel*, II, pp. 819-21.

31. So also Mosis, *Untersuchungen*, pp. 143-44; Japhet, *I & II Chronicles*, pp. 556-57, and other commentaries.

does not say where or how the veil is to be hung. So this must be understood from the tabernacle description.

The veil was included in Chr's treatment of Solomon's temple, because it established an important continuity between the tabernacle of Moses and Solomon's temple. The veil was symbolic of the tabernacle as a whole and of the most holy place in particular. With it was associated the most solemn activity of the high priest on the Day of Atonement (Lev. 16). This continuity theme also extended to the Second Temple and its cultus in a way that was not possible for the description of the temple in Kings. The modification of the Second Temple architecture, not yet evident in Ezekiel's temple (cf. Ezek. 41.3-4), reflects this accommodation to the Priestly Code.

At this point in his description Chr omits a large body of material covered by Kings (1 Kgs 6.31–7.14). First, he omits the description of the doors (6.31-35), both those to the inner sanctuary, because they would conflict with his inclusion of the veil, and also the doors to the nave. Temple doors are one feature that does receive some special notice in royal inscriptions. The treatment of the courts in 1 Kgs 6.36 and 7.9-12 Chr reserves for another place (2 Chron. 4.9). As indicated above, the dating in 1 Kgs 6.37-38 and the description of the palace in 7.1-9 are also omitted. The palace has no place in the continuity theme of the temple. It corresponds to nothing in the tabernacle narrative of Exodus nor to the Second Temple. It had to be left out here.

At this point in the Kings narrative the author shifts from the construction of the buildings[32] to the furnishing of the temple. For this purpose he introduces Hiram of Tyre, a skillful metal-worker in bronze, who proceeds to make several objects of bronze (1 Kgs 7.13-47). This figure undoubtedly inspired the Priestly writer's creation of the figures of Bezalel and Oholi-ab, who not only excelled in metalwork but in other crafts as well and were in charge of the complete construction of the tabernacle.[33] Chr combines Bezalel and Oholi-ab with Hiram (in the person of Huram-abi/Huram), who then is given all the construction skills and set over the whole project before it begins (2 Chron. 2.13-14).[34] However, unlike the tabernacle account (Exod. 36–39) where

---

32. In the oldest version, perhaps after the temple itself in 1 Kgs 6.36.

33. M. Noth (*Könige* [BKAT, 9/1; Neukirchen–Vluyn: Neukirchener Verlag, 1968], p. 148) suggests that 1 Kgs 7.13-14 was influenced by P, but the reverse seems to me much more likely.

34. See esp. the discussion of Mosis, *Untersuchungen*, pp. 136-38. Mosis sees

Bezalel is consistently the subject of the verb עשׂה ('he made'), and Kings where Hiram is the artisan of all the furnishings in 7.15-47, in Chronicles the conflation of sources has led to some confusion about who is the subject of the verbs of construction, Huram or Solomon.

Chr greatly abridges the description of the two pillars in front of the temple (3.15-17; cf. 1 Kgs 7.15-22). He also makes two significant changes. First, the pillars are no longer bronze, the product of a special metalworker. Chr is completely non-committal about the material used. Second, he almost doubles the height of the shaft, from 18 cubits to 35 cubits. If one accepts the figure of 120 cubits for the height of the vestibule in v. 4 as original to Chr's work, then it may explain the concern to increase the size of the pillars in front of it.[35] The pillars, however, were not a feature of the Second Temple or the tabernacle and were not of primary concern to him.

Chr next makes reference to a bronze altar 20 cubits square and 20 cubits high. This object is not mentioned in the descriptions of the furnishings in Kings, but a number of scholars have conjectured that a similar statement stood in Kings and was lost by *homoioarkton* of the verb עשׂה ('he made') for both the altar and the sea. The style of using three dimensions, with height expressed using קומה, is similar to that used in Kings elsewhere, and a bronze altar is explicitly mentioned in 1 Kgs 8.64 and 2 Kgs 16.14.[36]

This conclusion does not seem to me to be very convincing for a number of reasons. First, such a huge altar could not possibly have been made of bronze. It is an idealization and not an object that would have been known to the author of Kings. Much more is required of the description to make it intelligible. One would expect the description to be much longer, as is the case with Ezekiel's altar (Ezek. 43.13-17). Second, when Kings does refer to a bronze altar, it clearly has in mind a much smaller object for the king's personal use which could be moved. According to 2 Kgs 16.10-16, there was both a small bronze altar and a great altar whose exact size and building material is not

the modification of the name Hiram to Huram-abi as influenced by the name Oholi-ab.

35. Various ways have been suggested as to how Chr arrived at the figure of 35 (e.g. by the addition of length [18 cubits], circumference [12 cubits], and capital [5 cubits]). See Japhet, *I & II Chronicles*, p. 557.

36. See W. Rudolph, *Chronikbücher* (HAT, 21; Tübingen: Mohr, 1955), p. 207; followed by Williamson, *1 & 2 Chronicles*, p.210; Japhet, *I & II Chronicles*, p. 564.

specified. Kings knew the great altar as an innovation of Ahaz and therefore not part of Solomon's temple. It seems quite unlikely, therefore, that Chr derived this description of the altar from Kings.

The origin of the particular *form* of the altar description is not difficult to find.[37] In 2 Chron. 6.12 Chr follows Kings (1 Kgs 8.22) in referring to Solomon standing 'before the altar of Yahweh in the presence of all the assembly of Israel' to begin his prayer. But then Chr inserts a parenthetical remark, not found in Kings, in v. 13a, that is surely his own. He states: 'Solomon had made a bronze platform (כִּיּוֹר) five cubits long, five cubits wide, and three cubits high (קוֹמָתוֹ), and had it set in the court; and he stood on it.' This bronze platform, which is not previously mentioned and is a rather awkward addition to what has been taken over from Kings,[38] has the same form and pattern of dimensions as that of the altar construction in 4.1. What is the source for the description of this piece of furniture if it is not from Kings? The dimensions are a clear indication: it is derived from the description of the altar in the Priestly tabernacle construction in Exod. 38.1-2 (cf. 27.1-2): 'He made the altar of acacia wood, five cubits long, five cubits wide...and three cubits high (קוֹמָתוֹ)...and he overlaid it with bronze.' It is this text that became the basis, in abbreviated form, first for the bronze platform in 2 Chron. 8.13, and then for the large bronze altar in 4.1.[39]

The question still remains as to the origins of the dimensions for the large altar. Busink has suggested that the inspiration for this altar is the altar of the Second Temple, which in a source of the Hellenistic period (as reported by Josephus) was just this size but was made of unhewn stones.[40] Chr, under the influence of all the references to bronze altars, made the great altar of bronze in spite of its size. Even though his bronze altar is ten meters square, he still repeats the statement of Kings

---

37. See also Mosis, *Untersuchungen*, pp. 145-46.

38. That is especially clear from the repetition in v. 13b of v. 12, but with the change that Solomon now *kneels* in the presence of the assembly. The point of his standing upon the platform is thereby made superfluous.

39. The tabernacle account also knows of a bronze laver (כִּיּוֹר) for washing, which was closely associated with the bronze altar. Does this suggest the conflation of כִּיּוֹר in the sense of 'platform' with the bronze altar? Chr has a quite different altar and quite different lavers for washing in his Solomonic temple.

40. See Busink, *Der Tempel*, II, pp. 830-31. The reference in Josephus is *Apion* 1.22.198.

that the bronze altar that Solomon had made could not hold all the burnt offerings and other sacrifices (7.7; 1 Kgs 8.64).

The great bronze altar is clearly intended to establish continuity of cultic practice between the bronze altar before the tabernacle of the wilderness period and Solomon's temple. Just as Solomon offers sacrifices on Bezalel's altar in front of the tent of meeting at Gibeon before the altar was built (2 Chron. 1.5-6)—and the priests of David before him (1 Chron. 16.39-40; 21.29)—so Solomon does the same with the great bronze altar before the temple. There is also continuity with the Second Temple altar and all the cultic activity associated with it.[41]

Chr takes up the Kings' description of the 'molten sea' in a slightly modified form (4.2-5; 1 Kgs 7.23-26).[42] He then omits the mention of the ten stands in 1 Kgs 7.27-37, but he does include the reference to ten lavers (4.6), which in the Kings version were placed on the stands (1 Kgs 7.38-39a). Kings also gives the size, the fact that they were made of bronze and were distributed, five to the right (south side) of the temple (or nave) and five to the left (north side). Chr says nothing about their size or material and merely places them five on the right and five on the left; but he does not mention the temple. The omission of the stands from the description is curious, because they are mentioned in the summary in 2 Chron. 4.14.

While Chr greatly compresses the description of the lavers, he adds a remark about their function, which is not found in Kings. He states that the lavers are 'for washing in them, (and) what is used for burnt sacrifices they rinse in them. The sea was also for the priests to wash in it' (4.6). How are we to account for the inclusion of this ritual use of the lavers and the sea by Chr, while he at the same time omits the stands that seem necessary to the lavers on which they sit? The answer is in the description of the tabernacle. Exod. 30.17-21 speaks about a bronze laver on a bronze stand to be used for washing by the priests and placed between the altar and the tabernacle.[43] The frequent references to this laver always suggest a close association with the altar.[44] Chr has

41. It is not clear, however, what connection David's altar has with Solomon's (1 Chron. 21.26; 22.1; 2 Chron. 3.1), only that it identified the location of the temple as a whole.

42. See Japhet, *I & II Chronicles*, pp. 564-65.

43. The brief account of setting up the altar and the basin in Exod. 40.29-32 does not mention the stand, only the basin.

44. See also Exod. 30.28; 31.9; 35.16; 38.8; 39.39; 40.7, 10-11, 29-32; Lev. 8.11.

interpreted the sea and the lavers, which follow his statement about the altar, as both fulfilling the function of the basin for washing in the Mosaic law.

The original purpose for the sea during the history of its use was almost certainly not for washing. Its size and character suggest something quite different.[45] The lavers, whatever their exact use in the first temple, were very likely within the nave as the Kings text suggests. But this contravenes Mosaic law in which the washing must precede entrance into the tabernacle. Chr leaves the location of the lavers very vague for this reason. What is essential for him is to establish continuity between elements of the Solomonic temple and the Mosaic tabernacle.

Chr, in 4.7-9, departs from Kings by adding an account of the construction of ten golden lampstands (מנרות) 'as prescribed' and ten tables, and these are placed 'in the temple' (בהיכל), five on the right/ south and five on the left/north.[46] Chr also mentions the manufacture of a hundred bowls of gold. None of these are mentioned in Kings, and they do not fit the list of bronze objects made by Hiram. Chr then shifts to the construction of the court of the priests and the great court and their doors. As with Kings, one would have expected this detail much earlier in conjunction with the construction of the temple building, not the furnishings (cf. 1 Kgs 6.36; 7.12). Chr then reverts to the location of the sea (4.10), also mentioned in 1 Kgs 7.39b, which shows that this addition of 4.7-9 has been spliced into the temple description.

As we have seen previously in the case of so many other of Chr's additions, the above items are included here because he has drawn them from the tabernacle description. The making of the golden menorah and the table for the bread of the Presence are treated in Exod. 25.23-40 and 37.10-24, albeit in reverse order. The hundred 'bowls' may be a summary way of speaking of the list of dishes made for the table of the bread of the Presence (Exod. 25.29; 37.16). The change of the number of lampstands to ten is based on the summary statement in

45. See R. de Vaux, *Ancient Israel: Its Life and Institutions* (New York: McGraw-Hill, 1961), pp. 328-29. See also the informative remark by W. Burkert in his *Greek Religion* (Cambridge, MA: Harvard University Press, 1985), p. 86: 'On the Acropolis in Athens, the most important mark of the cult apart from the olive tree was the "sea", a little pool of salt water in a hollow in the rock…Here it is the symbolism of the deep which is important, rather than any practical use.'

46. The fact that the location 'in the temple' is given twice with both objects makes its omission with the lavers more conspicuous.

1 Kgs 7.48-50, repeated by Chr (4.19-22), but the latter extends the symmetry to the tables for the bread of the Presence, where Kings only has one table. Furthermore, the account in 4.7-9 has been anticipated in 1 Chron. 28.15-19 as part of David's plan that is passed on to Solomon. In this plan there is more than one golden lampstand and table for the bread of the Presence. This plan is what is meant by the remark that these objects were made 'as prescribed', 4.7, 20.[47] Elsewhere in his work, however, Chr seems quite insistent in maintaining the one table[48] and the one menorah,[49] as in the Mosaic tabernacle. His conflation of sources has led to a momentary inconsistency. There may have been a reference to the golden incense altar in Chronicles, as we have it in Exod. 30.1-10; 37.25-28. Not only does in also occur in the summary list of 4.19, but it is mentioned in David's plan of the temple, along with the other items treated here (1 Chron. 28.18).

This brings us to consider the remark about the courts in 2 Chron. 3.10. As noted above, the placement of this notice about the two courts is quite different from Kings, and both the terminology and description of the bronze gilded doors have nothing in common with Kings. Again we must turn to the Priestly tabernacle account for an explanation.[50] Following the making of the furnishings, the Priestly writer then mentions the making of the court enclosure that goes around the temple and separates it as a holy place (Exod. 27.9-19; 38.9-18). This inner court became the court of the priests in the Second Temple period, to which only they had access. This order of furnishings followed by the courts in the Priestly source is taken over by Chr. The Priestly writer says nothing about a 'great court', but Ezekiel (ch. 40) has much to say about both the outer and the inner courts. Yet the terminology used by Ezekiel is closer to that of Kings than Chronicles, and neither Kings nor Ezekiel describes the doors of the court, although Ezekiel gives an elaborate treatment of the gateways of the courts. It is more likely that Chr is reflecting the temple area of his own day.[51]

The whole section in 2 Chron. 4.11–5.1 follows rather closely the

47. See also Mosis, *Untersuchungen*, p. 143. He takes the remark 'as prescribed' to refer to Exod. 25.31ff.; 37.12ff.

48. Cf. 2 Chron. 13.11; 29.18.

49. Cf. 2 Chron. 13.11.

50. See Mosis, *Untersuchungen*, p. 140.

51. Williamson (*1 & 2 Chronicles*, p. 211) suggests some influence from Ezek. 40, but there seems little evidence of that to me.

text of 1 Kgs 7.40-51 with only minor differences. Some have argued that this section in 4.11-22 is a later addition,[52] but that does not seem altogether necessary.[53] The items in the plan of David in 1 Chron. 28.16-17 certainly suggest that 2 Chron. 4.19-22 at least belongs to the original, and if that is admitted, then there is little reason left not to accept 4.11-18 as well. One interesting modification is the *tables* (plural) for the bread of the Presence in 4.19 for the single table in Kings (7.48). This is clearly an adjustment to accommodate the ten tables in 4.8.[54]

For the whole of the building account Chr follows the scheme of the Priestly source, whereby God reveals everything in great detail to Moses and then the construction is actually executed by Bezalel. In a similar fashion David instructs Solomon in the details of the temple construction and its furnishings, which he has received from divine revelation (1 Chron. 28.11-19), concluding with the statement: 'The whole in writing because of the hand of Yahweh upon (him)[55] to accomplish/instruct in all the work of the plan (התבנית).' Since Solomon also has a master craftsman, Huram-abi (= Hiram), who is in charge of the whole building activity, there is a certain amount of ambiguity as to who is executing the divinely inspired plan—Solomon or Huram. When Chr refers to the ten golden menorahs 'as prescribed' in 4.7, he is probably thinking of the plan of David. But when he adds in 4.20, 'to burn before the inner sanctuary, as prescribed', he is thinking of the Mosaic pattern (תבנית) in the tabernacle account (Exod. 25.40; 40.22-25). This is a matter of some importance to him, as is evident in 2 Chron. 13.11.

---

52. See Rudolph, *Chronikbücher*, p. 205.

53. See Japhet, *I & II Chronicles*, pp. 560-63.

54. Williamson (*1 and 2 Chronicles*, p. 211) thinks that 'this is a mistaken assimilation to the tables of v. 8, which served a different purpose.' He suggests that the tables were intended as stands for the menorahs. This seems very unlikely, however, since the lampstands were never set on tables but were themselves 'stands' for lamps. It is true that, as indicated above, Chr mentions only one table of the bread of the Presence, just as he mentions one menorah in 2 Chron. 13.11. But in 1 Chron. 28.16 he indicates that there was more than one table for the shewbread.

55. So LXX; MT has עלי ('upon me'). *BHS* also suggests moving the *athnach* to this word.

Conclusion

The nature of Chr's historiography is deliberately and consciously ideological. Only one of his sources—the book of Kings—purports to describe the Solomonic temple. The information from this source he deliberately modifies to bring it into closer agreement with that of the tabernacle to create a more obvious continuity with the law of Moses in its Priestly form than would otherwise be the case. This is not just an exercise in antiquarian curiosity. It is an attempt to shape a portrait of the past, of a particular period as the constitutional age, that gives legitimation to the Jerusalem temple in a way that was lacking in the older Kings tradition. This is a historiography that is more akin to myth-making than to modern historiography, or even the best of classical historiography.

Such a method cannot be characterized as 'exegesis' or commentary. It is revisionist, reading into the past all the necessary structures and institutions, and ideological legitimation to support the later religious community. The Priestly Code had already laid down the foundation for this religious constitution. What was lacking was the specific continuity from this Mosaic law through the political and religious authority of Jerusalem. The Samaritan community or their predecessors could and did claim that continuity through the sanctuary of Gerizim. Chr's history is the Jerusalem community's attempt to establish the continuity of the Pentateuchal law in final form through Jerusalem.

JOASH OF JUDAH ACCORDING TO JOSEPHUS

Christopher T. Begg

2 Kgs 12.1-22 (EVV 11.21–12.21) tells one story of Joash of Judah: a God-pleasing ruler and temple renovator was eventually compelled to buy off invading Syrians and suffered assassination at the hands of his own 'servants'.[1] 2 Chron. 24.1-27, however, tells a rather different story of Joash, one involving his defection from the Lord and his murder of the son of his own earlier protector.[2] This essay will explore yet a third 'Joash story', that of Josephus in *Ant.* 9.157-172.[3] My investigation involves a comparison of the Josephan account with its biblical 'authorities' as represented by the following major witnesses: MT (*BHS*), Codex Vaticanus (hereafter B),[4] and the Lucianic (hereafter L) or Antiochene MSS[5] of the LXX, plus Targum Jonathan on the Former Prophets (hereafter TJ)[6] and the Chronicles Targum (hereafter

---

1. On 2 Kgs 12, see C. Levin, 'Die Instandsetzung des Tempels unter Joash ben Ahasja', *VT* 40 (1990), pp. 51-88.

2. See M.P. Graham, 'The Composition of 2 Chronicles 24', in E. Ferguson (ed.), *Christian Teaching: Studies in Honor of Lemoine G. Lewis* (Abilene, TX: Abilene Christian University Book Store, 1981), pp. 138-54.

3. For the text and translation of Josephus's writings, I use the edition of H.St.J. Thackeray, R. Marcus, A.P. Wikgren, and L.H. Feldman, *Josephus* (LCL; 10 vols.; Cambridge, MA; London: Harvard University Press: Heinemann, 1926–65).

4. For the text of B, I use the edition of A.E. Brooke, N. Maclean and H.St.J. Thackeray, *The Old Testament in Greek, According to the Text of the Codex Vaticanus*, 2.2 *I and II Kings* (Cambridge: Cambridge University Press, 1930) and 2.3 *I and II Chronicles* (1932).

5. For L 4 Kgdms, I use the text edited by N. Fernández Marcos and J.R. Busto Saiz, *El Texto Antioqueno de la Biblia Griega.* II. *1-2 Reyes* (TECC, 53; Madrid: CSIC, 1992). For L 2 Par, I use the apparatus of the Cambridge edition of Chronicles cited in n. 4.

6. I use the text edited by Alexander Sperber, *The Bible in Aramaic*, II (Leiden: Brill, repr. 1992) and the translation of D.J. Harrington and A.J. Saldarini,

TC).[7] I undertake this comparison with a range of questions in mind. How does Josephus deal with the many divergences between his two biblical sources in their respective treatments of Joash? Which text-form(s) of those sources did he have available in composing our segment of *Jewish Antiquities*? Why, how, and with what effect does he rewrite the biblical data on the king? My study is intended then as a 'prolongation' of the standard redaction-critical approach to Chronicles in which questions analogous to the above are raised concerning Chr in relation to his source, DtrH. Such an extension of redaction-criticism to encompass Josephus's version of biblical history might be thought an obvious move for biblical scholars to make, but in fact it has been undertaken only quite sporadically hitherto.[8]

To facilitate comparison, the material is divided as follows: (1) Joash introduced (*Ant.* 9.157-158[159-160] // 2 Kgs 12.1-4 [MT] // 2 Chron. 24.1-3); (2) temple repair (*Ant.* 9.161-165 // 2 Kgs 12.5-17 // 2 Chron. 24.4-14); (3) Joash's defection (*Ant.* 9.166-169 // 2 Chron. 24.15-22); (4) Syrian incursion (*Ant.* 9.170-171a // 2 Kgs 12.18-19 // 2 Chron. 24.23-24); and (5) closing notices (*Ant.* 9.171b-172 // 2 Kgs 12.20-22 // 2 Chron. 24.25-27).

Joash Introduced

Josephus's sources commence their respective introductions of Joash (2 Kgs 12.1-4 // 2 Chron. 24.1-3) with chronological indications: he accedes at age seven (and in the seventh year of Jehu, 12.2aα) and reigns 40 years (12.1-2a // 24.1a). They proceed to note the name of his mother (Zibiah of Beersheba, 12.2b // 24.1b) and conclude with a summary evaluation, stating that Joash 'did right in the Lord's eyes' due to the influence of the priest Jehoiada (12.3 // 24.2). Thereafter, 2 Kgs 12.4 mentions the continuation of worship on the high places under Joash, while 2 Chron. 24.3 speaks rather of the king's familial

Targum Jonathan of the Former Prophets (The Aramaic Bible, 10; Wilmington, DE: Michael Glazier, 1987).

7.　I use the text of TC edited by R. le Déaut and J. Robert, *Targum des Chroniques*, I (AnBib, 51; Rome: Pontifical Biblical Institute, 1971), and the translation of this by J.S. McIvor, *The Targum of Chronicles* (The Aramaic Bible, 19; Collegeville, MN: Liturgical Press, 1994).

8.　For one such attempt, see my *Josephus' Account of the Early Divided Monarchy (AJ 8,212-420)* (BETL, 108; Leuven: Leuven University Press/Peeters, 1993).

situation (Jehoiada provides him with two wives [see below], and he has sons and daughters).

Josephus's introduction in 9.157-158 first reproduces the data of 12.1-2 // 24.1 on the king's age at accession and the name of his mother and her birthplace. In line with his usual practice, Josephus 'delays' use of the sources' mention of Joash's length of reign until the end of his own account (see on 9.172). As with Chronicles, he has no equivalent to 12.2aα's synchronization (see above). In place of the stereotyped biblical expression about Joash's doing 'right in the Lord's eyes', he affirms that the king 'kept strict observance of the ordinances and was zealous (φιλοτίμιαν) in the worship of God...' In agreement with 2 Chron. 24.2, he qualifies this assessment via the appended phrase 'all the time Jōdas (= Jehoiada) lived' (cf. 12.2, where Joash did right 'all his days because Jehoiada...instructed him' [RSV]). Josephus (9.158) likewise follows Chronicles for its *Sondergut* item (24.3a) about Joash's marriages: 'And *when he came of age*,[9] he married two women whom the high priest had given him.' This notice is of interest for its indication of the text-form of 2 Chronicles 24 that Josephus utilized. MT 24.3a preserves the ambiguous וישׂא־לו יהוידע נשׁים שׁתים, which leaves unclear the referent of the pronoun לו-. Is it Joash or Jehoiada himself? LXX resolves the matter with its rendering, καὶ ἔλαβεν ἑαυτῷ Ἰωδᾶε γυναῖκας δύο. It would seem that in this instance Josephus had before him not the unambiguous reading of LXX, but rather the MT, which he 'clarifies' in his own way.[10] In any case, he does not reproduce the reference in 24.3b to the children begotten by Joash (or Jehoiada). In place thereof he introduces (9.158b) an extensive, provisional closing formula for his preceding account concerning Joash's accession and early reign (*Ant.* 140-158a // 2 Kgs 11.1–12.4 // 2 Chron. 23.1–24.3). It reads: 'This much, then, concerning King Joash and how he escaped the plot of Othlia and succeeded to the throne is all that we have to relate at this point.' Josephus's insertion of this formula has in view the 'interruption' of his Joash story (9.159-160), which immediately follows. The latter sequence represents his 'delayed' conclusion to the

---

9. I italicize elements such as the above that have no parallel in Josephus's sources; his insertion of this reference to Joash's maturation might reflect the fact that Joash was only seven at his accession.

10. The ambiguity of MT 2 Chron. 24.3a continued to generate controversy in Jewish tradition. See L. Ginzberg, *The Legends of the Jews* (Philadelphia: Jewish Publication Society of America, 1939), VI, p. 354, n. 11.

reign of Jehu (// 2 Kgs 10.32-36), last mentioned by him in 9.139 (cf. the closing formula 'such, then, was the state of affairs under Jehu' at the end of this paragraph).[11]

Temple Repair

2 Kgs 12.5-17 and 2 Chron. 24.4-14 both describe Joash's (financial) initiatives for the repair of the temple in considerable detail, though also with numerous divergences. The latter sequence opens (24.4) with a statement concerning the king's intentions: 'After this Joash decided to restore the house of the Lord.' Josephus' temple repair account (9.161-165) commences with an amplification of this Chronistic 'plus': 'As for Joash...he was seized by a strong desire to renovate the temple of God...'

2 Kgs 12.5-6 and 2 Chron. 24.4-5a recount a directive by Joash addressed respectively to 'the priests' and 'the priests and the Levites'. Here too, Josephus aligns himself with Chr's presentation, while also representing the king as using Jehoiada as his intermediary: 'summoning the high priest Jōdas, he commanded him to send the Levites and priests [priests and Levites, 2 Chron. 24.4]...' Subsequently as well, Josephus will highlight Jehoiada's role in the episode. The content of the royal directive differs markedly in the source accounts. In Kings, Joash enjoins the priests to collect, at the temple itself, various categories of monies[12] and to repair the edifice. In Chronicles, on the contrary, the priests and Levites are dispatched to 'the cities of Judah' to gather funds (2 Par, ἀργύρου) for temple repairs and are further instructed to 'hasten the matter'. Josephus agrees with Chr in reporting a 'mission' by the two groups of cultic officials 'throughout the entire country'. In his wording of the charge given the delegation, however, he incorporates language 'anticipated' from Joash's rebuke of Jehoiada in 24.6-7 (see below). Specifically, in Josephus's narration, those sent

---

11. On *Ant.* 9.159-60 in relation to 2 Kgs 10.32-36, see C.T. Begg, 'Josephus's Version of Jehu's Putsch (2 Kgs 8,25-10,36)', *Antonianum* 68 (1993), pp. 478-82. By reversing the sequence of 2 Kgs 10.32-36 (// *Ant.* 9.159-160, Jehu's later reign and death) and 11.1–12.1 (// *Ant.* 9.140-158, the accession of Joash in Jehu's seventh year; see 12.2), Josephus presents events in their proper chronological order, whereas the biblical account 'gets ahead of itself'.

12. On the terminology used for these, see L.S. Wright, '*mkr* in 2 Kings xii 5-17 and Deuteronomy xviii 8', *VT* 39 (1989), pp. 438-48.

out are told 'to ask *half a shekel* of silver [ἀργύρου] *for each person*[13] for the repairing and the renovation of the temple (cf. 24.4, which reads: 'money to repair the house of your God'), which had been left crumbling by *Joram* and Othlia and her sons'.[14]

Both biblical sources note the disregard of Joash's instructions on the part of their respective addressees. 2 Chron. 24.5bβ states, 'But *the Levites* did not hasten it', while 2 Kgs 12.6 records, 'But by the twenty-third year of King Joash *the priests* had made no repairs on the house.' Josephus, who earlier made Jehoiada the (direct) recipient of the royal injunction, likewise represents him as the one who ignores it, just as he also supplies a reason for his doing so: 'The high priest, however, did not do this, *realizing that no one would be well affected enough to offer the money...*' To this notice, in turn, he appends the dating indication peculiar to 2 Kgs 12.6 (see above). In 9.162 that date is associated with the confrontation between Joash and his heedless officials (see 2 Kgs 12.7-8 // 2 Chron. 24.6-7) as follows: 'when in the twenty-third year of his reign the king summoned...' According to 2 Kgs 12.7, those called to account by Joash are 'Jehoiada and the [other] priests', while 2 Chron. 24.6 has the king confront Jehoiada alone regarding the priest's failure to compel the Levites to collect the Mosaic tax (see above). Joash's summons in Josephus are extended to Jehoiada and the Levites. In both Kings and Chronicles Joash's confrontation of the hearers opens with the question of 'why' they have not done as directed. Josephus turns the question into an accusatory statement: 'after

---

13. This specification is inspired by 24.6, where Joash asks why the 'tax levied by Moses...for the tent of testimony' has not been collected by the Levites. The 'tax' in question is the one prescribed in Exod. 30.11-16 (cf. *Ant.* 3.194-196), i.e., 'half a shekel...for the service of the tent of meeting'.

14. This concluding reference to the damage done to the temple by Joash's predecessors represents an anticipation and adaptation of the king's later word to Jehoiada in 2 Chron. 24.7 ('For the sons of Athaliah, that wicked woman, had broken into the house of God; and had also used all the dedicated things of the house of the Lord for the Baals'). In his rewording of this statement Josephus has Joash acuse not only Athaliah's sons, but also the queen herself and her husband Joram of abusing the temple. Conversely, he leaves aside the more specific charge of 24.7b that the temple goods were used in Baal worship. This 'omission' is in line with Josephus's general tendency to pass over biblical references to 'cultic particulars' that a Gentile audience would not have found interesting. See Begg, *Josephus' Account*, p. 127.

charging them with having disobeyed his orders...'[15] He couples this
accusation with a renewed directive ('[he] commanded them in future
to look after the repair of the temple...'), somewhat reminiscent of
Joash's word to the priests in 12.8bβ ('hand it [the money they are no
longer to collect, 8bα] over for the repair of the house'). He has no
equivalent to the notice of 12.9 about the priests' 'agreeing' neither to
collect money nor to 'repair the house', the latter part of which would
conflict with the injunction just issued by Joash in his own account,[16]
but proceeds instead immediately to his version of the biblical notices
on the 'collection chest'. In 2 Kgs 12.10 it is Jehoiada, acting on his
own initiative, who takes measures regarding this chest, whereas in
2 Chron. 24.8 an unspecified 'they' do so at the command of the king.
In accord with his highlighting the role of Jehoiada in our episode,
Josephus follows Kings' presentation on the point. At the same time,
however, he introduces the priest's initiative with an elaborate
transitional phrase that itself picks up on, while also reversing, his
earlier mention of Jehoiada's awareness of the people's unwillingness
to contribute to the temple's repair (see 9.162). This inserted formulation runs: 'the high priest employed the following device for collecting
the money, which the people willingly accepted...' Thereafter (9.163),
he enumerates, with various minor embellishments, Jehoiada's measures regarding the chest cited in 12.10a: 'he made a *wooden* chest and,
having closed it on all sides, made a *single* opening in it. Then he
placed it in the temple[17] beside the altar [παρὰ τὸν βωμόν]...'[18] In
what follows, Josephus seems to rejoin Chr's account (24.9), where
'proclamation is made' to Judah and Jerusalem to bring the Mosaic tax
(cf. 24.6 and 2 Kgs 12.10b, 'and the priests who guarded the threshold
put in it [the chest] all the money that was brought into the house of
the Lord'). He does, however, specify the subject/source of the

15. Here, as so frequently elsewhere in *Antiquities*, Josephus recasts biblical
direct as indirect discourse. On the feature, see Begg, *Josephus' Account*, pp. 12-
13, n. 38.
16. Recall in this connection that Josephus has already 'anticipated' (elements
of) Joash's address to Jehoiada of 2 Chron. 24.6-7 in his version of the king's
opening directive to the high priest in 9.161.
17. Cf. the more complicated localizations cited in 2 Kgs 12.10 ('on the right
side as one enters the house of the Lord') and 2 Chron. 24.8 ('outside the gate of
the house of the Lord').
18. Cf. L 4 Kgdms 12.10, παρὰ τὸ θυσιαστήριον (B, παρὰ ἰαμειβείν).

'proclamation' as Jehoiada himself: 'Then he...told everyone to throw into it, through the opening, as much as he wished, for the repair of the temple.' In this presentation, Jehoiada's initiative as cited in Kings (12.10) is further accentuated. On the other hand, in contrast to Kings but in the line of Chronicles, Josephus represents ordinary temple visitors depositing their offerings directly in the chest rather than having the priests do this for them.

Josephus rounds off his mention of Jehoiada's 'command'[19] with a notice on its effect, inspired by 2 Chron. 24.10: 'To this request all the people (πᾶς ὁ λαός = 2 Par) were well disposed[20] (contrast 9.161, where Jehoiada realizes that no one would be well affected enough to offer the money), *and they collected much silver and gold, vying with one another in bringing it in.*'

2 Kgs 12.11 // 2 Chron. 24.11 describe, with divergent details, what was done with the contents of the collection chest. Josephus's parallel reads like an expanded conflation of elements from both source presentations:

> Then, when the scribe[21] and priest of the treasury [ὁ ἱερεὺς τῶν γαζοφυλακείων][22] had emptied the chest [κενοῦντες...τὸν θησαυρόν][23] *and in the presence of the king*[24] had counted [ἀριθμοῦντες;

---

19. Josephus uses the same verbal form (ἐκέλευσεν) for Joash's 'commanding' Jehoiada to dispatch the priests and Levites to collect the temple tax (9.161) and for the latter's 'commanding' the people to deposit their offerings in the chest (9.163). The usage accentuates the priest's stature.

20. Cf. 2 Chron. 24.10, 'all the princes and all the people rejoiced' (so MT L; B, 'gave').

21. 2 Kgs 12.11//2 Chron. 24.11 specify the 'scribe *of the king*'. By beginning immediately with mention of this official, Josephus leaves aside the respective transitional phrases of Kings ('and whenever they saw that there was much money in the chest...') and Chronicles ('and whenever the chest was brought to the king's officers by the Levites, when they saw there was much money in it...').

22. Josephus's designation for this second official reflects the title used in 2 Chron. 24.11, i.e., 'the officer of the chief priest' (LXX, ὁ προστάτης τοῦ ἱερέως τοῦ μεγάλου), as opposed to 2 Kgs 12.11 ('the high priest' [LXX, ὁ ἱερεὺς ὁ μέγας]), i.e., Jehoiada himself.

23. Cf. 2 Par 24.11, καὶ ἐξεκένωσεν τὸ γλωσσόκομον. 2 Kgs 12.11 does not mention an 'emptying' of the chest as such.

24. This reference to Joash's involvement in the disposition of the funds collected has no counterpart in either source but does underscore the king's continued concern with the temple repair project.

4 Kgdms ἠρίθμησαν] the sum that had been collected,[25] they put the chest back in the same place. And this they would do every day.[26]

The biblical accounts (12.12-13a // 24.12) continue with mention of a two-stage process of distribution of the collected funds to those working on the repair of the temple. In 2 Kgs 12.12 those initiating the process would appear to be the two officials cited in 12.11, whereas 2 Chron. 24.12 specifies that it was rather 'the king and Jehoiada [+ the priest, LXX]'. Josephus follows Chronicles on the point, incorporating its reference into a transitional phrase of his own composition: '*When the people had put in what seemed a sufficient amount of money,*[27] *the high priest* Jōdas *and King* Joas[28] *sent...*' In both 2 Kgs 12.12 and 2 Chron. 24.12, those initiating the distribution of the money to the temple workers act through 'middlemen' ('those who had charge of the work of the house of the Lord', Chronicles), to whom they confide the sums to be used in hiring various categories of artisans. Josephus dispenses with the biblical intermediaries and reports that the high priest and king themselves 'hired [μισθούμενοι; 2 Par, ἐμισθοῦντο] stonecutters [λατόμους, so 2 Par] and carpenters [οἰκοδόμους, so 4 Kgdms]'.[29] Following their respective shared notices on the hiring of temple workers, Kings and Chronicles diverge once again. 2 Kgs 12.13b speaks of additional uses of the collected monies: 'to buy timber and quarried

25. For this mention of the officials 'counting' the money, Josephus draws on Kings after following Chronicles for its *Sondergut* item concerning the 'emptying' of the chest. On the other hand, he leaves aside Kings' further reference, peculiar to itself, about the officials 'tying up the money'.

26. These last two items of Josephus's notice are drawn from the *Sondergut* conclusion of 2 Chron. 24.11. He does, however, omit the closing words of that verse: '(the two officials) collected money in abundance'. Cf. his anticipation of this in 9.163, i.e., (the people) 'collected much silver and gold'.

27. This phrase might be seen as Josephus's 'delayed' equivalent to the expression 'whenever they saw that there was much money in the chest' at the opening of 2 Kgs 12.11, which he passed over earlier.

28. Note Josephus's reversal here of the sequence in which 2 Chron. 24.12 mentions the two figures. Note too that he adds the name 'Joas' to Chronicles' title 'the king'. His designation of 'Jōdas' as 'the high priest' corresponds to the LXX plus ('the priest') in 24.12 (see above).

29. Josephus speaks of only two categories of artisans, while 2 Kgs 12.12b-13a mentions four (RSV 'carpenters and builders...masons and stone-cutters') and 2 Chron. 24.12 three (or four: 'masons and carpenters...and workers in iron and bronze...').

stone for making repairs on the house of the Lord, and for any outlay upon the repairs of the house'. 2 Chron. 24.13, on the contrary, proceeds immediately to describe the workers' efforts and their results: 'So those who were engaged in the work labored, and the repairing went forward in their hands, and they restored the house of God to its proper condition and strengthened it.' Josephus, for his part, follows Kings, even while condensing markedly: '[Jehoiada and Joas, see above]... ordered *great* timbers [ξύλα, so 4 Kgdms] *of the finest wood.*'[30]

At this juncture Josephus's sources evince an apparent 'contradiction': 2 Kgs 12.14 states that no money was used to make vessels of any sort for the temple; rather all money collected was distributed to the workmen (12.15), no accounting being asked of the supervisors because of their honesty (12.16). By contrast, 2 Chron. 24.14a affirms that, once the temple repairs were complete, the money left over was utilized in fabricating liturgical vessels. Faced with this discrepancy, Josephus (9.164) opts to follow Chronicles.[31] His version of 24.14 reads: 'And, when the temple had been repaired,[32] they spent the money[33] that was left over—*it was no small amount*—for bowls [κρατῆρας] and pitchers [οἰνοχόας] and cups [ἐκπώματα] and other vessels [σκεύη]...'[34]

Kings and Chronicles go their own ways also in their respective conclusions to the temple repair episode. 2 Kgs 12.17 ends its account with the notice that monies generated by the guilt and sin offerings

---

30. Note Josephus's embellishment of Kings' simple mention of 'timber' here.

31. Josephus's preference for Chronicles over Kings in this instance could reflect the consideration that the former's presentation underscores the magnitude of the sums collected—there was so much left over from the repair of the temple that a variety of vessels could be fabricated from the remainder. As such, Chr's notice points up the Jews' devotion to their temple in impressive fashion.

32. Josephus omits the indication of 2 Chron. 24.14 about the surplus money being 'brought before the king and Jehoiada'.

33. Literally 'gold and silver' (χρυσὸν καὶ ἄργυρον; see the same phrase in reverse order in 9.163: the people 'collected much silver and gold'). Cf. θυίσκας χρυσᾶς καὶ ἀργυρᾶς (2 Par 24.14a).

34. Of the four Greek terms in the above sequence, only the final, general one has an equivalent in 2 Par 24.14a. With the three previous, more specific terms of the sequence, compare, however, Josephus' (biblically unparalleled) enumeration of the items that Josiah directs the high priest Hilkiah to make from the money left over after the repair of the temple in *Ant.* 10.57: κρατῆρας καὶ σπονδεῖα καὶ φιάλας.

remained the property of the priests rather than being 'brought into' the temple. 2 Chron. 24.14b concludes rather, 'And they offered burnt offerings in the house of the Lord continually all the days of Jehoiada.' Here again, Josephus aligns himself with Chr's formulation: 'and they continued *day by day* to enrich the altar with costly sacrifices. Thus, so long as Jōdas lived [ἐφ' ὅσον Ἰώδας χρόνον ἔζη],[35] these things were done with the required care'.

Joash's Defection

In Kings, Joash's initiative on behalf of the temple (12.5-17) is abruptly juxtaposed with his humiliation in having to buy off the Syrians (12.18-19). Chr interposes between these two events an account of Joash's defection, which provides a theological rationale ('immediate retribution') for what befalls him. This Chronistic insertion stands in 24.15-22; Josephus's parallel is 9.166-169.

Chr's account of Joash's defection (24.17) opens (24.15-16) with a preparatory notice on the death (at age 130) and burial among the Judean kings of his mentor Jehoiada. In Josephus (9.166) an expanded version of this notice is incorporated into the mention of the royal apostasy itself. It reads as follows: 'But, after Jōdas died at the age [see 24.17aα] of one hundred and thirty years, *having been an upright man and good* [δίκαιος...καὶ...χρηστός][36] *in all ways*, and was buried in the royal sepulchres at Jerusalem [24.16, in the city of David with the kings] because he had restored the kingdom to the line of David,[37] King Joas proved faithless...'

According to 2 Chron. 24.17 Joash was induced to defect by 'the princes of Judah' who, following Jehoiada's death, appeared before the king to do him homage and to whom Joash 'hearkened'. Josephus, on the contrary, represents Joash going astray on his own volition: '[After the death of Jōdas]...Joas proved faithless in the service of God

---

35. Note the echo of 9.157, παρὰ πάντα τὸν χρόνον ὅν Ἰώδας ἐβίωσεν.

36. Josephus also employs the above collocation in *Ant.* 9.133; 10.100 (Jehoiachin); 11.183 (Nehemiah); 13.114 (Ptolemy Philadelphus). In all these other instances the order of the terms is the reverse of that in 9.166.

37. This motivation for Jehoiada's burial among the kings represents a specification of that given in 2 Chron. 24.16b ('because he had done good in Israel, and toward God and his house'), recalling the high priest's initiative in re-establishing the legitimate dynasty. See 2 Kings 11 // 2 Chronicles 23 // *Ant.* 9.140-156.

[προέδωκεν...τὴν ἐπιμέλειαν τὴν πρὸς τὸν θεόν].'³⁸ Thereby, he excludes the 'extenuating circumstances' that Chronicles posits for the apostate Joash (just as he makes the severity of the king's subsequent punishment appear all the more deserved). In 2 Chron. 24.18a the outcome of Joash's heeding the 'princes' is that 'they' together forsake the temple and begin serving 'the Asherim and the idols'. Josephus's presentation continues to portray Joash himself as the instigator of the defection, which, in turn, the historian describes in much more general terms than does 2 Chron. 24.18a. His statement on the matter runs thus: 'And together with him were corrupted [συνδιεφθάρησαν] the leaders of the people [οἱ τοῦ πλήθους πρωτεύοντες; 2 Par 24.17, οἱ ἄρχοντες Ἰούδα]³⁹ so that they transgressed against what was right and held among them to be the highest good.'⁴⁰

2 Chron. 24.18b-19 juxtaposes two notices on the sequels to Joash's defection: 'wrath comes upon' Judah and Jerusalem (v. 18b), and the Lord sends prophets of repentance whose 'testimony' goes unheeded (v. 19). Josephus effects a smoother linkage between the two items: 'Thereupon God, being displeased [δυσχεράνας]⁴¹ *at this change of heart in the king*⁴² *and the others*, sent [πέμπει; LXX, ἀπέστειλεν]⁴³ *the*

38. Contrast Josephus's statement (9.157) that Joash when under Jehoiada's tutelage ἐποιήσατο... περὶ τὴν τοῦ θεοῦ θρησκείαν φιλοτιμίαν. With the construction of 9.166 above, cf. Samuel's accusation of the people in *Ant.* 6.90, προδεδώκατε τὴν θρησκείαν καὶ τὴν εὐσέβειαν.

39. Josephus's statement about the king's self-corruption influencing the leaders (rather than vice versa, as in Chronicles) echoes his remark concerning the defection of Rehoboam in *Ant.* 8.252 (// 2 Chron. 12.1): 'For the morals of subjects are corrupted simultaneously (συνδιαφθείρεται) with the characters of *their rulers...*'

40. With the above 'generalization' of 2 Chron. 24.18's reference to the king and princes' 'serving the Asherim and the idols', cf. 9.161, where for Joash's statement of 2 Chron. 24.7b about the sons of Athaliah using dedicated temple objects 'for the Baals', Josephus has him simply aver that the temple 'had been left crumbling' by Athaliah's family. On Josephus's tendency to leave aside the 'cultic specifics' of the biblical account, see n. 14.

41. Josephus' other uses of δυχεραίνω with God as subject are *Ant.* 3.218; 4.107; 5.14; 6.91. With this reference to God's 'displeasure', Josephus clarifies the indeterminate biblical mention of 'wrath' coming upon nation and capital.

42. In this inserted Josephan specification of the object of the divine 'displeasure', note the continued emphasis on Joash as the primary guilty party.

43. As here, Josephus frequently introduces the historic present where his biblical source(s) have some past form. On this phenomenon, see Begg, *Josephus' Account*, pp. 10-11, n. 32.

prophets [τοὺς προφήτας]⁴⁴ to protest solemnly [διαμαρτυρησομένους; LXX, διεμαρτύραντο] *against their actions* and to make them leave off their wrongdoing [24.19 to bring them back (LXX, ἐπιστρέψαι) to the Lord].' He then (9.168a) greatly amplifies the concluding reference of 24.19 to the inefficacy of [the] prophets' words ('they would not give heed'):

> But they indeed were seized with so strong a love [ἔρωτα] and so terrible a desire [δεινὴν ἐπιθυμίαν]⁴⁵ for it [i.e. their wrong-doing; see 9.167] that,⁴⁶ heeding neither the punishment which those before them had suffered together with all their house for outraging the ordinances [ἐξυβρίσαντες εἰς τὰ νόμιμα],⁴⁷ nor what the prophets (see 9.167) had foretold, they refused to repent [μετανοῆσαι]⁴⁸ and turn back [μετελθεῖν] from the lawless course [παρανομήσαντες] which they had taken.

2 Chron. 24.20-22 (// *Ant.* 9.168b-169) exemplifies Joash's persistence in apostasy with its story of his execution of Zechariah, the son of his patron Jehoiada. That story commences in v. 20 with the spirit of God 'clothing' Zechariah, who addresses the people with an accusatory question and announcement of retribution. Zechariah's initiative, in turn, prompts an unspecified 'they' to 'conspire against him', which eventuates in their stoning him in the temple court at the command of Joash (v. 21), who thus shows himself completely 'unmindful' of the benefits done him by Zechariah's father (v. 22a). Josephus rearranges the sequence of 24.20-21 so as to throw into relief the king's reprobate directive: 'Moreover the king even ordered Zacharias, the son of the high priest Jōdas, to be stoned to death in the temple...'⁴⁹ To this

44. 2 Chron. 24.19 (MT and LXX) speaks of 'prophets' without the definite article; contrast *Ant.* 10.39, where Josephus reads '(God) sent prophets' in place of 2 Kgs 21.10's 'The Lord spoke through the hand of his servants *the prophets.*'

45. Josephus's one other use of the above phrase 'strong desire' is in 17.169 (of Herod's urge to scratch himself). Cf. the related expressions in 6.279 and 7.168.

46. With the above reference to Joash and the others having 'so terrible a desire' for their wrongful deeds, cf. the note in 9.161 that the king was 'seized by a strong desire (ὁρμή) to renovate the temple...' The reminiscence of that earlier formulation here in 9.168 underscores Joash's moral degeneration.

47. This precise expression occurs only here in Josephus. Cf. *Ant.* 4.13.

48. On this term and its *Wortfeld*, see the literature cited in Begg, *Josephus' Account*, pp. 31-32, n. 162.

49. With the above formulation Josephus turns the 'execution notice' of 2 Chron. 24.21b ('they stoned him...in *the court of* the house of the Lord') into the content of Joash's 'command' alluded to there.

mention of Joash's command drawn from 24.21b, Josephus next appends an anticipated version of 24.22a: 'unmindful of the good works [τῶν...εὐεργεσιῶν...λαθόμενος; LXX, οὐκ ἐμνήσθη...τοῦ ἐλέους] of his father...' Only thereafter does he come to relate the content of 24.20, making this the motivation for Joash's directive: '*because*, when God appointed him to prophesy,[50] he stood in the midst of the people [στὰς ἐν μέσῳ τῷ πλήθει][51] and counseled [συνεβούλευεν][52] both them *and the king*[53] to do right [τὰ δίκαια πράττειν],[54] and warned them that they would suffer heavy punishment if they disobeyed.'[55] The episode of Zechariah's martyrdom concludes in 24.22b with the victim's dying appeal, 'May the Lord see and avenge.' Josephus (9.169b) elaborates:

As he died, however, Zacharias made God[56] the witness [μάρτυρα; see διαμαρτυρησομένους, 9.167] and judge [δικαστήν; LXX, κρινάτω; cf. MT, וירדש] of what he had suffered in being so cruelly and violently

50. This expression is Josephus's substitution for the mention of God's spirit (LXX, πνεῦμα θεοῦ) 'clothing' Zechariah in 24.20a. The substitution exemplifies Josephus's tendency to avoid using the term πνεῦμα in reference to either the divine or human 'spirit'. See Begg, *Josephus' Account*, p. 123, nn. 769-70 and the literature cited there.

51. This phrase is similiar to the one used in *Ant.* 8.231 in Josephus' version of 1 Kgs 13.1, where a 'man of God' (called 'Jadōn' by Josephus) from Judah confronts (σταθεὶς ἐν μέσῳ τῷ πλήθει) Jeroboam I. Cf. 2 Par 24.20a, καὶ ἀνέστη ἐπάνω τοῦ λαοῦ.

52. In introducing his reproduction of Zechariah's words with this verb, Josephus, in accord with his standard practice, leaves aside the *Botenformel* of 24.20b. His avoidance of that formula, in turn, agrees with his tendency to eschew biblical references to the divine 'word'. See Begg, *Josephus' Account*, p. 20, n. 90.

53. In 2 Chron. 24.20b Zechariah's words are directed to the people globally; Josephus's singling out Joash for explicit mention here conforms with his consistent highlighting of the king's responsibility for the negative course taken after Jehoiada's death. Note again the substitution of indirect for the source's direct discourse.

54. This phrase echoes (positively) the negative formulation of 9.167, πλημμελεῖν εἰς τὰ δίκαια.

55. This phrase represents Josephus's (more determinate) version of Zechariah's closing words according to 24.20, 'Because you have forsaken the Lord, he has forsaken you'.

56. Here, as consistently elsewhere, Josephus substitutes '[the] God' for the Bible's 'the Lord'; on this feature, see Begg, *Josephus' Account*, p. 45, n. 218 and the literature cited there.

[βιαίως][57] *put to death in return for his good counsel* [συμβουλίας; see συνεβούλευεν, 9.169a] *and for all that his father had done for Joas* [cf. 'unmindful of the good works of his father', 9.168].[58]

Syrian Incursion

2 Kgs 12.18-19 and 2 Chron. 24.23-24 converge in their basic story line of a Syrian incursion that results in ignominious losses for Joash. At the same time, the two accounts differ markedly in their details. Josephus's version (9.170-171a) eclectically combines elements of both presentations (cf. his handling of the temple repair episode above).

In line with 2 Chron. 24.23aα ('at the end of the year the army of the Syrians came up against Joash'), Josephus's narrative opens with a transitional phrase that insists on the speed with which Joash's previous crimes were requited: 'It was not long, however, before the king paid the penalty [δίκην; see δικαστήν, 9.169] for his unlawful acts' [παρηνόμησεν; see παρανομήσαντες, 9.168]. He then proceeds to cite several details peculiar to 2 Kgs 12.18 (e.g. name of the king of Syria, his capture of 'Gath'). His notice on the Syrian incursion itself thus reads: 'For Azaēlos, the king of Syria,[59] invaded his [Joash's] country[60] and, after subduing Gitta [Γίτταν; 4 Kgdms 12.18, Γέθ] *and despoiling it*, he prepared to march against him to Jerusalem [2 Kgs 12.18: "Hazael set his face to go up against Jerusalem"]...'[61]

---

57. On this term and its *Wortfeld* in the Josephan corpus, see E. Moore, 'ΒΙΑΖΩ, ΑΡΠΑΖΩ and Cognates in Josephus', *NTS* 21 (1974–75), pp. 519-43.

58. Josephus lacks the embellishments on the circumstances of Zechariah's murder (e.g., its occurring on Yom Kippur; for this detail, see, e.g., TC 2 Chron. 24.20) and the 'seething' of his shed blood until the Babylonians finally avenged his slaying by executing many of the surviving Jews, as found in Jewish (and Christian) tradition. See S.H. Blank, 'The Death of Zechariah in Rabbinic Literature', *HUCA* 12-13 (1937–38), pp. 327-46.

59. This figure (called 'Hazael' in 2 Kgs 12.18) was previously cited by Josephus in 9.159 as the devastator of Jehu's kingdom. In his presentation, then, both the contemporary kings Jehu and Joash have their lands overrun by the same Syrian ruler in punishment for their disregard of God's laws (see 9.160, 170).

60. Cf. 2 Chron. 24.23aβ, 'The Syrians came to Judah and Jerusalem.'

61. Josephus lacks an equivalent as such to the *Sondergut* sequence of 2 Chron. 24.23b-24: 'They (= the Syrians)...destroyed all the princes of the people from among the people, and sent all their spoil to the king of Damascus. Though the army of the Syrians had come with few men, the Lord delivered into their hand a very great army, because they had forsaken the Lord, the God of their fathers.

Josephus likewise follows Kings' distinctive presentation in his account of Joash's 'buying off' the Syrians with the palace and temple treasures. He introduces his parallel to 2 Kgs 12.19a with mention of the psychological state that prompts Joash to act as he does: 'Joas, fearing [φοβηθείς] this [i.e. Hazael's advance on Jerusalem]...'[62] He then continues:

> [Joash] emptied [12.19, 'took'] all the treasuries of God and of the palace [βασιλείων; the codices MSPE read βασιλέων][63] and, taking down the dedicatory offerings [τὰ ἀναθήματα; 4 Kgdms, τὰ ἄγια],[64] sent them to the Syrian *to buy himself off* [ὠνούμενος] *with these from being besieged and endangering his entire power.*[65]

2 Kgs 12.19 ends with a laconic notice on the result of Joash's desperate initiative: 'Then Hazael went away from Jerusalem'. Here again, Josephus (9.171) elaborates: 'Accordingly the other [Hazael], *being persuaded by the very large amount of money* [τῇ τῶν χρημάτων ὑπερβολῇ],[66] did not lead his army against Jerusalem'.

Thus they executed judgment on Joash.' In so doing, he downplays the 'theological component' of the episode, which Chr highlights.

62. Also, Josephus elsewhere inserts references to the 'fear' that causes a king to either surrender Jerusalem to an advancing enemy or 'buy off' that enemy (see 8.258, 'because he feared him' Rehoboam admits Shishak; 8.304, 'fearing' [φοβηθείς] Baasha's invasion, Asa sends silver and gold to the king of Syria; 10.96, 'in fear of' Jeremiah's prophecies, Jehoiakim opens Jerusalem to Nebuchadnezzar).

63. Cf. 2 Kgs 12.19, 'all the gold that was found in the treasuries (θησαυροῖς) of the house of the Lord and the house of the king'.

64. Josephus omits the specification of 2 Kgs 12.19 that the 'votive gifts' in question were those dedicated by Jehoshaphat, Jehoram, and Ahaziah. Josephus's omission here is readily understandable, given the biblical (and his own) presentation of the last two of these three rulers as 'bad' kings. He passes over as well the source verse's mention of Joash's own 'votive gifts'—likewise understandable, given his immediately preceding portrayal of Joash's defection, which he borrowed from Chr's *Sondergut*. Note too that Josephus reverses the sequence of 2 Kgs 12.19, where the king's handling of the 'votive gifts' is cited before his dispatch of gold from the treasuries.

65. This inserted explication of the purpose for Joash's initiative underscores as well the king's humiliation.

66. This embellishment also accentuates the enormity of Joash's loss and humiliation. Cf. 8.305, where in his description of Asa's 'buying' Syrian assistance against Israel (// 1 Kgs 15.18-20//2 Chron. 16.2-4) Josephus reports that the Syrian king 'gladly accepted the large sum of money' (τῶν χρημάτων τὸ πλῆθος).

Joash's Death

2 Kgs 12.20-22 first gives the standard source notice for Joash (v. 20) and then its account of his violent death (v. 21), with appended mention of his two named assassins (v. 22a), his burial, and succession by his son Amaziah (v. 22b). 2 Chron. 24.25-27 rearranges the sequence of these items as follows: Joash's death (v. 25a), burial (v. 25b), names of his assassins (v. 26), source notice (v. 27a), and accession of Amaziah (v. 27b). In his own conclusion for Joash (9.171b-172), Josephus, in accord with his regular practice, dispenses with the 'source notice' of 12.20 // 24.27a *tout court*.[67] He introduces his account of the king's death with what seems to be a reminiscence of the *Sondergut* notice of 24.25aα (the Syrians depart from Joash 'leaving him severely wounded'; LXX, ἐν μαλακίαις μεγάλαις), that is, 'But Joas, being stricken by a very severe illness [νόσῳ...χαλεπῇ]...'[68] In that condition, Josephus then notes, the king 'was attacked by some of his friends [τῶν φιλῶν],[69] who had plotted [ἐπεβούλευσαν; 2 Par, ἐπέθεντο] against the king to avenge the death of Zacharias, the son of Jōdas,[70] and was done to death by them'. In limiting his narrative of Joash's assassination to the above points, Josephus leaves aside several further, though divergent, particulars of the biblical sources: the site of the murder ('in the house of Millo, on the way that goes down to Silla', 2 Kgs 12.21; versus 'on his bed', 2 Chron. 24.25) and the names of his killers, Jozacar and Jehozabad (12.22a // 24.26).[71] Rather, he proceeds immediately (9.172)

67. Presumably, he does this because his own presentation uses the Bible itself as its 'source'.

68. Josephus's formulation, it will be noted, leaves the 'source' of Joash's 'malady' quite indeterminate. Contrast 2 Chron. 24.25, which certainly seems to suggest that the Syrians were responsible for the king's 'wounds' (recall in this connection that Josephus has no parallel to the notice of 24.23 about the Syrians 'destroying all the princes of the people').

69. Some codices read though, 'the friends of Zacharias' (see Marcus, *Josephus*, VI, p. 92, n. 4; p. 93, n. a). Josephus's substitution of 'friends' for the biblical designation of Joash's assassins as his 'servants' (see 2 Kgs 12.21//2 Chron. 24.25aβ) conforms with his tendency to introduce the former, Hellenistic-Roman court title where his sources lack it (see Begg, *Josephus' Account*, p. 16, n. 54).

70. Cf. 2 Chron. 24.25, 'because of the blood of the son (so LXX; MT, sons) of Jehoiada the priest'.

71. Chronicles supplies, as well, ethnic designations for (what it takes to be) the mothers of the two assassins as cited by Kings, making one an 'Ammonitess' and

to the burial of the murdered king. On this point as well, Josephus was faced with a divergence between his sources. 2 Kgs 12.22bα avers simply that Joash was 'buried with his fathers in the city of David', that is, he received the regular burial accorded deceased Judean monarchs. By contrast, 2 Chron. 24.25b informs us that the apostate king—as he ends up being in Chr's account—was buried 'in the city of David', but 'not in the tombs of the kings'. As might be expected given his earlier inclusion of Chr's *Sondergut* account of Joash's defection, Josephus aligns himself with Chronicles on the point: 'And, though he was buried [θάπτεται; 2 Par, ἔθαψαν][72] in Jerusalem [12.22b // 24.25b in the city of David], it was not in the sepulchres of his forefathers [ἐν ταῖς θήκαις... τῶν προγόνων]...'[73] To this burial notice taken over from Chronicles, Josephus appends a final, brief invocation of Joash's defection: 'because of his impiety' (ἀσεβὴς γενόμενος).

In 2 Kgs 12.22b, notice of Joash's burial is followed immediately by mention of Amaziah's succession. Chr, on the other hand, interposes other material (24.26-27a) between these two items that stand in his 24.25b and 27b, respectively. Josephus follows Chr also in this regard, although his interposed material has a content peculiar to himself. Specifically, between his notices on Joash's burial and the accession of 'Amasias' at the very end of 9.172, he pauses to make use of a source chronological datum he had earlier passed over (see above). Whereas, however, 2 Kgs 12.1-2a // 2 Chron. 24.1 cites Joash's age at accession (7 years) and length of reign (40 years), Josephus, who has already adduced the former item (see 9.157), here in 9.172, in line with his regular practice, combines this with the latter one (previously skipped by him) in generating a figure for Joash's age at death, that is, 47.

Conclusions

Our findings on Josephus's story of Joash may be summarized under two main heads: the sources available to him and his reworking of

the other a 'Moabitess'. Josephus's non-mention of the biblical names is in accord with his tendency not to overburden his account with the names of minor characters whose peculiarity might prove offputting to Gentile readers.

72. Note Josephus's historical present form here, as opposed to LXX's aorist (see n. 43).

73. Cf. 9.166, where Jehoiada is buried ἐν ταῖς βασιλικαῖς θήκαις ἐν Ἰεροσολύμοις.

them. On the 'source question', the presence of *Sondergut* items from both 2 Kings 12 and 2 Chronicles 24 in *Ant.* 9.157-172 makes clear, first of all, that in this segment at least Josephus was drawing on each of these works.[74] This finding deserves to be underscored. It suggests that for Josephus Chronicles had an authority equal to Kings as a source of historical information.[75] Given that status, the former document could be used without more ado to supplement the latter's account and vice versa. In developing his own presentation, Josephus appears then to have been basically untroubled by the 'contradictions' between Kings and Chronicles that have so agitated 'critical' historians; for him the data of the two documents are simply complementary. This approach to the sources gives Josephus's version of biblical history its irremediably 'pre/un-critical' character—which is not, of course, to deny its great interest and importance in other respects.

On the other hand, however, given the overall agreement among the textual witnesses for the two chapters (MT, LXX, Targum), as well as Josephus's own paraphrasing tendencies, it is not possible to determine with any assurance the particular text-form(s) of his sources that Josephus was using in the passage at hand. I would recall, however, several negative findings on the question: Josephus either did not know or opted against the distinctive reading of LXX regarding the husband of the 'two wives' cited in 2 Chron. 24.3 (// 9.158), just as he gives no evidence of familiarity with the various peculiarities of TC (for example, on Zechariah's intervention; see TC 2 Chron. 24.20 [and n. 58]; cf. 9.169).

How then does Josephus deal with his sources for Joash? Most notably, perhaps, he freely alternates between Kings and Chronicles for the details of his presentation in those instances (i.e., the temple repair, the Syrian incursion, and Joash's demise) where those sources generally parallel each other but go their own ways in many particulars. In so

74. Compare the (odd) passing remark of E. Nodet ('Pourquoi Josèphe?', in *Naissance de la méthode critique. Colloque du centenaire de l'École biblique et archéologique française de Jérusalem* [Patrimonies: Christianisme; Paris: Cerf, 1992], p. 100), 'l'on peut...se demander s'il [Josephus] a vraiment connu les Chroniques...' Even on the evidence of Josephus's Joash story alone, there can be no doubt that he did indeed 'know' Chronicles.

75. For more on Chronicles as an authority for Josephus in *Antiquities*, see E. Ben Zvi, 'The Authority of 1-2 Chronicles in the Late Second Temple Period', *JSP* 3 (1988), pp. 73-76.

doing, Josephus evinces his intention of 'making room' for some special material from each *Vorlage*.

In addition, Josephus further modifies both the style/wording and content of his sources. Biblical parataxis becomes a better Greek hypotaxis, and direct discourse is consistently turned into indirect. Twice, he introduces historic present forms (πέμπει, 9.167; θάπτεται, 9.172). The names of minor characters (i.e. Joash's two assassins) are avoided, as is 2 Chron. 24.20's mention of 'the Spirit of God'. Chronicles' cultic particulars give way to more general formulations, while Joash's disloyal 'servants' are Hellenized into royal 'friends'. Joash's reference to the Mosaic 'tax for the tent of testimony' in 2 Chron. 24.6, 8 is specified, on the basis of the earlier biblical text to which the king alludes (Exod. 30.13), as 'half a shekel' (9.161). Instead of Joash's length of reign (so 2 Kgs 12.2 // 2 Chron. 24.1), Josephus reports his age at death (9.172).

On occasion, Josephus rearranges the sequence of source material (see, for example, his 'anticipation' of elements of Joash's second discourse on the repair of the temple [2 Chron. 24.6-7] in his version of the king's first pronouncement on the subject [9.161; cf. 24.5abα], as well as his rearrangement of the components of 2 Chron. 24.20-22a in 9.168b-169a). Under the heading of 'rearrangements' one might also recall Josephus's insertion of his parallel to 2 Kgs 10.32-36 (closing notices for Jehu, 9.159-160) within the body of his Joash narrative.

Josephus omits relatively little material common to both his sources (or of the extended *Sondergut* segment, 2 Chron. 24.15-22). In accord with his standard practice, he does, however, pass over the 'source notice' of 2 Kgs 12.20 // 2 Chron. 24.27a. Occasionally, too, Josephus simply omits items about which the sources differ, for example, the place of Joash's assassination (2 Kgs 12.21a vs. 2 Chron. 24.25a; cf. 9.171b). Under the 'omission rubric', one might also mention Josephus's amendment of his sources' presentations so as to focus on the narrative's protagonists (for example, high priest and king hire the temple workers directly, rather than going through overseers [9.164b; cf. 2 Kgs 12.11 // 2 Chron. 24.12]).

Josephus's additions to the biblical accounts are also rather minor. See, for example, the (provisional) concluding formula of 9.158b, the reason for the disregard of Joash's initial instructions (9.161; cf. 2 Kgs 12.7 // 2 Chron. 24.5bβ), and the characterization of Jehoiada as 'upright and good in all ways' (9.166). Beyond such instances of actual 'addition' to the sources' records, we also noted Josephus's more frequent practice of elaborating upon some bare biblical datum (for example, the wood procured for the temple [9.164; cf. 2 Kgs 12.13], the people's [eventual] enthusiastic response to the collection [9.162-163; cf. 2 Chron. 24.10], the hearers' disregard of Zechariah's admonition [9.168; cf. 24.19], and the prophet's dying words [9.169; cf. 24.24b]).

Having reviewed Josephus's various rewriting techniques in *Ant.* 9.157-172, we might now raise the wider question: given the application of those techniques, how does the Josephan presentation of Joash differ from the biblical one(s)? Overall, it might be said that Josephus goes beyond the Bible in accentuating the stature and activity of the two main characters, Jehoiada and Joash. This is particularly the case for the latter figure, whose initial zeal for God's law and temple he highlights, just as he does his subsequent, self-initiated (cf. 24.17-18) defection. In its concentration on the personage of Joash as a good man who comes to a bad end at the hands of an outraged deity, Josephus's story is one that both Gentile and Jewish readers could readily appreciate in light of their respective literary traditions.

INDEXES

INDEX OF REFERENCES

BIBLICAL REFERENCES

INDEX OF AUTHORS